THE UNCERTAIN PROFESSION

The Uncertain Profession

HARVARD AND THE SEARCH FOR
EDUCATIONAL AUTHORITY

Arthur G. Powell

Harvard University Press
Cambridge, Massachusetts
and London, England

1980

Copyright © 1980 by the President and Fellows of Harvard College
All rights reserved
Printed in the United States of America

Library of Congress Cataloging in Publication Data

Powell, Arthur G   1937-
   The uncertain profession.

   Bibliography: p.
   Includes index.
   1. Harvard University.   Graduate School of
Education—History. 2   Teachers colleges—United
States—History. I. Title.
LB2193.C414P68   370'.73'097444   79-26096
ISBN 0-674-92045-7

For Barbara

Preface

SURELY NONE of the social sciences spawned by the American university at the end of the nineteenth century has had a more volatile and
troublesome history than the field of education. During the 1890s
enthusiasts dreamed that education could become both a source of
professional authority and a valid liberal art. Despite some reluctance, most colleges and universities started to develop elaborate
education curricula. Their success in one sense was formidable.
Higher education soon destroyed the existing centers of formal educational study, the state normal schools. Yet, despite remarkable
growth, the triumph seemed hollow and tentative.

Decades before it became fashionable to attack professionals in
nearly every field as self-serving and against the best interests of
clients, university efforts to professionalize school careers encountered hostility and contempt. Although education made a significant investment in research, especially after 1910, its efforts to join
the company of legitimate liberal arts lost out to other newcomers
such as economics, political science, and sociology. Even when justified only as vocational skill, education was accused of technical
bankruptcy and anti-intellectualism. Later in the twentieth century, other critics berated the field for its alleged complicity in perpetuating social inequality. It was hard to detect whether education
had failed because of the poverty of its knowledge-base or because of
its conservative efficiency. Was education not yet a true profession,
or was it too much one?

Schools of education have been condemned more than studied.
We know little of the inner intellectual turmoil that made their
search for an authoritative subject and a respected profession so elu-
sive. Again and again uncertainty characterized their response to
fundamental concerns. What educational roles were most impor-

tant? How were education professionals developed? By what means was reliable educational knowledge produced? And what were the objectives education could reasonably achieve in American society?

This book does not analyze the experience of all schools of education, but endeavors to show why certain choices were made by one of their number and why uncertainty remained regardless of the choices made. For nearly four decades after 1890, Harvard University participated fully in the mainstream of education's national development as a subject and an occupation. Only in the 1920s did the increasing anomaly of education's existence in an elite university force Harvard to renounce mainstream traditions and to seek a more separate identity. Its gyrations became atypical but, even so, they exposed the endemic tensions of the enterprise as a whole.

PAUL H. BUCK first suggested this subject in his seminar on the rise of American social science disciplines. Afterwards, while serving as associate dean of the Harvard Graduate School of Education between 1968 and 1976, I was struck by the poignant parallels between policy struggles of the late 1960s and debates in the first half of the century. In my subsequent attempt to unravel education's complex history at Harvard, I am grateful to two generations of staff at the Harvard University Archives for their assistance and patience; to Wyman Holmes and Mrs. Francis T. Spaulding for granting me access to important papers before their deposit in the archives; to the many alumni who wrote personal letters and submitted course notes; to present and former officers of the School and University who willingly answered questions in person and by letter; and to the Faculty of Pedagogy, Philosophy, and Psychology at the University of Bielefeld, Germany, for providing ideal working conditions at a needed moment.

I profited greatly from thoughtful readings of all or parts of the manuscript in its various stages by Robert L. Church, Nathan Glazer, Michael B. Katz, Francis Keppel, Theodore R. Sizer, and Sheldon H. White. I am especially grateful for the criticism and support of David K. Cohen and Hugh Hawkins. Although I would like to blame these friends for the book's errors, I fear I cannot. Maria Rainho typed the manuscript with her usual precision, while Barbara Schieffelin Powell cracked the whip lovingly in good times and in bad.

A. G. P.
Cambridge, Massachusetts

Contents

ILLUSTRATIONS

(following p. 148)

All photographs are from the Harvard University Archives, except for Lincoln Filene (courtesy Wm. Filene's Sons) and Felix Warburg (courtesy American Jewish Archives, Hebrew Union College, Cincinnati Campus, Jewish Institute of Religion).

Charles W. Eliot	Felix Warburg
Paul H. Hanus	Walter F. Dearborn
Nathaniel S. Shaler	Alexander Inglis
Edwin H. Hall	John M. Brewer
Barrett Wendell	Frederick G. Nichols
Hugo Münsterberg	The School, on the steps
A. Lawrence Lowell	of Lawrence Hall, 1920
Henry W. Holmes	James B. Conant
James J. Storrow	Francis T. Spaulding
Joseph Lee	Francis Keppel
Lincoln Filene	Phillip J. Rulon

THE UNCERTAIN PROFESSION

Prologue:
Celebration at the Union

THE HARVARD UNION, Tuesday evening, February 17, 1920. The time of triumph seemed finally at hand. All Harvard officialdom had gathered for dinner, on the invitation of the Committee of the Board of Overseers to Visit the Division of Education, to celebrate the impending conversion of the Division into a Graduate School of Education. On a frigid winter night, elaborate pains had been taken to ensure a warm environment of good fellowship and good taste. Elegant courses followed one after the other: oysters, cream of mushrooms, filet of beef, endive salad, cheeses, fruit ices, and cake.

The impressive assemblage of nearly two hundred guests included veterans of four decades of debate over Harvard's proper relation to the nation's primary and secondary schools. At the center of attention was Charles William Eliot, nearing his eighty-sixth birthday but characteristically vigorous and opinionated. During the 1880s, many in the room could remember, President Eliot had made the reform of the lower schools a central priority for Harvard University. At first he had not thought that defining "education" as a separate university subject was an especially helpful means to achieve school reform. Many more direct methods to influence educational policy and practice had been available to Harvard, and had been effectively employed. But, in 1890, Eliot persuaded his reluctant faculty of arts and sciences to begin a small experiment in secondary teacher education. One of its elements was a new assistant professorship in the history and art of teaching. When visiting his son in Denver soon after, Eliot met an ambitious Colorado schoolman named Paul Henry Hanus, whose drive and sympathy with Eliot's ideas led to a Harvard appointment. Now, nearly thirty years later, many Union guests viewed the new School as a monument to both men's vision and zeal.

Paul Hanus contributed substantially to Eliot's various school projects in the 1890s and developed a strong hero worship for his famous patron. By 1901 Eliot secured tenure for him. Hanus thereafter dreamed of an enormous departmental expansion patterned after the growing colossus of Teachers College, Columbia University. But his aggressive advocacy, accompanied by apathy or hostility from other academic departments, led only to increased administrative autonomy without much increase in size. In 1906 a separate department (called a Division) of education existed, but it consisted of only two faculty members.

Eliot's school-reform activities enabled education to begin and survive, but not to flourish. Only when that reform spirit waned, supplanted by a new energy less connected to Harvard's immediate interests, did rapid growth ironically occur. The new reform spirit, which coalesced in the second decade of the century, differed profoundly from the first. It did not focus on the academic curriculum or on students who might one day attend colleges like Harvard; indeed it did not address or try to resolve college issues at all. It took its energy, rather, from the conviction of affluent businessmen-reformers that secondary education's mission must expand. They regarded the high school as American society's decisive institution for adjusting youth to the urban and industrial world of the twentieth century. Entirely new educational services, such as supervised play and vocational guidance, would be established to effect that adjustment.

The new ideological climate allowed Hanus to recast his department's mission in terms no less grand than the maintenance of the social fabric. By so doing he also found he could reduce annoying frictions with his Harvard colleagues over issues of academic teacher preparation. His professional identity became at once more satisfying (and more attractive to philanthropy) as he withdrew from academic curriculum reform in favor of school administration. His connections with local reformers eventually led to various gifts to expand the faculty. In the decade after 1907 the size of the department increased from two to seven members, and Hanus pressed for more expansion and greater autonomy from the faculty of arts and sciences. The large representation of business reformers assembled at the Union, such as A. Lincoln Filene and Felix Warburg, testified to the social relevance the Division's work had assumed.

Yet Hanus' personal triumph was only partial. Abbott Lawrence Lowell, who succeeded Eliot as president in 1909, was far less tolerant of Hanus' demands for expansion than his predecessor had been. An intense dislike arose between the two men, and President Lowell seized the first appropriate opportunity to remove Hanus from the Division's chairmanship. His young successor, Henry Wyman Holmes, was far more to Lowell's taste. A loyal and active alumnus of the College, anxious to please and to succeed, graceful in manner and in literary style, Henry Holmes eagerly provided staff support to Lowell, much as Hanus had done for Eliot earlier. While Holmes eased the Division's difficulties with Lowell, Hanus nurtured professional and personal contacts with Abraham Flexner of the General Education Board. In 1919 the board agreed to make a major gift to endow a Harvard graduate school of education, and Lowell appointed Holmes its first dean.

Holmes carefully planned the February dinner in collaboration with Jerome Greene, chairman of the overseers' committee and toastmaster for the occasion. Greene, an old Eliot loyalist and Hanus admirer, agreed that the moment was historic and should be made as memorable and dignified as possible. The Graduate School of Education would be the first genuine school of education in New England and would restore to Harvard the educational leadership many believed it had lost to Teachers College. It was the capstone to Hanus' life ambition, and a vindication of Eliot's statesmanship. The occasion demanded that the key voices of the Division's past be heard, symbolically to bless the enlarged role now before it.

The speaking began auspiciously. Governor Coolidge, unexpectedly a national hero for breaking the Boston police strike, personally conveyed the greetings of the Commonwealth. His theme was comforting: in economic competition with states blessed with more abundant natural resources, Massachusetts could counter with the resource of an intelligent citizenry. The prosperity of the Commonwealth depended on maintaining educational leadership at all levels. The Harvard School's opportunities for service were thus wide and deep.

Holmes had nervously prepared a twenty-page lecture for his ten allotted minutes. He eagerly seized on Coolidge's remarks and enumerated in solemn detail the range of services the School hoped to provide. Deeply religious — he had seriously considered the ministry as a career—Holmes recalled the hope of one of the Division's business boosters that education might provide the individual identity and social stability which an earlier and simpler society had obtained through the church. The opportunities to expand the ministry of schooling were dazzling. The Division had recently taken historic initiatives in fields such as vocational guidance and play. New initiatives in commercial and industrial education, in physical education, and in boy scouting were being planned. Programs to deal with children with special needs, such as the blind and feeble-minded, seemed likely as well.

Holmes emphasized that the School's ability to meet new social "demands" also required expansion of the traditional Harvard student constituency. Of course it was necessary to train leaders, but the School had to train educators wherever it could find them. It would, as a first initiative, admit women—the first time women could receive Harvard degrees. It would also reach out to ordinary teachers, even those who were not college graduates and hence ineligible for the graduate degrees the School would offer. Summer offerings would be expanded, a new extension program established, and a larger portion of regular instruction moved to the late afternoons and Saturdays.

Underneath Holmes's emphasis on service through expansion of both program and student constituency was his confidence in the intellectual maturity of the field of education. He recounted the rise of educational psychology since 1900, the development of tests, the use of documentary evidence and surveys to study administrative problems. Education was a normative science as well; it clarified what constituted a good school and a good society. The Harvard curriculum would thus undertake "no narrow peddling of methods for the schools as they now exist . . . To train for school work as a mere craft is one thing; to teach Education is another." With that confidence in the authority of professional knowledge, it was a moral imperative to increase the number of students who might be enlightened.

Unleavened by even the hint of humor, Holmes's prolonged sermon set the evening far behind schedule. Charles W. Eliot came next, "the first citizen of our country," as Wallace Buttrick affectionately dubbed him a few moments later. Eliot acknowledged his happiness and satisfaction at the occasion, and reminisced that in

1891 not a single faculty member believed that education could be taught. But his point was not to celebrate the intellectual maturity of the subject since that time, any more than confidence in its potential had been much of a factor in his decision to appoint Hanus. His point was to speak about the sources of educational progress and ultimately about power. "We have absolutely demonstrated in the course of the last fifty years that improvements in education come from the top. They are invented in the upper grades of education and thought, and then descend from these upper grades through the lower."

He had not contradicted Holmes, but his emphasis was on the politics of implementation rather than on the duty of serving the profession or of responding to social demands. Eliot envisioned the entire university, not just its department of education, as a source of new subjects and new methods of teaching. Yet, as in the 1890s he was much less preoccupied with the problem of discovering exemplary educational procedures than with the problem of disseminating good ideas once they were known. Eliot was confident that, at least in his time, Harvard had faithfully discharged its responsibilities for leadership over the primary and secondary schools.

Wallace Buttrick, president of the General Education Board, brought greetings from the foundation whose endowment gift of $500,000—conditioned on three times that amount being secured by Harvard—had caused the School's creation. Buttrick had long admired Eliot and Hanus; but insiders knew that the board's general secretary, Abraham Flexner, had been primarily responsible for the gift. Flexner was ill and could not attend, but his prestige and that of the board brought a legitimacy to education, a sense of coming of age on a par with older professions such as medicine, which elevated the confidence of the new School's faculty. Jerome Greene described the board as constantly seeking "the strategic point at which the largest possible returns can be made in terms of welfare for the country." Education was now considered such a strategic point. As a result the new institution would begin with an endowment larger than that of either the Law School or the Graduate School of Business Administration.

It was now well past ten o'clock. Greene cautioned Hanus to be as brief as possible. But Hanus was moved deeply by the evening, and especially by Buttrick's warm description of him as fighting, determined, and gritty. He announced that, despite the hour, he would speak longer than his allotted time, unless Greene stopped him, and discarded his prepared text in favor of more candid expression of his feelings. Most faculty colleagues had considered his subject a "sham" from the beginning, he said, and part of that reputation had clung to him personally up to that very night. He sarcastically ridiculed the "assistance" he had been given over the years by the faculty of arts and sciences. "We have received their scrutiny, sometimes their suspicion, always their criticism. I can not say that that criticism was always constructive." Through experience he had learned that the only way to eliminate destructive criticism was through education. He had "deliberately precipitated collisions" with his academic colleagues in order that "information might be provided, and when the flood-gates were once opened, it was given liberally." Tonight, he thought, was one occasion when the flood-gates were open. He would talk on.

Hanus praised Eliot, his colleagues in the Division, his students, the visiting committee, the General Education Board. He mentioned name after name after name, but never once Lowell's. Then he summarized his career. In the beginning, people naively assumed that his work was confined to teaching how to teach. The study of education was simply the inculcation of classroom technique. His own title had not been professor of education, he remembered with special bitterness, but professor of the history and art of teaching. Over time the study of education had happily outgrown its preoccupation with teacher preparation. It had become instead a "social force for the spiritual and material welfare of the individual and of society." The objectives of the Harvard Division had accordingly changed to train "leaders," such as educational specialists, school superintendents, principals, and college presidents. They would manage new functions specially designed to advance education's social purposes.

Hanus spoke with special warmth about his students. The best ones had been older men ambitious for leadership. The personal friendships Hanus had forged with these mature men were among the greatest rewards of his career. At the end he characterized education as "a great social force which must be analyzed to be understood, which must be organized and administered wisely to be effective. To train leaders in this analysis and in this organization and administration is the function of the new School and to it we consecrate ourselves afresh."

Now it was past eleven. Lowell at last stood up, noted the lateness of the hour, and thanked those who in his estimation were responsible for the new institution. For him its "parents" were not faculty, students, or former presidents, but the members of the visiting committee. They had "brought the idea of this child prominently forward," and the General Education Board had been its godparents. Lowell made no mention of satisfying a personal dream, for he had never actively wanted the School. Nor had he been sufficiently antagonistic to oppose the prominent individuals, some of whom were personal friends, who urged it on him just as they had underwritten the Division's growth.

Lowell viewed the School in the context of the century-old process of upgrading training in all fields that claimed professional status. Over and over again, he noted, other fields had altered their pattern of training from apprenticeship to academic schools where the "principles" of professions were organized and taught. Education, which was "always behind almost every other department of human effort," was now attempting to make the same shift. The test would come in the School's ability to teach principles of greater value than the knowledge gained through direct experience.

Lowell's central argument followed from this perspective. The School's effectiveness would depend above all else upon its ability to conduct educational research. Unlike Eliot, who could confidently recall a nearly endless list of educational inventions that Harvard had passed on to the schools, and unlike Holmes, whose concern was the widest possible diffusion of professional knowledge, Lowell doubted whether very much was actually known about education. "We act a great deal on presupposition, which is either inherited from the past or borrowed from the possible future . . . We get a comparatively little amount of knowledge that we can stand by." The "one thing" he wished from the School was to contribute to "our knowledge of the things which we need to know about so much and know about so little."[1]

Greene quickly declared the proceedings at an end, and the eminent gathering scattered into the night. John F. Moors, Fellow of the Harvard Corporation[2] and one of Lowell's closest friends, agreed with his wife on the subway ride to Boston that the president had made the only clear and appropriate statement. In contrast, Eliot later recalled that neither Hanus or Holmes had been at his best, and that the high point of the evening had been the quality of the audience. He had listened most carefully to Lowell, seeking clues to his real attitude toward the School and its chances for receiving his active support. Always suspicious of his successor, he was disappointed that he could not discern a position one way or the other.

Holmes was discouraged and fearful. After a sleepless night, he telephoned Moors the next morning to apologize for Hanus' emotional outburst and his slighting of Lowell. He regretted the "spirit of antagonism" which ran throughout Hanus' speech and sought Moors's assurance that it would have no long-term ill effects. Holmes had wished above all to avoid any appearance of hostility or discord and to emphasize instead warm sympathies and common commitments. His anxiety was not unreasonable. The different positions and feelings publicly exposed at the dinner expressed the polarities of increasingly bitter policy disputes then under private debate.

Hanus longed to be dean or honorary dean of the new School, if only as a brief courtesy before his retirement. Failing that, he wanted some official recognition of his role in the School's establishment, such as a Corporation resolution of appreciation or a salary advancement to the highest professorial level. He expected Holmes to secure that recognition, but Lowell would have none of it despite Holmes's approaches. Now Holmes began to see Hanus' escalating bitterness deflected in part toward himself. The two men already had subtle but potentially serious differences over whether the School should concentrate exclusively on training mature people for leadership positions in administration. The differences had surfaced briefly in their dinner remarks, but were covered over by their commitment to education as a social force and confidence in the maturity of education as a subject. Holmes did not want these internal disputes to get out of hand.

But Holmes's most serious policy conflict was with Lowell. Only five weeks before, the president had unexpectedly rejected all of Holmes's proposals for professorial appointments to the new School. It would be wise, Lowell had bluntly suggested, "to sacrifice something in the way of technical knowledge for the sake of academic caliber." Holmes suspected, with good reason, that the president "wanted to give our School a remote and lofty character, which would make it impossible for us to attract here the school men of the country." Protracted discussions had ensued about whether "technical" knowledge in education was as intellectually mature as Holmes claimed or as rudimentary as Lowell believed. Holmes boasted that "our profession has outgrown its tutelage to any other subject." At the time of the dinner the impasse still existed.

Other points of contention existed with the president. Holmes favored retention of the Ph.D. degree, which the Division had routinely awarded when it was part of the faculty of arts and sciences. But Lowell insisted that no other faculty could award that degree. One price of a new School at Harvard would be the invention of new degrees. Further, Lowell had ordered, over Holmes's vigorous protest, that the Division's thirty-year tradition of undergraduate teacher preparation cease within three years. Holmes was distressed at the hardness of Lowell's positions on such matters, and at his own inability to budge him. As a result of these confrontations, which he loathed as much as Hanus had relished, gnawing self-doubts began to surface. Holmes feared personal humiliation and harbored "wild thoughts" that somehow the School might never open at all.

John Moors thanked him for calling and counseled him not to worry. Hanus' discourtesy was not surprising. He "had had bitterness in his heart for so long that he could not divest himself of it even on an occasion like that of last night." Moors told Lowell later that day that some good might even come from the incident. Perhaps for the first time Holmes had seen Hanus "with our eyes but with some chagrin." There could be no lingering feeling that the University had treated Hanus unjustly. A better foundation for the new School could be laid.[3]

The celebration at the Union soon receded from memory. Holmes's anxieties seemed exaggerated. A fortnight later the Corporation officially voted to establish the Graduate School of Education. The educational press reported triumphantly that Harvard at long last was firmly committed to the graduate study of education.

1

Harvard and the Schools

THROUGH FOUR remarkable decades after 1869 Charles William Eliot presided over the conversion of Harvard College into a modern university. The faculty of arts and sciences was greatly enlarged. Curriculum expansion broadened the range of subjects included in university study and deepened their coverage through advanced specialization. Extension of the free elective system of course selection facilitated student access to the expanded curriculum. The University also upgraded standards for its professional schools and promoted the idea that collegiate education should precede professional training. Less deliberately but no less significantly it slowly encouraged graduate study and research.[1]

These now-familiar transformations were not easily wrought. Internal opposition often arose from members of the various faculties, from the Board of Overseers, and from prominent alumni. Looking beyond these internal political problems, Eliot knew that change within the University depended on change outside. Modern universities could not be "built in the air," he cautioned in his inaugural address. No "sudden reconstruction" could cause their appearance.

The conversion of Harvard to a university required, in particular, changes in the curriculum and teaching methods of the schools that sent students to it. A university characterized by a broader and more specialized curriculum needed students prepared for and willing to enroll in the courses the faculty wanted to teach. Because Eliot linked institutional self-interest to his personal conviction that the same educational principles applied equally to schoolboys and college men, the way was open for relentless downward extension of the curriculum emerging in Cambridge.[2]

At first the shaping of schools to meet these new needs seemed simple enough. The small number of local preparatory institutions had no other function but college preparation and followed Harvard's lead. The traditional required admissions examinations were the means through which changes in the desired intellectual preparation of freshmen were enforced on the schools. By the middle 1880s, however, the process of school control became more complicated. In part this was because the rapid pace of changing requirements in subjects like science outstripped the capacity of most preparatory schools to keep up. Schools needed technical assistance beyond the lesson of examinations. More important, Eliot enlarged the constituency of schools he wished to affect. The public high schools showed increasing interest in sending graduates to further study. Inordinately sensitive to Harvard's growth rate, Eliot decided that this larger body of institutions also had to be brought within the University's sphere of influence. Other University priorities, notably the desire to precede professional study with full collegiate preparation, heightened his interest in compressing and upgrading the schools' course of study.

By the end of the 1880s, required examinations alone seemed an unsatisfactory method of influence. Harvard's most significant new strategy was to advocate wider options in modern subjects as acceptable preparation for college. This would open up the possibility of Harvard attendance to students who could not meet existing requirements in the classics and mathematics. Still, for its influence on curricula to be maintained, Harvard had to shape all the major subjects taught in schools. In the 1890s Harvard initiated an unprecedented array of techniques to disseminate its ideas about proper curriculum content and educational method.

School reform became a central activity. At the extreme, the faculty of arts and sciences solemnly voted to endorse a curriculum for elementary schools, and prominent Harvardians suggested the desirability of direct university administration of preparatory schools. Less dramatic responses included detailed curriculum guides, summer teacher-education courses, a school inspection service, and a national curriculum report that celebrated the Harvard methods. By the late 1890s many Harvard professors believed that the University already had shaped the teaching in many schools, and was prepared to give forceful direction to American primary and secondary education for the next century.

As THE SCIENCES, modern languages, and history expanded their place in the Harvard curriculum, and as increased scholarly sophistication in the classics and mathematics rivaled that in the modern subjects, the traditional continuities between the College and its feeder schools weakened. In both content and methods, Charles Francis Adams, Jr., later remarked, preparatory schools "by degrees ceased to prepare for the College." Strong incentives existed for Harvard to remediate the situation. As the extension of course electives at Harvard eroded the academic monopolies older subjects had enjoyed, faculty competition for student interest and enrollments led to demands that the new subjects and the revamped older ones be taught earlier and better. With growing specialization in advanced courses, many faculty members wished to avoid the burden of elementary instruction in subjects taught little or not at all prior to admission. Schools should help to generate enthusiasm for unfamiliar subjects and teach a larger range of fields.[3]

The logic of Eliot's own educational convictions reinforced efforts to restore weakened instructional links between schools and the College. Although he was slow to endorse free choice of studies in secondary schools, Eliot argued from the first that schoolboys as well as college men should be exposed to all the major branches of modern learning. He did not deny the educational value of mathematics and the classics, but opposed their claim to be the sole source of culture and discipline. Broadening the curriculum of the preparatory schools would be a constructive educational reform quite apart from the benefits it brought to the Harvard faculty. Moreover Eliot drew no sharp distinction between schoolboy and college man with regard to classroom method. What worked for one would work for the other.[4]

In the 1870s Harvard could direct curriculum change in preparatory schools with relative ease. A few local institutions provided the College with most of its students. Half the freshmen entering in 1869 were prepared in seven nearby private schools or special-purpose public schools: Phillips Exeter Academy, Boston Latin School,

Cambridge High School, Phillips Academy in Andover, Mr. Noble's School, Roxbury Latin School, and Charlestown High School. Since their primary function was college preparation, curriculum was virtually considered the property of the College to alter at will. Harvard's admission requirements were more demanding than other colleges and thus determined the schools' academic program. Eliot took full responsibility for deciding that certain subjects, such as physics and chemistry, should be taught extensively in preparatory schools, while others, such as botany or geography, need not be. "Schools follow universities," he liked to say, "and will be what universities make them."[5]

Admission examinations were the traditional means for Harvard to enforce curriculum policy in the schools. Until the 1870s requirements had remained unchanged for a generation. All applicants were orally examined on prescribed works of Greek and Latin prose and poetry, on classical grammar and prose composition, and on mathematics and ancient history. Then three kinds of changes were rapidly introduced. New subjects were required, the content of previously required subjects was revised, and options were introduced among the examined subjects.

Between 1873 and 1876 English composition, French or German, and physical science were added as new requirements for admission. These subjects had previously been required for graduation from Harvard; the new policy was intended to push elementary instruction down into the schools. At the same time, Harvard encouraged prospective students to fulfill remaining college course requirements while in school by offering examinations in those subjects at the time of college entrance. Substantial changes in traditional requirements followed as well. Mathematics was stiffened to include quadratics and plane geometry. Instead of emphasizing the memorization of prescribed texts, classics examinations stressed sight translations of unfamiliar passages. Even examinations in the newer subjects were upgraded soon after they were first adopted. Prescribed books in English composition increased, a test to correct specimens of poorly written English was added, and an optional test encouraged experimental rather than textbook work in physical science.

The first examination option allowed schoolboys in 1870 to concentrate more heavily in mathematics or physical science instead of in the classics. Neither Greek nor Latin was made wholly optional, but now a somewhat different mixture of school subjects might prepare a boy for Harvard. Although the modernists on the faculty had won the first skirmish with the traditionalists, few applicants exploited the new possibilities since few schools taught advanced science or mathematics. In the early 1880s the faculty debated at extraordinary length whether Greek would become optional. After three years of bitter argument, the modernists won: entrance to and graduation from Harvard would be possible with no Greek. But the traditionalists succeeded again in requiring so much school mathematics in place of Greek that few students exercised the option.

Although Eliot first praised the preparatory schools for the speed with which they adjusted to Harvard's new and complex demands, the strain on them was apparent by the early 1880s. Many complained that admissions requirements to various colleges had become too diverse for individual schools to prepare for more than one or two institutions. Others pointed to the added costs of competent teachers for new or revised subjects, extra space for classrooms and laboratories, and new books and teaching materials. Some resented as well Harvard's aloofness and condescension. Eliot supported efforts to harmonize relations, minimize administrative confusion, and achieve greater uniformity in entrance examinations. After 1880, for example, the Association of Colleges in New England held conferences of college teachers in the various subjects and some uniformity in requirements was achieved. And in 1885 several principals, with Eliot's encouragement, established the New England Association of Colleges and Preparatory Schools.[6]

Nonetheless, Eliot was most concerned with the schools' academic performance. It was one thing to require prospective freshmen to pass certain examinations. It was quite another to assure that students would be prepared to cope successfully with those examinations. The problem existed for all the required subjects, but the most dramatic example was science. Physical science was first required for admission in 1876, when its content was defined as material from a textbook. But textbook science did not produce enough freshmen interested in pursuing science in college. Harvard enrollments, especially in physics, were discouragingly small in advanced courses. Eliot and most of the faculty in chemistry and physics believed the problem was caused by lack of school expertise in the kind of laboratory experimentation that had come to dominate Harvard science.

In 1885 Harvard began to encourage schools to abandon textbook memorization by developing a science admission examination based on laboratory skills. But the new examination was only an option for the old; it did not supplant it. Laboratory science, Harvard officials realized, could not be brought into the schools by legislative fiat alone. Not enough teachers knew about modern science; nor did enough laboratories exist to make teaching effective. Genuine reform in science teaching required University initiatives beyond examinations. Harvard had to provide technical assistance to schools lacking proper teachers and equipment. The physics and chemistry departments began to create curricula and teaching materials, and to consider how they might be disseminated to the schools.[7]

Such direct assistance in the 1880s was fully consistent with the educational role Eliot expected his faculty to play and with the assumptions held by many professors about their own responsibilities. In his inaugural address, Eliot emphasized that the "prime business" of professors was "regular and assiduous class teaching." But teaching was no routine activity, and anachronistic educational methods were a serious barrier to learning. Memories of his own frustrations as a Harvard undergraduate led Eliot to view the teaching of science "not from books merely, not through the memory chiefly, but by the seeing eye and the informing fingers." His chief success as a young scientist had been to write a text on laboratory methods of teaching chemistry.[8]

Older professors, such as the chemist Josiah P. Cooke, and younger men with research ambitions, such as the physicist Edwin H. Hall, were encouraged to work energetically on the reform of school curricula and teaching methods. In 1886 Cooke and Hall introduced to the Harvard curriculum two elementary science courses designed as exact models of courses they hoped the schools would replicate. Cooke prepared a lengthy booklet, *Descriptive Lists of experiments on the fundamental principles of Chemistry for use in Chemistry B, also for the use of teachers preparing students for the admission examination in Chemistry*, and Hall brought out a similar pamphlet on physics experiments. Each guide, later widely distributed by commercial publishers, told teachers what to do, what equipment was necessary, and how much it would cost. Hall's went through six editions over a quarter century. It was incorporated into the science section of the report of the Committee of Ten in 1893, formed the basis of the College Entrance Examination Board physics test in 1901, and stimulated the manufacture of cheap laboratory equipment for schools.

Direct contact with teachers was simultaneously encouraged. Years before Harvard organized a summer school, Hall offered a brief summer course within the physics laboratory for sixty teachers. Harvard professors in all fields offered in the schools spoke at teachers' gatherings and published articles on curriculum and methods. Hall became a prominent research scientist, but later concluded that school pedagogical reform had been one of the major achievements of the Department of Physics at the end of the nineteenth century. The same conclusion applied to other departments as well.[9]

THE HIGH SCHOOLS supplied few students to Harvard in the 1870s. Except for a few public institutions that functioned primarily as preparatory schools, the high schools were largely devoted to offering career advantages to those who would not attend college. Harvard officials assumed that stiffened admissions requirements would prevent all schools, except private academies and a few public classical schools, from sending their graduates to Harvard. In 1876 Eliot argued that public high schools should not even attempt to fit boys for college, and criticized Massachusetts schools that tried to combine the "high" and "preparatory" functions in a single institution.[10]

By the early 1880s, however, Eliot began to realize that the course of secondary education in America was not so self-evident. The constitutionality of using public funds to support high schools had been firmly established, and the sporadic opposition to tuition-free public high schools which had marked the 1870s had subsided. High schools were growing, and despite the paucity of their resources many sent at least a few graduates to Harvard. No Harvard official imagined that within a generation secondary education would become a nearly universal experience for American youth, but in the 1880s they realized that some boys in a surprisingly large number of high schools were interested in further study. Yet college admissions requirements, still dominated by the classics but now demanding more extended instruction in the modern subjects as well, were formidable barriers to most students in most high schools. In 1884, for example, Massachusetts' 228 high schools provided only 199 freshmen for the nine Massachusetts colleges. Such statistics were consistent with Eliot's assumptions during the 1870s. By 1884, however, Harvard attitudes and especially those of its president had begun to shift. Instead of accepting the gap between high school and college as appropriate and inevitable, Eliot viewed it as a "serious evil" that had to be remedied.[11]

Eliot had never wanted ambitious but impecunious or poorly located youth to be barred from college opportunities because they lacked access to a college preparatory course. In the seventies he had advocated the creation of regional public preparatory schools, special boarding schools, or scholarships to meet their needs. But none of those devices had materialized. Instead, private day and boarding schools were increasing and did nothing to provide collegiate preparation for the less wealthy. Statistics he gathered (and studied with great seriousness) indicated that both the total number and percentage of public school boys at Harvard was declining. In 1870 nearly 38 percent of the freshman class had graduated from public schools of various types. Ten years later that fraction had dropped to 29 percent and was only 22 percent in 1884.

Eliot's new sensitivity to the "broken connections" between Harvard and the high schools was fueled not merely by concern for Harvard's accessibility to less privileged students but by a more general fear that the University's own growth might be stunted. For Eliot the growth rate of Harvard College was a crucial index of the University's educational success and financial strength. Statistics on that rate provoked much anxiety in the mid-1880s. At no time in the period between 1871 and 1885 did the size of the freshman class increase in two consecutive years. Eliot blamed the spotty and lagging growth of the College in the 1870s on the effects of business depression, but by the 1880s he began to wonder whether liberal education was losing popularity in the country. If the colleges' relative hold on the people was shaky, then it was necessary to bring the colleges and the popular institutions of secondary education into closer contact.[12]

There were, moreover, an increasing number of private schools outside New England that seemed almost as cut off from Harvard admission examinations as the public high schools were. Eliot believed that the slight increase in Harvard's student body during his presidency had come not from New England but from the middle and western states. Apparently many alumni had left the East, improved or founded preparatory schools, and then organized them to prepare for Harvard. When Eliot became president, admissions examinations were given only in Cambridge. By the early eighties they were given in New York, Philadelphia, Cincinnati, Chicago, and San Francisco. But these distant institutions often had trouble meeting the Harvard requirements even if their students were located near an examination site.[13]

Eliot concluded that the most effective way to bridge the gulf between Harvard and the high and preparatory schools was to introduce into college requirements for admissions "reasonably wide options, so that some course or courses of study which will admit to college may be brought almost to coincide with a substantial high school course of study, laid out primarily for youth who are not going to college." This fundamental policy change acknowledged that the widening and deepening of admissions requirements achieved in the 1870s had had the effect of severely limiting the schools that could prepare for Harvard, even as the requirements had brought substantial improvements in curriculum and instruction to those few schools.

Most public high schools, and many private ones as well, could only send boys to Harvard if Harvard's requirements took reasonable account of their capacities. In the 1880s and thereafter, Eliot advocated "wide options" in admissions requirements no longer to accelerate the expansion of the Harvard curriculum, but primarily to increase the "number and variety of schools which fit boys for college." He also realized that wide options—assuming that Harvard continued to maintain control of the content and methods of the optional subjects—would guarantee curriculum influence not merely in a few preparatory schools, but in all secondary schools that wished to send boys to Harvard. This was a strategy both to increase the size of the undergraduate student body and to widen Harvard's influence over the content of secondary education in America.[14]

Since the first major casualty of Eliot's new policy was required

Greek, conservative classicists and their allies denounced the plan as a retreat from Harvard's influence on secondary education. The 1885 admissions revisions technically made Greek optional, but did not resolve the internal faculty battle over whether Harvard's influence on the schools was growing or diminishing. The same issues were fought with equal vehemence in the 1890s, following publication of the Report of the Committee of Ten and a new round of faculty debate over further options in admissions requirements. But for Eliot, the abandonment of Greek was a welcome price to pay for the more profound University influence on the schools that he hoped would follow. Almost overnight, his advocacy of wide options changed the opinions of many public school defenders who had attacked his earlier relegation of the high school to what they considered an inferior status. If Eliot was once the "most prominent opponent of . . . secondary education," wrote William A. Mowry, he was now its "wise, broad-minded and progressive friend."[15]

Closer attention to the school curriculum also seemed essential to resolve a related problem of institutional growth at Harvard. One of Eliot's principal objectives was to upgrade training for the professions by requiring the Bachelor of Arts degree as a prerequisite for admission to professional study in law and medicine. A major obstacle, in his judgment, was that the length of the curriculum in both the Law School and the Medical School was increasing at the very time that the average age of Harvard College graduates was rising. The result was that College graduates had to endure an inordinately long period of study before they could enter professional practice. Unless the average age of beginning doctors and lawyers was lowered, Eliot believed, the whole effort at professional upgrading might fail. Prospective professionals would not tolerate the long delay and would enter professional school directly after completing secondary education. That result would not only weaken medicine and law as true learned professions, but would threaten the growth and prosperity of Harvard College.[16]

The problem could be addressed by shortening the college course or the school course that preceded it. Eliot advocated both policies and believed that two full years could be "saved." Yet his campaign to reduce the undergraduate course from four to three years was one of his least successful efforts. Although the faculty voted in 1890 to reduce course requirements for the A.B., the overseers refused to

approve measures that seemed to weaken the College. They suggested that the proper place to save time was in the schools. By that
time Eliot was ready to oblige.

In an 1888 speech to the National Educational Association, his
first in fifteen years, Eliot opened a vigorous campaign to get the
"good secondary schools to fit boys for college better and in less
time." The result was to deepen his involvement in school-reform
issues at a national level and to provoke an interest in elementary
education as well as secondary. From the perspective of time saving,
he found the main weakness of pre-collegiate education to lie in the
grammar and elementary schools. Their school day was too short,
instruction was uninteresting and narrow, too little attention was
given to individual differences, and too much attention was devoted
to profitless memory work. Ideas Eliot had endorsed for colleges and
secondary schools now were applied to elementary education as
well.[17]

Again and again, as the eighties progressed, Eliot discovered that
crucial Harvard problems could be solved only by changing the
schools. The concern for curriculum continuity between traditional
preparatory schools and the College had been supplemented by the
desire to make Harvard accessible to graduates of a far broader
range of institutions. In addition, Eliot pursued a notion of professional upgrading that necessitated reform in even the earliest
grades. He never questioned Harvard's responsibilities to reform the
schools, claiming throughout his life that educational innovations
were always invented at "the top" and then "descended" to lower
levels. But the focus of Eliot's growing interest — he regarded the
work of "reforming and uplifting secondary education" as the "most
pressing" educational task in the United States at the beginning of
the 1890s — posed a serious procedural problem. Influence on local
traditional schools could be exerted through the familiar means of
required subjects and Harvard-produced curriculum materials. But
when public high schools, distant preparatory schools, and even
grammar schools posed problems that Harvard could not ignore,
the ways to exert control became more complex.[18]

THE NEW CONDITIONS caused school-reform efforts in the 1890s to
emphasize dissemination of the "Harvard methods." The most press-

ing problem was no longer the academic task of curriculum development but the political task of implementing existing ideas. Eliot encouraged faculty members to involve themselves directly with schools and teachers more than ever before, as an integral part of their roles as university teachers. At no time before or since was the Harvard faculty more extensively engaged in school improvement. Eliot dramatically increased his own participation in local and national school organizations, and commended the career of "professional educationist" to Harvard students as a worthy occupation.[19]

The work of Professors Albert Bushnell Hart and Nathaniel Southgate Shaler best expressed the new reform mood. Hart had earlier pioneered in improving the school instruction of American history. Now he contended that the Harvard faculty could more directly affect local schools by acquiring political power within them. He won election to the Cambridge School Committee and promptly convinced his colleagues to upgrade the grammar schools along Eliot's lines by introducing geometry, physics, and physical geography into the city's curricula. Hart persuaded Eliot to provide free short courses in the new subjects for Cambridge teachers, taught by the Harvard faculty, and eventually expanded teacher training beyond Cambridge through establishment of a standing committee on afternoon and Saturday courses for teachers. In 1892 the faculty of arts and sciences voted to endorse a broadened curriculum for grammar schools.[20]

Shaler also seized on the possibilities of in-service teacher education. His major interest, the Lawrence Scientific School, had been losing students throughout the 1880s and was in precarious straits when Shaler became its dean in 1891. Preoccupied with increasing enrollments, Shaler believed that well-trained schoolteachers with warm feelings toward Harvard were the key to securing a larger student body. Shaler inaugurated a curriculum within the Lawrence Scientific School to train high school science teachers, and created the Harvard Summer School as a vehicle to influence teachers in all fields.

But courses alone were not enough to forge loyalty to Harvard. In 1891 Shaler founded the Harvard Teachers Association to create "somewhat permanent relations between this institution and a large number of teachers in schools widely scattered over the country." The association sponsored dinners and conferences, published up-to-date lists of Harvard men in the schools, and provided some assistance in job placement. By the turn of the century, the dues-paying membership exceeded 400 and included a large number of Harvard faculty members. Fittingly enough, Eliot and Hart were the first faculty members Shaler recruited.[21]

Eliot realized that influence might be extended not only by bringing teachers to Harvard but also by bringing Harvard to the schools. The best-known alternative to entrance examinations as a means to determine college admission was a system of certifying schools pioneered by the University of Michigan. The method of assessing schools rather than individual students necessitated on-site evaluations of high schools wishing to participate. Some Harvard observers regarded school certification as a more effective tool to improve school instruction than college admissions examinations. Charles Francis Adams, Jr., who chaired the Overseers Committee on Composition and Rhetoric, was disgusted with the inability of Harvard freshmen to write clear English prose. Harvard's admissions examination only perpetuated the problem, Adams thought.

Examinations often shifted the burden of responsibility from the teacher to the student and made "skill in cramming supplant the art of education." Unremitting in his advocacy of more coercive policies toward schools to force them to produce good results, Adams suggested that perhaps twenty preparatory schools agree to place their entire program under the "supervisory control" of Harvard. Only through direct day-to-day management — which went far beyond the periodic visitation provided by institutions like Michigan — could Harvard hope to guarantee proper performance in its feeder institutions. Students who successfully completed approved programs would be automatically admitted to the freshman year at Harvard, just as students who successfully completed the freshman year were automatically advanced to sophomore status. Adams imagined extending his system to the primary level as well.[22]

Although Yale and Princeton moved in the general direction Adams advocated by encouraging the establishment of Hotchkiss and Lawrenceville schools, Eliot shied away from this more radical extension of university authority. He did not accept the premise that certification schemes guaranteed university influence more than examinations did. Moreover, unlike Adams, he wished to influence the largest possible number of high schools. No transfer of authority from a few local preparatory institutions to Harvard could address this larger objective. Yet Eliot also appreciated the uses of on-site inspection of schools and sought a scheme that would provide direct access without surrendering admissions examinations. Following an inspection of the various certificate systems in 1892, he persuaded the Harvard faculty to establish a Schools Examination Board.[23]

The Schools Examination Board offered secondary schools an official Harvard assessment of their "methods of instruction, discipline, and physical training, the proportionate attention given to each study, the quality and range of the books used, and the quality and quantity of the apparatus." When a school requested examination, the Board dispatched a team of Harvard professors to visit the institution for a few days. Their final report was not made public and, except for the expenses of the examiners, Harvard did not charge for its services. Eliot hoped the Schools Examination Board would "add to the influence of examination papers a direct friendly intercourse with the schools themselves." In addition, the Board might educate those Harvard teachers to whom the idea of school cooperation was relatively new.[24]

The Board was an inventive effort to open the schools directly to Harvard professors, but it faced problems from the beginning. Faculty members disagreed on how much pressure should be placed on schools to request examinations. Hart, for example, wanted approved schools to receive special preference in the awarding of freshman scholarships and Harvard to endorse publicly the work of outstanding school departments. Without such incentives, and with examinations costing schools between $120 and $150, the institutions seeking examination were largely confined to those already under the sway of "Harvard methods." More significantly, the Board's function to provide advice on proper content and methods was undercut by a far cheaper source of Harvard authority when the report of the Committee of Ten on Secondary School Studies appeared in 1893.[25]

After 1888 Eliot found the platform of the National Educational Association an effective means to disseminate his views to a wide audience. In 1892 he was appointed to the NEA's elite National Council of Education and suggested the idea of a committee to study the curriculum of secondary schools as they pertained to college admission. He was made chairman of that committee and drafted the famous report of the Committee of Ten. Eliot's report brought together the key educational ideas he had been advocating for five years: the necessity to introduce modern subjects and modern methods in schools on an equal basis with the older ones, the desirability of school elective programs that could satisfy college admission requirements, and the need to shorten the school course of study. Although it was sponsored by the NEA and was the collective responsibility of a distinguished group of educators, Shaler considered the report one more Harvard method to reform the schools. The Committee of Ten, he suggested, should be "properly regarded as a Harvard project." Edwin Hall cautioned care in mentioning the close similarity between the committee's recommendations and Harvard's requirements. The greatest opposition to the report, he feared, would come from those most opposed to the extension of Harvard influence.[26]

Probably the report of the Committee of Ten extended Eliot's influence on schools more widely than anything else he did. Yet it was designed to influence college admissions requirements as much as school curricula. The effect of the report at Harvard was to raise once again the policy issue of options in admissions requirements. How far would the faculty go to accept the position of the committee and its chairman? Although Eliot's position had not changed substantially since the middle eighties, he now became far more explicit. He hoped Harvard would count for admission ' any subject which is taught in good secondary schools long enough and well enough to make the study of it a substantial part of a training appropriate to the pupil's capacity and degree of maturity." The reasoning was clear: "colleges and universities, if they would retain a national character and influence, must be careful not to offer unnecessary obstacles to the admission of young men of adequate though diversified preliminary training."[27]

The battle over revision consumed much faculty debate for the rest of the nineties. What subjects could be presented for admission in place of Greek? The classicists had waged a successful rear-guard defense by making the available substitute for Greek—advanced mathematics—so difficult that few students exercised the option. But in 1898 the faculty voted that almost any subject could count in place of Greek. For the first time, many American high schools that could not afford a Greek curriculum could prepare for Harvard.[28]

Behind the Greek debate lay broader issues of what the ideal student constituency of Harvard really was and how the strategy to improve schools was determined by different conceptions of that constituency. All the combatants agreed that maximum Harvard influence was essential. Those who regarded the College's constituency as students in local preparatory institutions believed that requiring a few subjects was the best means to "compel" school improvement. Charles F. Adams, Jr., who had given up his hopes for admission by certification, hoped to stiffen admissions requirements in English to improve freshman performance. He and others believed that wide options in admissions constituted a retreat from Harvard's efforts to improve schools.

But men like Hart and Eliot, who imagined a national constituency of students and a correspondingly greater influence for the University, had abandoned the strategy of influence through a few required subjects. "It would not be wise for us," Eliot told Adams, "to jeopardize our hold upon middle state and western schools by demanding for admission things which they have never begun to teach." The objective of school influence had not changed, but it had to be adapted to a larger institutional constituency. By accepting subjects that most high schools taught, and by setting curriculum and pedagogical standards in each one, Harvard's influence would grow. Suspicious of claims that some academic subjects possessed greater educational value than others, Eliot was free to engage in such strategic planning without abandoning his conception of what made an educated man. The "guiding of secondary schools," he now concluded somewhat disingenuously, "can be better achieved by cooperation than by orders from the College."[29]

Throughout the nineties Harvard employed an impressive variety of strategies to increase its "hold" on the schools. Eliot still fought indefatigably for the reduction of study for the bachelor's degree from four to three years. But at the end of the decade he used as an argument the enormous improvement already made in secondary schools. "This development of secondary school training in the last few years is one of the most remarkable educational phenomena which I have seen in my time . . . We have more training underneath the college, and consequently may introduce the three years' college course without reducing the total sum of liberal training." Harvard, he said, had provided the leadership for reforming instruction in all the major school branches. Many agreed, including a Hartford High School teacher who wrote that all the preparatory schools were "under the sway of the Harvard ideas—whether we name them or not."

The growth of the College provided another index of success. Between 1886 and 1900 the freshman class doubled in size. Despite this increase, the percentage of high school graduates among freshmen remained constant. Hart wrote triumphantly that "never in the history of the University has it had such widely distributed, well-adjusted, and harmonious relations with the schools which prepare its students as at the present moment; never has the University contained such a large number of students from outside its immediate watershed; never has there been so large a number of schools and colleges scattered throughout the country sending students to this University." Shaler too was grateful for what had been done, but looked to the future: "If we have a mind to, we can take the lead and keep it for the next century in all that relates to the lower schools."[30]

2

The Harvard Normal

NO ONE WAS CERTAIN in the 1880s whether Massachusetts public high schools were the first step of a system of higher education or the highest step of the common school system. Eliot's efforts to draw them closer to the orbit of higher education were resisted by leaders of elementary education. Although Eliot's leverage was impressive, elementary education possessed competitive advantages. Through interconnected institutions such as state normal schools, professional associations, and specialized periodicals, many men had found it possible to build lifetime careers in a variety of roles above and beyond the feminized common school classroom. At the higher levels, these men had attained an occupational coherence and political influence far beyond what high school men could claim. And by expanding the normal school's training mission to include high school teachers, leaders of elementary education hoped to further extend their domain.

Identification with higher education was far preferable to many high school principals than affiliation with the lower schools. At the end of the 1880s a growing high school assertiveness focused on guaranteeing that high school teachers be college graduates. The recruitment strategy of secondary principals was to link high school teaching with traditional prestigious professions by establishing graduate-level training programs. Eliot sympathized with an objective that paralleled his own, although he opposed their advocacy of a new state-supported "high normal school" to achieve it. But eventually he agreed to initiate a small teacher education program as one more Harvard mechanism to promote school reform.

If Harvard had agreed to sponsor secondary teacher education, had it also agreed that education was a legitimate university subject?

Although Eliot had no doubt that authoritative educational knowledge existed, the issue of a separate subject was more complicated. Most contemporary efforts to elaborate a science of education rested on idealist thought that was in sharp conflict with Eliot's educational values. Counter-efforts to devise a more inductive and experimental educational science received little encouragement from Cambridge. Eliot cared far more about disseminating already-known educational principles than about searching for new ones. From his reformist perspective, a separate subject of education offered few tactical advantages and might even be self-defeating.

The surer path to enduring educational reform, it seemed, was to strengthen organizational continuities between higher education and the schools. Unifying the educational system under the benevolent leadership of higher education could best be achieved through concentration on individual school subjects, taught in similar ways and for similar ends from the upper elementary through the college years. Harvard began teacher education with no particular use for education as a subject and little confidence in it. The program's center of gravity would be departmental methods courses which drew on the instruction already offered by Edwin Hall, Josiah Cooke, and others. An additional faculty member to manage the new effort was essential, but his role was seen less as a teacher of a separate subject than as an administrative coordinator of all the new agencies simultaneously under development to implement school reform.

As MASSACHUSETTS high schools grew both in number and in student enrollment during the 1880s, their purposes became more blurred and confusing. Affected by downward pressure from the colleges and upward pressure from the common schools, the high schools gave little impression of separate and coherent institutional identity. Some of the "modern" subjects had first entered their curricula as extensions of what had been taught to younger children, only to be later modified as the same subjects were upgraded in the colleges. In contrast, Latin and advanced mathematics were taught when they were taught, because of historical associations with higher education. Organizationally, the high schools had taken on the graded character of the common schools, but their boundaries were fluid.

There was little agreement about where elementary education
ended and secondary began, and the upper boundaries of secondary
education were equally uncertain. By contending that liberal education applied to schoolboys as well as to college men, Eliot hoped to
shape this unclear situation to the advantage of the colleges. But he
faced energetic competition.[1]

The most powerful opposing force was the organized leadership
of Massachusetts elementary education. If Eliot imagined the high
schools to represent the beginnings of liberal education shaped by
university values and methods, John W. Dickinson, Secretary of the
State Board of Education, regarded them as the highest step of a
state system whose values and methods were set in the earlier grades.
Dickinson was prepared to enforce his conception of the high
school's identity, and his principal weapon was the state normal
schools. More than any other agency, the normal schools had advanced and regularized the still unusual idea of lifetime careers in
school work. These careers led progressively from classroom teaching in the common branches to more stable and influential positions
in administration, educational journalism, or normal instruction
itself. By the 1880s, after only four decades of existence, the normals
could claim as former students or faculty some of the most influential educators in the Commonwealth. Dickinson himself, a former
principal of Westfield Normal School, held the position created by
the already legendary Horace Mann. And the state's leading educational journal was edited by Albert E. Winship, an alumnus of
Bridgewater Normal.

As high schools increased, the normals grew interested in placing
their graduates as high school teachers. To that end they developed
optional four-year courses and upgraded their admissions standards. In the 1880s they also attempted to attract as students college
graduates who would study educational theory prior to teaching in
high schools. To Dickinson, the principles of teaching were everywhere the same, regardless of grade level. High school teaching,
therefore, required the same professional training as did elementary. Ideally, all teachers should be prepared in normals to instruct
both small children and teenagers. Many school board members
and teachers agreed with him. In Salem, for example, normal
school graduates were welcomed in the high schools. Board members made no distinction between qualifications needed for instruc-

tion at primary or secondary levels. Fully a quarter of high school principals did not believe college graduation was essential for high school teachers. In the early 1890s only a slight majority of Massachusetts high school teachers held college degrees.[2]

The assertive efforts of organized elementary education to penetrate high school careers and shape high school purpose were strongly resisted by many principals from the larger and faster-growing high schools. For reasons ranging from assessments of institutional function to a careerism of their own, they preferred to define high schools more through relations with higher education than through relations with the earlier grades. To them the possibility of college domination seemed frequently more an opportunity than a threat.

In part the orientation of these principals to university ideas of liberal education derived from the growing number of high school graduates who pursued additional education. The Malden High School, whose principal George E. Gay was one of their leaders, sent half of its forty-nine graduates in 1890 on to further study. Only seven of Malden's graduates entered college, for the high schools propelled graduates to professional schools and other formal training that by-passed the colleges. But this pattern of mobility did not diminish, and may even have furthered, the belief that high schools were expected to provide the foundations of modern liberal learning to those who would go either to college or on to some other kind of advanced training. High school growth in these years hardly challenged the assumption that the institution was fundamentally elitist.[3]

This expectation of selectivity helped to justify the preference for curriculum and pedagogical ideas derived from universities, and also suggested the desirability of new patterns of high school personnel recruitment. Whatever might have been the possibilities of Massachusetts normal schools in their formative years, by the 1880s they attracted large numbers of less educated and less privileged students. Men avoided them almost entirely, and the growth of women's colleges siphoned off from them an increasing number of ambitious and more privileged women. Male high school principals perceived a growing educational and social-class chasm between their own ambitions and the reality of the normal schools, and saw no benefits to be derived from closer affiliation with them.[4]

One index of the preferred identity of high school men was the changing shape of teacher associations. The vexing question of college admissions requirements triggered in 1867 a splitting off of secondary educators from the Massachusetts Teachers Association to form the Massachusetts Association of Classical and High School Teachers. The wish for even closer ties to higher education led directly to the formation in 1885 of the New England Association of Colleges and Preparatory Schools. An elite group of school and college officials with a self-perpetuating membership, the association perfectly expressed the wish of many high school principals to blur the distinctions between their own roles and those of college faculty and administrators.

Association leaders like John Tetlow, principal of the Boston Girls High and Latin Schools, and Ray Greene Huling, principal of the Fitchburg and later New Bedford High Schools, opened up lines of communication between high schools and Eliot. The association's proceedings were published in *The Academy*, established in 1886 as the first American periodical exclusively devoted to secondary education. In its pages, and at association meetings, schoolmen bound for university careers (such as the young George Lyman Kittredge of Phillips Exeter Academy) expressed their educational ideas. Similarly, university men like Albert Bushnell Hart underscored ties with high schools by defining all the teachers of youth as potential professional experts. In its earliest meetings the association emphasized policy issues such as uniformity of college admissions requirements. But near the end of the 1880s it turned its attention to the equally charged issue of the high school teaching career and the qualifications necessary to pursue it.[5]

No member of the New England Association described the problem of career more bluntly than Horace M. Willard of the Howard Seminary in West Bridgewater. Secondary education most needed, he thought, teachers of "the noblest native endowment, supplemented by the highest possible culture." Teachers should be drawn from the pool of individuals whose education and ambition for "honor and fame" would routinely lead them to consider careers in the traditional learned professions, business, or science. Yet Willard saw little in secondary teaching to attract a collegiate elite. The job itself lacked autonomy. Instead of stimulating "individuality, ideas, independence, originality, study, investigation," high school teaching was a "mechanical routine" characterized by a "machine of supervision, organization, classification." The job lacked dignity and permanence because it was subject to the whims of capricious school boards or arrogant headmasters.

The school machine not only suppressed individuality but stifled personality. Willard decried the tendency of teachers to be recluses rather than men of affairs *"en rapport* with the live issues of the day." Confined to the company of the young and the powerless, they easily became autocratic and dogmatic. Their isolation extended to relationships with other teachers. Instead of colleagueship and cooperation, Willard found a "critical or jealous spirit and an ungenerous rivalry."[5]

In effect Willard warned that high school teaching resembled teaching jobs in the lower grades far more than those in the colleges. What could be done? Most principals agreed that the one indispensable step was to ensure that all high school teachers be committed college graduates. If the function of the high school was to commence liberal education, then the principal qualification for the high school teacher was, as Tetlow put it, "prolonged contact with liberal studies . . . as the result of a collegiate course of study." But even when college graduates did take high school jobs they often regarded teaching as a temporary expedient to earn money to do something else. Uncommitted and frequently ineffectual, they were a far cry from the nobly endowed teaching force Willard desired.[7]

Schoolmen like Horace Willard, John Tetlow, Ray Greene Huling, and George Gay all agreed that the college recruitment problem could be solved only if teaching more closely resembled other attractive professions. Crucially, their approach was rarely to seek direct changes in the unattractive, uncompetitive aspects of the teaching job that Willard had identified. Instead of eliminating unprofessional characteristics from high school teaching, they found it more feasible to add professional ones to it. The career could best be made to resemble a true profession, they argued, by establishing specialized training. When Willard asked rhetorically whether teaching was really a profession at all, his immediate evidence for the negative was not unprofessional characteristics of the job, but the unprofessional absence of specialized preparation for it. A sympathetic committee of the Massachusetts Board of Education succinctly linked successful recruitment of college graduates with specialized training. Such training would make teaching "more dig nified and attractive in the eyes of the pupils whom the colleges are annually sending forth. It would raise it at once to the ranks of a learned profession, worthy to command the best talents and the loftiest intelligence." The lure of specialized training was the expectation that its existence alone would have a more powerful recruitment effect than any other policy intervention.[8]

By 1890 it was a commonplace that specialized training was indispensable for any occupation that wished to call itself a profession. The New England Association first addressed the problem in 1888, when it asked Charles Kendall Adams to review recent developments outside New England. Adams, an historian active in the movement to confer professional status on that field, was a professor at the University of Michigan at the end of the 1870s when Michigan first began to offer instruction in education. Its effort, and similar ones in other western universities, was less a response to the professional ambitions of high school teachers than a university strategy to shape the high schools as preparatory institutions.

Adams endorsed the basic idea that education could be studied as a separate subject and introduced similar courses at Cornell when he became its president in 1885. His argument for such courses before the New England Association did not touch on the problem of career among high school men, but instead emphasized how the college-level study of education could be a useful weapon in the war upon low standards in grammar schools that Eliot had declared only a few months before. Despite his appeal for education in terms of collegiate self-interest, Adams impressed his audience by contending that education should be propagated to New England colleges. Near the end of 1889 a coherent movement to establish specialized training for secondary teachers gained momentum in Massachusetts. Tetlow, Huling, and a few other members of the association eventually convened a special conference of high school masters and other interested parties to recommend a course of action. Their discussions in January 1890 clearly exposed the gap between leaders of larger high schools and defenders of normal school expansionism.[9]

Although the principals agreed that the main qualification for high school teaching was the knowledge that came from a college education, they argued that additional professional training was essential. The most important training was supervised practice. George Gay suggested that professional training be conducted within a high school. The teachers of teachers would spend part of their time in regular high school instruction, part of their time in supervision, and part in classroom instruction of prospective teachers. The key to success, he asserted, was the integration of training with actual practice in a single location. J. W. MacDonald of Stoneham, who sought the same ends, proposed a four-year graduate program above the A.B. in which the first year would be spent in study and the final three in supervised classroom teaching.

No one spoke about the desirable content of the more theoretical study of education usually called pedagogy. In part this was because few knew what it was. *The Academy* had lamented that almost no literature existed in English on secondary education. But, whatever the content of education might be, its details were irrelevant to their purposes. In the light of their interest in recruiting a larger number of committed college graduates to high school teaching, what mattered most was how specialized training would be organized. Three possibilities were suggested. Secretary Dickinson and state agent George A. Martin defended the existing four-year programs of the normal schools to train high school teachers. Others proposed that one or more colleges establish chairs of pedagogy. Most of the principals favored a new graduate-level "high normal school," financed by the state but entirely separate from the existing normal schools.

Dickinson emphasized the unity between the high schools and common schools and the principle that all grades of teachers should receive the same professional training. Martin added that more students would enroll in the normals' high school preparation programs if only public pressure for trained teachers could be increased. The existing normals, he stressed, were fully adequate to the task. Even college graduates might attend normal classes containing students who themselves were not high school graduates. Arranging this would involve only "details of administration." In any case, Martin contended, "Sincere seekers after truth have never found any part of the present normal school work degrading because of its littleness."

A cascade of rejection greeted this position. All the high school men believed that college graduation was essential for high school teaching, and all found it absurd to contend that college graduates might seek subsequent professional training in an existing normal school. They had not done so, and never would because normal work was dreary, childish, and trivial. The only question worthy of debate was whether the colleges, and particularly Harvard, might establish a program in pedagogy, or whether a new state institution should be established. Principals M. C. Lamprey of Easton and A. S. Roe of Worcester believed that teacher education should occur within the undergraduate colleges, since a postgraduate course would require financial sacrifices that most candidates could not or would not make. A new graduate normal school ran counter to the objective of recruiting more college graduates into teaching.

But most of the others disagreed that colleges were the best site. MacDonald noted that true learned professions had schools, not chairs, and that it seemed unlikely that any college was prepared to establish a school of pedagogy. Unlike Lamprey, he did not fear erecting more difficult obstacles to entry. These obstacles would happily exclude those who were "poor in more than one sense." Principal A. K. Potter of Middleboro agreed that a separate institution "might do much toward elevating our work to the dignity of a true profession and might attract many who are now repelled by the fact that teaching is so often a last resort for those unable to spend longer time in preparation for a profession." The function of extended training was primarily to recruit the able student with career options, regardless of what other benefits training might also convey.

In any event, the issue of action by Harvard seemed already foreclosed. In remarks at the New England Association meeting just weeks before, Eliot had opposed the idea that specialized training in education be introduced in colleges or universities. Harvard was already making a substantial contribution to teacher education, Eliot emphasized, without any formalized courses in pedagogy. It was "by developing new methods of teaching subjects that colleges make teachers best equipped for their work." Eliot added, however, that he had no objection to the development of a truly high normal school elsewhere.

Quite apart from Harvard's intentions, the principals knew that most high school teachers were women and would likely be women for the foreseeable future. A Harvard initiative would offer limited recruitment potential. The proposed high normal school, in contrast, would be coeducational. The overwhelming consensus of the special conference was to petition for the creation of a new state

institution open only to college graduates and completely independent of the existing normals. Curriculum details would be left to the
Board of Education.[10]

Despite a half-year struggle before the Massachusetts legislature
in 1890, the high school men could not forge an effective alliance to
favor their proposal. Dickinson had no desire for a new state institution that ran counter to his fundamental beliefs. He preferred a
smaller initiative at Harvard if that would defuse the larger internal
threat. Eliot withdrew his casual early support of the high normal
school. He now argued that the state would not provide enough
money for anything but a "cheap high normal school," which would
inevitably fall into the hands of Dickinson and his allies. Having
recently determined that elementary schools took too long to accomplish too little, Eliot blamed the normals and claimed it was ludicrous to entrust an additional and more complex task to the state.
Dickinson and others countered that elementary teaching was superior to that in high schools, and Eliot was more fiercely denounced
by elementary school spokesmen than ever before. Privately Eliot
lobbied to prevent Dickinson's reappointment as Secretary to the
Board of Education.[11]

Contemporary observers regarded Eliot's opposition as critical to
defeating the high-normal-school bill. A disappointed John Tetlow,
who had failed to persuade Eliot that opposition did nothing to advance secondary teaching or check the normals' influence, pointedly
advised that he was now responsible for suggesting a better scheme.
Boston's school superintendent Edwin Seaver remarked that the
obvious answer to Eliot's financial argument was to establish high
school teacher training in a university already blessed with rich and
varied resources. Such action, Seaver went on, would be in the "intelligent self-interest" of higher education, for it would help close
the "widening gap" between colleges and schools that so concerned
Eliot. Seaver knew Eliot personally and assured the high school men
that Harvard's president had spoken off the top of his head when he
had previously rejected the idea of formal teacher education at Harvard. Eliot's mind, Seaver was sure, was still open.[12]

The time in fact was propitious for Eliot to reconsider his position. The overseers were about to reject the faculty's proposals to
shorten the undergraduate course; in the wake of that rejection
Eliot's concern for shortening the school course increased. He was

now convinced that school reform was the highest University priority. Successful opposition to the high normal school did little to reverse expansion of the existing normals. Possible passage of the bill during the next legislative session would only produce a weak institution that Dickinson would control. A specific Harvard initiative in teacher education might deflect pressure for a state institution and would be one additional weapon in Harvard's growing fight to disseminate its ideas to the schools. If Harvard took the lead, teacher education might be shaped in Massachusetts on Eliot's terms. It was hardly surprising that in the fall of 1890 Eliot asked the Harvard faculty to consider creating "a possible Normal Course of one year designed to meet the demand of those who sought legislative action from the General Court in 1889/90 in favor of such a project." Colleges such as Wellesley took similar action. The state Board of Education soon concluded that no further requests to the legislature for a new institution need be made.[13]

WHEN HARVARD PLANNED its "Normal Course," the case for including education within the widening curriculum of the modern university seemed compelling to many Americans with no special brief for normal schools. Charles Francis Adams, Jr., had proposed a decade before that universities teach education just as they taught dentistry, mining, and agriculture. Adams sensed the futility of local reform efforts that relied exclusively on the isolated efforts of a few charismatic leaders. He had tried just that approach in bringing Francis W. Parker to the Quincy schools, but saw how Parker's efforts were undercut by established schoolmen more concerned with the system and mechanical methods than with child-centered pedagogy. The way to overcome a mechanical system, Adams believed, was to substitute a scientific one. A large class of enlightened professional leaders could be nurtured if the universities would establish chairs of pedagogy to train them. Parker's example made Adams confident that a useful field of pedagogy existed. There was "just as much a science in developing the more ordinary faculties of the human mind as there is in raising crops or extracting minerals from the earth . . . The operation of the child's mind, the natural processes of growth and assimilation which go on in it, its inherent methods of development and acquisition, must be long and patiently studied."[14]

Professor Edmund J. James of the University of Pennsylvania, a leader in the movement to advance economics as a social science, was sure that a science of education was possible too. Universities were the only institutions capable of advancing knowledge about education. Normal schools were mere "distributing reservoirs" for ideas evolved elsewhere. The organization of educational knowledge into a separate university subject, James believed, would signify that teaching no longer was a "simple, bald handicraft" and would generate interest among university students where none had existed before. Moreover, the time teachers invested in studying the field would discourage them from grasping at some other calling at the first opportunity. James went beyond Adams to suggest a role for education in liberal as well as professional studies. It could offer the same kind of mental discipline as was available through other philosophical or moral sciences. Armed with such arguments he found it astonishing that Harvard, which seemed to teach everything else, had neglected education.[15]

Several universities began to act by the late 1880s. Cornell imported Michigan's example to the East. Columbia's president failed, despite repeated attempts, to convince his trustees to introduce the new field but encouraged a young protégé, Nicholas Murray Butler, to continue the battle. By 1887 Butler had created a new institution, the New York College for the Training of Teachers, which he hoped to affiliate with Columbia and develop on a grander scale. In 1890 New York University opened a school of pedagogy. When Stanford opened the next year, it included a department of the history and art of education. Three years later John Dewey established a department of pedagogy in the University of Chicago.

While these university efforts accelerated, leaders of the existing organized profession also advanced the claim that education constituted a complex intellectual subject. The claim had been made earlier in the century by well-educated Massachusetts men who promoted educational reform and the establishment of normal schools. But the normals at first had backed away from the idea. The poor preparation of most students militated against serious attention to education as a scholarly field. By emphasizing easily communicated procedures such as object teaching, the normals acknowledged the limited background of their constituency. But if devices and techniques constituted normal instruction, normal leaders began to emphasize that practical methods were not derived from merely "empirical" raw experience but rather from immutable laws of mind. Even if a "science of education" was not easily accessible to normal students, the leaders claimed it existed and justified the normals' growing ambitions.[16]

John W. Dickinson produced at the age of seventy-three a treatise that defended his methods by explicating the mental laws from which they stemmed. He had spent his life developing, teaching, and promoting the methods. His career was propelled not by theoretical explication, but by practical advocacy of the one true educational method, a variation on object teaching called the "analytic objective" method. Dickinson thought the entirety of elementary education consisted of facts that could be taught by "presenting the objects with which the facts are found connected." He pioneered the use of blackboards to teach facts not associated with concrete and visible objects, but with relationships among objects. Unusually committed to his method, he once suggested that each Williams College teacher be assigned a personal classroom so that alumni could better remember the particular doctrines of individual professors.[17]

Dickinson's career was wholly isolated from higher education, which he always considered a threat to the upward extension of normal ideals. But the careers of other leaders of elementary education were boosted by links they established with colleges and universities. For these men, more direct attention to the "science of education" was far more essential than to Dickinson. William T. Harris, the famous St. Louis school superintendent, United States Commissioner of Education, and Hegelian philosopher, did not hold a university appointment but retained extensive personal and professional university connections throughout his career. The best example of the normal school man who emphasized educational science as he entered a university environment was Professor William H. Payne of the University of Michigan.

Payne was arguably the first American university professor of education, nearly the only one in the early 1880s, and certainly the best known by the end of the decade. Self-educated beyond the academy level, Payne ascended to Michigan following service as teacher, principal, editor of the *Michigan Journal of Education*, normal school principal, and superintendent of schools. His remarkable mobility exemplified the career possibilities made feasible by expansion and organization within elementary education. Acutely sensitive to his pioneer role in converting a normal background to a successful university career, Payne argued for a true profession of education in terms that anticipated the Massachusetts high school men. From his university setting, Payne contended that the normal schools' stress on "mechanical exactness and expertness" produced a "machine" rather than teachers of "freedom and versatility." The secret to achieving professional status was to emphasize the complex principles that constituted educational science. At Michigan, Payne tried to teach only theory. The task of converting principles into practice was left for students to work out on their own. True professionals were taught to *do by knowing*. Only quacks professed the dogma that one learned to *do* by *doing*. His own professional role was to codify the principles of educational science, and he published widely to this end in the 1880s. One measure of Payne's success in adapting a normal background to the modern university was his later appointment as president of Vanderbilt University.[18]

By the end of the eighties the possibility of a complex university-based subject of education had been raised by reformers and university men, and by members of the organized, normal-oriented profession. Eliot readily endorsed the importance of expertise in education, the value of professional educationists, and the centrality of the university as the source of educational knowledge. One colleague even imagined Eliot himself as the ideal professor of education and urged him to teach it at Harvard. But Eliot had always been dubious about education as a separate academic field. Nicholas Murray Butler thought him the logical person to prepare an article for the opening issue of *Educational Review* arguing against the possibilities of a science of education. Eliot demurred from this theoretical exercise, but could not avoid the practical task of deciding what role education as a subject would play in Harvard's new Normal Course.[19]

ELIOT WAS SUSPICIOUS of a subject of education despite his firm belief in the existence of authoritative educational knowledge. The philosophic substance of American educational science seemed to him profoundly wrong. The core of that science was a sustained defense of German idealism against the materialist threat of Herbert Spencer. Spencer's strident individualism, his utilitarian emphasis on science rather than on classical studies, his abandonment of consciousness and will to evolutionary determinism, and his religious agnosticism were all central targets for schoolmen primarily interested in the development of moral character. Payne, for example, emphasized the inner forces that "predetermined" man toward upward growth and condemned the view that man was a "passive victim of environment." He fought the decline of the classical curriculum, the disinterest in metaphysics, the waning faith in religious ideals, and the threat to moral stability posed by an unyielding practicality. Dickinson, whose idealism led him to define the main goal of elementary education as self-control, steadfastly maintained that reasoning powers should be encouraged only during secondary education. When he oversaw Westfield Normal, Darwin and Spencer were banned.[20]

Yet it was precisely Spencer's educational theory that gave Eliot philosophic backing for his emphasis on reasoning as an educational aim, expansion of the university curriculum and especially of science, the inductive method of teaching, and individual development through appeals to student interest and free choice of subjects. Eliot, moreover, was utterly unsympathetic to speculative methods that permitted educational theorists to derive a science of education from personal introspection rather than from direct experience. For Payne and Dickinson the sole source of knowledge about mind was conscious reflection, and both believed that knowledge of mental principles was "well-settled." For Eliot the educational value of particular subjects of instruction had to be determined by practical experience with those subjects over time, not by theoretical deductions from first principles. Even the important role idealist thinkers ascribed to historical study as a source of new educational knowledge had little appeal for him. Close examination of educational history would merely yield evidence of anachronistic bad practice. The past could offer no lessons on teaching modern subjects in modern ways.[21]

Although the science of education in 1890 was dominated by introspective study of mind and by history, Eliot was aware of newer pressures to observe and analyze contemporary educational data. Many advocates of educational science from outside the organized profession, like Charles F. Adams and Edmund James, assumed that

the field would employ inductive or Baconian methods rather than
a priori speculation. Eliot himself had helped to promote inductive
pedagogical study by consenting in 1881 to Harvard sponsorship of
a lecture series on pedagogy and philosophy by the young psychologist, G. Stanley Hall. Earlier than any other American, Hall began
to link German inductive psychology with the study of pedagogy.

After a youthful infatuation with Hegel had passed, G. Stanley
Hall took the first American Ph.D. in psychology under William
James. Fresh from a second academic journey to Germany, this time
to study under Wundt, Hall told his lecture audiences (including
Adams) that education should be studied through observation of
"facts or phenomena" rather than through "theory accepted before-
hand." Science meant a process of investigation rather than an
orderly arrangement of principles. Soon afterwards Hall launched
the child study movement in America. Some idealists like Payne refused to embrace child study, but other schoolmen perceived that
Hall's inductive approach might lend immense authority to teaching and also confirm older truths of the introspective tradition. The
notion of science could be more opportunity than threat, and teachers were urged to collect data about pupil behavior and characteristics.[22]

Despite pockets of pedagogical enthusiasm for an inductive educational science, the attitudes of local academicians whom Eliot
knew best were far more reserved. By 1890 even Hall had become
dubious. Increasingly preoccupied with creating pure experimental
psychology, Hall left the Johns Hopkins University in 1888 to become founding president of Clark University. By then Hall viewed
pedagogy only as one branch of applied psychology whose content
could easily be determined once pure psychology became firmly
established. Having no intention to establish education within the
Clark curriculum, he abandoned child study and admitted that
existing pedagogical literature was "dreary, and would be fatal to
the cause if introduced into the university course." Hall's reluctance
to endorse education as a separate field worthy of inclusion into his
own university, despite his reputation as America's leading advocate
of inductive educational study, was not lost on Eliot. That judgment, moreover, was confirmed by the Harvard professors to whom
Eliot turned for counsel: William James and Josiah Royce.[23]

William James regarded education as a mixture of the "mighty and aspiring generalities" of idealist philosophy and the "puerile concretes" of normal school technique. He knew William T. Harris and found his Hegelianism "tedious" and "preposterous," though Harris personally charmed him with an "innocence and apostolic disposition." James was equally dubious about Hall's experimentalist confidence in "jawbreaking German laboratory-articles" but, like Hall himself, saw no significant tendency toward a separate inductive pedagogy. Although he reluctantly agreed at Eliot's request to offer lectures on pedagogical psychology in the proposed Normal Course, James claimed no special pedagogical knowledge and would cover only the habit, association, apperception, and attention topics in common psychology.[24]

Josiah Royce, the idealist philosopher whom Eliot chose to chair the faculty committee to develop Harvard's Normal Course, shared James's skepticism about excessive claims of any philosophical school. After Eliot turned down Butler's request to argue against a science of education, Butler approached Royce with greater success. In the same weeks that Royce labored with the practical questions of determining what Harvard's program in teacher education should be, he wrote down his view that no distinct science of education existed, or could exist, from which rules of educational practice might be derived. All attempts to formulate a separate science of education, Royce contended, assumed that the function of the field was to supply valid rules of procedure for teaching the young. This was true regardless of whether they relied on older, deductive, unified theories of mind or whether they looked to the fragmented monographic literature of recent experimental psychology.

But, he cautioned, the "lesson of the historical as well as of the biological sciences is that when you undertake to discuss the growth of a complex organism you must not expect to deduce all the wealth of the details of this life from your account of the general type of the growth itself." Modern psychology might indeed provide valuable knowledge of general aspects of human growth. The distinctive characteristic of teaching, however, was its concern for the particular situations of individual pupils and individual teachers. In teaching, the "detail" was more important than the "type." There could be no science of education "that will not need constant and vast adaptation to the needs of this teacher or of that, constant modification in the presence of the live pupil, constant supplementing by the divine skill of the born teacher's instincts." Teachers most needed to know just what "science abstracts from and ignores." Since the act of teaching dealt with unique people and situations, true pedagogy was an art.

Royce thus undercut the main issue of pedagogical debate in 1890. Instead of discussing the means by which education could become a true science, he attacked the very notion that any separate subject could contain principles directly applicable to instruction. By noting how pedagogical systems inexorably produced faddist endorsement of this or that "true" method, he sought to resurrect the place of personal insight and experience opposed by both speculative and inductive camps. Royce stressed that he did not claim that psychology or philosophy had no value for teachers. Knowledge of these fields could offer general guidelines and prevent gross error. Ignorance was indefensible. Moreover, though he spoke in places of "born" teachers, Royce also claimed that the skill needed to practice the art of teaching—skill to adapt teaching strategy to the particulars of classroom situations—was similar to the *method* of modern psychological research. Psychology's value to a teacher was more to "train his power of diagnosis, than to equip him with abstract pedagogical rules." The effective teacher should be a "naturalist," skilled in the "habit of observing the mental life of children for its own sake, and of judging the relative value of its moods and tendencies."

Royce thought that the very attempt to create a separate field of education focused misguided attention on universally applicable principles. The knowledge of mind teachers needed could be gained through the study of psychology itself, along with the skill of mental diagnosis that came from understanding psychological method. Royce believed that teachers needed well-formulated ethical ideals along with knowledge of psychological method, but the best way to learn these was through the church or through university courses on ethics. Thus he could oppose a separate science of education but simultaneously favor university action to train teachers

When William James made his own position more explicit in his later lectures to teachers on psychology, he followed Royce's lead. He opposed the idea that psychology or pedagogy could yield "definite programmes and schemes and methods of instruction for immediate schoolroom use." Good teaching could not contravene general laws of psychology, but knowledge of psychology did not guarantee effective teaching. The essential skills were artistic: a "happy tact and ingenuity to tell us what definite things to say and do when the pupil is before us." But James stopped short of embracing psychological method as proper training for the teacher's art. He regarded abstract and analytical psychological observation as contradictory to the concrete and ethical attitudes he associated with good teaching, and opposed the child study effort to make teachers classroom experimenters.

Royce never explored further his suggestion—so different from Payne's theoretical emphasis—that aspects of the teaching art might be advanced by university instruction. One of the common criticisms of Massachusetts normal schools was that they neglected practice teaching in favor of inculcating method, and one of the strongest recommendations of high school men who advocated secondary teacher education was to incorporate observation and practice as central elements. Yet neither this nor other organizational means to further the teaching art were suggested by Harvard's pedagogical planners.[25]

BEYOND THE INTELLECTUAL reservations of respected colleagues, Eliot lacked enthusiasm for an inductive alternative to speculative educational science because he saw education's task as advocacy rather than as analysis. Never an active proponent of research as a Harvard priority, he valued it even less in a field where implementation of the known seemed much more pressing than discovery of the unknown. He never explored the political possibility that a separate subject of education might organize and codify the reforms he wanted. Instead he hoped to disseminate sound educational principles by incorporating them into existing school subjects.

The very nature of Eliot's reform agenda suggested the political advantage of dispersing its educational content into the various school subjects. In the nineties he applied University-derived innovations to younger and younger age groups. The grammar school curriculum, he asserted, was too narrow. Insufficient attention was paid to science and modern foreign languages. Too much attention was paid to memory work rather than to development of reasoning power. Individual differences and interests were everywhere ignored. This characterization of the problem suggested the remedy.

Education at all levels had to be *unified*. The way to get school systems to resemble modern universities pedagogically was to reshape them to resemble universities organizationally.

To institutionalize university influence, Eliot wished to encourage role similarities among educators at all levels. He advocated specialization of teaching according to academic subjects even in the lower grades, preferring competence to teach one subject across a wide age range over competence to teach many subjects to a single age group. He urged that school faculties be organized by the university departmental system. Leading teachers would become department chairmen, and young assistants would teach small groups under the direction of regular teachers. Eliot supported tenure and higher salaries for teachers, and hoped modern superintendents (like university presidents) would preside over faculty meetings and be responsive to faculty sentiment. By encouraging school systems to adopt university procedures, Eliot hoped to increase the authority and intellectual excitement of the teacher's job and thus recruit and retain better-educated (especially male) teachers. At the same time, the departmental organization would build far stronger channels of downward influence from higher education. Normal-oriented schoolmen fully understood and bitterly protested Eliot's "aristocratic" attempt to guarantee university domination.[26]

It was hardly surprising that the Harvard Normal Course which emerged in 1890-91 aimed mainly to redeploy existing departmental resources. The faculty authorized thirteen short courses in the proper content and methods of subjects usually taught in secondary schools. "Skilful teachers," Eliot explained, "should be able to give some account of their methods for the benefit of those who are beginning to teach." The courses would be controlled by the departments and given by the regular faculty. Male graduates of colleges or scientific schools could enroll in one or several. Although no credit would be offered, special certificates would be awarded to those who completed the work.[27]

Where departments felt a special stake in the schools, they readily accommodated themselves to a newly labeled but essentially familiar task. Cooke and Hall agreed to teach methods in chemistry and physics, and Hart agreed to carry the burden in history. One professor who had spent a career promoting the sight reading of French thought there was "really nothing I could do more easily than to lecture to teachers upon French teaching." But it was harder to stimulate interest in departments with less prior involvement in school reform. The English entrance requirements, for example, were mainly in composition although literature was the main interest of the English Department. (Indeed, the department had been severely criticized by an overseers committee in 1884 for offering instruction in written English "grossly unworthy of Harvard University.") Professor LeBaron Russell Briggs, who set the admissions examination, thought the secret to teaching composition was not a method but a teacher with a "clear head, an enduring conscience, an elastic enthusiasm, and uncommon commonsense." Unlike Hall, Hart, and Cooke, he saw little continuity between his Harvard academic instruction and the work of the schools. Briggs thought too much energy would be required to master two separate spheres of educational activity. Only with great reluctance did he agree to help teach a methods course.[28]

Whenever possible, the faculty tried to disassociate its effort from teacher education elsewhere. It struck out the word "Normal" from final program descriptions and overturned Royce's recommendation that women be admitted to the lectures. It endorsed, by the divided vote of 28 to 14, Royce's suggestion that Eliot consider a new appointment in the "art of teaching." The vote hardly endorsed education as a university subject. Royce was tired of moderating faculty disagreements and wanted someone else to administer the program. The final job title of "history and art of teaching" carefully excluded "science," which was to be covered by separate lectures by James on psychology. Eliot announced that the faculty had little interest or confidence in pedagogy as a subject, and he endorsed the new position mainly for its administrative convenience. The increasing pace of Harvard's school reform activities required added staff support. Schools had to be visited, the Harvard presence extended in teachers' associations and institutes, the anticipated growth of teachers in summer courses attended to, and the new program conducted. The faculty made sure that control over teacher education rested not with the new instructor but with a faculty committee chaired by Royce.[29]

G. Stanley Hall once suggested that the best way to develop a university teacher of pedagogy was to select a bright young man with some teaching experience, and arrange for him a thorough course of educational study at home and abroad. Eliot's approach to filling the Harvard position revealed no such elaborate ambition His son, a Denver minister, recommended one of his parishioners when Eliot was a house guest during a western speaking tour The candidate was invited to meet the president, and after dinner Eliot suddenly offered a five-year assistant professorship. The astonished appointee was not particularly young, had no degree beyond the B.S., had never studied abroad, and had taught pedagogy jus long enough to decide to give it up. Nonetheless Eliot saw in him other qualities more germane to Harvard's special needs.[30]

Paul Henry Hanus, then nearing his thirty-sixth birthday, had emigrated as a young boy from Prussia to Wisconsin. His stepfather was a mining entrepreneur who moved around the country with his family as new opportunites opened up, and Hanus attended common schools in rural New York, Wisconsin, and Colorado. At twelve he became an apprentice druggist in Denver for three years, received his secondary education at a Wisconsin normal school, and then worked for a year in a New York drug-import business. Energetic and ambitious, Hanus studied chemistry, physics, algebra, and geometry in the evenings at Cooper Union. His stepfather was successful enough to finance his enrollment at the University of Michigan, where Hanus continued to concentrate on science and mathematics. Following graduation in 1878 he returned to Colorado to teach a year in a Denver high school, spent a year as instructor in mathematics at the new University of Colorado, and then resigned to establish a drugstore. In 1881 he returned to the university as a full professor of mathematics, publishing in 1886 a treatise on *Elements of Determinants*.

From time to time Hanus was sent by university authorities on speaking tours throughout the state to drum up grass-roots support for higher education. At the same time, he conducted teachers' institutes on the various subjects of school instruction. 'As time went on," he later recalled, "I found myself much more interested in studying schools than I was in studying mathematics." Hanus resigned from the Colorado faculty in 1886 to become principal of a Denver high school. Thereafter he identified his career more and more with education, and reached out beyond Colorado to secure

minor administrative positions at the Chicago and San Francisco
NEA conventions in 1887 and 1888. In 1890 he turned down a
mathematics professorship at the University of Wyoming and accepted instead the professorship of pedagogy at the new Colorado
State Normal School at Greeley.

But he found the work at Greeley disappointing. His scientific
background collided with the assumptions of the normal school. He
was expected to teach psychology, principles of pedagogy, and history of pedagogy. Knowing nothing about any of these subjects, he
felt completely uncomfortable with the available deductive and
speculative literature. He was most comfortable with practical responsibilities such as advising how to teach reading and arithmetic,
and directing Greeley's "model school." When his old Denver principalship became vacant in early 1891, Hanus decided to return to
it. Then he met Eliot and received the chance of his life.[31]

Hanus' main appeal to Eliot was probably the scientific biases
that both men shared. Here was a devoted schoolman committed to
observation and induction rather than to introspective theorizing.
Lacking the means to continue his scientific interests through graduate study, Hanus had pursued them instead through amateur
botany, geology, and zoology—and finally through education.
Above all he believed in the preeminence of facts. Hanus passion-
ately sought out and classified fossils, ferns, mollusks, snakes, and
bird skins. As an educator, he believed students learned through
examining particulars, observing, comparing, inferring, expressing,
and applying. That is, they learned by "doing rather than through
verbal instruction." School curricula should be broadened, he
thought, beyond the traditional disciplinary subjects to embrace the
external world. Pedagogy itself had to abandon speculative theorizing in favor of studying schools as they "actually were."

Hanus' experience well prepared him to link various levels of education and advance the unity of educational practice. His career
had been propelled forward by the rapid expansion of public education in Colorado in the 1880s. By 1891 he was experienced in virtually all aspects of that system and had been chosen president of
the Colorado State Teachers Association. His ready confession of
pedagogical ignorance was, to Eliot, a source of strength. Although
Royce urged him to familiarize himself with modern psychological

and philosophical literature as quickly as possible, Eliot cared little about this academic preparation. Seeking primarily an effective ally in the school reform movement, the president was far more concerned whether Hanus' ignorance of Greek would affect his ambassadorial relations with conservative Massachusetts schoolmen.[32]

3

Transformations in Professional Identity

EVERYONE WAS PUZZLED by what Hanus' role would be. His subject and duties were only vaguely defined. He was not sure what to teach, nor was it even certain that instruction would be a central responsibility.[1] But very quickly a role took shape that seemed both comfortable and appropriate. Hanus functioned as an amplifier for Harvard's school reform movement. The content of his instruction generally followed Eliot's educational line, and his administrative duties reinforced links among the various mechanisms used to deepen Harvard's school influence. Moreover, he became the equal of other colleagues after his courses were counted for regular academic credit and attracted an undergraduate audience instead of the anticipated graduate constituency of prospective teachers.

The stability of the amplifier role depended on the stability of University sentiment for school reform. In the late 1890s Harvard's commitment to shape school practice began to weaken. Many of the problems that had originally stimulated Eliot's interest now seemed under control. And the growing sense that scholarly research was indispensable for faculty advancement made participation in school reform professionally unwise. Above all, Eliot's central tenets of student freedom and vocationalism were subjected to counterattack by faculty members urging a return to discipline and structure. Hanus' work symbolized an educational ideology increasingly on the defensive within Harvard. He survived by reshaping his role to fit the new circumstances.

The most dramatic change was the emphasis he gave to training experienced administrators at the graduate level rather than prospective teachers in Harvard College. Administrative training expanded his own political influence and self-esteem at the same time that it caused far less collegial friction than had teacher education. Significantly, school administrators seemed more important than teachers because their role was to direct education conceived of as a "social force." At the turn of the century Hanus' substantive interests shifted from promoting closer links between Harvard and the lower schools to promoting a variety of educational services for the mass of youth who would never attend college at all. In the mid-nineties his characteristic duties included managing the Schools Examination Board and expanding the Harvard Teachers Association. Within a decade he had allied himself with powerful social reform forces in Boston, helped organize a Social Education Congress, chaired a state Commission on Industrial Education, and led the executive committee of the Boston Vocation Bureau.

These role changes had important consequences inside Harvard. Hanus' program gradually won greater administrative autonomy within the faculty of arts and sciences. Nevertheless, he realized that other universities were rapidly surpassing Harvard in their commitment to education. As his own ambitions soared he became more frustrated and embittered by Harvard's unwillingness to underwrite major expansion. Ominously, the appointment of A. Lawrence Lowell to the presidency in 1909 promised an even more troubled and uncertain future.

A skeptic about pedagogy in a skeptical environment Paul Hanus' most immediate Harvard problem was to decide what to teach. Cautiously he adopted the familiar curriculum plan developed by Michigan's William H. Payne in the early 1880s. Payne at first divided education into "theoretical" and "practical" spheres but by 1882 had removed history from theory to form a third division of instruction. For Payne history conferred special advantages. Its respectability as a "culture subject" might ease education's own acceptance into the university curriculum. History could stimulate professional pride by associating schoolmen with an "honorable and honored ancestry." Above all Payne used history to attack contemporary materialism, thwart inductive investigation, and emphasize that valid educational truth was already imbedded in previous human experience. With history separated from educational theory, Payne defined theory as the study of mind. His practical course, unwanted but necessary, treated methods and school management. Charles Kendall Adams commended Payne's tripartite curriculum to the New England Association in 1888, and it was subsequently accepted in most early formulations of educational study in New England colleges.[2]

Although Hanus borrowed familiar categories, his approach to all three courses departed strikingly from Payne's. History attracted him for some of Payne's reasons, but he regarded it as a source of new facts about thought and practice rather than as a defense against modern science. At first he imagined that history would be his central scholarly pursuit once he gained access to the resources available in Harvard libraries, and educators elsewhere reinforced that expectation. Hanus accepted Nicholas Murray Butler's invitation to prepare a volume on the impact of Rousseau's educational ideas. He also began to translate Comenius' "Didactica Meagna," which William T. Harris agreed to publish in his International Education series. But despite this encouragement Hanus' historical interest quickly waned, and he abandoned both writing projects. He continued to believe in history's value in educational studies, but privately resolved to give up teaching it as soon as someone else could be found.[3]

If Payne regarded the study of mind as the core of educational theory, Hanus never evinced any interest in psychology. He pursued neither Royce's suggestion to become a psychological collaborator of James nor James's willingness to withdraw if Hanus himself wished to lecture on psychology for teachers. Hanus repudiated introspective psychology but lacked training and interest in the newer inductive psychology. Instead of undercutting his ambitions, James's lectures in psychology strengthened the reputation of the teacher education program and freed Hanus from the need to define educational theory in primarily psychological terms. Without psychology as an organizing principle for theory, Hanus was forced to "spin largely from my own substance." His course treated educational aims and the best means to achieve them by drawing on his Colorado experience and his growing involvement with the Harvard school reform movement.[4]

Immediately upon his arrival in Cambridge, Hanus was swept into a variety of coordinating and promotional activities. Shaler made him secretary of the Harvard Teachers Association, and he rapidly extended its membership and reputation through well-organized annual conferences. He administered the Schools Examination Board, visited schools remote from Cambridge to stimulate applications and administer admissions examinations, helped Shaler build a teacher education curriculum in the Lawrence Scientific School, and taught Cambridge grammar school teachers in Hart's in-service program. Hanus provided Eliot with information for educational speeches and correspondence and was himself in constant demand as a speaker. As the principal link between all the school reform activities, Hanus reinforced their connections and amplified their impact. No sooner had Eliot enunciated his goal to "unify" education at all levels than the Harvard Teachers Association devoted a meeting to the idea and tried to build a membership roster ranging from grammar school to university representatives.

Not surprisingly, Hanus' notions of educational theory paralleled Eliot's. The basic aim of education, he argued, was individual usefulness and happiness. For each individual, these ends were reached by harmonizing "his interest and capacity with his life work." The secret was informed vocational choice. The means to ensure this were a broadened curriculum during all the school years, more electives, and greater reliance on inductive teaching. Like Eliot, Hanus emphasized specific policy reforms rather than theoretical justifications for them and was especially wary of psychological faddism. Herbartian categories were pretentious, child study sentimental, and laboratory psychology limited in its implications for method.

At certain points their thinking diverged. Eliot believed that many subjects could develop general intellectual power and refrained from ranking them according to their educational value. Hanus tended to regard power as specific to particular fields and considered "ethical" fields concerned with institutions, ideals, and conduct as more educationally valuable than fields dealing only with external nature. Yet his reliance on interest as the catalyst for all academic achievement, and his conviction that vocation was the main source of personal fulfillment, overrode his hierarchy of subjects and led him to celebrate the widest curriculum and the largest choice. In later years he acknowledged again and again the profound intellectual impact Eliot's ideas had made on him.[5]

Hanus' most creative efforts were concentrated in the third area of educational study that Payne had labeled the "practical" and

Harvard called the "art of teaching." Dramatically reversing Payne's priorities, Hanus dreamed that the future center of gravity of the field would be educational practice. As a confirmed naturalist used to discovering ferns and classifying rocks, nothing seemed more obvious than to observe educational activity as it occurred, collect facts about it, classify those facts, and then assess their meaning. Aware that educational practice meant far more than teaching technique, Hanus broadened Royce's idea of teacher-as-naturalist to include observation of significant educational endeavor outside classrooms and psychology. By defining education as the study of a complex social institution, he hoped to demonstrate that the art of teaching possessed as much cultural value as any other subject. Payne had placed his bets on history to make education a legitimate liberal art. Hanus bet instead on education as a contemporary social study. Within one year he changed the title of the "Art of Teaching" course to "Organization and Management of Public Schools and Academies."

Observation and fact collecting became Hanus' best-known initiative. He urged students to observe as much classroom teaching as possible, asked Eliot to establish a laboratory school to gather "actual facts," and proposed an additional course wholly devoted to observation. In the absence of funds for a laboratory school, he secured permission for his students to observe in local classrooms. Hanus dispensed with course texts on practical methods and replaced them with school documents and reports of investigating committees such as the Committee of Ten. Course examinations were dropped in favor of extremely long term papers which demanded comparisons of curriculum practices in different school systems. When he created a pedagogical seminar in 1893 to consider topics of special interest, he used local school reports to analyze curriculum policy.[6]

These early efforts to define his instructional role and disarm collegial skepticism won for Hanus a cautious sympathy among a small faculty majority. His suspicion of pedagogical panaceas, practical appeal to induction, general espousal of Eliot's educational beliefs, and conscientious management of Harvard's school links reassured the faculty of like persuasion that normal school thought had not penetrated Harvard Yard. The earliest test of faculty acquiescence was perhaps the most crucial he ever faced. The three education courses, organized as regular half- and full-year offerings rather than as short courses, drew in 1891-92 only four teachers with sufficient interest, time, and funds to complete the work. Embarrassed by the small numbers and the anomaly of an assistant professor whose instruction could not count for academic credit, Royce's supervisory committee persuaded the faculty to count all three toward the A.M. degree. The faculty also voted in 1892 to count the history and theory courses toward the A.B. By a margin of one vote, the faculty one year later accepted the practical course for bachelor's credit as well.

Fairness alone probably explains the active support of men like Royce and James, but larger institutional issues were also at stake. Shaler wanted to develop an undergraduate teacher education program to boost enrollments in the Lawrence Scientific School. Credit for the education courses was necessary to implement his plan and he led the faculty debate in favor of granting it. More generally, Shaler hoped to end the continuing faculty debate about the time needed for professional studies by establishing the principle that explicit vocational preparation was a legitimate function of the A.B. course. Despite Hanus' contention that his courses had cultural as well as vocational value, few faculty actions in the nineties better symbolized endorsement of undergraduate vocationalism than the decision to count all of Hanus' instruction toward the A.B. degree.[7]

These votes created an unexpected and indispensable undergraduate market to make up for lagging graduate enrollments. In 1896 Hanus persuaded Boston school authorities to waive the year of experience normally required to take high school teacher's examinations for Harvard College graduates who had passed appropriate education courses. His triumph revealed how quickly Harvard had dropped its assumption that teacher education was a graduate function. In the same year Hanus strengthened his undergraduate appeal by establishing practice teaching courses in collaboration with the towns of Newton and Brookline. A year later Eliot organized an Appointments Committee to handle the growing requests for nominations for teaching jobs. The committee discerned both rising undergraduate interest in secondary teaching and the rising value of education courses in ensuring access to public school positions. In 1897 a group of Radcliffe College[8] friends became sufficiently interested in teacher education to pay a second Harvard instructor,

George Herbert Locke, to repeat education courses at Radcliffe. By 1901 the courses had grown to 236 undergraduate enrollments compared with only 76 graduate ones. Three fourths of the undergraduates in Hanus' least vocational courses said that they took them for vocational preparation.[9]

PAUL HANUS' instructional and managerial performance won him a second five-year appointment, but after 1895 he had to contend with new forces emerging in the faculty. Increasing research specialization and a growing reaction against undergraduate freedom and vocationalism gradually challenged Eliot's Harvard. School reform in general, and undergraduate teacher education in particular, symbolized educational values criticized by an articulate faculty minority. The environment that had permitted Hanus to function now turned against him.

The short departmental methods courses were originally regarded as far more important than Hanus' pedagogical instruction. But most attracted few students and became increasingly marginal after the education courses secured credit and attracted undergraduate degree candidates. Although Hanus urged that departmental instruction be incorporated into the regular undergraduate curriculum alongside his own courses, the departments were unwilling to enlarge and regularize their involvement in teacher education. Nor was any pressure put on them to do so. Royce's committee regarded its diplomatic duties at an end when the faculty accepted Hanus' courses on an equal basis with all other offerings. Only Shaler seemed committed to methods courses for credit. Upon his request, Hanus organized a course on science methods for Shaler's teacher education curriculum. Shaler then led the successful faculty debate to count that course toward undergraduate degrees.

Despite Shaler's enthusiasm, many colleagues thought that the course usurped departmental responsibility. Hanus himself was the official instructor and staffed the course with experienced school science teachers in addition to the few Harvard scientists he persuaded to participate. Edwin Hall warned him that credit courses in methods as such were a grave mistake. The elementary physics course had been created as a model for schools and embodied departmental opinion on proper method. No additional instruction was necessary; in any case it was injudicious to import non-Harvard teachers to instruct in Harvard methods. Hanus thereafter backed away from offering in his name other methods courses with local teachers as staff, and attempted once more to persuade departments to offer them. Despite the lure of a small financial subsidy that Eliot made available, only classics, French, and German showed interest. A few such courses were irregularly given until 1907. Other professors, even those who cared about explicit method in their own instruction, feared that Hanus' actions betrayed a preoccupation with methods divorced from content.[10]

The problem of organizing instruction in methods, whether separate from content or combined with it, was symptomatic of a broader shift in faculty priorities. By the early nineties, the director of the physics laboratory no longer measured its success by the number of students enrolled in elementary courses but by its capacity to turn out well-trained professors and investigators. Even Edwin Hall, while appreciating Eliot's personal support for his efforts in school reform, lamented in 1895 that "whatever reputation I may have made in this way has probably done me more harm than good among college men, who are not, as a rule, interested in the work of preparatory schools." Because Hall was an experimentalist as well as an educator he survived the shift in values. Others were less fortunate. By the end of the century the chemistry department saw no further need to continue an elementary course corresponding to the admissions requirements or to keep the instructor who taught the course. To no avail, Joseph Torrey, Jr., argued that the teaching of elementary chemistry was as much of a specialty as was chemical research. Even established champions of school reform, like Shaler and Hart, were regarded as insufficiently scholarly by departmental colleagues.[11]

At the same time that research priorities helped to undercut methods instruction, faculty members opposed to undergraduate electives, specialization, and vocationalism began to attack Hanus' regular courses. Still a faculty minority during the late nineties, these critics associated Eliot's values with the erosion of community and social order in American life. Harvard's individualism seemed to Professor Hugo Münsterberg little more than "mercenary utilitarianism and selfish materialism." Münsterberg urged schools and colleges, instead of catering to vulgar self-interest, to develop virtues such as truth, harmony, unity, beauty, and duty. Professor Barrett Wendell, a mildly eccentric Boston aristocrat, hoped to restore the "moral" function of Harvard College by reestablishing discipline, good taste, and continuity with the past. Professor LeBaron R. Briggs believed that the goal of school and college education was to "establish character" and to make "moral character more efficient through mental discipline."

The details of their criticism were as varied as their backgrounds. Münsterberg, a German experimental psychologist brought in by James to develop a psychological laboratory, embraced Hegelian idealism as much as he did modern science. Wendell, an English professor with no training beyond his Harvard A.B., was forever preoccupied with his New England ancestry. Briggs, another English professor, served with distinction as dean of Harvard College in the nineties and thereafter as dean of the faculty of arts and sciences and president of Radcliffe. He cared more about the inner quality of the College than the situation of the larger society.

Yet these diverse men were drawn together by the themes of less free choice, less appeal to interests, less vocationalism, more curricular structure, more attention to academic rigor, and more concern for the total impact of an educational environment on moral character. If Shaler, Hart, and Hall had earlier pursued educational reform to promote their particular subjects, Münsterberg, Wendell, and Briggs later demanded reform to promote holistic notions of well-rounded character. The first group welcomed the study of education as a hopeful ally. The second thought education embodied everything they hated.[12]

The very idea of education as a specialized field contradicted their sense of what good teaching comprised. They all believed that specialization and vocationalism could best be combatted by teachers who themselves were less specialized, less preoccupied with vocational objectives, more well-rounded, and more idealistic. These qualities were not the outcome of brief, specialized technical training but were expressions of personality gradually formed by the entirety of educational and social experience. Everyone agreed on the importance of thorough scholarship in the subjects to be taught, although Münsterberg went much farther than most in advocating two years of graduate study for high school teachers. But they stressed that passion and commitment were equally indispensable, and that scholarly specialization too often produced uneducated teachers devoted solely to reproducing their narrow interests in students.

Münsterberg emphasized emotional rapport and ethical maturity. Teachers of the very young needed tact, patience, and understanding, while teachers of older students needed to fuse their love of subject with higher ideals of truth and beauty. Briggs agreed that the "man of intelligence and self-sacrifice who bends his energy to teaching boys will soon get enough scholarship for the purpose; whereas no amount of scholarship can make up for the want of intelligence and self-sacrifice." Professor George Herbert Palmer contended that failure in teaching was less often the result of technical ineptitude than of "personal defects."[13]

Barrett Wendell went so far as to argue that specialized teacher education would only recruit inferior people. A vigorous personality was required to attract and hold student attention. But vigorous college youth would see that teaching careers required them to renounce normal ambitions for wealth, power, "virile contest," and influence among equals. Only later in life, when their energy had been sapped by more demanding occupations, might such men be drawn to the "comparative retirement of academic seclusion."

Even if most critics did not share Wendell's unusual logic, they believed that Hanus' courses attracted academically weak students and required little work. Münsterberg condemned Hanus for meeting his courses fewer hours than was customary, and for granting additional credits without requiring extra work. Hanus bitterly denied the allegations, but he went on to assign longer and longer student term papers to eliminate the criticism. Eliot had to intervene to advise that the written work was excessive. Yet the beliefs persisted, for Hanus in fact was an easy grader and the judgments about his students' capacities were often made by administrative officers in a position to know. They reinforced the critics' attitudes at a time when concern for academic standards was growing within the Harvard faculty.[14]

Hanus' courses also generated hostility because of what they taught. If their existence exemplified the Harvard policies of specialization and vocationalism, their content propounded those very principles as educational truth. When Hanus attacked the special educational claims of Greek, his students dutifully reported the criticism to their Greek professors who angrily protested that he was undermining their subject. When Hanus asked teachers to reflect consciously on their educational aims, Münsterberg retorted that no committed teacher would submit to such overt utilitarianism. Clarifying aims would not develop better teachers, only their capacity to "talk about the purposes of the new education till all is covered by beautiful words."

When Hanus spoke of the value of psychology for teachers, in the cautious terms of Royce and James, Münsterberg denied that psychology had any value for teachers at all. In ringing phrases that won the affection of both normal-dominated journalism and William T. Harris, Münsterberg celebrated emotional empathy and derided psychology's modern tendency to "dissolve the personality into elements." When Hanus defended the elective system, and even set his seminar to gathering facts about its efficacy at Harvard, Münsterberg, Briggs, and Wendell all called for its abandonment. And when Hanus defended methods courses, Wendell rebuked him before the faculty with such vitriol that he found it necessary to apologize for his unforensic behavior. "The chief trouble," Wendell said after he had calmed down, was "old-fashioned ignorance, not neglect of 'pedagogy.' "[15]

Above all else the critics loathed the naive optimism of modern education. They contended that the appeal to electives, student interest, and inductive methods of teaching had not achieved the results that Eliot and Hanus claimed. Briggs complained that the elective system mainly made elective the habit of studying. Münsterberg argued that there were bad individual interests as well as good ones and that the elective system permitted "selfish enjoyment." Wendell observed that Harvard students were becoming "flabbier and flabbier in mind."

Like Briggs, Wendell cared deeply about educational methods at the college level and pioneered in the use of daily themes to teach English composition. Still, he argued that such modern methods were rarely judged by their results. He attacked the optimism that buttressed attempts to teach more and more subjects and create more and more graduate schools. Was all this formal education superior to the education offered by life experience? Did not deliberate education have limits that advocates of modern methods scarcely perceived? Even in his own field Wendell was pessimistic about what he had accomplished and suggested that perhaps English composition could never be effectively taught. He called for more experimentation, more caution, more attention to results. His attack on Eliot's administration, and on the education courses, was not a sign of disinterest in the educational process but rather a rejection of particular ideas. As Eliot's ideas faced more internal attack, Hanus' intellectual alliance with them became a liability.[16]

After 1900 these currents of faculty concern helped to create a less favorable climate for school reform. Professors interested in research were simply uninterested in schools. Critics of Eliot regarded Harvard College as the focus of reform efforts, not the schools. In the waning years of Eliot's presidency these critics began to cohere into a more potent political movement. Under the leadership of Wendell's closest friend, Professor Abbott Lawrence Lowell, a more structured, more rigorous, less vocational undergraduate curriculum began to take shape. By 1909 Lowell had forged enough political support to become Eliot's successor.

But the erosion of school reform was not wholly the result of newer faculty priorities. The remarkable growth of Harvard in the 1890s largely solved the problems of student recruitment and the ordering of professional studies. In the last decade of his presidency Eliot devoted less and less attention to the reforming of school subjects and instead stressed the limits of Harvard's direct influence on schools. Eliot understood that Harvard could not affect the public high schools by narrow prescription of studies but thought that wide options — with content and method still determined by Harvard ideas — could retain and expand influence on a looser basis. After 1906, when small decreases in the number of undergraduates raised once again the question of Harvard's hold on the schools, the University began to retreat from the inevitability of required Harvard admissions examinations. In 1906 the faculty voted to accept as an option the examinations of the new College Entrance Examination Board. Five years later it adopted an optional plan of admissions which distinguished between the quantity of work done, as assessed by a certificate, and the quality of the work, as assessed by four examinations with wide choices.[17]

The Schools Examination Board, in part a victim of the Committee of Ten, made its last visiting trip in 1896. Hart's in-service program for Cambridge teachers grew into an extension program, but its purpose shifted significantly. What had begun as an effort to re-train Cambridge teachers according to Harvard methods became, in the early twentieth century, an effort to provide general culture in fields, such as art and Russian literature, utterly unconnected with school curricula. Perhaps more than anything else, the death of Nathaniel Shaler in the spring of 1906 marked the end of an era. Shaler had been Hanus' most enthusiastic faculty supporter and closest faculty friend. No one had defended more strongly the elective system and the place of vocational studies in the undergraduate curriculum, and no one better exemplified opposition to both research specialization and more structured liberal education. Soon after his death the Lawrence Scientific School was absorbed into the faculty of arts and sciences and its undergraduate teacher education program abolished.[18]

NEAR THE END of the century Hanus had begun to contend that Harvard should train superintendents and high school principals as well as teachers. As undergraduate teacher education absorbed increasing faculty criticism, administrative training became a haven from collegial attack as well as a new source of students and influence. Eventually, too, administrative careers seemed better fitted than teaching careers to carry out Hanus' educational reform program.

The education courses had always attracted practicing and aspiring administrators in small numbers. The *New England Journal of Education* characterized administrative participants as "the most progressive of the secondary school men about Boston." Students such as Ray Greene Huling had been among the first to sound the call for secondary teacher education in New England. Both Hanus' seminar and course on organization and management provided a unique institutional structure for secondary administrators to explore contemporary issues among peers. Like the New England Association of Colleges and Preparatory Schools and the campaign for postgraduate teacher education, Hanus' advanced courses enabled high school men to construct an environment for themselves on terms strongly identified with higher education. The *Journal* remarked on the "high tone of professional ideals, achievement, and fellowship" maintained in the seminar and published the best papers of its senior participants.[19]

The needs of career schoolmen seemed substantially different from those of young undergraduates. In 1896 Hanus invited Brookline's superintendent Samuel T. Dutton to lecture o older students who did not take practice teaching. A year later Dutton and Huling taught the course themselves when Hanus was on leave. Finally in 1898 the organization and management course was divided into separate sections for prospective teachers and aspiring superintendents or high school principals. Since Hanus' pedagogy gave great attention to the impact of vocational interests on academic achievement, it was natural for him to structure his own curriculum according to the jobs students wished to secure.

Curriculum differentiation between teachers and administrators indicated group differences in age, experience, and commitment more than it indicated the existence of separate fields of professional knowledge. Both course sections tended to read the same school documents and reports of investigating committees. The common thread of instruction for everyone remained curriculum policy, especially the problems of arranging the modern subjects in high school programs and the problems of unifying practice and procedure across the entire span from elementary to higher schooling. Of course Hanus gave some attention to purely administrative matters, such as strengthening the executive powers of city superintendents at the expense of school boards. But the separation of administrators from teachers in advanced courses took place well before the creation of a specialized administrative literature.

Separate administrative instruction conferred practical benefits on both Hanus and the student participants. Enrollment became a new means for experienced students to create educational reputations and thereby a new way to promote careers. Normal schools frequently served a placement function, and Hanus was quick to point out that many normal graduates became superintendents. Now university courses enabled ambitious secondary schoolmen to shortcut the informal processes of establishing reputations beyond their local communities. "Successful and ambitious teachers," Hanus wrote in 1899, were "naturally turning to the university for the training which they need to enable them to compete successfully for all the higher positions in the profession." The crucial placement function enhanced Hanus' reputation too, as he was increasingly called upon to recommend candidates for important administrative positions. By 1900 the *New England Journal of Education* noted that "several important selections of superintendents and high school principals this season have established beyond question the efficacy of the department of education at Harvard University under Professor Paul H. Hanus. The man who takes that course and wins the respect and confidence of President Eliot and Professor Hanus is as sure of a good position as any man can be of anything."[20]

Administrative training, furthermore, generated far less faculty hostility than did teacher education. Eliot strongly endorsed the idea to "aim distinctly at training superintendents." Eager to further educational unity by associating the superintendent with the university president, Eliot sensed that superintendents needed to be regarded as experts qualified to assume "full charge of the intellectual and moral management of the schools." Efforts to reform the Boston School Committee after 1897, largely led by Harvard alumni, advocated a powerful, expert superintendent and a weak school committee as the best method to guarantee honesty and efficiency. Although the Harvard Appointments Committee relied mainly on departmental judgments for its recommendations of young graduates for teaching positions, it consulted Hanus about the "more important part of his work, the training of men for principalships and superintendencies of public schools." The committee's secretary found far greater faculty sympathy for this function because it was "a subject in which they are not deeply interested." (But he quickly withdrew the word "sympathy" to say merely that "apathy has succeeded hostility.") Administrative training dampened faculty hostility because it encroached on no job-placement or curriculum territory traditionally occupied by the faculty of arts and sciences.[21]

Above all, the positive appeal of administrative training grew out of a new set of educational problems which assumed a larger role in Hanus' thought near the end of the century. Teachers dealt mainly with individuals in classrooms; administrators were charged with directing education as a "social force." As Hanus began to distinguish between social and individual objectives, and to pay closer attention to the first, the mission of the administrator rose dramatically in importance. At the same time, the distant connections between the new social concern and the older concern for curriculum reform further reduced overt discord with other faculty members.

Years before John Dewey's pathbreaking lectures on the school and society in 1899, optimistic evolutionists applied biological language of adaptation to the traditional American interest in the social impact of public schooling. They concluded that schools could help prepare individuals to meet the social and economic dislocations of modern industrial life. Albion W. Small of the University of Chicago, for example, advanced his "sociological" position in the course of a sarcastic attack on the Committee of Ten's objectives and pedagogy. By restricting the content of education to the "abstract phases of reality" represented by modern academic disciplines, Small believed that the Ten ignored social objectives beyond the cultivation of intelligence. It also ignored the pedagogical truth that learning required "action in contact with reality." Brookline's Samuel T. Dutton was appalled by individual competitiveness and growing class conflict during the 1890s. He stressed character rather than intellect, cooperation instead of individuality, as the ends toward which all youth should be "socialized."[22]

When Hanus first distinguished between individual and social objectives in 1897, he claimed no originality of viewpoint in defining the latter as capacity to "adapt every individual to the civilization of his time." The decision to speak out was probably stimulated by fears of social disorder provoked by the bitterly contested national presidential election campaign months earlier. Where he had previously regarded secondary education as the preserve of an ambitious minority of youth bound for business or the professions — although not necessarily for college — he now regarded some secondary education as essential for all male youth. Schooling would equip youth to resist entrapment as the "prey of the demagogue and the social agitator." It was essential to foster a "wise conservatism" to promote suspicion of "plausible but fallacious solutions" to social problems. The 1896 election results mandated education to combat anarchistic license and socialist utopianism.

But Hanus intended no sharp break from his commitment to individualism and the principles of the Committee of Ten. He had defended expanding the curriculum to include modern academic subjects in order to arouse interests, especially vocational interests, among a minority of youth. Now a further expansion was necessary to appeal to interests of all youth. He called for the introduction of manual training and commercial subjects to develop awareness of the scope and principles of various industrial callings. He advocated systematic attention to good citizenship through school instruction in economics, government, and education—subjects ignored or downplayed in the Committee of Ten's deliberations. And he urged that secondary education be conducted within "comprehensive" institutions to inculcate common values and mend a split social fabric.

Despite his anxiety, Hanus' older commitments to individuality, the modern academic subjects, and intellectual development softened his emphasis on social order. The essence of social adaptation was to maximize possibilities for constructive individual choice rather than to impose some convenient concept of social necessity upon individuals. Hanus was fully aware of the dangers of constraint in education—he vigorously opposed the growing assault on the elective system within Harvard—and of the ease with which social adaptation could become social manipulation. Citizenship aims, he emphasized, did not call for patriotic propagandizing. Vocational aims did not require explicit vocational training. The appeal to vocational interests might well strengthen vocational commitment, but was equally a pedagogical device to develop intellectual power. His flat and restrained prose style, deliberately modeled after Eliot's, lacked the enthusiastic flourish of Small or Dutton, who called on educators to make society over and socialize the child. When the themes of social adaptation began to dominate educational thought after 1900, Hanus' efforts to link those new aims with older cultural and intellectual ones made him seem "conservative."[23]

Even though Hanus stressed the intellectual continuities between academic curriculum reform and emerging social aims, the new priorities nevertheless hastened the dominance of administrative training over teacher training. He never officially downgraded teacher education as a significant departmental responsibility, but delegated to others more responsibility for practice teaching and abandoned all efforts to develop courses in the teaching of the various academic subjects. He turned over the course in history of education to his young colleague, Arthur Orlo Norton, who had replaced George Herbert Locke. And he urged Norton to redirect historical instruction away from pedagogical classics toward an analysis of the "gradual evolution of educational needs" at various stages of history and the ideas, schools, and universities that arose to meet those needs. Norton's subsequent efforts to define history of education as a branch of social and political history instead of a branch of philosophy shifted its orientation from problems of instruction to problems of administrative policy. Hanus devised a new undergraduate course on the organization and administration of education as a branch of state and municipal affairs. He also removed from his theory course most topics on educating the individual, such as classical educational theory and educational psychology. When he finally abandoned the theory course entirely in 1913, all of his instruction was in school administration.[24]

The social role of schooling legitimized additional specialized administrative functions that further differentiated the education curriculum in the early twentieth century. The separate sections for administrators and teachers in the "practical" course soon became entirely separate courses. The course for administrators was then further divided into separate courses for high school principals, elementary principals, and superintendents. If Hanus regarded himself as a specialist in administration at the turn of the century, by 1910 he saw himself mainly as a specialist in the superintendency. Moreover, he also endorsed — but could not yet implement — training in the administration of kindergartens, physical education, vocational education, and the process of vocational selection. The management of schooling had become rational social intervention and school administrators had become pedagogical engineers. As new social needs were identified, Hanus assumed that the most appropriate response was to create new social institutions. A colleague wrote approvingly that education was "progressing very properly according to the Spencerian formula — continuous differentiation of function in a constantly growing unity."[25]

The pro-normal *New England Journal of Education* viewed with caution and unease the rise of specialized university training in educational administration. It admitted that the professional characteristics of the teacher and administrator were different. But whereas it agreed that teaching expertise was enhanced by professional training, it was less sure of the sources of administrative capacity. Should the big-city administrator be a young man pedagogically trained at Harvard or Clark? Should he be a "veteran . . . with extended experience, whose incorruptibility is demonstrated, and who has the genius for faithfulness to every detail?" Or should he possess a combination of training and experience in small communities?

At the end of the century the *Journal* regarded the question as puzzling and still open. Five years later it lamented the growing professional segregation between teachers and administrators and the rise of "class conscious superintendents." The *Journal* might mourn the collapse of John W. Dickinson's dreams of normal school power. But Paul Hanus had no doubts about the unusual opportunities for social service opening up before him. Moreover, his zeal was matched by a powerful cohort of Boston reformers who intensified his commitment to social adaptation.[26]

JOSEPH LEE shared Barrett Wendell's Brahmin disgust for the modern city, his yearning for a rural past where individuals were both self-reliant and selfless community members, and his brooding doubts about the role of old families in the new Boston. Yet the two men reacted in strikingly different ways to a common situation. Wendell withdrew to the world of books, self-consciously cultivating the roles of impractical man of letters and sardonic commentator on urban barbarism. Blaming modern education for the sapping of individual character, he urged a return to traditional discipline and delighted in the assault on Eliot's Harvard by his politically astute professorial friends.

By contrast Joseph Lee found his calling during the 1890s as an indefatigable reformer and attempted to improve society through a many-sided deployment of his considerable fortune. Celebrating the outdoor life rather than bookishness, Lee converted memories of his physically active and socially serene boyhood into a comprehensive program of social reform. Modern educational reform, as exemplified by Eliot's Harvard and by institutions like the kindergarten, seemed not a threat to character but the best hope to enhance it in urban civilization.[27]

Lee endorsed sharply contrasting approaches to reform. At times individual choice had to be repressed. Certain threats to responsible character could best be extinguished by legislation. By helping to found and support agencies like the Massachusetts Civic League and the Immigration Restriction League, Lee became a pivotal figure in movements to prohibit liquor, vice, billboards, and immigration. But he simultaneously regarded human nature itself as the source of good character. The careful liberation of natural tendencies was as much his reform strategy as was direct compulsion. This thoughtful man, who loomed large in the intellectual and political history of American racism, was also one of the most vigorous advocates of child-centered educational reform.

Lee's wife, Margaret Cabot Lee, a kindergarten teacher, introduced him to the theories of Frederich Froebel which he found confirmed by G. Stanley Hall's instinctual psychology of child development. Primal drives seemed universal human characteristics; for Lee they also became the key to social reform. If inborn drives toward struggle and power could grow into constructive heroism, if instincts for expression and creation could mature as workmanship and vocational pride, and if native tendencies to loyalty could develop into teamwork, then social progress would be assured. Lee attacked Hugo Münsterberg's belief that instincts had to be overcome. In contrast, they had to be cultivated to "grow in their natural direction." Gradually Lee concluded that education, if defined as a stimulant for such growth, could unify all his disparate reform interests. He campaigned for more kindergartens. And through tireless advocacy of play facilities for children and youth he became known as the father of the playground movement in America.[28]

Like many other reformers, Joseph Lee saw the public schools as appropriate institutions to continue the reform enterprises begun by private philanthropy. The school superintendent of the future, he imagined, would replace the minister as the spiritual leader of American communities. Near the end of the century, he became involved in political efforts to restore Brahmin control over the Boston School Committee. Lee's intimate friend and college classmate, John Farwell Moors, founded the Public School Association in 1897. Armed with Moors's organizational talents and Lee's money, the Association attracted younger civic leaders to school politics. The most important of these was James Jackson Storrow.

Another of Lee's boyhood friends, Storrow practiced law in the nineties. But after joining the banking house of Lee, Higginson and Company in 1900, he had more time for reform and especially for educational reform. Storrow won election to the Boston School Committee in 1901 and moved to keep schools open beyond normal hours as social and educational centers for their surrounding neighborhoods. Infuriated by the capture of the cumbersome School Committee by Irish Catholic forces in 1904, Storrow and Lee successfully engineered state legislation to reduce the size of the School Committee from twenty-four to five members. The political result was a sweeping victory for the Public School Association and a decade of Brahmin control over the Boston School Committee. Storrow became chairman in 1906, and in 1908 Lee himself began nine years of elected service.[29]

By 1900 Lee, Moors, and Storrow began to explore the connections between urban school reform and Harvard. When Münsterberg denounced modern education, the elective system, the study of pedagogy, and the kindergarten, Lee rebutted him. Lee argued that the elective system expressed the same sensitivity to youth's basic needs as the kindergarten and endorsed the study of education for promoting understanding of child nature. He advocated a pedagogy of doing not learning, of action not acquirement, and attacked Münsterberg's effort to frustrate nature with imposed academic culture. When Hanus looked for affluent Bostonians to buy more education books than the Harvard College Library thought prudent, Joseph and Margaret Lee, as well as Moors, agreed to help out.

More significantly, they began to regard education at Harvard as a supporting service for their own reform ventures. Lee asked Hanus to provide undergraduate volunteers for boys clubs and to gather information on what cities and school systems were doing about play facilities. When Storrow decided to restructure the Boston School Committee, he turned to Hanus to analyze city school organization and make policy recommendations. By providing two graduate students to do this work—Henry Wyman Holmes (who joined the education faculty in three years) and Frank Thompson (who became superintendent of schools in Boston)—Hanus participated directly in the Boston reform movement. Simultaneously, he demonstrated his emerging professional role of supplier and selector of educational talent. The casual nature of these early connections between the Boston reformers and the education department became regularized after Harvard's Board of Overseers created a "visiting committee" for education in 1901. Margaret Lee and Moors were members from the outset. Storrow became chairman in 1905. All three gave small sums for books, scholarship assistance, and department publications.[30]

The most dramatic evidence of the department's use to Boston reform came in 1907 when the Lees guaranteed the five-year appointment of a new faculty member to promote the kindergarten cause. Disappointed by the slow growth of the kindergarten, Joseph and Margaret Lee were on the prowl for imaginative dissemination methods. At first they persuaded Harvard officials to compare for them the undergraduate records of students who had and had not attended kindergartens. They dropped this early example of quantitative policy analysis after preliminary findings suggested a possible negative relation between kindergarten participation and Harvard class rank. The Lees then decided to install on the Harvard faculty a "prophet" to win disciples for the Froebelian cause. Stipulating that the source of the gift remain anonymous, Lee explained that it would be counterproductive for people to know that he had "succeeded in introducing my fad into the college (however true that may be)." Although Hanus had little enthusiasm for prophets, he was convinced that his department could not ignore the social functions of elementary education. He also longed for an additional colleague to begin specialized training of elementary principals. Recognizing a unique opportunity for expansion, Hanus persuaded Lee as well as Eliot to accept as the new appointee his young protégé, Henry W. Holmes.[31]

Hanus' contacts with the Boston reformers deepened his sympathy for the causes they espoused. He praised the efforts of "benevolent and clear-sighted members of the community" to provide supervised playgrounds, kindergartens, vacation schools, and neighborhood community centers. At the end of 1906 he served on the executive committee for the Social Education Congress, an emotional peak of Boston confidence that systematic education could throw back the "forces of evil" loose in the modern city. Although the central theme of the congress was that school instruction in social cooperation would eliminate both upper-class greed and lower-class envy, virtually all of the reform strategies devised by Boston philanthropists were discussed and approved. One concrete result was an alliance between Hanus and Robert Woods, the dean of Boston settlement house reformers and a close friend of Storrow and Lee, to establish a fellowship in social education at Harvard. The stipend enabled one of Hanus' students to spend a year at Woods's South End House to learn about "various new phases of educational work, whether under public or philanthropic auspices, which are designed to bring it, on every side, into closer quarters with the actual needs of the community." The first holder of the fellowship became Storrow's private secretary and political confidante.[32]

Hanus participated most fully in urban educational reform through the Massachusetts campaign for separate industrial training schools. Until 1906, vocational education was not a major priority for reform philanthropy, although it had not been entirely ignored. In the mid-nineties, for example, Joseph Lee connected vocational happiness with strength of character. The end of formal apprenticeship and the growth of unions restricted access to various trades, and Lee endorsed a variety of new formats for trade training. But he recognized that the nature of modern industrial work was as much a problem as the processes of access to it. "A man's best years and his best strength," Lee wrote, "the main force with which his character and his life are to be built up if he is to have any character and live any life worth living—are spent upon his daily work; and if that work fails to make him a return in life and character, or if such return is meagre and inadequate, his best chance for the reward that we all are dimly striving for is lost." Many jobs plainly offered no such return, creating a problem Lee thought philanthropy had to address. He went out of his way to praise companies that acted on the idea that work should express an individual's "mind and character." Lee endorsed schemes such as profit sharing and involvement of workers in management decisions. Educational reform required changing industry to meet the creative needs of workers as well as fitting youth to industrial needs.[33]

But the Massachusetts industrial education movement dealt mainly with entry processes to the trades. The catalytic event was the 1906 report of a state commission concerned with how Massachusetts industry could compete with other states by enlarging its pool of skilled labor. A survey conducted for the commission revealed that 25,000 Massachusetts youth between the ages of fourteen (the upper limit of compulsory schooling) and sixteen were out of school and out of productive work. This sensational disclosure gave the campaign for vocational education an educational and social mandate that nearly overshadowed the economic. Vocational education would get a large number of shiftless and ignorant youth off the streets.

Further, since the survey data also suggested that these youth chose to drop out of school not because parents needed their labor but because they found school profitless, the commission endorsed the creation of new vocational schools entirely separate from existing high schools. The Massachusetts legislature created another commission charged with persuading local communities to establish separate trade schools under its direction rather than that of local school boards, and offered partial state subsidies as an incentive. Hanus had just returned from a Munich sabbatical where he had studied with enthusiasm its trade continuation schools Now better known through his Boston connections, he was chosen by the governor to chair the state Commission on Industrial Education.[34]

Hanus eagerly performed the role of salesman for separate industrial schools. He had become dissatisfied with manual training's distance from vocational education and, by 1908, had endorsed vocational preparation in the upper grammar grades and the last two years of high school. Now, impressed with German models and confronted by the specter of 25,000 youths out of school and work, he quietly dropped his democratic opposition to separate trade schools. Equal opportunity could only be achieved he concluded, by luring youth to new institutions that gave single-minded attention to vocational preparation.[35]

In speech after speech across the Commonwealth on behalf of the commission during 1907 and 1908, Hanus emphasized that the chief source of personal usefulness and happiness was vocation, and that the main incentive to educational achievement was interest. When these principles were applied to a new class of adolescents less ambitious, more reluctant to attend school, and more immediately faced with vocational decisions than the traditional high school constituency, the pedagogical result was a more direct appeal to vocational interests. In earlier writings about the older constituency, Hanus emphasized the close ties between academic subjects and vocational purposes. With the new group in mind, he portrayed existing high schools as exclusively "cultural" with no connection at all to industrial pursuits. A new educational approach was necessary not because high schools were inundated by a new and highly visible class of youth but because that class avoided the schools.

Hanus remained uninterested in psychology and was never enthusiastic about the biological theories of adolescence put forth by G. Stanley Hall. Yet Hanus' social and economic observation that youth was a "critical period" was reinforced by Hall's conception of

adolescence as a distinct and crucial life stage. Though more interested in the education of teenagers than young children, Hanus had
earlier followed Eliot's lead in emphasizing *continuities* between
grammar, high school, and college education. His definition of
youth had embraced a wide age range. Now he tended to define
youth as a distinct class with distinct needs. Since the fourteen-to-
sixteen-year-old period of occupational shiftlessness seemed precisely the time when "the plasticity of earlier years gives place to
stability," the need for a specialized educational response seemed
self-evident.[36]

Unlike Joseph Lee, who regarded trade schools as only one means
to develop vocational commitment, Hanus emphasized what schools
could do alone and unaided. His reliance on schooling was more the
result of professional faith in the potency of formal education than
of a narrow conception of vocation. Like Lee he regarded vocation
as not just the source of a living but the source of a fulfilled life, and
attacked the tendency of American industry to convert workers into
machines and to be satisfied with shoddy products. Recalling the
sturdy and skilled artisans of bygone days, he advocated rational
careers for all workers in which stages of vocational progress could
be planned and insights into work's broader theoretical meaning
could be developed. Schooling to foster life-enhancing careers in all
workers was very different from narrow skill training. Hanus envisioned a broad curriculum for industrial schools, in which subjects
like science, mathematics, English, and civics were studied through
their connections with particular vocations. The development of
"industrial intelligence," business ethics, and even cultural interests
were just as important as concrete job skills.[37]

Nothing guaranteed positive connections among vocation, happiness, and usefulness better than a wise choice of career. Hanus
imagined the first half of an ideal four-year trade school to be a
"preparatory school" in which youth could explore a variety of possibilities and finally choose one vocation according to "natural taste
and capacity." He successfully enlisted Eliot's support for the commission's work—reversing the direction of influence that had prevailed through most of his Harvard career—but shied away from
Eliot's blunt recommendation that teachers have authority to "sort
out the boys and girls, assign to each the trade at which he or she
seems best adapted, and the law should then compel these children

to be trained for these trades." Although Eliot subsequently endorsed informal sorting over compulsion, the issue of choice in vocation remained central in the campaign for industrial schools. The
New England Journal of Education, profoundly suspicious of any
movement in which Harvard played so prominent a role wondered
whether it was accidental that the zeal for vocational schools was
"confined almost entirely to those whose children will never go to a
vocational school." Concluding that separate trade schools would
limit the options of the poor, the *Journal* remained an implacable
foe of the Commission on Industrial Education.[38]

During 1907 Hanus began to distinguish further between the
problem of providing vocational training and the problem of helping youth to develop vocational interests. The latter concern was
encouraged by a commission member, A. Lincoln Filene, who
shared Hanus' Prussian ancestry along with his conviction that vocational experience was the key to personal happiness. Filene and his
brother owned a large Boston department store. With Lincoln Filene primarily responsible for personnel, the store pioneered in precisely the directions Lee advocated to improve working conditions
and involve workers more directly in management decisions. Although Filene had not attended college, he became connected with
many of the reform causes of Lee and Storrow. As his relationship
with Hanus ripened into friendship, he introduced him to a philanthropic project that dealt directly with the issue of vocational
choice.

With the financial backing of Lincoln Filene and Mrs. Pauline
Agassiz Shaw, and the strong support of James J. Storrow, the Boston reformer Frank Parsons established a Vocation Bureau in 1908
to advise youth about career choice. Parsons' approach to what he
called the "vocational guidance" of youth was developed through
settlement work, not schools, and the Vocation Bureau was located
at the Civic Service House. But his attitudes were similar to Hanus'.
Both men emphasized the need for new institutions to adapt individuals to the conditions of modern society. Both stressed the importance of free choice of career and the necessity to make information
available about the characteristics of occupations and the interests
and aptitudes of individuals.

Parsons imagined vocational guidance as sufficiently crucial and
complex to define an entirely new professional career, and he

argued that the proper location for the function should be in schools rather than in philanthropic settlement houses. Immediately intrigued, Hanus served with Filene on the Vocation Bureau's executive committee and soon became its chairman. Even without the state backing that assisted the Commission on Industrial Education, the Vocation Bureau effectively promoted the idea of guidance. Within a year of its founding, vocational counseling was introduced in the Boston schools.[39]

THE DRAMATIC SHIFT in Hanus' professional role in the decade after 1897 raised new questions about the place of education within the Harvard curriculum. As his interests moved away from both academic curriculum reform and undergraduate teacher education, he urged independence for his courses from the Division of Philosophy which had sheltered them since 1892. If education was "a concrete fact rather than a matter of abstract contemplation or speculation," the label of philosophy was absurd. Hanus also resented his misleading academic title of "history and art of teaching" and the numerous squabbles within the Division of Philosophy, especially with Münsterberg, over student programs, course approvals, and the allocation of graduate financial aid.

Most colleagues agreed that his courses were "grotesquely misplaced" and no one in the Division of Philosophy feared a loss of prestige if Hanus withdrew from it. Even so vigorous an opponent as Barrett Wendell did not object to education's presence within the University as long as it was completely separate from the faculty of arts and sciences. In 1899 education became a quasi-independent department within the Division of Philosophy, and the courses were all relabeled. More important, Eliot secured Hanus' promotion to a full professorship two years later. Always sensitive to the difficult situation he had placed Hanus in, Eliot respected him for his loyal advocacy, his ability to increase enrollments, and perhaps for the faculty enemies he had made. Eliot certainly wished to vindicate the judgment he had made a decade before, although he was cautious enough about internal opposition to turn down Hanus' request that the professorship be called "Education" rather than history and art of teaching. Still, Eliot concluded that the promotion settled "on a permanent basis what has been the doubtful question of providing at Harvard systematic courses in Education."[40]

Despite the triumphs of greater administrative independence and an assured personal career, Hanus was increasingly frustrated by the widening gap between his sense of education's social mission and Harvard's modest investment in it. By the end of the century Harvard's efforts lagged far behind those of other universities. Harvard had been among the first eastern universities to offer instruction in education. Its national competition in 1891, perceived mainly to be Clark and New York University, had no special advantages or head start. But during the nineties the subject grew rapidly at most institutions of higher education. By 1902 Hanus helped John Dewey found the Society for College Teachers of Education. Three years later he founded the New England Association of College Teachers of Education.

Hanus most envied the rise of education at the University of Chicago and, especially, at Teachers College. After its formal alliance with Columbia University in 1898, Teachers College became the unquestioned international center of the university study of education. By 1905, when Harvard's instructional budget in education was roughly $5000, Teachers College spent nearly $282,000. Compared with Harvard's $500 investment in financial aid, Teachers College allocated $8000. Exclusive of a special methods faculty (of which Teachers College had twenty-four and Harvard none), the education staff of Teachers College consisted of eighteen persons. Harvard's department then included Hanus and Arthur O. Norton.[41]

Embarrassed at being distanced so decisively, Hanus pressed Eliot to expand the department once his tenure was assured. By 1903 Hanus regarded departments of education as transitional stages in an evolutionary development toward schools of education. He proposed that $2.5 million be raised to create a school of education under the control of the faculty of arts and sciences. Although LeBaron R. Briggs warmed to the idea of separation and counseled Hanus on how to proceed, Eliot quashed the scheme. He advised Hanus to "neither talk nor think" about a separate school, for Harvard was already overburdened with too many schools and would consolidate when the opportunity arose (as it did four years later when the Lawrence Scientific School was merged into the faculty of arts and sciences).

Eliot never understood Hanus' belief that Harvard was "losing ground" in educational influence. Faculty approval of an independ-

ent department, Hanus' tenure, Corporation willingness to continue
the second faculty position after the Radcliffe gift ran out, and the
slow but steady growth in enrollments were all indicators of substantial progress. Eliot now regarded education as a perfectly suitable
study for the A.B., A.M., and Ph.D. degrees, but believed its value
as a separate subject was limited. The proportion of technical information needed in educational careers seemed far less than in occupations like medicine, law, or divinity. The basic professional
knowledge needed in education was still, after all, knowledge of a
subject to be taught. Without Hanus' enthusiasm for social adaptation, and no longer preoccupied with the school reform movement,
Eliot sensed no inconsistency between what Harvard was providing
and national educational needs.[42]

Hanus counterattacked with the familiar argument that Harvard's "hold" on prospective students would be lost to Columbia and
Chicago if it failed to control the allegiance of teachers. Eliot would
only concede that the University might accept a school of education
if a single giver were to provide the entire sum without a public
campaign. Three years later, with Storrow installed as visiting committee chairman, Hanus pressed his case once again on a smaller
scale. This time he made no mention of a separate school. Despite
Storrow's support, Eliot remained unconvinced and criticized
Hanus for adopting the "exaggerated and undesirable standard" of
Teachers College. Professor Charles Homer Haskins, on the other
hand, was disappointed at the absence of mention of a separate
school. Like Wendell and Briggs, he wished to distinguish professional from liberal education and urged Hanus to think of a "graduate school of education parallel to our existing graduate schools."
The proposal got nowhere, but in 1906 education became a division
completely independent of the Division of Philosophy.[43]

Eliot was not prepared to underwrite expansion or to authorize
fundraising efforts. Yet he had not entirely closed the door. The
main initiative would have to come from the Division itself or its
friends. But here the contrast with Teachers College was especially
discouraging. The Division did not collect its own tuition revenue, a
major source of income for the expanding New York colossus. Even
if it had, the tuition potential for Harvard seemed relatively small.
Teachers College profited not only from its location in a more popu-
lous area, but also from state and city certification requirements in

the New York region which encouraged attendance. Efforts by the Massachusetts state department of education in the nineties to secure legislation requiring professional training for teaching jobs were defeated by traditions of local control. Moreover, the reputation won during the early growth of Teachers College stimulated for it a national enrollment pool in the first decade of the century. By 1904-05, Teachers College enrolled 250 graduate students and 800 undergraduates, compared with Harvard's 31 graduate students and 85 undergraduates. Nothing frustrated Hanus more than the loss of Harvard College alumni to the greater range of graduate educational opportunities at Columbia.[44]

Lacking tuition income as a source of revenue, Hanus' main hopes for expansion lay with private philanthropy. There too Chicago and Teachers College far outstripped the Harvard effort. Between 1892 and 1897, for example, annual giving to Teachers College rose from $24,000 to nearly $70,000. Its physical plant alone was worth over $1.4 million. Wealthy social reformers like Grace Dodge had enabled Teachers College to expand in its early years. But Harvard's early commitment to academic curriculum reform neither solicited nor excited philanthropic interest. Even when Boston social philanthropy began to discover the education department, the embrace was exceedingly tentative. Despite the fundraising potential of the overseers' visiting committee, the contributions of the Lees, Moors, and Storrow during the first decade of the committee's life were minuscule in comparison with Teachers College beneficiaries. All scholarships and library books totaled only $3000. Hanus took hope from the Lees' support of Holmes after 1907, but Lee had other Harvard interests to which he had given much more.[45]

Hanus' ability to match in fundraising persuasiveness Teachers College counterparts like Nicholas Murray Butler or James Earl Russell was hindered by personality traits that grew more pronounced as his frustrations mounted. Without much humor or personal flexibility, he did not try to disarm criticism by forging personal relationships with real or imagined faculty adversaries. Deadly serious, he resorted instead to principled appeals in defense of the rightness of his cause. When the Appointments Committee seemed to recommend teaching candidates with strong scholastic records regardless of whether they had taken his courses. Hanus asked the faculty to instruct the committee to give preference to his students, provided their scholarship and personal qualities were satisfactory. Even his friends disliked faculty motions phrased to secure an explicit vote of confidence in one member, and Shaler successfully moved to table it. Later on, Hanus chose to mark the annual anniversary of the creation of the Division of Education by dinners celebrating emancipation from bondage.[46]

As his schemes for sudden expansion were frustrated, Hanus became more belligerent and embittered. Eliot recognized but did not mind his "small defects in disposition and manner," but A. Lawrence Lowell openly clashed with him after 1909. Lowell's mandate to restore intellectual tone to the College and dismantle rampant vocationalism threatened education's immediate self-interests. The new "concentration" and "distribution" system of course selection, which replaced the elective system in 1909, threatened education enrollments. Since there were not enough education courses to constitute a concentration (nor had Hanus ever favored undergraduate specialization in education), and since the rules of distribution prescribed certain areas of study, undergraduate freedom to select education courses became more constrained. Lowell, moreover, had no sympathy for vocational courses in Harvard College. Shortly after his inauguration he told Hanus that history of education should properly be given in the history department, psychology of education within the department of psychology, and administration within the department of government. At the same time, he turned down Hanus' latest request to raise funds for a separate school of education.[47]

Beyond these educational differences, Lowell perceived Hanus' belligerence as evidence of a tactless and unpleasant disposition. Far closer personally to the visiting committee reformers than Eliot had been, Lowell left no doubts with them that he was "very thoroughly dissatisfied with the condition of the Education department" and that the source of his dissatisfaction was the "existing personnel." He installed his close friend John F. Moors as head of the committee, not to advocate Hanus' cause but to provide inside information on how to change things. Moors reluctantly accepted the assignment — there seemed little he could accomplish where such antagonism prevailed — but clearly shared Lowell's views. The most impressive quality of Hanus, Moors thought, was his extreme interest in his field. "He seems to have faith in it of the kind which ought to move mountains, yet one has a feeling that for him the mountains will not move."[48]

At the end of Hanus' second decade at Harvard the magnitude of his professional redirection seemed drowned out by growing uncertainty about the Division's future. The "discreditable inferiority" of Harvard's efforts in comparison with other universities was painfully apparent both to Hanus and to outside observers. A new president was hostile to him on both educational and personal grounds. The fragile ties to Boston wealth were undercut by Lowell's friendships with the same people. Hanus believed he was hated by Lowell and most of his faculty colleagues. Regarding Lowell as little more than a pompous aristocrat, Hanus anxiously awaited the president's first opportunity to act directly on the Division's fortunes.[49]

4

The Rise
of Educational Science

THE UNEXPECTED RISE of educational research after 1910 broke the stalemate between Lowell and Hanus and enabled the Division once again to serve University, or at least presidential, aspirations. Throughout most of the school reform movement the sources of valid educational knowledge seemed clear enough. Knowledge was derived from the collective practical experience of the Harvard faculty. Knowledge was codified and transmitted through President Eliot's annual reports and the reports of prestigious national bodies such as the Committee of Ten. Systematic educational research, by contrast, was not considered an especially important source of educational authority. Eliot had little personal interest in research. Paul Hanus also believed that the most prominent methods of educational inquiry available in the nineties, history and psychology, were remote from serious issues and life experience.

Yet the idea that knowledge was based on consensual codification of successful experience became increasingly vulnerable after the turn of the century. As secondary education expanded and newer social objectives emerged, Hanus detected disagreement and fragmentation of authority. His first response was to call for more prestigious committees to unify educational doctrine. But he also urged greater attention to the actual results of different educational procedures. When his 1911 survey of the New York City schools caused his own professional authority to be ridiculed as biased opinion, Hanus concluded that educational knowledge required more impregnable foundations. It needed above all the quantitative certainty of modern science. He always remained dubious about educational psychology, but believed that the newer field of measurement promised truly objective educational authority.

President Lowell similarly hoped that educational science, by which he meant statistics, would validate the many educational reforms he proposed for Harvard College. Lowell's growing interest in educational research enabled him to see new possibilities for the Division of Education. He substituted educational statistics for educational history as a faculty specialization, installed a more congenial chairman in Hanus' place, and encouraged a variety of projects to advance educational science. Between 1911 and 1914 the Division experienced a remarkable transformation in morale. Even Hanus attempted to retool himself as a measurement expert.

But the Division's intentions were never identical with Lowell's. Hanus and his rising young colleague, Henry W. Holmes, tended to regard research as one professional tool for practicing schoolmen, rather than as a full-time function of its own. And eventually Holmes began to have second thoughts about whether educational science could really become the primary source of valid educational knowledge.

DESPITE HIS DEVOTION to fact gathering and early determination to take up scholarly pursuits once immersed in Harvard's superior facilities, Paul Hanus' first two decades in Cambridge were marked by an absence of concern for research. He advocated a "model" school to exemplify sound contemporary practice rather than a laboratory or experimental school to search out new ideas. When Professor Thomas N. Carver suggested that Hanus' 1906 case for faculty expansion could be strengthened by emphasizing the importance of inquiry, Hanus took him to mean that nothing was known about education and a larger department was therefore unnecessary. Although Carver protested that his point was intended to support education's expansion and applied equally to any of the new social sciences, Hanus still would not revise his document to include the case for research.[1]

Elsewhere systematic educational inquiry was no longer considered exotic activity. In the mid-1890s the leading center of American educational research was at nearby Clark University, where child study flourished under Stanley Hall's intense leadership. Research had also become an explicit priority at Teachers College. Yet neither Harvard's educational mission nor its institutional climate encouraged similar developments. The task at Harvard was to implement good ideas already known, not to find new ones. Eliot never pushed Hanus to engage in inquiry—to complete, for example, the historical studies he had originally agreed to make—nor judged him adversely because he did not do so. Although Eliot valued research as a university function and created an environment in which research became a central activity of many faculty members, he did not view it as essential in the field of education.[2]

Nor did Hanus' faculty colleagues often suggest that inquiry was required to illuminate or improve educational practice. Psychologists such as James and Royce continued to argue that psychology's principal value to teachers lay not in its content but in its method of sensitizing teachers to be judicious observers of individual differences and complex situations. Such skepticism did not attract graduate students interested in the connections between psychological research and education. They gravitated elsewhere, to Clark or to Columbia.

In his own instruction Hanus incorporated the psychological skepticism of James and Royce, along with their personal distaste for Hall. Well into the twentieth century he continued to characterize both child study and experimental psychology as "fads" with limited educational value. The analytic quality of laboratory psychology would not illuminate the complex totality of the schoolroom where behavior was emotional and volitional as well as intellectual. Child study by contrast was excessively sentimental. The devoted Worcester teachers who collected masses of data "ought to be chloroformed at the age of forty." Hanus disputed Hugo Münsterberg not because he envisioned a large role for psychology in education, but because Münsterberg rejected in the nineties even the modest function Royce and James were willing to ascribe to it.[3]

Even when Münsterberg later shifted ground and endorsed applied research in the Harvard Psychological Laboratory, his administrative moves only confirmed Hanus' suspicions that psychology offered little to education. The young Harvard psychologist of animal behavior, Robert M. Yerkes, reluctantly agreed to teach a course on educational psychology in the Department of Psychology in 1910. The subject did not really interest him, but he understood that increasing his enrollments would increase his prospects for reappointment. Yerkes worked to confine educational psychology exclusively to topics in heredity and eugenics, and longed for the day when someone else would be commandeered to teach those aspects of the subject concerned with "nurture." In such circumstances, the relations between the education and psychology departments grew more distant. Yerkes' course had no connection whatever with Hanus' work. In 1910 educational psychology was not included among the four basic fields required for students pursuing the Ph.D. degree in the Division of Education.[4]

Even had greater institutional interest existed in educational research, Hanus' promotional responsibilities consumed nearly all his time and made protracted scholarly work difficult. He was expected to teach every summer, manage the Harvard Teachers Association and its elaborate annual meeting, visit schools as secretary of the Schools Examination Board and as a Harvard admissions representative, organize and supervise practice teaching, serve on professional committees, give speeches, and engage in a large correspondence concerning job placement and other subjects. He chaired the state Commission on Industrial Education while carrying a full teaching load. For six years he did all this alone; for ten more with just one colleague. His publications were by-products of this varied public advocacy; he worked speeches or lectures into articles and then published the collected articles as books. To have accomplished these administrative tasks and also to have pursued creative scholarship would have required resources of intellect and literary capacity that Hanus did not possess. When Henry W. Holmes joined the Division in 1907 Hanus urged him to protect his time carefully or he would have no chance for personal scholarly development.[5]

Of course Hanus' research attitudes were not wholly shaped by institutional climate or role demands. Blind forces did not push him in directions he found distasteful. Whatever his scholarly intentions might have been in 1891, contemporaries soon sensed that he preferred teaching and the public role of advocate and organizer to private scholarship. But however much this was true, Hanus was never insensitive to the crucial issue of a widely accepted body of expert educational knowledge. Indeed his disinterest in research stemmed in part from the conviction that systematic university research was not the principal means to provide the field of education with authoritative knowledge.[6]

Hanus believed that the research strategies available to explore education touched the margins but not the center of the new subject. What made education distinct and justified its inclusion in universities was neither past experience nor the nature of mind, but the vast conglomeration of practices and institutions connected with carrying on education in contemporary American society. The problems of this vast practical activity, not the problems of history or psychology, both defined and justified the field, in the same way that economics and government as academic fields were defined and justified by the significance of ongoing business and political activities.

Since the problem of how secondary education should be organized and conducted was then preeminent, the field of education had to suggest authoritative solutions. But how? Again and again Hanus advocated direct examination of all the facts of educational reality rather than abstract and distant speculation. The educational world was a chaotic storehouse of ideas and practices — isolated, competing, wise, unwise. To bring order from chaos, the facts of experience had to be organized. Once diverse experience was observed and assessed, thoughtful men would agree on its meaning; the facts would speak for themselves. Then isolated procedures could be related, successful experience distinguished from unsuccessful, wise theories separated from unwise. The establishment of authoritative knowledge meant the unification of belief through the codification of good practice.

With such strong beliefs in the power of facts to generate agreed-upon guiding principles if only collectively analyzed, Hanus' ideal model for educational inquiry was not the research study but the authoritative committee. He regarded the major NEA investigating committees of the nineties, and especially the Committee of Ten, as the most promising means to codify educational knowledge. The Committee of Ten's conferences in each of the academic subjects brought together varied experts. Such ingenious administrative procedures were the key to successful codification. The Committee of Ten seemed the first effort in American history to "give collective expression to eminent professional authority on an educational question."[7]

But when criticism of the elective system mounted within Harvard, and the emerging social function of education began to conflict with the Committee of Ten, Hanus properly worried that educational consensus was eroding. In a striking speech to the NEA Department of Superintendence in 1902, he bluntly warned that increasing disagreement endangered the further growth of professional status. Without consensus on educational principles there could be no authoritative defense against "persistent, usually well-meant, but pernicious meddling with the details of school work by school committees, parents, newspapers, and other lay influences." Consensus and "definite guidance" were still possible; thoughtful educators could still agree. The main problem was that professional committees tended to work in isolation. Insufficient attention had been given to building on the work of previous committees and establishing "cumulative influence." Professional doctrine had to be frequently reformulated, perhaps every ten years. A new NEA committee to carry out that reformulation was essential.

Yet professional authority could not be secured through the consensus of informed judgment alone. Hanus also asserted that his field lacked a "body of recorded educational experience." Here he defined experience more narrowly than before, as "results actually achieved." Hanus urged the superintendents to cooperate with one another in experiments to measure the attainments of pupils taught in different ways. The facts would still speak for themselves, but the facts would be organized data on pupil achievement rather than the experiential insights of educators. Comparing education to physics and biology, Hanus stressed that such studies of results would have a "convincing value which no amount of assertion beginning 'in my school,' or 'so far as my experience goes,' or 'I believe,' or 'in my opinion,' could possibly have." Five years earlier the journalist Joseph Mayer Rice had scandalized the same group with a similar argument. Clearly influenced by Rice's ideas, Hanus now endorsed them as a new means to strengthen professional authority. Impressed by his courage in agreeing that educational procedures had to be justified by educational results, Rice in turn praised Hanus' speech and published it in *The Forum*.

Hanus suggested that his proposed new NEA committee could record educational experience as well as secure a new consensus on educational doctrine. Although the committee was established with Hanus as its chairman, it never received the NEA financial backing he thought essential and never completed its task. Meanwhile he decided that the attacks on the elective system at Harvard had to be met with evidence of its results. He conducted through his seminar a survey of the impact of the elective system on Harvard alumni. Research conducted through history and psychology still seemed peripheral to contemporary educational problems, but the measurement of results had become a valuable tool to strengthen professional authority.[8]

But Hanus' tentative interest in systematic measurement was hardly a clarion call to replace common-sense reasoning by complex statistical methods. He was unfamiliar with contemporary innovations such as normal curves, standard deviations, and coefficients of correlation. In his study of the results of the elective system, he used a questionnaire to ask Harvard alumni their opinions. A simple count seemed a reliable method because the respondents were all educated men who possessed "the habit of making correct statements on matters of importance." If younger investigators elsewhere insisted that facts became scientific only when subjected to controlled experimentation or to statistical analysis, Hanus continued to rely on judgment and reasoning to convert facts into authoritative knowledge.

He never considered his endorsement of separate industrial schools, for example, to be based on personal opinion. It was rather a considered professional judgment based on direct observation of Munich continuation schools, the inability of American high schools to attract non-college-bound youth, the existence of a class of shiftless youth, and the evolutionary principle that schools could serve an adaptive function in modern society. When Hanus listed in 1908 the most promising methods and tendencies in educational work, he made no mention of research but emphasized industrial education, social settlement work in relation to schooling, raising salaries, and centralizing authority and responsibility in school management.[9]

Outside Harvard, in contrast, a new enthusiasm for the professional uses of quantitative procedures grew rapidly in the first decade of the century. Young administrators flocked to Edward L. Thorndike's courses on measurement at Teachers College, first introduced in 1902. They perceived that measurement and quantification had enormous potential for establishing unchallengeable administrative authority in a time of growing school enrollments and expenditures. In 1904 Thorndike published his pathbreaking *An Introduction to the Theory of Mental and Social Measurements.*

When Harvard offered no instruction at all in measurement or educational psychology, the department that taught those subjects at Teachers College enrolled more students than any other.[10]

A local example of this tendency was the work of superintendent Frank E. Spaulding in Newton. Spaulding was thoroughly committed to replacing Newton's preoccupation with college preparation with the newer notion of developing each individual regardless of future destination. Soon he proposed significant new expenditures for an industrial school and a technical high school. Anxious to succeed in a conservative, cost-conscious system widely known as the burial ground of superintendents, Spaulding cultivated a political style to appeal to the business-dominated school committee and aldermen who controlled the pursestrings. Instead of stressing broad philosophy and playing down costs, he relentlessly emphasized "how the largest educational returns could be secured for every dollar expended." His detailed justifications for even small expenditures and emphasis on efficiency enabled him to transform the Newton schools without ever having a proposed budget increase rejected. Well before the efficiency movement became in 1911 a national craze to apply Frederick Taylor's ideas of scientific management to the schools, Spaulding was applying the same quantitative rhetoric to increase expenditures in Newton with enormous success.[11]

Spaulding regarded new knowledge as a professional weapon and looked to major departments of education to help supply it. His practical rather than scholarly perspective helped push Hanus from a vague to a vigorous exponent of research. In 1909 Spaulding urged the Harvard Division to undertake "profound study, as scientific as possible, of the greatest variety of practical educational problems." "We are spending enormous and rapidly increasing sums of money on public education," he argued. "If we give serious thought to the matter, we must realize that the basis and results of the expenditures need careful investigation." When Hanus arranged for him to present his ideas to the Society of College Teachers of Education, Spaulding chastized university education departments for not conducting research on administrative problems. They should ally themselves with progressive local school systems not merely to establish practice facilities for novice teachers, but to gain opportunities for research within the schools. Hanus immediately endorsed the idea of a "working partnership" extending beyond practice teaching. "The way to study school administration," he wrote, "is to study school administration, and not to study the social and philosophical sciences." He arranged for Spaulding to teach his courses when he was on leave in 1911-12 and sent administration students to Newton to work on research problems as part of their professional training.[12]

During 1911 the Division's interest in educational research noticeably accelerated. Hanus became more comfortable with research as he saw its uses for administration and revised his list of departmental needs to include a professorship in experimental pedagogics and an experimental school. Harvard's enthusiasm mirrored the new professional attention given educational science by the efficiency fad, but decisive local events help to explain the new mood. In the spring Hanus accepted an invitation to direct an unprecedented inquiry into the operations of the New York City public schools. More than anything else he had ever done, the inquiry would test his claim to possess authoritative educational knowledge. He was nervous and more willing than before to explore "objective" methods. The leave of absence he had to take, moreover, gave Lowell an opportunity to define for the first time his own stance toward the Division's future. As Hanus sought to vindicate in New York two decades of the university study of education, Lowell sought ways to invigorate a moribund department. From contrasting perspectives the central issue for both men became the sources of educational knowledge.[13]

THE SCHOOL SURVEY movement was one expression of the general enthusiasm for science, quantification, efficiency, and results that pervaded American education after 1910. Surveys were typically conducted by university professors of education or foundation staff outside the school systems under scrutiny. They focused attention on more universalist claims to expertise than resided in local experience or tradition. The new role of outside consultant dramatized the claim of university departments of education to possess special knowledge unavailable to practicing schoolmen. In 1910 Hanus had conducted one of the earliest surveys for schools in Montclair, New Jersey. His method was to collect facts about local conditions and assess them against the consensus of accepted educational doctrine.

If Hanus confidently characterized surveying as "pedagogical engineering," he was also well aware how values and politics could undermine educational authority. Earlier for example, he had been certain that industrial training in Massachusetts high schools was "bad intrinsically," but he nonetheless faced heated opposition from other educators who also claimed professional expertise. Although he attributed opposition to separate trade schools to ignorance of the facts and to political attempts to preserve the power of the state board of education, it was still true that the opposition was successful.[14]

The New York City schools posed a much greater challenge to professional authority. The value conflicts that authority was asked to resolve were more powerfully represented than anything Hanus had previously encountered. Indeed, the New York survey itself was intended by its sponsors as a political weapon in their warfare on alleged fiscal profligacy in the schools. The Board of Estimate and Apportionment, the city aldermen responsible for approving school budgets, opposed Superintendent William H. Maxwell's constant requests for additional appropriations. William H. Aller, director of the efficiency-minded New York Bureau of Municipal Research, had convinced the aldermen that a survey would surely attribute bloating budgets to inept management rather than to genuine educational needs.

A school survey would not only promote ideals of economy and efficiency, Allen believed, but also enhance the power of the Bureau of Municipal Research and the political fortunes of the aldermen. President John Purroy Mitchel headed the aldermen's committee on school inquiry, but he privately gave Allen the responsibility to ensure that the survey would have the anticipated effects. Thus the New York inquiry did not originate with a board of education or with school officials, but with their enemies. Suspicious from the beginning, defenders of Superintendent Maxwell sought vindication for his policies, while Allen maneuvered behind the scenes to underscore the schools' wastefulness and neglect of scientific management.[15]

The high political stakes and bitter personal rivalries magnified the pressure on Hanus. The pro-Maxwell *New England Journal of Education* suggested that Hanus could become the "man of the hour" only by avoiding criticism of "one of the noblest professional personalities in the educational world." By affirming the "life, the spirit, the power, the glory" of the New York schools Hanus would become privileged to enter "into the great work of Dr. Maxwell." At the same time, Allen persuaded Hanus to devote his early weeks to analyzing the Board of Education's new budget requests and preparing critical questions for the aldermen to put to school officials in forthcoming budget hearings. Hanus complied reluctantly, for he wished to separate educational from purely fiscal concerns. Besides, he was preoccupied with the enormous task of organizing and staffing an effort that employed eleven specialists besides himself and eventually cost nearly $100,000. In the end Hanus' tepid efforts disappointed and angered Allen. School officials survived the budget hearings unscathed.[16]

Thereafter Allen and Mitchel attempted to win Hanus' sympathy for their position by threatening to cut off funding for the inquiry. When Hanus arched his back, Allen retreated and tried instead to control the text and distribution of the survey's results. When preliminary galley proofs of the eleven reports were first available in the summer of 1912, Allen obtained copies and prepared for Mitchel's use critical questions and requests for revisions prior to final printing. Hanus, now convinced that a conspiracy was under way to alter his findings and ruin his reputation, would not respond. But Mitchel angrily retorted that the aldermen, who were paying for the inquiry, had every right to demand more data if they saw fit. The Committee on School Inquiry publicly rebuked Hanus, refused to print one report it found particularly offensive, and printed the rest with the unanswered questions appended.[17]

Some of Hanus's associates believed there had been no need to alienate the Committee on School Inquiry and that his principled appeals to professional independence naively misunderstood urban political realities. By refusing to deal with Mitchel's concerns, and by refusing literally to speak with Allen, Hanus encouraged city hall antagonism at the very moment when the survey's results provoked equally hostile reactions from school officials and their apologists. The Committee on School Inquiry, for example, disliked the various reports for recommending new programs that would substantially increase school expenditures. Above all they disliked the argument that the schools were an agency of the state rather than a department of city government.

This doctrine of state control, as developed in the report of Yale professor Ernest Carroll Moore, was completely rejected and Moore's report was not even printed by the aldermen. The Committee on School Inquiry then commissioned two eminent experts on municipal reform to restudy the problem. When their analysis was completed, Moore himself perceived that the two reports agreed "pretty completely as to the essential facts," but disagreed "radically as to the meaning of these facts." The aldermen's experts believed in "centralized municipal government" while Moore advocated the independence of city school systems from municipal control. It was hardly surprising that Superintendent Maxwell considered Moore's report the best and most important of all. But those who disagreed could cite Moore's own words to prove that his conclusions represented mere opinion rather than scientific authority.[18]

Although the issues changed, the same criticism was applied by defenders of the schools to other recommendations with which they disagreed. Hanus and his associates, thought the *New England Journal of Education*, were men of "well-defined opinions" who used facts only to ascertain how far the New York schools met their standards. The survey recommended, for example, the abolition of the Board of Superintendents in favor of a supervisory council consisting of teachers and administrators. The grounds were that the existing board discouraged communication between teachers and the central school administration, even though cooperation under leadership was "essential to good supervision." But Associate Superintendent Andrew W. Edson bitterly complained that Hanus presented no scientific evidence for his "preconceived and doctrinaire point of view that fails to take in the entire situation and is more visionary than practical . . . Its makers evolve from their inner consciousness a panacea for all ills that the New York school system is heir to as they see it." Moreover, Edson complained that none of the investigators had extensive city school experience and were motivated only to attract attention and large consulting salaries.[19]

Maxwell himself attacked the "arrogance" of university education professors and reserved special scorn for Hanus' advocacy allegedly without concrete evidence of results, of separate industrial schools and electives in the elementary schools. Most critics admitted that substantial efforts had been made to collect data on pupil achievement. The arithmetic tests of S. A. Courtis, for example, were given to 33,000 pupils, but such data rarely informed major policy recommendations. Maxwell could attack recommendations for their lack of scientific evidence while simultaneously lambasting "university theorists" for their "mania for collecting statistics." "The best results of education," Maxwell thought, "—the development of concentration, initiative, and devotion to duty—are not measurable in statistical terms."[20]

Hanus won the support of professors of education like Chicago's Charles H. Judd and of lay organizations like the Public Education Association which resented the intrusion of efficiency advocates into school affairs. But modest praise could not mask the fact that the professional authority of education had been denounced on the very grounds Hanus himself had long used: its claim to knowledge was based upon opinion rather than on evidence. The considered judgment of experienced observers of educational facts had proven highly vulnerable to hostile attack. In consequence, fact gathering had to become more systematic, controlled, experimental, and quantitative. The only valid authority for education was modern science. In a draft letter to Mitchel that Hanus chose not to send, he wearily admitted: "At the present time there is no criterion to settle who is right on many of the educational questions contained in our report, except the judgment of educational specialists. Your staff represents such judgment . . . we know that on many questions our judgments must be subjected to further confirmation."[21]

Hanus reflected on the lessons of New York in a speech before the Department of Superintendence in early 1913. He recalled his appeal a decade before to ground educational authority in recorded experience. That need was now more compelling than ever. Principles of education were authoritative only in the limited sense that they were a "serious attempt at generalizations from contemporary procedure in progressive school systems; and hence they are at least definite hypotheses, the validity or the falsity of which can be established by carefully collected and well-organized future experience." The older effort to base authority on a consensus of experience and judgment had to be abandoned. "Unless the validity of educational opinion is established by verifiable data which any technically informed person can appeal to, we are practically helpless." Since "exact measurement in education, the necessary basis of a science of education," was only in its beginnings, the emerging priority for a university department of education seemed clear enough. On his return to Harvard Hanus resolved to inaugurate "much statistical and experimental study."[22]

As HANUS' enthusiasm for educational research grew through the trauma of his New York experience, the same enthusiasm emerged in Cambridge during his absence through the pressure of A. Lawrence Lowell. If Eliot cared mainly to implement existing ideas in the schools and expressed little interest in measuring outcomes, Lowell took seriously the possibility that educational research might both suggest and validate reform in Harvard College. Lowell's persistent efforts to build an undergraduate climate conducive to intellectual pursuits led him toward deliberate pedagogical innovations that broke sharply with Eliot's laissez-faire attitudes. Eliot's policies emphasized relationships among educational institutions and the widening of individual choice at all levels below the professional. Lowell hoped to manipulate educational processes at the college level to "bring the strongest possible influence for good to bear upon the student, instead of merely offering opportunities to be seized or neglected as he may please." All the extraordinary reforms Lowell introduced — the concentration and distribution system, the comprehensive general examination, the tutorial system, the reading period, freshman dormitories, and the House system — were educational strategies to achieve specific objectives. Although no one was brave enough to suggest that he teach courses in education, Lowell was nonetheless one of the most self-conscious pedagogical engineers of his generation.[23]

Lowell's interest in educational research was confined almost exclusively to the measurement of results. Just as Hanus in New York longed for the surety of quantitative data to validate his doctrines and disarm opposition, so Lowell saw quantification as a tool to confirm his hunches and demolish lingering pro-Eliot sentiment. He experienced no sudden conversion to educational science in 1911. He had used statistical methods in his earlier political science research and had cleverly gathered questionnaire data as a faculty committeeman to reinforce his positions. He then concluded that statistics was the most promising method of educational science, since individual variation was so immense and uncontrollable. The vast collection of Harvard records at Lowell's disposal seemed a remarkable storehouse of data awaiting creative analysis.

Lowell himself initiated such analysis at the beginning of his presidency. One of the most unpleasant characteristics of undergraduate student culture was its "tendency to disparage the high scholar." By comparing undergraduate rank in class with later success in professional school, Lowell demonstrated a close correlation he hoped would suggest that hard work in college paid off later on. He also wished, as had Eliot, a younger student body in Harvard College. But whereas Eliot sought to achieve this by reducing both the college course and the school course preceding it, Lowell urged statistical analysis of academic and disciplinary records to validate his hypothesis that younger students performed better and were less troublesome than older ones. With this knowledge, parents might take steps to ensure earlier attendance of their sons.

Since Lowell had no time to conduct this study himself, he asked Henry W. Holmes of the Division of Education to do it for him. The results confirmed Lowell's beliefs. More important, a new function had been found for the Division: it could be a center for institutional research. Increasingly, Lowell spoke out on the parallels between the advancement of knowledge in education and medicine. Only a century before, medicine was still a battleground for theory. Then scientific methods had brought great and sudden progress. It was now "high time that the same progress should take place in education. We ought to pass from the stage of theory, however plausible, to that of scientific knowledge."[24]

Hanus' unpaid leave of absence in 1911-12 gave Lowell his first chance to apply these beliefs to the Division without spending extra money. He invited Edward Thorndike to be visiting professor for a year. Thorndike's appeal lay not in his role as educational psychologist but in his "experimental and statistical" work. When his commitments prevented Thorndike from accepting the position, Lowell turned to Walter Fenno Dearborn of the University of Chicago. In two statistical papers relating school and college grades, Dearborn had demonstrated that grades were distributed along a normal curve and that college students maintained the same relative class rank they obtained in high school. Dearborn's work exemplified Lowell's hopes for educational science, but Dearborn too was unavailable for the visiting post. Temporarily rebuffed, Lowell turned back to Hanus and Holmes the task of finding a replacement; Frank Spaulding was appointed.[25]

That fall Lowell decided not to reappoint Arthur Norton and tried for Thorndike on a permanent basis. A more committed and productive scholar than either Hanus or Holmes, Norton was still neither an original historian nor an inspiring teacher. Hanus and Holmes urged his promotion anyway, for they admired his devotion and regarded his subject as "an approach to the study of education from the social side which no other branch . . . can offer." But Lowell rejected not only Norton but his subject. History was not a useful means to develop educational science. "We do not teach the history of medicine or of law," Lowell advised Holmes, 'because we have plenty to do to acquaint students with the principles and problems of medicine and law. One reason why the history of education has been considered so important in the training of teachers is that we have had so little so far to teach them about the way that things should actually be done."[26]

Thorndike declined Lowell's offer of a professorship in part because his Teachers College salary exceeded the Harvard maximum, and the president now invited suggestions of other candidates to develop work in educational statistics. Robert Yerkes anxious to give up instruction in educational psychology, befriended Holmes and argued that Lowell's preoccupation with statistics was a great mistake. It took no great genius, he claimed, to "take the data which are available in University Hall at present and intelligently and even ingeniously, perhaps, make them contribute to the advancement of education." Far more important than statistics was experimental educational psychology, in which Lowell had shown no interest whatever.

Yerkes' candidate for the position was his friend John B. Watson of Johns Hopkins University. Watson was willing to devote himself to "experimental pedagogy" and, Yerkes confided, could be lured to the Division. With Watson appointed, Yerkes promised to join the Division himself and apply their mutual interests in animal behavior to the education of humans. Holmes was impressed by the apparent sincerity of Yerkes' protestations of interest and friendship, but he had not heard of Watson — whose famous proclamation of behaviorism was not made until 1913 — and in addition shared Hanus' and Lowell's disinclination to connect laboratory psychology with educational progress.[27]

Like Yerkes, Hanus and Holmes had little interest in mining the statistical ore of Harvard College. They could not renegotiate the demise of history as a field, but at least they wanted a colleague who would investigate and evaluate school problems in schools. Their ideal candidate was William Chandler Bagley of the University of Illinois, who had a Ph.D. in psychology along with long experience in normal schools and interest in educational problems. But Bagley was unknown to the psychologists Lowell consulted, and his name was dropped. One candidate appealed to Lowell for his statistical work, to the Division for his experience with schools, and to the Harvard psychologists for his laboratory interests: Walter F. Dearborn. Dearborn also had the advantage of a strong reference from Thorndike — "the man I should recommend for my place at Teachers College should anything happen to me." Although he had turned down a visiting appointment the year before, he now accepted Lowell's offer of a five-year assistant professorship.[28]

Dearborn's training was far more specialized than that of previous Division teachers. In college he developed interests in visual perception and the reaction time of the eye. Following graduation from Wesleyan in 1900 — five years after Thorndike and six years after Charles Judd left Middletown — Dearborn took a Columbia psychology Ph.D. and subsequently an M.D. in Germany. His special interest was the quantitative measurement of human capacity. His doctoral dissertation analyzed reading behavior through photographs of eye movements obtained from a specially designed camera, and he soon became interested in the psychology of intelligence and in educational testing. His statistical studies of grading were clearly peripheral to his larger experimental interests, though there is no evidence that Lowell knew or cared about his psychological work. Lowell's interest was exclusively statistical. "I feel that there is a great chance of doing work of that character," Lowell wrote him, "and perhaps no better place to do it than there is here."[29]

THE SUDDEN RISE of educational science dispelled anxiety that Lowell might reconstruct or even dissolve the Division. Within a year the gloomy forebodings of early 1911 were replaced by the euphoric hope of a new alliance between presidential and departmental interests. Already Lowell had indicated that the Division, which had been "very little developed" in the past, might now become developed "much more fully." Even Hanus confessed that the president's attitude was "decidedly good." As this transition occurred, no one worked more indefatigably to use educational science to improve the Division's position, and no one profited more directly from the outcome, than did Henry Wyman Holmes.[30]

Holmes's chance for leadership came when Lowell appointed him acting Division chairman in Hanus' absence. Keenly anxious to remain forever at Harvard, Holmes hoped to impress Lowell by replacing confrontation with cooperation and even deference as departmental strategy. Only thirty, he had already demonstrated a sensitivity and charm in marked contrast with Hanus' bitter and blustery manner. Holmes's Harvard College studies had been mostly in philosophy and literature, ending with the academic success of a *magna* degree and election to Phi Beta Kappa. He enjoyed considerable social success as well, penetrating some of the best clubs and literary societies. When a career flirtation with the ministry faded, he took an A.M. under Hanus and became in 1904 principal of a Brookline elementary school. Two years later he was made head of the English department at the Boston High School of Commerce.

In 1907 Holmes abandoned the career line which headed toward a high school principalship to fulfill his greater ambition of joining the Harvard faculty. An enthusiastic participant in alumni affairs, he often demonstrated the social grace, elegant wit, and eloquent prose style which readily suggested administrative presence and intellectual power. During his four years on the Harvard faculty he pursued no research, but spoke widely on kindergarten issues and on the need to reconcile objectives of individual development with newer concerns for social adaptation. Yet he fully anticipated a scholarly career, planned to take off a year in 1912 to begin doctoral study, and debated whether to learn the new educational science or to stay with the older philosophical and ethical approach.[31]

Sensing that inquiry was the key to education's future at Harvard Holmes pledged the Division to carry its "full share in the founding of a real science of education." Through his efforts, both the 1911 meeting of the New England College Teachers of Education and the

1912 session of the Harvard Teachers Association were devoted for
the first time to educational research. An air of anticipation excited
the latter gathering, where Edward Thorndike and the well-known
efficiency expert Leonard Ayres discoursed in Lowell's presence on
the professional promise of measuring results. Only a year before
the meeting's theme had been whether vocationalism threatened
cultural ideals. Since no one had argued that it did, the meeting
had been a boring failure. Yet within a few short months all educational attention came to focus on the far more exciting question of
"educational products." "The day of the educational engineer," one
speaker exulted, "is at hand."[32]

Holmes persuaded Storrow to finance publication of monographs
reporting on Division research and convinced Joseph Lee to help
subsidize a formal research collaboration with the Newton schools.
Already at work analyzing student records for Lowell, Holmes encouraged his seminar to study "by exact methods, problems in the
teaching of English composition, spelling, and hand writing, in the
management of children's study habits, in the development of an
exact terminology for the mental traits required in elementary
school work, and in the causes of lack of interest in school activities." The Division accepted an unprecedented request of the department of economics to study its own teaching, a project that
Lowell encouraged as another example of institutional research. By
early 1913 a discerning student praised the "complete transformation" of the Division and the fact that its faculty distrusted "all
conclusions which are not the product of experiment under closely
and rigidly controlled conditions." With Dearborn now in Cambridge the official aims of the Division, unchanged since Hanus had
added administrative training in 1898, were revised to include "original investigation and experiment." Holmes's acting chairmanship,
to his embarrassment and Hanus' chagrin, was made permanent.[33]

When rhetorical advocacy of research began to be supplemented
by actual research activity, most participants anticipated that educational science would confer clear benefits in a relatively short
time. Hanus wanted to shore up the flagging expertise of the pedagogical engineer; Lowell wanted to validate internal Harvard reforms; and Holmes promoted institutional development. For each
the pursuit of educational research was justified by its hoped-for
contribution to the advancement of professional authority. Holmes

and Hanus attempted to guarantee this linkage and guard against academic irrelevance by defining research as a professional rather than a scholarly skill and by focusing research activity on the solution of practical problems. Harvard, they said, had no interest in training a separate class of researchers but wished to make research skill a professional tool for all responsible school officers. Hanus called on Dearborn to abandon his interests in "laboratory psychology" and feared that the warm reception the psychologists gave him — his courses were cross-listed in the catalogue and he received space in the psychology laboratory — masked a devious plot to lure him away from educational concerns. Lowell also made plain to Dearborn his preference for analysis of Harvard grade data over laboratory psychology.[34]

The most important research enterprise was the cooperative arrangement with Newton for which Joseph Lee paid half the costs of a research fellow. William Setchel Learned, who received the third Ph.D. degree in education awarded by the Division, became what Holmes called the "first university expert in experimental pedagogy attached to a city school system in this country." Learned's job in Newton was not to conduct research himself, but to stimulate and consult with classroom teachers who initiated research projects. He encouraged teachers to formulate a problem, to devise new procedures of instruction or class organization that might solve it, and to develop measuring instruments through which the results of the new procedure could be compared with the old. After a year Learned had no concrete results to report, but this did not matter. The production of new educational knowledge was only one contribution that research could make to professional development. More important, Learned thought, was encouraging and stimulating teachers "to a new view of the possibilities, opportunities, and obligations of their position." The principal product of the Newton enterprise was not research but professional self-esteem. Holmes fully agreed that the goal was "arousing teachers in service to the need of a professional attitude toward their own work."[35]

By conceiving of research as professional uplift, Learned and Holmes demonstrated how vocational ideals shaped implementation of educational science at Harvard. Learned's doctoral dissertation was a sociological and historical inquiry into the sources of skill and status of secondary school teachers in Germany. Convinced that the

rapid development of education at the university level had not upgraded the status of the American high school teacher, and even
fearful that an actual decline had occurred, Learned hoped to
apply German lessons to America. Among the many differences between secondary teachers in the two countries was the German habit
of "continuous mental enrichment." Perhaps that same habit could
be inculcated in American teachers by encouraging them to do research. Learned, of course, was aware that research findings were
perhaps as significant as professional self-confidence. But he saw no
reason why thoughtful teachers could not add research with relative
ease to their repertoire of professional skills (just as he was shifting
his own professional interests from primarily historical analysis to
experimental pedagogy). At a time when quantification was emphasized as never before, the conduct of educational research was assumed to be a realistic possibility, and even a duty, for educators
regardless of their previous training. Indeed, when Learned and his
successor left Newton because of better job offers elsewhere, Frank
Spaulding persuaded Holmes and Hanus themselves to take over the
work and assume more initiative in instigating research projects.[36]

Holmes was nearly finished with analysis of the relation between
age and performance among Harvard undergraduates. Hanus, true
to his word, had inaugurated two research studies after his return
from New York. He believed that the most promising instrument for
educational research was the achievement test, since establishing
the validity of any classroom procedure depended on techniques to
measure its results. Hanus administered the Courtis arithmetic tests
to adults and developed short tests to measure progress in learning
Latin. But research in Newton, especially if it meant mounting projects instead of just advising classroom teachers, would be enormously time-consuming. In an ingenious example of administrative
skill, Holmes contended that he and Hanus could enter Newton only
if an additional Harvard faculty member assumed all instruction in
secondary education and all supervision of practice teaching. Then
he persuaded the visiting committee to guarantee the salary of the
new appointee.[37]

The Newton opportunity was a significant test of the Division's
commitment to research. But despite their success in freeing themselves from burdensome involvement in teacher education, neither
Holmes nor Hanus commenced any research in Newton and the

formal collaboration ended after only two years of existence. Spaulding left for Minneapolis in 1914, and his successor was less interested in investing Newton funds in research. More important, Hanus and Holmes were unwilling to pursue research seriously. By 1914 Hanus was fifty-eight years old and frequently in poor health. A major shift in career role, despite his rhetoric, was not attractive. Moreover, he found congenial scope for his noninstructional activities in consulting and conducting surveys. After New York he never again agreed to investigate a city school system, but took on smaller institutions like Hampton Institute where his basic educational values would be accepted at the outset by those in charge. Near the end of his career he regarded research only as one of eleven functions a graduate school of education should perform.[38]

Holmes also found other activities more attractive and pressing. He never found the time to earn a doctorate and instead devoted himself unflaggingly to the administrative work he had grown to enjoy. He won Lowell's growing respect through tireless fundraising activities, personal cultivation of the visiting committee, and speech-making on behalf of Harvard College. Personally warm and witty, confident and comfortable with faculty colleagues in different fields, able in oral debate and even more compelling in written discourse, Holmes won new respect for both himself and the Division. One student gushed that he possessed "one of the sweetest, purest, and most guileless natures I have met." The reward came in 1917 when Lowell made him a full professor. A year later Lowell vetoed a job possibility for Holmes in war-related work. Even his temporary absence would mean greater responsibilities for Hanus and a disastrous setback for the administrative progress that had been achieved.[39]

While the lure of administration hastened Holmes's withdrawal from research activity, he also grew more suspicious of the claim that educational science was the principal source of professional authority. Scientific zealotry in experimental psychology or quantitative measurement might as easily impede as advance the profession and the practice of education. Holmes felt more comfortable with the "older sort of study, in which the approach is from ethics and general reflection upon values and ideals." He opposed deterministic claims that science could identify educational objectives or alone guarantee effective teaching. Men were not mechanisms whose behavior could be fully explained or predicted by scientific procedure. Although emphasizing that there need be no antagonism between educational science and educational reform, he nonetheless sensed an inescapable tension between scientific values of control and educational values of advancing moral freedom.

"So long as we think of education as a process to be in any degree mechanized or carried forward in a purely quantitative fashion," he cautioned, "we may nurse the hope of Pestalozzi that a 'method' may be found whereby the tyro or the untrained — Pestalozzi expected to use retired soldiers — shall be enabled to work the miracle with every child." Overconfidence in scientifically derived mechanisms or methods led to neglect of the true sources of educational effectiveness and diminished the role of teachers. He reassured Joseph Lee that the Division had not lost its head over tests and scales. "I believe insight, common sense, and a broad sympathy will always be indispensable in teaching and in the study of education. When we know all the 'facts,' we shall still have to teach, and the facts won't tell us all we need to know about what we are teaching for." For all its potential usefulness in guaranteeing educational authority, Holmes sensed an ironic and darker side of educational science. It seemed to legitimize a new gap between scientific experts and the masses of teachers who merely did what they were told. For Holmes, who believed that the advancement of education required teachers "of a power which would bring distinction in any other reasonably-chosen calling," science could take away as much as it gave.[40]

As Hanus and Holmes reassessed their intention to pursue scientific activity, responsibility for educational research at Harvard increasingly fell to Dearborn alone. At first his interests seemed more consistent with the Division's than Hanus dared imagine. Dearborn agreed that research was a weapon in the arsenal of practicing educators and offered a course to provide teachers, principals, and superintendents with the "technical skill and practice" to undertake research studies in their own schools. His own interests shifted away from laboratory studies of eye movements. Deeply influenced by the medical studies he had completed in Munich just prior to assuming his Harvard duties, Dearborn began to emphasize clinical investigation of physical and mental infantilism and other developmental disorders by employing new intelligence tests, X-ray photographs, and records of physical measurements.

These clinical interests led him out of the laboratory, to the delight of his colleagues, and into hospitals, schools, and mental institutions to seek out subjects to test. The link between this work and educational practice was obvious, since schools increasingly demanded "standards" of normality and abnormality to classify students and assess the efficacy of their teaching procedures. At the same time, Dearborn successfully avoided Harvard statistical records. Lowell remained hopeful that eventually he would concentrate on this data, and advanced him to a professorship at the same time that Holmes was promoted.[41]

But the connections between Dearborn's work and professional practice became more strained as time passed. Faced with the dilemma of small enrollments in his research courses, he began to advocate training a new category of research specialists. They would work full time in school systems on problems of clinical measurement and experimentation. Less attention would be given to equipping teachers and administrators to do this work themselves. He also laid plans for a major research project that would emphasize repeated measurements of development on the same individuals. The time dimensions required for a longitudinal study suggested deferred results and deferred utility. And the proposed scale of the project involved research management responsibilities that further removed Dearborn from central involvement in the training of teachers and administrators.

Once the euphoric rhetoric of 1911-12 had subsided, research at Harvard took on characteristics significantly different from initial expectations. It became the province of one man. It became connected with specialized careers distinct from teaching and administration. Its capacity to guarantee professional knowledge seemed less imminent and more risky. Rather than recasting faculty behavior to any lasting extent, research enthusiasm was a temporary but crucial interlude. Its effects were the growth of presidential support, a shift in the Division's leadership, and a mood of optimism and confidence among faculty and students. Eventually, that new mood pervaded the visiting committee itself.[42]

5

New Careers for
the Socialization of Youth

THE INSTITUTIONALIZING of social reform replaced the brief passion for educational science as the Division's most significant activity in the decade after 1914. Financial support from an invigorated visiting committee enabled the faculty to grow from three to seven members in two years. With these new resources Harvard converted the social aims espoused by Hanus earlier in the century into courses, programs, and careers. The reform movement sought the "socialization of education." Educational objectives, that is, were defined by the social roles of responsible adults. The expanded Division of Education aimed to establish and to staff new educational services to assist youth in acquiring the proper social roles.

Through a range of institutional innovations—the junior high school, supervised recreation, vocational guidance, and commercial education—the Division proposed to extend adult supervision over an increasing fraction of the life experiences of young people. These particular fields were chosen not through calculated planning but were responses to special opportunities. None of them addressed intellectual or cultural objectives. The connections Eliot had hoped to build between higher education and academic school curricula were wholly ignored. The Division now seemed to want nothing whatever to do with academic education. It lamented that only financial constraints prevented, for the time being, additional expansions in Boy Scout work, agricultural education, industrial education, and religious education.

The new fields forged a significant alliance between reform thought and the advancement of the education profession. The expanded notion of educational services promised exciting new careers for adults. The faculty no longer wished merely to train teachers,

principals, and superintendents; they wished to create new specialized jobs. The older roles had antedated the creation of university
departments of education. Training programs did not cause their
existence but helped to promote occupational mobility. With the
newer, more specialized social fields the situation was different.
Vocational guidance careers, for example, rarely existed anywhere
in 1914. Reform seemed to require administrative invention more
than scientific analysis. The Division of Education soon became
more entrepreneurial and propagandistic.

WHEN HOLMES enthusiastically embraced university administration,
his intellectual interests shifted away from the kindergarten toward
social philosophy. Like many educators who matured early in the
century, he was preoccupied with reconciling personal freedom with
social responsibility. How could the best elements of an older tradition of unbridled, selfish individualism be preserved amid newer
calls for social cohesion and cooperation? Holmes found his basic
answer early and held to its essentials for the rest of his life. From his
undergraduate study with Royce, and his extensive reading of
Dewey and Froebel, he viewed man from the idealist perspective of
"loyal member" rather than "isolated individual." Never child-
centered in orientation, Holmes defined proper individuality by the
quality of the social roles people played: "father or son, employer or
employee, neighbor, fellow-worshipper, citizen." The highest purpose of schooling was to enhance youth's capacity to perform distinct social roles. The "socialization of education" meant nothing
more than redirecting educational objectives toward the "actual
duties of life." Of these duties, vocation was the most important.[1]

The practical implications of Holmes's social views differed little
from those of Hanus. But the possibilities for extensive implementation were brighter after 1912 than ever before because the visiting
committee began to assume a larger role in the Division's financing
and policy formation. Clearly Lowell's new interest in the Division
was decisive in causing the change, although Holmes's capacity to
cultivate members was important as well. Visiting committee meetings became more frequent and better attended as Holmes bom-
barded members with reports and position papers. Lowell himself
directed that lists of wealthy prospective members be prepared. The

committee's size doubled between 1910 and 1915. Older members such as Joseph Lee, James J. Storrow, and John F. Moors grew more committed and enthusiastic. New members such as Felix Warburg and Lincoln Filene, both appointed in 1913, joined them to form a body of affluent and opinionated advisers.[2]

Felix Warburg best exemplified the new mood. A prominent New York investment banker, trustee of Teachers College, and former member of the New York Board of Education, he reflected Lowell's desire to broaden the committee's geographical base and increase its financial potential. Accustomed to the energetic growth of Teachers College, Warburg immediately pressed his fellow committee members and Lowell himself for concrete evidence of Harvard's commitment to the Division. He did not want to waste his time on a stagnant operation. Although he contributed his first $1000 nearly a year before he could attend a meeting, he made subsequent support contingent on Lowell's written support of further growth. The lure of lucre inspired Lowell to characterize the Division as "an exceedingly strong, energetic and progressive department which will reflect very high credit upon the University." But to Warburg even this astonishing assessment smacked of satisfaction with the status quo. He pressed on for an unambiguous endorsement of future development. Eventually Lowell signed an acceptable letter that Warburg himself had largely drafted.[3]

Warburg was as aggressive about educational policy as he was about institutional commitment. Like most of his fellow members, he believed that the social conditions of modern life — industrialization and the end of apprenticeship, population concentration, immigration — required schools to provide new services that previously had been handled informally in other ways. He urged the Division to develop offerings in vocational education, vocational guidance, and recreation. Virtually all of the visiting committee's policy discussions dealt with educational services for the masses of youth whose formal education would terminate no later than the end of high school. None of the members made any connection between the work of the Division and the college-preparatory activities of high schools. Teacher education for the academic subjects continued, but the committee showed interest in raising funds to underwrite supervision of practice teaching only to free regular faculty to promote the socialization of education. Research was rarely mentioned. Again and again Warburg emphasized that the financial support essential to growth would come to the Division only when it emphasized the social and vocational problems that interested businessmen.[4]

All of the important members had public reputations as social reformers of one sort or another. There is no evidence that they wished to fit youth to be mere cogs in the industrial order. An exemplar of old wealth like Joseph Lee saw social efficiency as a tactic to restore strong individualism. Lincoln Filene had an iconoclastic commitment to the sharing of power among employees in his own business. Holmes admired their collective sense of social responsibility and concern for the less privileged. He regarded them by no means as rich amateurs but "in one way or another specialists in Education."[5]

The reborn visiting committee subsidized two faculty additions in 1913 and 1914. It guaranteed the first five years' salary of a professor to fill Arthur Norton's place, and it provided the salary of an assistant professor in teacher education. The new faculty members, Ernest Carroll Moore and Alexander James Inglis, increased the department's complement from three to five members. They represented philosophically contrasting approaches to further institutional development.

Ernest Moore was the last generalist appointed to the education faculty, the last individual who imagined himself able to range widely over all educational subdivisions as Hanus had once done. Still in his early forties, Moore had studied philosophy and taught education at Berkeley, had been superintendent of the Los Angeles schools, and in 1910 had been asked to teach education at Yale. Hanus knew him through their participation in the New York inquiry where they shared a common enemy and a common dissatisfaction with their professional lives in Cambridge and New Haven. Moore wished more colleagueship. Hanus saw that he could cover both history and philosophy, as well as participate in research projects and school surveys.

Despite this range of skills and a formidable teaching reputation, Moore's work always seemed remote from the Division's central priorities. In part the gap stemmed from his incomplete commitment to Cambridge. Moore and his wife disliked the industrial cities of the East and were constantly homesick for California. His attempt to protect urban schools from political control, which caused such tension in the New York inquiry, was based in part on the wish to insulate city schools from city influences. Moore hoped urban schools could create an "artificial environment in which many of the shortcomings of [the] natural environment may be overcome." No one was surprised when he resigned, after four years at Harvard, to become head of the Los Angeles State Normal School.[6]

His loss was not considered disastrous. Moore's philosophical pragmatism had led him to endorse an individual-centered view of education sharply in contrast with the emphasis of nearly everyone else in the Division on social tasks and social roles. In his assaults on traditional bookishness and his contention that education should prepare students for the lives they would probably lead, Moore was at one with his colleagues. But when he discussed the objectives of education, he emphasized training individuals to use their minds actively, learning by doing, and knowledge as a tool to solve problems. Processes of learning were always at the center of his conception of objectives. Moore agreed that desirable social behavior such as morality, citizenship, and vocation might be indirect outcomes of a pragmatic emphasis on the active construction of experience, but these goals were distant and secondary. Given the chance to develop one new course around his special interests, Moore offered "Methods of Study and Their Applicaton," an attempt to apply pragmatic notions of the learning process to the common academic subjects. When he resigned, the course died. Holmes then took over instruction in the philosophy of education and resolved to convert it to educational sociology. In 1920 he relabeled philosophy "Social Policy and Education." In these ways the Division effectively remedied the "defects" of Moore's individualist philosophy.[7]

In contrast to the cool reception accorded Moore's pragmatism, the social emphasis of Alexander Inglis won him enormous success. At first his anticipated role was much narrower. Inglis had been recruited from the Rutgers University education department in 1914, on Thorndike's recommendation, to supervise practice teaching and to lecture on teacher preparation. But he harbored scholarly ambitions beyond teacher education. The new scheme of course differentiation that Holmes had designed to justify a full-time faculty position in secondary education gave Inglis his opportunity. By removing practice teaching and problems of initial teaching from the existing course on secondary education, the latter could exclusively emphasize broad issues of policy and appeal to experienced students unconcerned with classroom teaching skill. Freed to focus exclusively on theory in what he considered his most important course, Inglis began to develop his lectures into a major book.

Inglis' 1918 *Principles of Secondary Education* became the Division's most successful intellectual product. Inglis was a member of the reviewing committee of the NEA's Commission on the Reorganization of Secondary Education, whose famous report "Cardinal Principles of Secondary Education" appeared the same year. The arguments of the book generally paralleled those of the report, and Inglis' reputation both inside and outside the Division soared following favorable reviews and steady sales. Two years before the commission's report Inglis had introduced a new course on the reorganization of secondary education. In 1920 he gave up altogether the training of beginning teachers. By then he had also received a professorship and had become, in the eyes of Holmes, the most eminent member of the staff.[8]

Inglis' reputation depended less on the originality of what he had to say than on the authority his scholarly labors gave to ideas that were already commonplace in educational discussion. The *Principles* scrupulously assessed a vast literature on history and the social sciences to discern the implications of valid findings for the conduct of secondary education. Yet its central theses were only elaborations upon Inglis' 1911 doctoral dissertation at Teachers College on the rise of the high school in Massachusetts. The preparation of that study apparently transformed him from a successful high school classics teacher and textbook writer to a leading theoretician of the socialization of education. The history of the high school in Massachusetts seemed a textbook example of how principles of social evolution worked themselves out. When society accumulated new "needs," the high school became its chosen instrument to meet them. As society's "formal agency of adjustment" of youth to responsible adulthood, the high school would guarantee society's "stability and . . . the direction of its own progress."

Educators had become aware of their obligations to use the school as a social instrument at the very time when social change was accelerating. Inglis defined educational aims by the categories of social behavior that Hanus and Holmes had used since early in the century. In 1915 he distinguished three kinds of important behavior:

the civic, the vocational, and "those activities of life which cannot be considered directly and immediately civic or vocational." Never pleased with the value of this third category, Inglis pejoratively labeled it "individualistic" but later called it worthy use of leisure time.

His extreme social perspective made him hope that even leisure activities would be as "well controlled" by educators as civic and vocational behavior. "Vice and social degeneracy" would surely occur if youth were permitted to fend for itself. Although Inglis and Moore differed profoundly on the centrality of the individual in educational policy, on this point they were in solid agreement. Through the artificial environment in which individual learning could flourish in the city, Moore also hoped youth would be safeguarded from the "agencies of destruction" that hovered all around. Both individualist and social efficiency advocates concurred that, by extending the domain of adult supervision, the educator would help to protect urban American youth.[9]

INGLIS ENVISIONED his contribution to the socialization of education as scholarly rather than as direct action. He was as proud of the methodology of the *Principles* as he was of its recommendations, and hoped his "unified theory" would place secondary education on as solid an intellectual foundation as economics or sociology. In place of mere advocacy he offered dispassionate summations of conflicting scholarly viewpoints. But even Inglis could not wholly avoid the organizational implications of his analysis.

A careful review of the psychological literature on child development, for example, caused him to reject Stanley Hall's position that the transition to adolescence was relatively abrupt. Most evidence pointed to both a gradual process of change and a substantial variability among individuals undergoing it. Like Eliot and Hanus before him, Inglis wanted to extend downward the influence of secondary education and advocated a six- rather than a four-year period. But the presence of a physically heterogeneous population between roughly the seventh and ninth grades suggested the desirability of a special kind of secondary education to correspond with this special period of development. Psychology had revealed the need for the junior high school! Inglis became a leading proponent of three-year

junior high schools and devised a separate Harvard course to prepare specialists to administer the new institution.[1c]

Faculty members appointed after Inglis made direct action to
socialize education their preeminent concern. The expansion of the
faculty began with the appointments of Dearborn, Moore, and
Inglis, and culminated with appointments in play, vocational guidance, and vocational education between 1915 and 1922. Joseph Lee
donated in 1915 a new position in play and recreation. In the same
year Lincoln Filene persuaded his allies in the vocational guidance
movement to do the same. Soon after, the Vocation Bureau of Boston itself was absorbed in the Division of Education. In 1920, after
years of advocacy by Warburg and Filene, the Division announced
plans to enter vocational education by annexing a Boston school
that trained teachers for commercial subjects. Two years later that
objective seemed met by the appointment of a tenured professor in
commercial education.

Once before, Joseph Lee had used the Division to propagate his
reform ideas, but his sponsorship of Henry Holmes in 1907 was only
intended to bring the kindergarten message to undergraduates who
would become influential decision makers even if they did not become career educators. By 1915, when publication of *Play in Education* confirmed Lee's reputation as the leading authority in the
field, he saw Harvard's potential contribution in more professional
terms. By inculcating play ideals in administrators and teachers,
and by training a new cadre of playground directors at the graduate
level, the play movement could be institutionalized in the schools
and perpetuated beyond the lives of enthusiastic but mortal philanthropists.

After calculating how the central figures in the play movement
could best be utilized, Lee concluded that a Harvard faculty presence would accelerate influence at a "geometric ratio — the teaching of teachers being the most effective point to apply one's power,
unless one could put in another link and be the teacher, we will say,
of Aristotle." Lee had no intention of delegating selection of his collaborator to anyone else and announced that only one individual
was really suitable for the position. If Lee was the leading philosopher of the play movement — he received a Harvard lectureship
and briefly taught without salary — its leading practitioner was
George Ellsworth Johnson.[11]

Lee first met George Johnson in the mid-nineties, when the latter abandoned early starts in schoolteaching and the ministry to find religion in the child study movement at Clark University. As a special student Johnson described and assessed hundreds of games played in the Western world. Unlike Inglis, who wished to be regarded as a contributor to social theory, Johnson was a loyal disciple of Stanley Hall and wished only to unravel the practical implications of child development theory for the conduct of play. Hall thought that Johnson's careful codification and ratings of games were more responsible than anything else for converting development theory into practical play activities teachers could undertake.

Johnson's subsequent career was primarily as an administrator. His Clark connections propelled him to various superintendencies in towns around Boston, where his hallmark was always to emphasize the educational value of play and playgrounds. Between 1907 and 1913 he was superintendent of playgrounds in Pittsburgh, organizing there what Lee considered the best city system of playgrounds in the country. At the age of fifty, he decided to train individuals to do the organizational work he had done with no specialized training. He was director of plays and games in the New York School of Philanthropy before Lee recruited him for Harvard.[12]

Johnson spent the bulk of his adult life building playgrounds rather than theory, and his main Harvard course was called "The Administration and Conduct of Play and Recreation in School Systems." But his attitude toward play theory shaped his conception of play administration in important ways. As he grew older, he gave greater attention to the value of play for adolescents as well as young children, stressed the social as well as the individual benefits of play, and above all emphasized the significance of adult supervision of play activities. These emphases were all related. Unlike Hugo Münsterberg, Johnson was optimistic about the constructive potential of biological instincts. He wanted to encourage their development through play. Yet he increasingly felt that city life warped unfolding instincts. The city environment tended to transform instincts from "our greatest security" to "the source of greatest danger." Inborn tendencies toward competitiveness and loyalty, for example, could be expressed as easily through youth gangs as through camping. Dancing had degenerated from a "form of prayer" to a "form of preying on the innocent by human beasts."

Increased play facilities alone did not solve the problem. Adult supervision was essential. When Johnson confronted a Pittsburgh boy repeatedly arrested for stealing apples, the boy confessed that he stole because he loved being chased by the police. Immediately Johnson understood. A perfectly natural urge was at work, but Tim's "love of the chase" needed channeling by trained adults into more constructive directions. Even the country boy needed guidance and direction. Spontaneous pick-up games on rural fields lacked the educational value of organized, well-coached athletics. The need for supervision increased with the age of youth. The ultimate aim was nothing less than "socializing the instincts."

The centrality of adult supervision suggested that one community agency — the school — should coordinate play services. Each school system needed a director of play and recreation. Johnson had no doubt that supervised play was a better means to develop desirable social behavior than activities in regular classrooms. American history was no more valuable in teaching citizenship than the supervised recess. With his older commitments to child-centered explanations of growth as well as to Lee's individualist values, Johnson sometimes wondered whether adult control and the rejection of spontaneity encroached adversely on individual initiative. But in the end he did not consider this a serious problem. American society needed nothing so much as well-coached baseball teams.[1]

Despite the advantages conferred on Harvard by Joseph Lee's financial backing and national visibility in the play movement, the goal of institutionalizing play ideology in the public schools proved very difficult to achieve. How could desirable activities like camping be promoted through the schools? What was the proper administrative relation between the Boy Scouts or YMCA and the schools? What career lines were possible and appropriate for educators interested in supervising recreational programs? Despite his administrative experience, Johnson was not a clever entrepreneur but a kindly gentleman who loved teaching. Lee realized this and had been willing to assume the promotional burden of the new enterprise. "I could beat the drum," he explained, "while Johnson sat inside the tent."

But Lee's oversight of the operation was soon deflected by other enthusiasms. The connections between Johnson's instruction and attractive career lines were never clear. Small enrollments were the most obvious manifestation of the problem, which was compounded by Lowell's refusal to open the play courses to undergraduates on grounds that they were highly vocational and hence inappropriate for liberal education. Holmes tried to imagine how a larger market could be created for Johnson's instruction. He thought the Boy Scouts could be incorporated into the public school's regular curriculum and considered developing Harvard programs for Scout and YMCA workers. And he explored collaborative programs with other parts of the University to train experts in physical education and health education, vague job categories that overlapped with yet were distinguishable from play and recreation itself.

At the same time, he encouraged Johnson to develop instruction in child development to recruit a younger and less vocationally oriented clientele. But even this administrative solution created headaches, for Lowell and the Harvard psychologists had no enthusiasm for an undergraduate course which, in the 1920s, continued to endorse Hallian theory (including "cultural epochs") as scientifically valid. The debate about counting the child development course for college credit ceased in 1920 when the Division of Education withdrew from the faculty of arts and sciences; but the question of how Johnson could maximize the organizational impact of play continued to perplex Holmes throughout the 1920s.[14]

As THE DIVISION expanded to include play and recreation, it eagerly embraced a similar opportunity in vocational guidance. Here the moving spirit was Lincoln Filene, who had urged a course in guidance ever since his appointment to the visiting committee. In 1915 Filene helped persuade the aging philanthropist Pauline Agassiz Shaw to donate a three-year faculty position in guidance. At that time university instruction in vocational guidance was rarer than instruction in play. Yet Harvard's guidance effort far more successfully addressed the organizational requirements of creating a new educational service. Part of the difference lay in the personalities and ages of the faculty involved, but guidance at Harvard was also pushed forward by its intimate association with the traditions of the Vocation Bureau of Boston.

By 1915, seven years after its establishment, the Vocation Bureau was the center of the guidance movement in America. As a clearing house of information, the bureau collected and published informa-

...on about the characteristics of occupations. As the promoter of a national movement it helped organize the first national conference on vocational guidance in 1910. This led in 1913 to establishment of the National Vocational Guidance Association and, inevitably, a periodical. The bureau also helped create the Boston Employment Managers' Association, a group of businessmen interested in vocational selection and on-the-job training. And it persuaded the Boston schools to establish a vocational guidance department

The bureau's director, Meyer Bloomfield, believed that guidance was as much the responsibility of social settlements and industry as it was of schools and that its clientele should include adults as well as youth. He dreamt of a new profession of vocational counselors steeped in facts about job requirements and economic conditions, and hoped they would work in a wide variety of social settings. Bloomfield believed the competent counselor should be conversant with contemporary educational literature, but he placed greater emphasis on familiarity with economics, labor relations, and sociological topics such as urban housing. Gradually Bloomfield became more interested in how industry itself could provide guidance and training to employees. He suggested that employment management could become the focus for vocational guidance, and in 1917 resigned from the bureau to establish his own consulting firm on industrial personnel counseling.

The Vocation Bureau was then absorbed by Harvard and renamed the Bureau of Vocational Guidance. At first Bloomfield's policy directions were retained. Stimulated by federal contracts available after America entered World War I, the trend toward out-of-school guidance for adult workers continued. Vocational guidance became virtually indistinguishable from on-the-job vocational education. The Bureau of Vocational Guidance published booklets to recruit shipyard workers, investigated employment problems of disabled soldiers, offered training programs for employment managers and Americanization courses for workers, and developed a plan to train plant foremen. But when Bloomfield's successor was also lured away by private industry, John Marks Brewer stepped in and shifted the bureau's interests firmly and permanently toward schooling. Just as Johnson imagined the public school as the center for supervised play services, Brewer imagined it as the sole basis for organized vocational guidance.[15]

Hanus first brought guidance into the Division's curriculum in

1911 when Bloomfield taught a course in the summer school. But Bloomfield could not initiate guidance instruction during the academic year because he was disliked by Lowell and faculty at the Harvard Business School. Pauline Agassiz Shaw's gift was designed to surmount this obstacle by apprenticing to the bureau a noncontroversial doctoral student who would join the faculty upon completion of his thesis. John Brewer had no idea he would receive this unique opportunity when he began studies toward a Ph.D. in education in 1914, but Hanus had no difficulty in recruiting him to the unexpected career of university specialist in vocational guidance.

Brewer was a thirty-seven-year-old Los Angeles high school teacher seeking to focus his varied interests in the socialization of education. His special enthusiasm was the extracurriculum. Active in California boys' clubs, summer camps, and vacation schools, Brewer experimented with student government methods in which adults delegated decision-making responsibility in order to develop self-control in youth. Later he incorporated his ideas into public high schools. A reformer in adult as well as student government, he was instrumental in introducing the city-manager form of government to Inglewood.

Like George Johnson, Brewer wanted to incorporate into formal school programs, under the direction of trained adults, youth activities traditionally peripheral to schooling. No Harvard faculty member displayed more overt hostility to the older academic curriculum. Brewer emphasized that the high school's only true function was to prepare for "specific duties of life," that these duties were mainly vocational and civic, and that "culture" as an educational objective did little more than perpetuate social divisions and economic inequality. For Brewer, education had to be socialized not to keep the masses quiet but to give them practical skills to live independent and happy lives. "We teach about the volcanoes of South America," he sneered, "but not about volcanoes of factory towns." And he wondered why ninety-six of every hundred Americans needed, in accord with the American economic system, the permission of the other four to work.[16]

Following his apprenticeship in the Vocation Bureau and a two-year stint at Ernest Moore's Los Angeles State Normal School, Brewer returned permanently to Harvard in 1919 to teach vocational guidance and administer the Bureau of Vocational Guidance.

His exclusive interest in the "school phases of guidance" was the result of personal experience, social ideology, and institutonal pressure. Unlike the previous leaders of the bureau, Brewer knew schools very well and industry hardly at all. He disliked the blurred conjoining of guidance and vocational education which seemed an inevitable by-product of using industry as an institutional site for guidance. Brewer always urged a clear distinction between vocational guidance as self-determination and vocational education as training. The bureau's work in employment management and industrial training, moreover, was resented by the Harvard Business School. Holmes wanted to avoid internal squabbles at all costs in the months when he was on the verge of achieving a graduate school of education. Despite some awareness that the philanthropic costs of abandoning an industrial base to the Business School might be substantial, Holmes agreed that the on-the-job aspects of vocational guidance would cease.[17]

The presence of a distinct "bureau" within the Division, with a budget of $13,000 in 1919, an advisory board, and two full-time staff in addition to Brewer and a secretary, gave vocational guidance special leverage and shaped the ways Brewer spent his time. Despite the withdrawal of industrial support the bureau made money through sales of publications, fees from short training courses, and annual gifts from Filene. With the profits, Brewer subsidized publication of the *Bulletin of the National Vocational Guidance Association* and assured Harvard of favorable publicity as a national center of the guidance movement. The bureau also subsidized publication of booklets on occupations which were distributed free to schools. In effect, Brewer managed a service and dissemination agency that consumed as much of his time as did formal instruction.[18]

Brewer self-consciously used the bureau as a political agency to promote the cause of vocational guidance, and his writings reinforced his preoccupation with administrative change in the schools. He produced dozens of articles advocating guidance along with a school text on occupations and a training text for guidance specialists. His most influential work was his dissertation, published in 1918 as *The Vocational Guidance Movement, Its Problems and Possibilities*. While Inglis tried to construct theory, and Johnson drew practical implications from Hall's theories, Brewer fixed his attention on the procedural problems of establishing school guidance programs. Characteristically, he began and ended with definitions — the six stages of vocational guidance and the eleven steps needed to inaugurate an adequate program. Once the steps and stages were fully understood — Brewer required of his students rather precise recall of his terminology — students would be better equipped for their primary professional mission of starting up a new school service. Brewer later recalled that perhaps his greatest contribution to vocational guidance was defining it.[19]

Brewer hoped that vocational guidance would not merely add to the existing school program but would transform it. If vocation was the central experience in a man's life, then vocational guidance should permeate all of education. Rather than confine vocational guidance to advice on job selection, Brewer regarded education itself as only another name for guidance rightly conducted. In later years he tried to elevate the idea of "education as guidance" into systematic educational theory; now its main use was to justify administrative schemes for guidance to penetrate the academic curriculum. Teachers of any subject were advised to use "vocational needs" as a criterion in the selection of course content. If English teachers considered the "vocational implications" of literature, they might infuse life into a subject whose most notable effect, Brewer thought, was to drive youth out of school.

The "life-career class" on occupations and the use of extracurricular activities to teach vocational awareness were additional devices to incorporate guidance into the regular school program. Vocational counseling itself was but one of several activities to further vocational guidance. The role of the counselor was as much to promote and coordinate activities like the life-career class as it was to advise individual students. Like Meyer Bloomfield before him, Brewer was vague about counseling skill beyond the possession of information about jobs and the economy. Bloomfield conceived of the actual process of counseling as "organized common sense," confined exclusively to matters of vocational decisions, and Brewer did not deviate from that model.[20]

Above all, both men emphasized that the counselor's proper role was nonauthoritative and nondirective. Youth should never be told what to do. The aim of guidance was self-guidance. Brewer was a consistent critic of psychological testing, especially after it achieved public notoriety during World War I. He was always suspicious that tests could be used to classify youth and push them toward occupations that only adults wanted them to enter. The more elaborate expert diagnosis became, the more convincing and controlling expert prescription would be. Brewer defined the skill of the ideal counselor more by social attitudes and administrative techniques then by knowledge of tests or mental measurement, and organized the content of his courses accordingly. The need to create vocational guidance in schools seemed vastly more compelling than the need to elaborate the counselor's technical skill. Unlike Johnson, Brewer could never reconcile adult expertise with youthful freedom. As course enrollments grew, book sales mounted, and new requests for advice and materials poured into the Bureau of Vocational Guidance, Brewer took increasing pride in his unusual entrepreneurial success. The preeminence of advocacy over science rested on a clear moral base.[21]

COMPARED WITH PLAY and vocational guidance, Harvard's entrance into vocational education was delayed and reactive. The desirability of a curriculum initiative in vocational education had been regularly endorsed by the visiting committee since Warburg and Filene joined it. But no one offered money to add a Johnson or a Brewer. Nor, in the years between 1913 and 1917, did Harvard have a clear idea of what a curriculum thrust in vocational education should be. The Division lacked the intimate links with the center of the vocational education cause — the National Society for the Promotion of Industrial Education — that it had forged with the national leadership of play and guidance. Felix Warburg was the chief proponent of vocational education, but preferred to push Teachers College's dominance of this field rather than Harvard's. He schemed to "domicile" the National Society at Teachers College and make its head a Teachers College professor, much as Filene and Hanus domiciled the Vocation Bureau at Harvard.

The pivotal event that clarified the shape of vocational education, helped define career lines within it, and eventually governed Harvard's entry into the field was passage by the Congress of the National Vocation Education Act in 1917. The Smith-Hughes Act, as it was commonly called, provided federal support to states on a matching basis for salaries and training of vocational educators in four distinct areas: industrial education, agricultural education, trade or commercial education, and household arts or home economics. By establishing financial incentives and by creating a Federal Board for Vocational Education to provide technical advice and encouragement, the Smith-Hughes Act gave the vocational educators an enormous political triumph that guidance and play advocates could only regard with envy.[22]

The Smith-Hughes Act gave a huge boost to commercial or business education in the public schools and presented Harvard with a wholly unexpected opportunity. At the moment when rapid national expansion of an undeveloped field of public schooling seemed likely, Hanus noticed a Boston institutional base on which Harvard might build as usefully as it had built upon the Vocation Bureau. Earlier in the century Lucinda W. Prince had established training classes to prepare saleswomen for Boston department stores, supervisors of saleswomen, and teachers of retail selling. By 1918 the Prince School of Education for Store Service was affiliated with Simmons College and was regarded as the best (albeit nearly the only) institution to prepare graduates of women's colleges to be "store educational directors" or personnel managers for retail business. Smith-Hughes encouraged the Prince School to emphasize the teacher-education possibilities of its work and to strengthen its ties to Simmons. Mrs. Prince helped the Federal Board for Vocational Education prepare a booklet on the need for school courses in retail selling, and the board encouraged her to train continuation school teachers and hence become eligible for federal support.

Hanus and Holmes concluded that the future of the Prince School loomed larger than its past and knew that officials at Teachers College had privately agreed not to develop commercial education if Harvard did. By acquiring an instant training capacity in a new field, the Division could achieve for one area of vocational education what it simultaneously was attempting in play and guidance. "This," Holmes concluded, "is a social demand we can not ignore." Hanus easily persuaded Mrs. Prince that annexation by Harvard was more in her interests than continued affiliation with Simmons. The Division offered increased prestige, graduate credit, Harvard degrees, and financial stability. The last point especially impressed the Boston merchants and officers of the National Retail Dry Goods

Association, who jointly underwrote the Prince School's substantial deficits. In 1920 Holmes negotiated an agreement to absorb the Prince School completely in two years.[23]

Eventually Holmes hoped to acquire faculty members in the other divisions of vocational education, and even sought foundation support to create in pastoral Cambridge a center for agricultural and rural education. But the immediate priority, once the decision to absorb the Prince School had been made, was to acquire a regular faculty member able to advance the cause of commercial education. Mrs. Prince suggested that the only individual of truly national stature in the field was Frederick George Nichols. In 1922 Nichols was persuaded to join the faculty as a tenured associate professor.[24]

At age forty-four, Frederick Nichols had brilliantly demonstrated how a resourceful young man without educational advantages could convert the growing national interest in vocational education into an impressive career. Unlike Johnson and Brewer, whose interests were turned to special fields at mid-career by graduate-level university opportunities, Nichols enjoyed no educational opportunities at all beyond attendance at a rural academy. Yet he parlayed his academy skills of stenography and bookkeeping into progressively more responsible school positions. He accurately regarded himself as the quintessential self-made man. He never applied for a job beyond his first one and was, after that, the first incumbent in virtually every position he held.

Perhaps his most risky and decisive move was to abandon the world of proprietary business schools, where most business education took place early in the century, for the undeveloped frontier of public education. In 1903, at age twenty-five, Nichols resigned the principalship of a large private shorthand school to organize a commercial department for the high school in Schenectady, New York. Two years later he created the position of director of commercial education for the Rochester schools, and two years after that he organized a department of commercial education for the state of New York. Upon establishment of the Federal Board for Vocational Education he was appointed its first assistant director for commercial education. When Pennsylvania created a state commercial education department, Nichols became its director in 1920.[25]

Nichols' energetic promotion of commercial education in each of his jobs expanded his reputation and helped generate his next assignment. In Rochester he devised a work-study curriculum in commercial education. In Albany he prepared a new state syllabus. When the junior high school opened up a younger market for commercial education, Nichols was quick to advocate a course on "junior business training," just as Brewer advocated a life-career class in guidance. Nichols first tried out the course in Rochester, promoted it in speeches and articles in Washington, prepared a complete syllabus for it in Pennsylvania, and published a text soon after he arrived at Harvard. In the depths of the Depression, sales of *Junior Business Training* earned him an annual royalty of $5000.[26]

He never needed to offer elaborate arguments to justify the educational centrality of vocational concerns, for his remarkable career was premised on and confirmed that centrality. Nichols was ideologically comfortable with his new Harvard colleagues, although he argued with Inglis that the seven "cardinal principles" had unfairly slighted vocational education. (Once, in defining the aims of education for high school youth, Nichols borrowed all six social-efficiency objectives of the cardinal principles but dropped its single concession to older intellectual aims, command of fundamental processes.) For the most part, however, Nichols confined his teaching and writing to specific problems within his field. Much as his colleagues formulated educational goals by identifying specific life activities, Nichols formulated the content of the commercial curriculum by identifying specific vocational activities that comprised work in commercial firms. The central reform thrust of his career, apart from advocacy of more commercial education, was to improve the high school commercial course by selecting curriculum materials according to the tasks people performed.

Again and again he argued that, as business education moved from proprietary to public school, it had perpetuated outmoded emphases on elite business skills such as bookkeeping and stenography. Most boys and girls were employed in jobs that required neither of those skills. A study he conducted while in Washington indicated that only 12 percent of students who studied bookkeeping and stenography in school could use them on the job. Nichols' conclusion was obvious: only the most able minority should be allowed to study these subjects. The rest should study what would "function" in their actual employments. A central task for universities was to classify and standardize existing commercial jobs and the specific skills required to do each one. Nichols took the lead in advocating differentiated school curricula to prepare for new kinds of business jobs such as clerical work and retail selling.

Nichols recognized the selective process inherent in curriculum differentiation. As the tasks required to do a job became more specific and identifiable, and the construction of a school curriculum easier, the jobs themselves ironically became more "routine" and low-paying. More desirable business jobs were harder to break down into skill components. He had no intention to exclude from the commercial curriculum general business and academic instruction, "since future advancement as well as present employment must always be kept in mind when setting up courses of business training." Yet the direction of reform was always toward more specific and less vague preparation. General training had to give way to "definite vocational training suited to the requirements of junior office and store-workers." Nichols thought that Brewer was naive and irresponsible in urging counselors to provide facts but not advice. As he took up his Harvard responsibilities, he looked forward to analyzing job skills in ever more minute detail.[27]

Having promoted commercial education at the highest levels of city, state, and federal authority open to him, Nichols regarded his Harvard opportunity as the fitting culmination of his career. He made more speeches and published more articles than anyone else on the faculty. He gained control of the commercial education section of the *Vocational Education Magazine* upon his move to Cambridge just as Brewer controlled the organ of the guidance movement. At Harvard Nichols hoped not only to increase the demand for his field, but to supply it as well. The central use of the university, for this man whose own educational opportunities had been so limited, was to enable him to reproduce himself. Although he valued the Prince School as a recruiting source, Nichols' personal interests were not to train young teachers but to develop leaders of commercial education at the city, state, and federal levels. The professional wisdom acquired in twenty years of educational work would now be efficiently transmitted, he hoped, to a larger band of disciples eager to occupy the new positions his relentless advocacy had helped open up. As for his other specialist colleagues, experienced and ambitious students to amplify the growth of his field were indispensable.[28]

6

The Graduate School
of Education

HARVARD'S ACADEMIC CLIMATE contributed to education's emphasis on specialized career roles to manage the socialization of youth. Lowell's adamant opposition to undergraduate vocational training forced Holmes to seek new student markets out of fear that education enrollments would otherwise shrivel. Enlarging the number of graduate students seemed the best strategy. No graduate market was more promising than the teachers in local high schools. And no recruitment argument was more alluring than the usefulness of graduate study to assist career transitions from teaching to administration or to one of the newer specializations. The ultimate recruiting magnet was an entirely graduate school of education. The idea of separating the Division from the faculty of arts and sciences was consistent with Lowell's notions of proper university organization and the Division's sense of its best hope for growth. In 1920 a $2 million endowment secured the establishment of the Graduate School of Education.

Holmes believed that the impact of a professional school depended on the number of students it attracted. At first he assumed that a substantial source of students would be young college graduates preparing to teach in high schools. Yet the Division's own history cast doubt on that prophecy. Despite the fact that education courses had been established at Harvard to prepare college graduates for teaching, very few graduate students were ever inexperienced teachers. Holmes often said that the classroom teacher was the central educational role for which Harvard offered preparation. But the reality, which became even more apparent after the new School opened its doors, was that student demand for graduate teacher education was virtually nonexistent. Holmes cared genuinely about teacher education and fought to perpetuate it at Harvard by maintaining an undergraduate program and by exploiting the opportunity offered by the Prince School to train commercial teachers. But Lowell dashed his efforts.

Instead, the student body of the Graduate School of Education became dominated by experienced teachers. The faculty regarded this development as advantageous, and soon the special needs of older students determined curriculum policy. Part-time study became nearly universal. The timing of instruction to accommodate part-time students became the central issue of curriculum planning. Technical courses of immediate applicability were developed far faster than theoretical or research courses that no one would take. Lowell was dubious about the School's tendency to equate the needs of education with the needs of experienced teachers and was especially concerned about the erosion of commitment to educational research. From time to time he intervened in appointment decisions, but only to slow down the pace of events rather than to reverse its direction. Meanwhile, the new School's enrollment, financial prosperity, and reputation all increased faster than Holmes's fondest expectations. By 1924 the School's mission and constituency seemed secure.

PRESIDENT LOWELL's academic priorities ensured that the expansion of vocational training for specialized career lines would find curriculum expression only at the graduate level. There was nothing inherently "graduate" about courses on the junior high school, play, guidance, or vocational education. The faculty knew perfectly well that the largest potential student market for those fields were youth workers, social workers, and industrial workers who possessed little or no higher education, much less a bachelor's degree. But Lowell defined undergraduate education at Harvard as exclusively liberal and defined liberal education as inherently nonvocational. It had become axiomatic that explicit vocational training at Harvard would exist only at the graduate level if it was to exist at all. Lowell demanded that all of the new specialized education courses be closed to undergraduates, and he sharply questioned the continuing availability to undergraduates of practice teaching.[1]

Administrative implementation of Lowell's views threatened the

accessibility of education courses to Harvard and Radcliffe undergraduates. When Holmes became Division chairman in 1911 he
worried more about the enrollment effects of the concentration-
distribution system than about Lowell's intervention in faculty appointment policy. The slight growth in enrollment experienced by
the Division in the first decade of the century was due exclusively to
increases in undergraduate registrations. In only one year of the
decade had undergraduate enrollments slipped below 60 percent of
the total. But in 1911-12 sophomores revealed their course preferences under the new plan for the first time, and the results seemed
disastrous. Not one planned to concentrate in education, and only
one planned to take as many as two education courses. The entire
sophomore class registered for only three education courses in 1911-
12, as compared with forty-two sophomore registrations the year
before. Total course enrollments from all categories of students fell
nearly in half, from the record 450 set in 1910-11 to only 239.
Undergraduates accounted for most of this drop. Graduate enrollments declined slightly, in part because Hanus was on leave. But the
percentage of total course enrollments by graduate students rose
from 26 percent to 41 percent, the highest graduate fraction since
the late 1890s.[2]

The enrollment crisis occupied much of Holmes's administrative
attention over the next five years. On the one hand he schemed to
circumvent the new system's restrictions on free choice and restore
education's pre-Lowell undergraduate complement. He encouraged
students to request, for example, special joint concentrations in
which some education courses were included, and justified the procedure by distinguishing between "vocational training" and liberal
education pursued "on the basis of a vocational purpose." Always at
his confident best in decorous verbal sparring, Holmes won several
committee battles on particular petitions.

But he was astute enough not to put his main energies into a rear-
guard campaign to resurrect Eliot's Harvard. He knew the Division's
future progress required a substantial increase in the number of
graduate students. Here the past record was embarrassingly weak.
Graduate student registrations and hence graduate course enrollments had been unstable and unpredictable, rising and falling from
year to year with no discernible pattern. Between twelve and twenty-
four graduate students might register for some fraction of time each

year and specify education as their major interest. By 1911 a total of sixty-two individuals who had focused mainly on education had received the A.M. degree during the prior fifteen years. Two had achieved the Ph.D. in education.[3]

Hanus blamed his failure to attract a sizable graduate constituency on both the small size of the faculty and the unwillingness of New England states and municipalities to require education courses as a condition of employment or promotion. Holmes ignored these impediments and doggedly pushed practical administrative responses. He tried to remove the obstacles that separated the Division's offerings from a potential graduate constituency. The education courses had been scheduled in the mornings, like most instruction in the faculty of arts and sciences, even though practicing teachers could only take courses in the late afternoons. Under Holmes most were rescheduled. In addition, he expanded summer enrollments, on the premise that students who first registered in the summer might continue as A.M. candidates in the regular term. From two summer courses enrolling seventy-one students in 1911, education mounted ten courses enrolling 179 students in 1915. With less success Holmes argued that in-service teachers should pay less tuition than other students.[4]

Besides removing obstacles to the attendance of graduate students, Holmes tried to add incentives to attend. As an advertising lure he attempted to recast the image of the Harvard A.M. from a cultural degree to a professional one. He formulated specific course sequences that prepared for various administrative jobs and proposed that the A.M. be awarded with specific designation given to the field of study undertaken. He failed in the latter effort because most members of the faculty of arts and sciences disliked the suggestion that the A.M.'s purpose was vocational. But he eventually succeeded in a related effort to persuade his colleagues to count summer courses toward Harvard graduate degrees. The inability to count any summer work toward the A.M. had long placed the Division at a competitive disadvantage with institutions like Teachers College. Holmes's triumph in the faculty debate, which astonished him as well as older allies like A. B. Hart and Edwin Hall, was achieved through "calm, genial, and pertinacious" forensic skill, and promised to have a substantial impact on the enlarged but still modest summer education clientele. At the same time he successfully lobbied the Boston School Department to count completion of the Harvard A.M. in education (when preceded by some undergraduate courses) as the equivalent of two of the three years of experience required to teach high school in Boston.[5]

As Holmes pressed the advantages of graduate study to make the A.M. degree more attractive, he relied on arguments that emphasized the deficiencies of undergraduate education study. Graduate study in education was *better* than undergraduate. With an enthusiasm that suggested personal conviction as well as acquiescence to Harvard political realities, Holmes applied arguments used to justify deferring professional training until after college to the field of education. Deferral guaranteed higher scholastic standards and more mature career choices. It avoided encroachment on studies "justly required" for a liberally educated individual. And, demonstrating how quickly professional controversies of a quarter-century before had been settled, Holmes noted that "the vocation that calls for an early training is lowered in the estimation of thinking men."

Just as Holmes undercut the idea that undergraduate professional preparation was wise policy, so he also withdrew from the idea that undergraduate education courses provided nonvocational liberal education analogous to economics or political science. The appointments of Inglis, Johnson, and Brewer inaugurated an era in which the Division's purposes became narrower and more specialized. Its tasks, Holmes told the visiting committee near the end of 1915, were now "wholly professional."[6]

Enrollment trends by 1915 indicated that the Division was finally able to recruit graduate students in reasonable numbers. In the five years ending in 1915-16, graduate students and graduate course enrollments both tripled. As many master's degrees were awarded between 1913 and 1917 — sixty-two — as in all the years prior to 1911. Doctoral study rose as well; twenty Ph.D.s were awarded between 1912 and 1920 compared with two earlier recipients. Undergraduate enrollments also recovered from the shocking setback of 1911, with the result that total Division course enrollments rose to 834 in 1916-17 as compared with 239 in 1911-12. Plainly the Division had underestimated the ability of undergraduates to fit into their schedules the courses they wished to take. Moreover, twice as many Radcliffe undergraduates enrolled in education courses in the five-year period after 1912 than in the five years before 1912. The

Radcliffe fraction of undergraduate enrollments increased from 29 percent to 45 percent between 1912 and 1917. In sharp contrast the graduate population remained overwhelmingly — 94 percent — male.

Holmes interpreted these trends in terms of the logic that dominated his own rhetoric and appointment decisions. The existence of a graduate market had been confirmed. The increased undergraduate interest was rewarding but burdensome. In May 1915, just after the visiting committee authorized faculty appointments in play and vocational guidance, Warburg and Holmes won Lowell's agreement to separate the Division from the faculty of arts and sciences and form a new Graduate School of Education. The logic of separation seemed clear to everyone and provoked no disagreement.

When Hanus first proposed a separate school of education in 1903, he had in mind something like the Lawrence Scientific School, which had maintained a prominent undergraduate program. By 1915 Lawrence was long dead and with it the notion of a variety of undergraduate options at Harvard. Holmes then accepted the more restricted idea of an institution open only to college graduates. He was willing to apply to education the newer Harvard model of professional training as an exclusively post-bachelor's experience. Like Hanus, he craved independence from the faculty of arts and sciences. Independence would signify acceptance of education's professional claims, would be a potent lure to attract more graduate students, and would guarantee the end of debilitating administrative squabbles with his academic colleagues.

Nor was Lowell opposed to separation. Although his recent interest in education was based primarily on its research potential, he had accepted without question the visiting committee's gifts intended to expand the faculty in explicitly vocational directions. In 1911, Lowell could easily have phased out the Division. Yet all his actions afterwards furthered expansion and the growth of forceful internal advocates. But clearly the expanding Division contradicted his beliefs of what the faculty of arts and sciences should include. Separation would eliminate a vocational cancer from Harvard College, a cancer whose growth could be charted by undergraduate enrollment data.[7]

Although Lowell approved the idea of a new school he did nothing to bring it about. After 1915 Holmes's most compelling administrative problem was to find money to start the institution. With research his main interest, Lowell did not intend to establish a school dependent for its survival on tuition income. In a significant reversal of Harvard policy and an astounding deviation from the practice of other schools of education, Lowell insisted that nearly all of the new school's expenses be met from endowment income. He further stipulated that the school could not exist until the entire endowment was raised. (In 1912 85 percent of the expenses of Teachers College were met by tuition income.) In order that fund-raising for education not conflict with higher-priority Harvard projects, Lowell refused to authorize any public solicitation until at least one third of the needed endowment was in hand. His friend John Moors, soon to become a fellow of the Corporation, resigned from the visiting committee chairmanship in 1917 because his colleagues pushed too aggressively for a fund raising campaign that Moors feared would undercut a larger University canvass about to begin.[8]

Despite tepid central support and the disruption of campaign activities by World War I, an endowment of $2 million was secured by the end of 1919. This substantial achievement—larger than the endowments of the law or business schools—was the result of one single breakthrough that combined enviable connections and sheer luck. When Hanus encountered difficulties during the New York inquiry, he found allies among prominent friends of public education who disliked the Bureau of Municipal Research's relentless cost-consciousness just as much as he did. The crucial link between Hanus and these sources of political and financial influence was Jerome Greene, who had once been Eliot's secretary and personal choice as his successor, and who remembered Hanus affectionately as one of Eliot's staunchest allies. Greene was a trustee and the first secretary of the Rockefeller Foundation, and also a trustee of the Rockefeller education philanthropy, the General Education Board. Afterwards he joined the New York office of James J. Storrow's banking firm, and Storrow persuaded him to succeed Moors as chairman of the visiting committee and of the endowment drive. Storrow also arranged to free Greene from business duties in order for him to run the campaign.

Through Greene Hanus met Abraham Flexner, the prominent medical reformer who joined the staff of the General Education Board in 1913 and promptly conducted an investigation into the

Bureau of Municipal Research (which had received Rockefeller support). Hanus and Flexner agreed on New York educational issues and liked each other personally. Over the years the bonds of respect and affection deepened, especially after Hanus successfully conducted a survey of Hampton Institute for the General Education Board. Flexner knew of Hanus' frustrations in Cambridge and of his dream for independence from the faculty of arts and sciences. When the board's interest switched to secondary education—it established the Lincoln School at Teachers College—Flexner indicated that it might be willing to express its confidence in Hanus through a major gift to Harvard.[9]

The problem of securing a gift from the General Education Board was less one of persuading its trustees to vote the money than of persuading Lowell to apply for it. Embittered at the board's rejection of various Harvard requests for medical endowment, Lowell refused to permit further applications unless guaranteed in advance that the request would be approved. When Abraham Flexner signaled in March 1919 that the trustees would act "favorably, promptly, and generously" to a Harvard education application, this condition was met. But Lowell also knew that Flexner could not deliver the entire endowment and that any gift would be conditioned on Harvard's capacity to raise the remainder. The act of applying to the General Education Board would officially commit the University to a financial effort it had not been willing to assume before.

Here Holmes, Storrow, Warburg, and Greene all reassured the president that the remaining money could easily be raised. Everyone agreed that a total of $2 million was a reasonable objective. The board was willing to supply $500,000. Holmes and Warburg persuaded Lowell to contribute from Harvard endowment funds the additional sum of $500,000, whose interest yielded roughly what the University was already spending on the Division. The remaining million would be obtained, Lowell was assured, from the visiting committee itself and others it would discreetly solicit. After a month's reflection Lowell finally decided that an application would be "wise and safe," and the General Education Board's $500,000 gift was promptly made.

Lowell's caution about the second million was fully justified. By midsummer all of the Division's prospects had announced their intentions and only $150,000 more had been raised. Warburg had been the biggest hope, but he regarded the new institution as a Boston enterprise and would only match whatever Storrow gave. Storrow could manage only $50,000. The committee's two most vigorous workers for the endowment together produced only a third of what Holmes had counted on. Filene and Lee, moreover, were more interested in particular enthusiasms than in the new school as an institution. Their annual giving continued but they provided no endowment. When the Division's only recourse seemed a more public campaign, the directors of the other, larger Harvard Endowment Fund drive quickly intervened. They did not want a separate, competing education campaign, and eliminated the need for it by absorbing education in their own effort. For all practical purposes the Graduate School of Education's existence was at last assured. The relabeled Division officially began its new work in September 1920, with Holmes installed as its first dean.[10]

DESPITE THE FINANCIAL cushion provided by the endowment, Holmes believed that the influence of the Graduate School of Education would primarily be determined by the size of its student body. The more teachers and school officers it could reach, the greater the public service it would render. The conviction that strength lay in numbers in part reflected the concurrent emphasis on promoting specialized professional careers and services. But it also exposed considerable anxiety over whether the School would draw. Even in its peak year before the war, the Division had attracted only forty-two full-time equivalent graduate enrollments. Its new curriculum did little more than upgrade to graduate status all the courses offered previously. Would more students attend?

Of course the endowment assured institutional survival without any students at all, under Harvard's "every tub on its own bottom" system of fiscal decentralization. Two millions' endowment generated $100,000 income annually, compared with the Division's expenses of $36,000 in 1919-20. But students symbolized success and impact. Moreover, drawing power influenced the School's political capacity to add additional faculty. In the winter of 1920 Lowell postponed Holmes's proposals for a near doubling of the faculty partly on grounds that no one could yet foresee whether student demand would justify and help support such an expansion.[11]

The School expected to exert far more powerful recruitment lures than the Division. In contrast to Teachers College and Chicago it was an exclusively graduate institution, although Yale's new department of education also banned undergraduates. When the School was established, Chicago's Charles H. Judd is supposed to have exclaimed that the field of education at last had donned a dress suit. To mark its separation from the faculty of arts and sciences, the School devised new professional degrees, the master of education and doctor of education, which it hoped would symbolize education's prestige and autonomy. Summer study was fully countable toward graduate degrees. Most significant of all, women students for the first time became eligible to receive Harvard degrees. Lowell had accepted that historic shift in University policy since the beginning of discussions about the proposed school.[12]

Yet the new procedures created their own uncertainties. Everyone feared that new degrees might be regarded as less prestigious than the older A.M. and Ph.D. regularly offered in all other major schools of education. The final decision to create the doctor of education was made only after last-ditch efforts to retain the Ph.D. were rejected by Lowell. The Division and its doctoral alumni were divided between those who believed new degrees would celebrate the liberation of professionalism from the ' skirts of the philosophical faculty" and those who contended that a new degree given for essentially the same work as the Ph.D. was a disastrous professional defeat. Holmes fought to retain the Ph.D., but Lowell saw little reason to deviate from Harvard's policy of academic decentralization which gave a monopoly on the Ph.D. to the Graduate School of Arts and Sciences. Lowell's application of the concept of academic decentralization was exceedingly selective. The School had hoped to create its own summer school and to realize the profits that summer enrollments brought to institutions like Teachers College. But Lowell agreed only to include the word "education" in the summer school's name. Whatever profits accrued continued to flow to the faculty of arts and sciences alone.[13]

Above all else Holmes feared that the School might be unable to attract young students to prepare for high school teaching. Although education courses at Harvard had first been established to provide college graduates with teacher preparation, they had never attracted such students in numbers. During the years of rapid graduate expansion after 1913, only 7 percent of education graduate students took practice teaching. Even the undergraduate practice teaching registrations were small, and Holmes acknowledged that more than half of the Harvard College graduates who entered secondary teaching took no education courses at all.

The Division's failure in teacher education recruitment seemed in part the product of its own lack of will. Holmes admitted that the training priorities of the Division had drifted away from teacher education. The ideological commitment to the socialization of education was in principle translatable to classroom concern for curriculum and pedagogy. Yet the focus of faculty attention was to provide additional administrative services rather than to reconceptualize older teaching fields. Classroom teaching was not a central interest of any of the major appointments made after Ernest Moore. When the completion of the endowment drive enabled Holmes to plan to double the faculty, he refused on grounds of policy to elevate "special methods" in the secondary curriculum fields to full-time faculty positions. After 1920 the Graduate School of Education introduced a limited array of special methods courses during the academic year, but the individuals who taught them were normally considered not regular members of the faculty but part-timers whose career lines lay outside the faculty of education.[14]

Pervading the neglect of teacher education was pessimism about the possibilities of making high school teaching truly professional. Holmes saw a yawning gap between the theoretical desirability of graduate training for teachers and the reality of low salaries that made the goal impractical. Eliot had endorsed secondary teaching as a career worthy of Harvard students, but Lowell doubted whether it could attract Harvard graduates. There were not economic prizes to be won in teaching, he noted, nor did the schools appear as "charitable institutions" to which the young would devote their lives as public service.[15]

During the second decade of the century men sensed that fewer students from Harvard and colleges like it were entering the public secondary schools and that candidates for teaching jobs had become more "narrow, uncultured, crude" than before. The *New England Journal of Education* traced the reduction of Harvard numbers and influence to the decline of the practice of taking on temporary teaching stints prior to commencing more permanent careers. As teacher preparation became more formalized and teaching itself more secure, such tentative forays were frowned upon. The development of similar processes of rationalized entry to other occupations reduced the need for temporary employment in teaching. Most Harvardians now entering teaching, the *Journal* argued, were those fully committed to education. In one sense this was a triumph for the reformers of the late 1880s who regarded uncommitted teachers as a major problem. But, ironically, the increasing constraint on spontaneous choice perhaps reduced the recruiting pool and altered its characteristics. Barrett Wendell had feared that the substitution of organization for spontaneity in teacher recruitment would repel desirable candidates. Could he have been right?[16]

With so much of the Division's attention focused on the career development of those who had already made irrevocable commitments to lifetime educational work, it was not surprising that Holmes cared far less for the intricacies of initial recruitment than had earlier proponents of university teacher education like Horace Willard or Ray Greene Huling. When a fellow of the Corporation, Thomas Nelson Perkins, suggested that the main problem of teacher education was to improve the type of person who entered teaching, Holmes countered with a fundamentally different perspective. Perkins, like Willard and Huling, viewed education courses as devices to recruit and sort out the committed. Holmes contended that the courses were now capable of changing anyone into a true professional.

The key to professional upgrading was professional training itself, not the raw material that sought it out. Holmes also made plain that he was talking about the impact of training on "standards and character" in addition to mere technique. "When loyalty to a great cause is really kindled in anybody's mind and heart, it goes a long way toward making a new person out of him." Yet the gap between the dramatic claim that training might *make* new persons and the Division's actual neglect of teacher education was very wide. A more realistic indication of dominant priorities was Alexander Inglis' success in securing a junior faculty colleague to relieve him of any responsibility for practice teaching. In persuading his choice for the job to abandon schoolteaching for a career in a school of education, Inglis counseled that it was best to get out soon. An able person would be sick of kids by the time he was thirty-five.[17]

The desire for a large enrollment forced Holmes to confront anew the complex problem of attracting inexperienced teachers. Initially, he hoped to retain the Division of Education alongside the Graduate School of Education to continue undergraduate teacher preparation. Lowell quashed that suggestion immediately. At Harvard even initial teacher preparation would be a graduate function only. Of course Holmes expected that at least some college graduates would risk a full year of graduate study in preparation for teaching. But the postwar teacher shortage made him pessimistic; in 1919 he renewed his appeal that undergraduate teacher education be continued despite the impending demise of the Division. This time Lowell granted practice teaching and a few other basic education courses a three-year reprieve within the faculty of arts and sciences. Yet when the new School opened its doors in 1920, even Holmes was astonished by the small numbers of prospective teachers who attended. The practice teaching course enrolled only four graduate students. Holmes attempted to extend the undergraduate reprieve, but this time Lowell refused to reopen the question. In 1923 thirty years of undergraduate teacher education at Harvard ended.[18]

The one remaining hope for initial teacher preparation was the Prince School, whose students garnered over one third of the sixty-four master's degrees awarded by the Graduate School of Education in its first year. The singular advantage of the Prince School was that its subject matter, "store practice and organization," was not taught in liberal arts colleges. Liberal arts graduates who wanted to teach retail selling had few institutional alternatives to attendance at the postgraduate Prince School. A steady and sizable student market seemed guaranteed by the amalgamation of the two institutions.

But full amalgamation was repeatedly delayed. Lowell wondered if instruction in how department stores were organized and how salespeople should behave was really of graduate grade. "We do not profess," he pointed out, "to give every grade of instruction, but only that which is appropriate in a university." The question had really not occurred to Holmes, since most of the Prince School students were graduates of the better women's colleges. Although he retorted that the Prince instruction was conducted in a "thoroughly competent and broad-gauged fashion which makes it worthy of a graduate student," Lowell deferred approval of complete absorption and continued for another year the informal collaboration of 1920-21.[19]

Even informal collaboration became more troublesome by the fall of 1921. Belatedly the Corporation discovered that the Prince School arrangement violated fundamental University rules. Prince students who received Harvard Ed.M. degrees rarely took more than two Harvard courses, since neither the Prince curriculum nor the Prince faculty had any official Harvard status. This casual relationship offended no one at the School of Education, where *de facto* consolidation was taken for granted, but it conflicted with the Harvard requirement that all degree candidates take a full year of Harvard instruction given by Harvard faculty. To remain eligible for the Ed.M., Prince School students would have to take a full year of Harvard instruction in addition to the one-year Prince course. Alternatively, the Prince courses would have to be made Harvard courses and the Prince faculty given Harvard teaching appointments.

Both Mrs. Prince and the faculty of the Graduate School of Education favored the latter course of action, which defined the full absorption they had had in mind from the beginning. But Holmes now realized that he could hardly break the University's taboo against women faculty members when the particular issue was offering instruction that Lowell doubted should be given by anyone at Harvard. He continued to believe that Prince instruction was perfectly suitable for the Ed.M., but now began to backtrack to find some formula acceptable to both Lowell and Mrs. Prince. His solution was to maintain the Prince School as a separate unit within the Graduate School of Education, drop the suggestion that Prince faculty receive Harvard appointments, and involve Harvard faculty in a few Prince courses just enough to relabel them as Harvard instruction.[20]

In his attempt to placate Lowell and save the Prince School connection, Holmes alienated Mrs. Prince and the dry goods merchants who impatiently watched the erosion of what they had understood were firm Harvard commitments to absorb the school. The merchants angrily rejected Holmes's new proposal, and Mrs. Prince characterized him as procrastinating, indecisive, and inexperienced. In fact, Holmes became increasingly perplexed by the entire situation. The intellectual grounds for much of his defence of absorption were removed by Frederick Nichols himself. After his professorship was assured, Nichols sided with Lowell on the crucial issue of the difficulty of Prince School courses. Demonstrating the charming candor that characterized his Harvard career, Nichols noted that "because most of the students in Mrs. Prince's School are college graduates it does not follow that the work they are doing is of a graduate character." Nichols did not think that it was and scoffed at the notion that graduate degrees were essential to prepare teachers of retail business.

Undercut by America's leading expert in commercial education, and unable to formulate any other satisfactory compromise, Holmes astonished everyone by announcing that the best solution was for the Prince School to withdraw totally from Harvard. Now Holmes's own colleagues vented their rage at his leadership. They demanded that he reconsider his rejection of what had been a unanimously favored Harvard plan for over five years. Holmes subsequently reversed himself again and agreed to support any compromise that a faculty majority could endorse. But the negotiations had already collapsed. Lowell made it known that he would use his good offices only to restore the Prince connection with Simmons, and that Harvard withdrawal seemed prudent under the circumstances.[21]

Humiliated by the blunt personal criticism he had received, Holmes nevertheless saw his indecisiveness not as weakness but as evidence of his growing understanding of the unique limitations and opportunities of a graduate school of education at Harvard. The Prince fiasco was a watershed experience. Combined with other events it revealed to Holmes the destiny of his institution. Nichols had persuaded him that it was fruitless to argue, at least to Lowell, that the Prince curriculum possessed sufficient intellectual complexity to be labeled graduate study. If the School of Education was unable to offer graduate credit for such subjects to young college graduates because they were of a "lower type," and if the School could not recruit young college graduates for teacher preparation in conventional academic fields, then it was unlikely that many young and inexperienced college graduates would attend the Graduate School of Education at all.

Nearly half the Ed.M. recipients in 1922 were Prince School students. With this group eliminated, Holmes concluded that his School "must become an institution for the training of teachers and school officers already experienced, who are seeking advancement to higher posts or a broader understanding of their work and greater efficiency in it." Enrollment projections prior to the School's opening had optimistically hoped for as many as 37 percent young and inexperienced students. By 1922 everyone understood that these numbers were impossible to achieve. In 1921 the median age of students was thirty-three. A year later less than 6 percent of the enrollment — excluding Prince students — lacked teaching experience.[22]

THE EMERGENCE of a predominantly older and experienced student body provoked no faculty discontent. Indeed the virtual elimination of younger students, who in most previous years had constituted a majority of the Division's clientele, was regarded as a blessing that freed the faculty for its more important work of instructing mature educators on the way up. John Brewer's only fear was f teacher preparation one day became popular among young college graduates, the burden of providing it would seriously reduce the School's effectiveness. And though Holmes never assumed that experienced students were superior, he quickly concluded that their dominance was inevitable. From the viewpoint of numbers alone, the absent youngsters were never missed. Within three years of its opening, 340 students were registered at the School during the academic year for some fraction of time, and the institution's accumulated cash surplus was $75,000.[23]

Holmes began to argue that experienced students had special needs which the curriculum must meet if their numbers were to increase further. The two most essential needs were part-time study and practical instruction. Holmes also asserted that meeting these career needs of experienced teachers was the same thing as meeting the needs of the schools themselves. This remarkable linkage perfectly expressed the faculty's conviction that the important jobs in education were those which managed the socialization of education. They were jobs entered at midcareer, after a stint of schoolteaching was completed, and after specialized training was secured at institutions like Harvard. It was far more important to attract older educators committed to professional advancement than young novices whose leadership years were decades away Ideally, Harvard wanted students whose professional mettle had already been tested. "We mean to train the leaders," Holmes assured the president, "as soon as we can get them to come to us."[24]

Experienced students almost inevitably were part-time students. The financial rewards of school careers simply did not permit full-time study. Strategies adopted earlier to boost graduate enrollments now appeared to be fixed conditions for the graduate study of education. After the Prince School debacle, all courses were rescheduled to meet in the late afternoon or on Saturday. As a result part-time registrants increased by 116, while full-time increased by six. The fraction of full-time students steadily decreased in the early 1920s. The expanded summer courses in education grew to over 900 enrollments in two years. Nearly 300 summer students considered themselves candidates for the Ed.M. In addition, Holmes won Lowell's approval to establish an extension program independent of the University Commission on Extension. Designed for a part-time constituency somewhat distant from Cambridge, the extension program was conducted in cooperation with the Boston University School of Education. Nearly 600 students enrolled in 1922-23, in courses conducted as far west as Chicopee. In a year extension enrollments doubled.[25]

Within the School only the venerable Charles W. Eliot, then at eighty-seven a member of the visiting committee, openly condemned these efforts to maximize the School's part-time constituency. He could not understand why so much attention was given to the preferences of local schoolmen. The direction of constructive change in the schools had always been from the universities to the schools. Holmes's efforts seemed to reverse that direction.[26]

The needs of experienced teachers affected the content as well as the timing of instruction. Training had to fit teachers for well-defined positions. Unlike lawyers and businessmen, teachers could not count on the "development of general or unspecified ability" to secure their advancement. Holmes distinguished sharply between the fundamental and technical fields of study within the education curriculum. He personally believed that the "best fruit of any professional training is a professional consciousness" formed by studies like history, sociology, or philosophy. But he knew that the best way to attract experienced teachers was to expand the technical or practical side of the curriculum. Technical specialists like Hanus and Inglis, he pointed out, represented far greater drawing power than either Dearborn or himself. His proposals for faculty expansion gave greatest priority to additional senior appointments in administration and secondary education. With the exception of social theory or sociology, where he proposed a full professorship to combat the "individualistic" view of education, Holmes saw no reason to expand any of the fundamental fields. They simply would not draw students. Until the mid-1930s the only instruction in history or philosophy of education was offered by part-time visitors.[27]

The preoccupation with student needs was the *coup de grace* for educational science at Harvard. Retreating from an older position, Holmes announced that school jobs provided little opportunity for scientific investigation. Practitioners and scholars formed two distinct groups. The School's primary mission was to help the former. Charles Judd had urged Holmes to fight to keep the Ph.D. degree on grounds that education was a "science on a par with every other science" found within faculties of arts and sciences. Judd wanted the Graduate School of Education to emphasize "advanced professional types of research" rather than "lower types of professional administration." Judd grew puzzled and disappointed about the trend of events in Cambridge. And when Holmes asked a visiting professor to assess the School's curriculum in 1923, he found the weakest areas to be history, philosophy, and psychology.[28]

Lowell was also displeased with the explicit repudiation of scholarship and research for practical training. When Holmes requested what he expected to be routine presidential approval for his professorial recommendations for the new School—he had already informally offered professorships to three men outside Harvard—Lowell shocked him by turning back every name and challenging the basis of his appointment policy. "Is it not of very great importance," the president asked, "that this School should start with a feeling on the part of the Faculty of Arts and Sciences that it is really of university grade, and that its instructing staff are not merely skilled in the technique of education but are on a scholarly level with that of the Faculty of Arts and Sciences?" Would it not be wise to "sacrifice something in the way of technical knowledge for the sake of academic caliber?"

Offended by Lowell's unexpected intervention, Holmes at first protested that he had recommended a major appointment in the fundamental field of social theory. But Lowell had no interest at all in the socialization of education and began speculating on the possibilities of persuading an eminent English philosopher to teach educational theory in America's Cambridge. Now frightened more than ever, Holmes asserted that any foreign eminence would only confer a "remote and lofty character" on the School and even deter the "school men of the country" from attendance. Harvard could "assume no attitude of detachment toward the work in which we have heretofore made common cause with the very men whose respect we most want to keep." If Lowell demanded a distinguished scholar, Holmes assured him that John Dewey was acceptable to schoolmen. But when the president indicated his distaste for Dewey, the matter was dropped.[29]

The appointment impasse grew more serious as weeks passed. The faculty had expected Frank Spaulding to become professor of school administration, but without a firm Harvard offer Spaulding accepted instead the chairmanship of Yale's new department of education. Nor would Lowell relent and approve Stephen S. Colvin of Brown University as professor of secondary education or President William T. Foster of Reed College as professor of education and social policy. What could Holmes do? He never found it easy to show anger or to be blunt, and his frustration with Lowell was accompanied by sheer fright. The School's existence had not yet been officially approved. Nor had his expected appointment as dean. Nothing was really secure. He judiciously obtained unsolicited letters to Lowell supporting his position and persuaded Lowell to call an unusual conference of the Corporation, visiting committee, and the Division's full professors to discuss the disagreement over appointment policy. Yet Lowell held all the cards and conceded only that he would impose no appointments on the School against its wishes. None of Holmes's major appointment recommendations was resurrected.[30]

Then Lowell took the offensive and proposed that the only new full professor should be a specialist in statistics. The absence of research interests among Holmes's recommendations was even more serious than their lack of academic caliber. The School of Education, Lowell confided, should be "a place to add to our exceedingly slight knowledge of education." Holmes now feared that Lowell's only concern was to make the School "a research institution pure and simple." He had the wit to counter Lowell's suggestion of a distinguished Englishman with the opinion that a young American might cost less money, not require tenure, and be more promising in the long run. A frenzied search produced Thorndike's nomination of his young colleague and former student, Truman Lee Kelley. But Lowell preferred to defer a decision until he had investigated English possibilities in person that summer. When he returned with no English statistician in tow, Holmes could hardly conceal his relief. It was now too late to make any appointment for the next year, though Lowell continued to argue that the most important thing the School could do was study the "actual results of different forms of teaching."[31]

Holmes now understood that some investment in research was essential to placate the president. Throughout the twenties, he reminded him of the School's constant concern to find an acceptable statistician. Beyond this he decided that the best way to conduct research in a professional school was to concentrate all institutional resources on a single highly visible project. The most likely candidate was Dearborn's projected study of children's physical and mental development. Holmes helped Dearborn procure $10,000 from the Commonwealth Fund in 1922 to commence the twelve-year Harvard Growth Study. A major longitudinal effort, the Growth Study sought to discover true patterns, and therefore correct standards, of human development by repeated measures on the same individuals over time. Throughout the 1920s research at the Graduate School of Education was virtually indistinguishable from conduct of the Growth Study. True to his promise of concentrated effort, Holmes devoted all his fundraising energies to the study, which consumed in addition nearly $100,000 from the surplus of the School. Lowell never doubted that the Growth Study was the School's most important activity.[32]

Despite the School's inability in 1920 to add professorships in the technical fields, Lowell's intervention did little damage to the professional mission. The president imposed neither foreigners nor statisticians. His veto of Holmes's faculty proposals was a fairly well-kept secret that did not diminish the favorable publicity generated by the new institution, its new degrees, and its historic accessibility to women. Moreover, Lowell approved without dispute Inglis' promotion to a professorship, the promotions of Brewer and Johnson to tenured associate professorships, and the appointment of Nichols to the same rank two years later. The programmatic initiatives of the 1914-1916 period became permanent institutional fixtures.

By such decisions Lowell indicated his willingness to tolerate opinions consistently and profoundly at variance with his own. He believed in intellectual rigor and hard work as educational goals. He defined democracy as liberty rather than equality. He defended individualism and suspected social efficiency (though he endorsed vocational education). Above all Lowell celebrated self-education and loathed the prolongation of childhood by required schooling and adult supervision. If Hanus had amplified Eliot's ideas, Holmes and his colleagues contradicted Lowell's. But Lowell did not seem to care. The public schools simply did not interest him. By 1919, the Massachusetts Commissioner of Education lamented the "impassable barrier" between proponents of secondary education for "fortunate" youth and defenders of secondary education for "all classes of society." Everyone knew where Lowell stood. In a rare appearance later before the NEA's Department of Superintendence, Lowell lambasted public schoolmen for making education easy, ignoring the talented few, and spending too much money.[33]

Lowell's tolerance of differences, or indifference to the issues, made possible an unusually cohesive and congenial senior faculty of education. Harry "The Deke" Holmes, Jim Johnson, Al Inglis, Jack Brewer, and Nick Nichols all shared similar social attitudes and a common bond with experienced students poised to assume larger responsibilities. After 1922, research was contained in Fenno Dearborn's Growth Study, which freed everyone else for professional instruction and advocacy. Only Hanus was embittered. Stung by Lowell's graceless refusal to acknowledge in any way the decisive role he had played in the School's creation, he sullenly retired in the spring of 1921. But his situation was atypical. Elsewhere the mood was one of pride and confidence. The new institution showed astonishing growth rates in its regular, summer, and extension programs, and accumulated a substantial profit. John Moors thought Holmes too smug, but outside opinion soon confirmed the School's self-satisfaction. In 1925 a respected survey already ranked it behind only Teachers College and the University of Chicago in the national pecking order.[34]

Charles W. Eliot

Paul H. Hanus

NATHANIEL S. SHALER   EDWIN H. HALL

BARRETT WENDELL

HUGO MÜNSTERBERG

HENRY W. HOLMES

A. LAWRENCE LOWELL

JAMES J. STORROW

JOSEPH LEE

LINCOLN FILENE

FELIX WARBURG

WALTER F. DEARBORN

ALEXANDER INGLIS

JOHN M. BREWER

FREDERICK G. NICHOLS

THE SCHOOL, ON THE STEPS OF LAWRENCE HALL, 1920

JAMES B. CONANT

FRANCIS T. SPAULDING

FRANCIS KEPPEL

PHILLIP J. RULON

7

*The Formation
of Educators*

AFTER 1924 the Graduate School of Education dramaticaly repudiated the training policies that had sustained its growth. It resolved
to replace part-time mid-career students with young, inexperienced
full-timers. It proposed a core curriculum of fundamental principles rather than an elective curriculum of technical procedures.
And it celebrated a training sequence in which all professional study
occurred during a single two-year period immediately following
completion of a liberal arts college course.

The policy thrust after 1914 had been to bring about the socialization of education by means of new school services and new school
careers. The policy thrust after 1924 was to strengthen training procedures within the Graduate School of Education in order to convert
aspiring novices into effective educators. The focus of reform shifted
from external entrepreneurialism to internal pedagogy. Instead of
transforming the organization of schooling, the Graduate School of
Education would transform the adults who worked in schools. Never
before had the faculty displayed such supreme confidence in the
capacity of deliberate training to alter professional behavior.

How could such an astounding policy reversal have occurred so
suddenly? All along the School had underestimated the pressure on
it to conform to traditions of other Harvard professional schools.
More important, Henry Holmes's judgment of the national professional movement in education changed profoundly in the middle
twenties: he glumly concluded that its promise had not been fulfilled. Despite two decades of expansion and socialization, the secondary schools seemed in decline. Intellectual objectives had been
sacrificed, he thought, and the moral justification for the socialization of education ignored. Schools of education, including Har-

vard's, had to accept much of the blame. Their graduates possessed only narrow techniques, not broad insight or moral commitment. They had also relegated classroom teaching to a routinized role that helped to guarantee education's ineffectuality.

By the end of the twenties Holmes was brashly confident that Harvard had finally found the way to educate educators. But he began to wonder if anyone besides himself really cared. The profession itself was caustic toward his efforts. His colleagues became weary and disunited. And President Lowell, in whose name so much of the new scheme had been advanced, seemed unable to appreciate the brilliance of the idea or the policies necessary to bring it to fruition. By 1931 Holmes found his School not the object of professional veneration but engaged in a desperate race against time.

AS ENROLLMENTS continued to increase, Holmes confidently turned his attention in 1924 to securing better facilities than the decaying building shared with the Business School. He wanted education included in a forthcoming University drive to enable various departments to construct new quarters. But Lowell curtly repudiated his overtures. The Graduate School of Education would not be permitted to seek new funds until it had "proved conclusively the value of its work." The president's criticism suddenly shifted from the issue of research to the issue of training. Did not the School's constituency of part-time older students preoccupied with practical courses contradict Harvard's understanding of how proper professional preparation should proceed? Had not experience confirmed that superior preparation stressed "fundamental principles" rather than "tools of the trade"? Did it not also demand young students willing to learn those principles in protracted study at the very beginning of their careers?[1]

Lowell believed that professional schools could only be defended if the knowledge required in an occupation could be made into a "scholarly subject by itself." Only then could formal schooling be justified over apprenticeship or informal experience. If professional schools merely taught academic subjects borrowed from other fields, or practical techniques that intelligent men could readily acquire on the job, they had no place in a major university. Lowell's model of excellence was the Harvard Law School, which he had attended in the 1870s. There Dean Langdell had abandoned the academic traditionalism of jurisprudence to define law as a science whose principles could be understood by tracing their development through cases. When the Business School was established later on, Lowell urged it also to treat business as a separate scholarly subject rather than as a collection of existing academic fields such as political economy. After initial efforts to define a business curriculum by distinct jobs or by types of business proved unsuccessful, the Business School emphasized functions common to most firms such as production, finance, marketing, accounting, and statistics. Lowell was immensely pleased by this separate yet scholarly formulation of a business curriculum.

Above all Lowell admired the law and business schools for the intellectual demands they made on students. Understanding legal principles required training in the arts of close scrutiny and discriminating classification. Through its attention to decision making and problem solving the Business School also developed reasoning skills of rapid analysis and synthesis. Lowell praised its use of carefully prepared problems, astutely relabeled as "cases" to suggest the intellectual rigor of the Law School. Yet when he examined the Graduate School of Education he saw no comparable effort to develop an intellectually demanding subject. Its curriculum contained either academic subjects borrowed from older disciplines, such as psychology and history, or practical techniques that hardly demanded extensive mental effort, such as play and guidance. Besides, how could the School ever make education into a rigorous scholarly subject when its part-time students were preoccupied with ongoing jobs and with acquiring immediate skills to advance their careers? Virtually all law and business students studied on a full-time basis and most had graduated from college only months before commencing professional study.[2]

Holmes and his colleagues found Lowell's constant analogies to other Harvard professional schools absurdly overdrawn. Perhaps a lengthy preservice training was appropriate in free, competitive fields where economic rewards were high. But in a public service characterized by "cooperative effort in a system," where the community supplied the clients and paid the bills, no such financial incentives prevailed. In addition, the nature of educational careers precluded overattention to general or fundamental training. Law-

yers and businessmen might survive unspecialized preservice education because their initial career responsibilities involved "minor
tasks." By contrast the initial educational job, classroom teaching,
was not only highly significant but carried from the first day all the
responsibilities demanded over a career. If a graduate failed as a
teacher in his first year or two of service, Holmes warned, "no general knowledge of Education will enable him to advance to higher
posts in the profession or save the School from disrepute."[3]

From his retirement Hanus reiterated that "leadership in education cannot come from any kind of training given to people right out
of college." The School should not deviate from its chief mission of
providing "service to teachers already advanced toward positions of
responsibility." Many alumni agreed that the ideal professional student was "the promising educator of between 35 and 45 years of age,
who has already a fine body of achievement to his credit," and were
wary about any policies that might discourage their attendance. Already they noted a disquieting tendency to replace older "big men"
on the faculty with less well-known younger men. Moore had never
been replaced at all, and Hanus had been succeeded only by his
unknown young protégé, L. O. Cummings. The crowning blow
came in 1924, when Inglis died suddenly and was replaced not by a
prominent national figure but by his assistant, Bancroft Beatley,
and another young instructor, Francis Trow Spaulding. Why would
ambitious schoolmen enroll at Harvard if their teachers were
younger and less experienced than they were? Would not the School
be left with an unsatisfactory collection of callow youngsters or
jaded "hospital cases"? Young students, to these alumni, were liabilities.[4]

Yet Holmes was perfectly willing to make a renewed effort to attract greater numbers of younger students if that would please the
president and win his support for a new building. In 1924 he initiated planning for a curriculum option designed for younger, full-
time students. But a year later Holmes stunned the Harvard community by proposing a more far-reaching reorganization. Instead of
merely adding a program for full-time inexperienced students, he
suggested that the entire School be transformed to conform to the
training pattern of other Harvard professional schools. The large
numbers of part-time teachers the School had attracted in the past
may have meant more professional service, he reflected, but not

necessarily the most important or desirable form of service. Instead of courting success through meeting immediate demands as they appeared, he advised the School to seek success through "whole-time students, especially men." The length of the master of education degree should be doubled from one to two years. In two years the School could offer graduates of liberal arts colleges an integrated program of professional training that provided complete career preparation without any further period of extended study. The program would contain a common curriculum covering one year of fundamental subjects plus advanced specialization.[5]

Perhaps because Lowell's endorsement made reorganization seem inevitable, and because Holmes's proposals did not suggest that older students be specifically excluded, the faculty approved the policy shift with little debate or recorded disagreement. Only Brewer raised doubts about whether the field of education, which had attracted so few full-time young students to a one-year Ed.M., could suddenly lure such students to take a two-year degree. In the visiting committee Felix Warburg feared that the scheme would "limit the Harvard service to the teachers of the community and the country," and Lincoln Filene agreed. But Lowell rejoined that the best service Harvard could render was "training a limited group in the best possible manner." The discussion was closed. By mid-1926 the faculty and the governing boards approved the new policies. Full-scale implementation was planned to begin in the fall of 1927.[6]

Decades later old men still debated how such an astonishing turnabout could have happened. Brewer always thought that Lowell himself had engineered a successful plot to destroy the School's growth and financial prosperity. However plausible in theory, Brewer's assessment is not supported by surviving evidence. Lowell at first was dubious whether so radical a step was wise, and Holmes had to persuade him that the risk was worth taking. In fact Holmes himself instigated the reorganization and staked his entire reputation on its eventual success.

One motive was purely administrative. In 1924 the faculty assumed that a special curriculum for full-time beginners could easily be grafted onto the School's existing organization without seriously disrupting it. But planning for such a program within the one-year confines of the Ed.M. proved exceptionally difficult. Everyone agreed that general training should supplement rather than supplant preparation for particular careers. Any new curriculum just for beginners thus carried a triple burden. It had to define education's "fundamental principles" beyond already required courses in social policy and psychology. It had to ensure proficiency in the first educational role normally undertaken, classroom teaching. And it had to provide training for whatever eventual educational roles students coveted, such as administration or other specializations. No one knew how all this could be done within a year.[7]

At the same time, Holmes noticed other institutional trends that disturbed him and, he knew, would soon disturb the president. The question of women was particularly troublesome. Though the School was an authentic pioneer in securing Harvard opportunities for women, the fear of a feminized enclave was ever present. Holmes had little doubt that the School's reputation and success within Harvard was directly proportional to its dominance by males. He never considered any woman for a regular faculty position throughout his twenty-year deanship. Women students were welcomed so long as they did not exceed an intuitive critical mass. During the School's first three years, their fraction held at a comfortable 38 percent, but in 1923-24 it rose dramatically to 48 percent. The Ed.M. was plainly in reach of many women and they threatened to become a majority.

Another ominous trend was the shifting character of the doctor of education degree. Before 1920, when the Division of Education offered the Ph.D. degree, the doctorate signified constructive research power and was intended for students pursuing mainly university careers. The new Ed.D. was designed to serve similar ends, despite rhetorical claims that its purposes were professional rather than scholarly. This distinction was chosen to create the appearance of a functional difference between Ph.D. and Ed.D. when in fact no such difference existed; it soon proved confusing to students and faculty alike. The School rarely explained that it did not regard a professional doctorate as antithetical to research any more than it regarded a scholarly doctorate as synonymous with research. Indeed, it endorsed a professional doctorate at the same time it contended that the highest *practitioner*'s degree was the Ed.M.

Despite official claims that the Ed.D. was research-oriented, doctoral enrollments grew rapidly. During the twenties only Teachers College and New York University awarded more education doctorates than Harvard. But most doctoral students were interested in senior administrative positions in school systems rather than in university careers. They did not want research training, and the School bent its policies to meet their needs. By 1922 doctoral candidates were informally assured that official requirements in French, German, biology, psychology, and the social sciences were not nearly as exacting as they seemed and might even be waived in favor of work experience. The faculty also discarded the preliminary examination that had determined admission to doctoral candidacy. Research training was downgraded just as research as a faculty activity had been.

This unofficial trend only magnified education's deviation from the Harvard norm. With just a single exception, none of the University's other professional schools offered a doctorate for covert practitioner training. The growing gap in actual research commitment between Ph.D. and Ed.D. degrees was also plain. Yet if unofficial practice isolated the School from Harvard custom, official policy tended to isolate the School more and more from other schools of education. Already some schools of education had devised Ph.D. tracks for prospective practitioners. Still worse, others were contemplating using the Ed.D. as an explicit practitioner's degree while retaining (as Holmes could not) the Ph.D. as a research degree. By 1924 Holmes was convinced that dramatic action was essential to reverse the internal and external trend toward a practitioner doctorate and to solidify forever the Ed.M. as the highest practitioner degree in professional education.[8]

A two-year Ed.M. seemed a partial solution to all these problems. There would be time enough for both Lowell's fundamental principles and the specific training desired by the faculty of education. The longer program might discourage creeping feminization. Finally, it might upgrade and thereby preserve the Ed.M. as the highest practitioner's degree, especially if research standards for the Ed.D. were simultaneously tightened. Holmes candidly acknowledged the "directing pressure" of Harvard tradition in stimulating the reorganization.

YET HOLMES's new enthusiasm for what he called the "Business School ideal" expressed more than a tactical response to University pressure. As he elaborated the advantages of the new scheme, he developed a coherent argument that went far beyond fearful kow-towing. To some extent he rationalized political necessity as moral imperative. But his explanations were not mainly for public relations effect. They built upon ideas he had held long before the two-year plan seemed propitious, and he continued to extol them years after all possible personal or institutional benefits had been squeezed out.[9]

Until the middle 1920s Holmes took great pride in the enormous expansion and transformation of American secondary education which had paced his adult life. The ideals of prolonging schooling for an ever-increasing proportion of youth and socializing youth to develop capacity to play adult roles had shaped the Division's expansion. The Division and School had helped to convert those ideals into school functions manned by cadres of trained adults. Expanding professional opportunities seemed equivalent to improving secondary education. This connection had justified the School's preoccupation with the size of its enrollment even when endowment income no longer required a large student body for institutional survival.

But by the end of 1924, Holmes publicly entertained growing doubts about the progress of American secondary education and the contribution that schools of education had made to it. As schooling became more universal, it abandoned important intellectual and cultural values. As schooling became more socialized, it neglected genuine social ideals. Instead of engines of reform, schools of education had become obstacles to it. The shattering realization that the organized profession—including his own institution—was less the solution and more the problem led him to extol radical reorganization as a national professional obligation rather than as a Harvard political tactic.

Holmes had never assaulted the life of the mind as a plaything of social privilege, as had Brewer, nor did he regard academic education as simply irrelevant to his professional interests, as had Nichols. On the contrary, he loved literature and the arts, quoted Latin whenever an appropriate occasion arose, and cautioned against extreme versions of social efficiency. He had little respect for David Snedden, the movement's apostle, and once urged William Heard Kilpatrick to accept mathematics' intrinsic value in enhancing self-understanding as one of its legitimate functions. Holmes's sense of a serious decline in intellectual standards in the high schools was caused, more than anything else, by the startling exposés of William S. Learned of the Carnegie Foundation during the twenties. Learned, who tried to document the academic inferiority of American high schools as compared with European institutions, exerted more influence on Holmes than anyone save Lowell. In late 1924, having just read Learned's most recent work, Holmes concluded that the "educational ideal is not the ideal of an easy equality or a low level of achievement" and that "safeguarding of standards" had become a serious dilemma in universal education.[10]

As Holmes reworked the materials of his course on social policy and education, his commitment to social efficiency became increasingly strained. Continuing to see the ends of socialization in moral terms — truly free individuals chose to cooperate with one another for the common good — he began to perceive that much that passed for social efficiency conflicted with this conception of social freedom. He spent less time differentiating among social roles like vocation and citizenship and more time lamenting the "privilege, prejudice, fear and greed" rampant in the 'present unsatisfactory direction of human life." Education focused too exclusively, he said, on adjusting individuals to existing society. It needed to explore how society must change to help education produce free individuals committed to purposeful, socially cooperative lives. Hardly a political radical, Holmes believed he had cleverly finessed the charge of using education to impose his personal world view. He contended that he sought merely a society that would enable education to be morally effective. Still, he thought educators had to advocate measures that looked toward "greater security of life and property, toward a larger production and a juster distribution of wealth, toward fuller sharing in the common life and the common purpose by all sorts and conditions of men, and toward the increase of beauty everywhere."[11]

Holmes had never expected that mass secondary education would produce in twenty years an American society of socially cooperative free people. But he was shaken by the idea that aspects of his own profession were, even if unintentionally, subverting that goal. Before the American Association for the Advancement of Science, he made his strongest attack on the consequences of education's heady embrace of science. The preoccupation with "materials and techniques" in measurement and administration, backed up by stimulus-response psychology, implied a "mechanistic or deterministic view of mental action" sharply contrary to the objective of freedom education should try to cultivate.

Science and technique not only embodied wrong conceptions of educational ends. Their very prominence caused teachers to avoid careful study of aims, values, and social conditions. Further, they legitimized a scrappy, disconnected course-by-course pattern of professional instruction appropriate to the learning of specialized procedures but disabling for the consideration of complex value questions. The time had come, Holmes argued, to "insist anew on the value of the philosophy of education — using the term philosophy to imply the study of aims, more particularly the study of the ideal of human life toward which we wish education to move the world."[12]

The dominance of methods, procedures, and techniques had one further disastrous consequence. It subtly legitimized the relegation of the teacher to a lesser, ancillary role that mechanically applied to masses of students procedures developed by a few experts. No wonder most teachers were "uneducated, poorly prepared for their work, understanding its significance but superficially, lacking in distinction and personal power." The profession *itself* had confined them to this role. Craftsmanship meant little more than work on "small, mechanical tasks, under close supervision." The teacher was a routine worker charged with executing orders handed down from above. If the teacher's own role contradicted the values of freedom and cooperation that Holmes sought for the larger society, how could those values be transmitted to pupils? Plainly the role of the teacher had to change if the social objectives he coveted were to have any chance of realization.[13]

Through such reasoning the Business School ideal became more attractive. Wise and effective professionals needed not just tools and techniques, but a "comprehensive grasp of the entire educational enterprise." The goal was to train "educators rather than mere craftsmen in schoolkeeping," that is, professionals who could interpret any issue, policy, or decision in terms of its impact on ultimate educational ends. Harvard's training efforts to date had not even attempted to scale these pedagogical heights. Degree-getting had depended only on collecting credits in disconnected courses spread out over indeterminate periods of time. But now, instead of putting mere "patches" on students, Harvard would *form* them through full-time, prolonged, and integrated study: "knowledge, understanding, skill and outlook are to be fused into an active whole." The goal was no less than to make a "profound and visible difference" in the professional behavior of every student who attended, to create literally a new man (or perhaps woman) in education. Holmes ironically thought that single-purpose normal schools, despite their modest academic pretensions, had nonetheless *formed* students more effectively than the huge university schools and departments of education that were replacing them.[14]

A longer training period would not only provide time to form professional skill but also would restore the classroom teacher to his central educational position. If all educators were trained together in one intense experience at the very outset of their careers, then the cooperative and common aspects of educational work would take precedence over the specialized and hierarchical aspects. Holmes believed that the pattern of part-time, mid-career, and highly specialized training had actually reinforced a professional job hierarchy in which the classroom teacher was only a routine worker under the expert direction of principals, supervisors, and superintendents. When all educators received their training at the same time, and when much of it consisted of common study of fundamentals, the teacher might become a true "expert, acting with an increasing measure of independent judgment concerning individual cases and the work of groups for which he is responsible. '

Holmes's opposition to hierarchy won strong endorsement from Hanus' young replacement in school administration, L. O. Cummings, whose principal instructional theme was to oppose the excessive power wielded by superintendents. Cummings argued against applying to education principles of power derived from war and business. A chain of command was justifiable only in situations characterized by the presence of "opposing force, competition, the question of life and death, and immediacy of action." By introducing "human relations" to the administration curriculum, Cummings hoped to make superintendents self-conscious leaders who would expand the role of teachers in policy making. He repudiated the notion that educational expertise increased in direct proportion to distance from classrooms. Holmes took similar comfort from John Dewey's conviction that teachers themselves were the only "channels through which the consequences of educational theory come into the lives of those at school." If teachers were regarded merely as channels of "reception and transmission," education would never occur. The key to educational success lay not in external techniques or procedures, Dewey thought, but in the teacher's "attitudes and habits of observation, judgment, and planning."[15]

Holmes's analysis was profoundly critical of the professional movement in which Harvard had proudly participated for nearly four decades. An era was over, he said, an era when schools of education were "conquering their territory and admitting hordes of immigrants." Now Harvard was seceding from that movement to inaugurate a new era of standards and effectiveness. It was not surprising that Holmes's colleagues across the country greeted his proposals with almost universal condemnation and ridicule. Chicago's Charles Judd, who exemplified to Holmes scientific determinism and elitism, roundly attacked Harvard's continuing obsession with practitioner training and new obsession with schoolteachers. Harvard's "only defensible position," Judd asserted, was to advance the science of education through research. A great university school of education should reduce its role in teacher education rather than expand it. Judd personally had "no interest in this group at all."[16]

Judd's interest in research was atypical. Other educators stressed the absurdity of applying Harvard's law and business model of professional training to the field of education. Why, they asked, should the highest practitioner's degree be the master's? James E. Russell of Teachers College and Stanford's Ellwood P. Cubberley both agreed that a clear distinction should be made between programs aimed at professional fitness and research. But they contended that both functions could be performed at the doctoral level, either by use of the Ed.D. and Ph.D. degrees or by establishing different tracks within the Ph.D. Why should undergraduate study in education be discouraged? Education was firmly established as an undergraduate field everywhere in the country except at a tiny number of Eastern colleges. Why require two graduate years when most education candidates, because of undergraduate study, possessed the equivalent of two years of education at the end of a single graduate year? Why was work experience prior to university study so detrimental? Stuart Courtis contended that work experience was a positive good, since it enriched study by adding to it maturity, motivation, and perspective. Russell believed that at least three years of teaching experience should precede training for administrative or specialized positions.

Why was a single period of complete preparation wise? In fields like law, medicine, and engineering, Russell argued, young professionals learned new skills through on-the-job supervision by superiors with a stake in the quality of work done by their juniors. Nothing remotely comparable existed in schoolkeeping. If teachers wanted to learn new skills or move up the career ladder, their only guide was "another professional course." Schools of education could never be unified around a common theme. They were "in reality a collection of professional schools, intended for different types of students and for quite different ends." Training had to come in mid-career when educators needed it, not all at once before particular career objectives were known. And what evidence was there that any students would attend such a bizarre program? Why should anyone spend two years in Cambridge when a master's could be obtained in one year everywhere else? Russell counseled that "the length of a professional course of any kind is determined not so much by ideals which may seem reasonable, but by the economic return that can be expected by those who pursue such study." He added that Harvard might not only lose students, but attract mediocre ones who would try to make up by elongated training what they lacked in native ability.[17]

These caustic reservations did not deter Holmes and seemed only to confirm how far ahead of conventional thinking his proposals really were. No one else seemed willing to grasp the conditions necessary for a genuine process of professional formation or to recognize the importance of upgrading the education and role of teachers. "What we mean by 'success,' " he concluded, "is not what they mean at T.C." Even the dire prediction that a two-year terminal master's would not draw generated little anxiety. In the short run, Holmes conceded, enrollments would probably fall. But endowment income, which covered 75 percent of basic expenses in 1925, could offset temporary reductions in tuition. The accumulated surplus of more than $100,000 was a further safety valve. Holmes predicted that the School could absorb deficits for at least five years. By then the new plan would have commended itself to the profession and to employing authorities. Still, it was prudent over that period to declare a moratorium on adding new faculty positions and fields.

A moratorium was consistent with the reorganization's principles as well. Harvard's task was no longer wild expansion in new areas of service, but internal curriculum development to bring the ideals of professional formation to fruition.[18]

WHEN THE REORGANIZATION was implemented, the Graduate School of Education revised its admissions policies to conform to those of the business and law schools. Before 1927 it automatically accepted anyone with a bachelor's degree and prescribed extra courses ("conditioning") for those from weak institutions. After 1927 it automatically accepted only graduates from a list of quality institutions and assessed the undergraduate records of everyone else on a case-by-case basis before taking action. Within three years its rate of acceptance had fallen from 98 percent to 86 percent.

Yet no one expected that selectivity in admissions would be an important factor in the success of the new plan. The modern idea of selective admissions was only dimly perceived in the University. The common assumption in admissions policy was that anyone who met a particular criterion could gain admission; the issue was the nature of the criterion. Only when the number of qualified applicants exceeded available places—an astonishing luxury through much of the history of higher education—did the system break down and new ideas emerge. When that first happened at the Business School, the initial impulse was to accept qualified students in the order in which their applications were received. But this soon seemed less sensible than comparing qualified applicants to each other. By contrast, the Law School continued for many years to admit all qualified students to its first-year class and deal with the numbers problem by large-scale failures thereafter. Since the Graduate School of Education never experienced a surplus of qualified applicants until after World War II, its awareness of how selective admissions helped to determine student performance lagged behind the rest of the University. The responsibility of making a "profound and visible difference" in graduates fell to the curriculum alone.[19]

The task of curriculum building consumed an extraordinary portion of faculty energy for more than a decade. The entire success of the School's radical adventure, Holmes reiterated again and again, depended on the curriculum's ability to transform novices into edu-

cators rather than mere craftsmen. A core curriculum of fundamentals was crucial to provide the breadth of understanding and
skill in judgment that enabled educators to analyze constructively
the myriad issues they would face as members of committees, participants in general discussions, and as advisers to parents and colleagues on matters of large policy. "Every teacher," Holmes urged,
"ought to be capable of taking part in the cooperative formulation
of educational policies. School work is more highly cooperative than
any other great social undertaking, even religion, even government." Because teachers as well as administrators would experience
the core curriculum and come to possess understanding and judgment, the lines of hierarchy within the profession would be blurred
beyond recognition.[20]

Holmes had not lost confidence in the maturity of professional
knowledge in the technical fields of practice. He merely questioned
its sufficiency. Only rarely did curriculum building directly address
issues of technical specialization. The faculty created a required
field "apprenticeship" to test technical proficiency once it had been
acquired, but this was a minor element in the reorganization and
was frequently waived. Field work was considered a method of evaluation rather than a method of training. When Holmes and Lowell
spoke of Harvard professional ideals, they thought primarily of law
and business, where field work was virtually nonexistent, rather
than of medicine, where it was indispensable. To them the burden
of university training in education was to establish its superiority
over practical experience, not to bring practical experience into the
university. Brewer cleverly tried to minimize the new plan's adverse
effects on part-time experienced students by maximizing the academic credit they might receive through field experience undertaken as part of their regular jobs. But Holmes correctly judged this
maneuver as a threat to the new professional ideal and quashed it at
the discussion stage. Only in the 1950s did medical training become
the preferred professional analogy for training in education, and
field work consequently more respectable.[21]

The paramount curriculum question was to identify those fundamental principles that guaranteed breadth of understanding and
soundness of judgment. Lowell had always argued for fundamentals
in the context of a unique scholarly subject whose subdivisions
neither duplicated existing academic fields nor emphasized narrow

procedures. Educational measurement perfectly exemplified such a subdivision. More specifically, Lowell thought the main divisions of education should address "what subjects should be taught, at what time, and how, for the development of the human intelligence at various stages of its growth." None of this struck Holmes as especially helpful. Three of the School's existing curriculum divisions had names borrowed from academic disciplines (history, philosophy, and psychology) but the content of those fields already seemed thoroughly professionalized.

Educational psychology, for example, duplicated nothing offered in the faculty of arts and sciences. History hardly existed at all, in part because of low student demand and in part because of Lowell's antipathy. And philosophy was represented not by an academic philosopher, but by Holmes's own efforts to integrate moral philosophy, sociology, and economics around the theme of social policy and education. Moreover, Lowell's insistence that technical fields be sharply segregated from the fundamentals had the effect of minimizing treatment of social problems in courses like school administration, secondary education, guidance, and play. Indeed, Lowell's ideas about education's basic divisions gave preference to the individual rather than society, to intellectual aims rather than other educational objectives, and to academic subjects and methods instead of social and economic determinants of educational effectiveness.[22]

The Graduate School of Education, Holmes concluded, had already organized many of education's fundamentals into courses but had been unable, in a one-year curriculum, to require them. The faculty committee planning the core curriculum had little trouble deciding that the two required courses under the old plan, psychology and social policy, should continue to be requirements, and that measurement and individual development should be added. Measurement was a political accommodation to Lowell; few faculty members thought it was as essential as did the president. A required course in individual development capitalized on Johnson's teaching ability as well as on his availability, since there were so few advanced students in play. The faculty hoped this course might also bring Dearborn's Growth Study more to the center of the curriculum. Initially Dearborn agreed to co-teach the course, but his research commitments intervened to prevent his participation. Most of the faculty would have also preferred a required course in history, but no one but Norton was available to teach it and the idea was dropped.

A far harder planning task was to determine the fundamental principles contained in the technical courses In the absence of any agreement among these fields on either their own fundamentals or on the intellectual relationships among them, elementary courses in one tended to repeat material covered by elementary courses in the others. Advanced courses, in addition, tended to repeat materials taught in the elementary ones. There was, Holmes admitted, too much "overelaboration," and too many courses which "overlap and which are divided merely on the ground that one is taught from this angle and another from that." Fundamentals contained in the technical fields had to be distilled out and their order made more sequential. But consensus was difficult to achieve. At first virtually every faculty member contended that a significant portion of his subject was sufficiently fundamental to be required of everyone. How could one assess the validity of such claims and group disparate materials in an orderly way? Academic pragmatism sought compromise through a new two-semester required course which would cover everything by means of guest lectures from most of the faculty. The responsibility of the course instructor was not to teach but to coordinate. No one knew what to name the effort, though eventually "Educational Institutions and Practices' was settled on. The issue of history's place as a fundamental was resolved by including a few lectures on it in this course.[25]

Even after the faculty agreed on a core curriculum of six courses, comprising three fourths of a year's work, the job of curriculum development had only begun. Exactly how was the core expected to transform novices into educators? What discernible proficiency or mastery was it intended to guarantee? How would it make alumni profoundly and visibly different from those of other institutions? When Dearborn defended a required course in measurement, he had in mind the development of practical skill in statistics, testing, or experimentation. Others disliked the cursory treatment of so many topics in the course on institutions and practices, and favored intense study of a few subjects such as school finance. But these objectives were attacked as excessive specialization and rejected. After only one year Dearborn's goal of skill training was abandoned in favor of a general survey of measurement issues. Although Holmes opposed use of the core to develop specialized skills, he recognized that his priority objectives of understanding and judgment themselves had to be defined and assessed much more precisely. Problems of instructional technique and assessment soon preoccupied curriculum planners as much as problems of the core's content.[24]

They gave brief consideration to developing a unique method of instruction analogous to the case method. But even apart from its expense, the case method's applicability to education seemed limited. Some faculty members questioned the appropriateness of a method designed to teach decision making in a profession where the implementation of decisions was perhaps more difficult than the decision itself. Lowell himself doubted the relevance of the case method, believing that educational principles were more likely to emerge from mathematical analysis of large numbers of examples than from detailed analyses of particular cases. No other dramatic instructional procedure presented itself. Consequently the familiar course pattern of lectures and small-group discussions continued unchanged. Instead of new methods of teaching, Holmes emphasized the importance of faculty cooperation and commitment to the core. It was essential that everyone know exactly what was going on in all the required courses. It was even more essential that the faculty be "worked up" to regard these courses as the most significant instructional service of the School.[25]

Holmes thought he could solve the problem of demonstrating the results of the core curriculum by adapting one of Lowell's most significant pedagogical innovations, the general examination. The general examination was one of many antidotes to the disconnected education of the elective system. General examinations were administered at the close of formal education independent of course examinations. They aimed to assess power to apply and reason rather than to remember and regurgitate. The president commended the idea to all University departments and found an especially receptive audience in Holmes. Unless the School of Education set some kind of goal or test toward which all the parts converged, Holmes reasoned, the effort to "unify and coordinate" instruction might merely put parts of the whole "next to each other like bricks in a pile."[26]

The faculty voted to require a general examination as part of the new plan of study, but its pedagogical and evaluative functions were immediately undercut. In 1928, after the core curriculum had been in operation for only a semester, the faculty voted to eliminate all required courses and to rely instead on the general examination to *define* the core that all educators should know. This embarrassing retreat from the well-publicized core curriculum was a political triumph for technical specialists. They were unhappy about the small role their various fields played in the required curriculum and anxious about the threat that the core posed to their existing introductory courses. By arguing that the general examination rather than course requirements should define the core, they gave themselves another chance to establish a larger portion of their specialized offerings as fundamental.

Faculty specialists in secondary education and administration contended that the general examination should cover everything taught in their existing introductory courses. Vocational educators believed that the general examination should cover not only the history, laws, and social purposes of vocational education but also specific definitions of practical arts, industrial arts, tryout courses, and corporation schools. The faculty in English and music education demanded the inclusion of topics from their fields. In such circumstances, the hard-pressed committee charged with setting the general examination had little choice but to create many questions and offer students wide latitude among those they might answer. Nearly three fourths of the sample questions distributed prior to the first general examination on education's fundamentals were drawn from the technical fields. In addition to the six originally required core courses, the School's catalog listed seventeen courses that provided appropriate preparation for the general examination.

Reliance on the general examination thus exposed the faculty's inability to agree on what the fundamentals of education were and how they could compactly be organized for instruction. The problems of overlap and repetitiveness, and therefore of thinness and superficiality, seemed if anything worse than before. With considerable exasperation Holmes estimated that proper preparation for the general examination theoretically required twelve courses – though no one took them all – and that materials in at least ten of these could be condensed into four courses and taught by a single man. The problem, he finally admitted, seemed to be "the state of our subject." It was not yet possible "to be certain of what should be taught in Education; our knowledge has been, and is, defective. In consequence, everyone tends to teach everything."

Moreover, the problem of accommodating faculty views on what the general examination should cover detracted attention from the examination's role in assessing how well students could apply and relate what they studied. General examination questions had the same essay format as regular course examinations. Many faculty members thought that course grades, which embraced a variety of measures such as examinations, papers, and class performance were far more reliable assessment instruments than a single examination. Was a general examination anything more than a status symbol? One young faculty member in measurement wondered whether Harvard College had done anything more than "pick up a few questions sufficiently vague and broad to be comprehensive, have them elegantly printed and sit back beaming patronizingly on the educational world." Amid such cynicism Holmes urged a renewed effort to find the core, even if it involved "intellectual discomfort, extra work, and compromise of views and desires."[27]

But he also began to dream of new ways to shape student behavior beyond the formal curriculum. Professional formation was caused not only by explicit instruction but by the environment in which students lived. Students learned from peers as well as courses. The characteristics of the School's physical setting could subtly stimulate a heightened and intense professional consciousness. All around the School's shabby quarters in old Lawrence Hall was visible evidence of the educational value of proper surroundings. On the Boston side of the Charles River Vanderbilt Hall arose in 1927 as a medical dormitory, dining hall, and lounge. The extravagant new Business School plant was in full operation. Just in front of Lawrence, the monumental undergraduate "houses" were under construction. To the rear, the extensions and remodeling of the Law School's main building had just been completed. The logic behind this activity, to Holmes, was not the lust for luxury but sober awareness of the educational impact of community living. He dreamed that similar elegant surroundings might one day be possible for the Graduate School of Education, and hired an architect to make preliminary sketches of a commodious plant.

All the buildings had to be in Georgian style. The dormitories were modeled after the undergraduate houses, with impressive dining halls and resident masters. On the walls of an elaborate assembly hall "memorials and portraits would be slowly gathered." Adjacent athletic facilities were indispensable. "The plant should have a unity, a visible coherence, and in all its architectural arrangements it should lend itself to a totality of many-sided influence upon the students and the Faculty." Here indeed would be "no pedagogic factory but a gracious place in which to live and work." One problem jarred Holmes's fantasies of a campus that educated. Somehow the presence of women seemed inconsistent with the spirit of community and colleagueship he longed to establish. Moreover, their numbers had risen to an alarming and unacceptable 54 percent by 1928-29. It was not financially judicious to bar women completely from taking courses and paying tuition, but it made sense to bar them from residence in the dreamed-of plant and also from Harvard degrees. The ultimate emulation of the Harvard professional ideal—proposed in deepest secrecy—was to abolish women's unique eligibility for Harvard degrees.[28]

THE IMPACT of either formal or hidden curriculum depended, Holmes believed, on the "united effort of a staff that works effectively together." Faculty morale was critical, and nothing determined morale more than promotion to higher rank in return for exemplary institutional service. Near the end of the twenties only Holmes and Dearborn held full professorships No appointments to tenured associate professorships had been made since Nichols arrived in 1922. Numerous personnel decisions were pending, and Holmes judged all of them in relation to furthering the professional objectives of the reorganization. Yet Lowell was far less certain that training ideals should govern faculty advancement. Although he publicly praised the School's efforts to upgrade training, he usually coupled his praise with hopes that the School would nonetheless become a center for educational research. He confided to John Moors in 1927 that the quality of the faculty of education was not nearly as high as it should be, and was determined to prevent an unsatisfactory situation from worsening.[29]

The two perspectives first clashed around the case of L. O. Cummings, whom Holmes recommended for tenure months before the new plan was officially to commence. Cummings seemed to exemplify all the faculty virtues needed for the plan to succeed. Although he published almost nothing and disliked writing, he was an effective teacher of school administration and a constructive participant in school surveys. More important, Cummings brought "high standards, honesty of judgment, and careful analysis of problems" to policy discussions within the faculty. Time and again Cummings' opinions had carried most weight in debates over revising doctoral requirements or shaping the objectives of the reorganization. Yet Lowell was wholly unresponsive to this line of reasoning. He insisted that Cummings publish something of significance if he wanted a promotion, but also doubted the legitimacy of school administration as a proper field of study in a school of education. The main principles of administration seemed common to all human organizations. Why should an education school develop and teach them, when they were pursued elsewhere in the University?

Beset with anxiety, Cummings angrily refused to run Lowell's gauntlet and announced his intention to resign immediately unless he was promoted. Near panic at the prospect of losing his best young faculty member only weeks before the new program began, Holmes virtually begged Lowell "for the 1st and last time" to relent. Disaster was temporarily avoided when Lowell compromised on a nontenured associate professorship designed to give Cummings time to show his scholarly mettle. But he never wrote and resigned two years later just before Lowell could fire him, to seek a new position where he could work "without the fatigue that comes from unrecognized efforts."

Everything about the Cummings affair depressed the dean: his inability to move the president, the bitter attacks he endured from Cummings and Hanus who blamed the outcome on his own unpersuasiveness, the weakened position of the School in the field of administration. He hoped to repair the damage through a dramatic major appointment, but how could he please the profession and win Lowell's approval at the same time? Perhaps he could find a "social philosopher who is willing to spend his life training superintendents of schools." But his own colleagues warned that any senior appointment other than an experienced city superintendent would make Harvard a "laughing stock" and drive students away. Confronted with such polarities the natural course of action was to do nothing at all. Soon Harvard's professional reputation in school administration vanished almost entirely.[30]

The most depressing effects were perhaps on faculty morale, which plummeted further following the treatment of the play advocate George Johnson. No faculty member supported the reorganization more loyally or was more beloved. In 1929 Johnson was sixty-seven years old and ill. He had not written a book since his late fifties; but he now coveted promotion to a full professorship for the additional income it would provide to pay doctors' bills. To Holmes the issue was clearly drawn. If Lowell denied his promotion he would "spread the corroding sense that universities, like republics, are ungrateful." The risks Harvard was taking to set new standards required keeping the faculty "united and enthusiastic." The great man standard of faculty promotion only encouraged selfish competition and diminished "the power of the faculty group as a whole." Yet once again Holmes could not budge the president, who concluded that Johnson's earlier writings were below professorial standards anywhere else in the University. Still teaching two years later to pay his bills, at age sixty-nine Johnson died without his promotion. Play and recreation then vanished from the curriculum without a trace.[31]

Both John Brewer and Frederick Nichols learned to their dismay that even prolific writing did not guarantee promotion. By the middle twenties Brewer took considerable pride at the record of his efforts to advance the guidance movement. His pathfinding book on vocational guidance had sold over 7000 copies, his school text on occupations over 70,000, and another text on training counselors was just finished. Brewer advised more doctoral candidates than anyone else. By 1930 he could boast that fifty-four students taught vocational guidance at the college level and more than a hundred were full-time guidance practitioners in the schools. The Bureau of Vocational Guidance undertook a variety of school service activities and continued to publish the official journal of the Vocational Guidance Association.

Yet when Brewer first raised the question of promotion, Lowell told him that all this work was little more than propaganda with no established basis in research. The president advised him to shift his energies from instruction, text writing, and the administration of bureau affairs to statistical analysis of the qualities needed for occupational success. In particular, Lowell doubted Brewer's claim that vocational education and vocational counseling were essential to occupational competence. Character, as developed by rigorous intellectual activity, might be far more important. But the question was open and could only be answered by research.

Of course Brewer was shaken by an attack that seemed to proceed from fundamental assumptions so far from his own. What was wrong with advancing a cause if the cause was just? Was not such advocacy the very essence of professorial responsibility when the School's goal was to help reform secondary education? Why should he be penalized by Lowell's personal opposition to social efficiency and not be judged instead by "standards recognized in schools of education"? And was not the task of *implementing* decisions a distinguishing characteristic of the education profession?

Brewer further resented the suggestion that only statistical research provided valid educational knowledge. He described his own methods as sociological and philosophical; they involved "analysis, hard thinking and the development of wisdom." The fruits of such methods sometimes appeared to be superficial and obvious after they were published, he admitted, just as most important discoveries were really quite simple. But Brewer claimed that his "analysis of the six steps of vocational guidance, the application of guidance to other fields of life activity, the analysis of skill, technical knowledge, and social understanding, and the analysis of the various activities" were all contributions of major significance to educational practice. He was totally opposed to more statistics, tests, and scientific expertise in guidance. Was it wise to stake the future of guidance on "highly technical knowledge in the mind of the expert, leading to rather definite advice"? Or was the essence of guidance to "enrich the child's life and then allow his purposes, decisions, and activities to unfold"? Statistics merely expressed the longing for a "modern form of fortune telling."[32]

Holmes had earlier regarded propagandizing the guidance cause as a legitimate function of the University and shared some of Brewer's reservations about educational science. But he nonetheless refused to press the promotion on Lowell until Brewer had conducted more research. It was now essential to move beyond "mere reiteration of the arguments for guidance" to establish hard evidence for some central contention of the movement. Nothing better expressed Holmes's personal shift from the ideals governing the School in 1920 to the ideals of the reorganization. In the late 1920s Brewer seemed an institutional liability, a symbol of an era that was over. His devo-

tion to promoting a cause through emphasizing administrative procedures stood in dramatic contrast to the contemporary emphasis on
broad understanding and judgment.

Brewer remained loyal to the tradition of part-time, mid-career
training and fought for the interests of experienced, older students
wherever possible. He might have won Holmes's support despite his
beliefs, but he argued them all with an extremism which—when
coupled with his Christian Science opposition to medicine—seemed
unreasoned and unbefitting an academic community. Yet he too
coveted his promotion and tried to win Holmes's backing by inaugu-
rating some research. When that proved disastrous, he focused instead on a major philosophical work, *Education as Guidance*. But
that book, a social efficiency effort to define educational objectives
in terms of the "present life activities of healthy, normal boys and
girls," was also a self-acknowledged critical failure. Brewer finally
rested his case for promotion on the pioneering entrepreneurialism
he was best at, but time only hardened Holmes's opposition to him.
In 1931 Brewer was told that he would never be promoted, that
Lowell would never raise his salary, and that he should consider
resignation. It was no longer sufficient, Holmes told the perplexed
Lincoln Filene, to define a professor's role by "the preaching of a
gospel or the encouragement of the clan."[38]

In sharp contrast to Brewer, Nichols enthusiastically embraced
research as a weapon in the fight to advance commercial education,
and Holmes never doubted his qualifications for a full professorship. By means of the research technique of activity analysis, Nichols
hoped to find out exactly what people did in office jobs. Through
questionnaires filled out by workers and employers, researchers
learned that most office tasks consisted of filing and indexing, han-
dling mail, billing, recording, and using a calculating machine—
not the bookkeeping and stenography that most school curricula
still emphasized. Research thus seemed to provide important backing for the curriculum changes Nichols advocated. Lowell appears
to have been wholly uninterested in any of this, but in an unexpected quarter Nichols became an active symbol of the essence of
the Graduate School of Education.

Abraham Flexner in early 1930 was completing a section on
schools of education for his forthcoming comparative study of
American and European universities. Only a decade before Flexner

had staunchly defended the possibilities of schools of education, and imagined that philanthropic foundations might guarantee excellence in a few of them just as they had upgraded leading medical schools. But now he had painfully changed his mind. In reasoning that partly paralleled Holmes's own reconsiderations, Flexner argued that specific job preparation, in combination with an uncritical acceptance of scientific testing and measurement, had produced "atomistic training . . . hostile to the development of intellectual grasp." Instead of scholarship, schools of education taught only technique, administration, and socialization. Teachers College seemed the worst offender, but Flexner sought assurances from Holmes that the same evil tendencies did not prevail at Harvard. Eager to exploit the opportunity to show off the reorganization and gain welcome publicity, Holmes submitted to Flexner the work of Nichols and his graduate students as evidence of how a serious research base could undergird a technical specialization.

But commercial education research only confirmed Flexner's worst fears. Why was such enormous energy devoted to the proposition that school curricula should mirror a nearly endless list of adult job activities? Were not most of these activities "piffling little problems, which every man settles in his own way and with his own horse sense"? If schools of education devoted their time to discovering everything that people did in their lives in order to teach it to them in schools, neither they nor the schools would have time left for the "study and mastery of ideas." Was not the logical next step solemn research on "cleaning nails, lacing shoes, filling fountain pens, or anything else that anybody above the level of a moron would absorb and do in the course of the barest living"? Flexner thought he had discovered why intelligent people rarely went into education as Education. It was simply too boring and trivial. To label Nichols' activities research just because he collected data was a ludicrous parody of real research.

Holmes calmly replied that Flexner had not glimpsed the constructive reforms that might flow from Nichols' efforts. Did he not know that millions of dollars were wasted teaching shorthand to millions of girls who did not need it? Perhaps policy issues in commercial education seemed simple to sophisticated men, but professional workers in the field had to treat them with utmost seriousness and not aloof condescension. There was no escaping the proposition that "professional students in Education have got to learn what to do and how to do it." For his part Nichols believed that elitists like Flexner and Lowell would never appreciate the problems of upgrading training for nonelite occupations.

In fact, Nichols' interest in clerks was a serious detriment to his own prospects at Harvard. The job of clerk never paid enough to support a head of household, was held mainly by women, and was only a stepping stone to more attractive business positions. Lowell's key adviser on the question of Nichols' promotion belittled his preoccupation with an unimportant occupation and neglect of the minority of commercial workers who would rise to more responsible jobs. Lowell refused the promotion. Yet even in defeat Nichols kept on with his method and constituency. In a subsequent questionnaire study of the traits needed in effective secretaries he concluded that intelligence, accuracy, personality, judgment, efficiency, loyalty, and executive ability were all important. Flexner was only surprised that Nichols did not also counsel on the proper secretarial use of spitoons; his conclusions seemed self-evident to "anybody but a jackass."[34]

All these rebuffs not only affected staff morale but cast broader doubts on how seriously the president really took the School's efforts to transform itself. The ultimate test of support was not his response to particular appointment recommendations, but his attitude toward a new fundraising campaign designed to complete the reorganization. In the summer of 1929 Holmes, assisted by Dearborn and Spaulding, initiated an elaborate proposal to raise $5 million to construct a new campus and expand the faculty to forty-four members. In all his life Holmes took no writing project more seriously. The drafts that emerged during 1929-30 expressed all the themes of the School's new mission with greater coherence than before, and were shrouded in prestigious secrecy because of the controversial proposal to ban women from Harvard degrees.

During this period of intense anticipation Holmes tried also to placate Lowell's concern for research. Despite the safety-valve moratorium on new faculty appointments, he decided finally to resolve the continuing problem of statistics. Truman Lee Kelley, then a professor at Stanford, was awarded the first full professorship since Inglis' promotion a decade before. When Kelley's request for an additional junior colleague, Phillip Justin Rulon, was granted, the School suddenly had created an entire new research department to complement Dearborn. Had additional funds been available, Holmes was prepared to invite Boyd Bode, the educational philosopher, to another professorship. Hopefully Lowell would be encouraged by these efforts to stimulate research as well as training and would endorse the $5 million campaign.

But Lowell completely repudiated the campaign document and would not approve a fund drive. He ignored all the careful rhetoric about complete training for young full-timers, about the capacity of curriculum and environment to form educators out of novices, about the School's courageous and risky pioneering. Nothing mattered, Lowell said, except the "quality of the men on the staff." He recalled how the Harvard Law School in the 1870s consisted of only five teachers and yet revolutionized the teaching of law. They would not have accomplished more "had there been forty-four of them. Their building, too, was not so large as the one you now occupy." Yet the Law School had not proposed expansion "until it had demonstrated beyond question the quality of its work."

With unaccustomed rage, Holmes desperately shot back that it was no longer possible to question the value of the work of the Graduate School of Education. To ignore the "historic turning point" embodied in the reorganization in favor of a vague attack on the faculty was patently unfair. It was too easy for outsiders to underrate a faculty of education. His was "far better than average." He resubmitted the planning document for reconsideration, but this time Lowell was even more direct. "I regret very much to say this," he wrote with cold finality, "but I really think it would be wise for the present to improve what we have and lay foundations rather than talk about a superstructure." But how, Holmes wondered, could one work enthusiastically at foundations if no hope existed for a superstructure? There was no answer. In the spring of 1931 all hopes of expansion were shattered. The planning document was renamed the "Boo-Boo." After Lowell retired two years later, he confided to the overseers that the Graduate School of Education was like a "kitten that ought to be drowned."[35]

8

Professional Training
and Institutional Disaster

THE HEADY MOOD of pedagogical pioneering had turned to doubt and anxiety by the early thirties. The issue was not only whether Harvard's training procedures could actually transform raw novices into polished educators visibly superior to the products of other schools of education. Even more important, did Harvard official-dom or school boards across the country really care if they could? As the faculty of education itself began to wonder whether Holmes's ambitious game was worth the candle, disunity and defensiveness steadily rose. Discouraged but not defeated, Holmes eagerly seized on a new means to prove the merit of Harvard's scheme. Having failed to secure either a stable core curriculum or a grand new campus, he now focused all his energies on quantitative measurement of the outcomes of professional training. The final product rather than the instructional process dominated institutional attention.

The subsequent rush to build objective and unchallengeable tests of acquired professional skill was accompanied by debilitating new dilemmas that eventually destroyed the two-year Ed.M. and threat-ened the School's primary commitment to professional training. In the years immediately after the 1927 reorganization, the size of the student body was considered less important than its youthfulness, lack of school experience, and commitment to protracted full-time study. Financial security seemed guaranteed by endowment income and the substantial surpluses accumulated during the early twenties. But once the Depression's full effect was felt in 1932, Holmes's wor-ries about enrollment became financial rather than programmatic. He cared more about how many students attended than about their characteristics.

Moreover, James Bryant Conant's accession to the Harvard presidency in 1933 abruptly altered senior-level debate on the problems and purposes of the Graduate School of Education. Unlike his two immediate predecessors, Conant began his labors as a professional scholar rather than as an educational reformer. As a chemist, he had thought little about the uses of educational research or the conditions of adequate professional training. But he was suspicious of the effects of "methods" courses on proper academic preparation of school teachers. And he equally regretted that schoolteachers enrolled in master of arts programs in the Graduate School of Arts and Sciences distracted that institution from training Ph.D. researchers. Even though the content of teacher education had not been a serious issue at Harvard since the turn of the century, Conant made it the center of his initial dealings with the School of Education. By 1936 he persuaded the faculties of arts and sciences and education to sponsor jointly a new degree, the master of arts in teaching, consciously designed to eliminate all the difficulties he associated with the Ed.M. and A.M.

The establishment of the M.A.T. shattered the logic of the two-year Ed.M. If Harvard offered a separate graduate degree just for beginning teachers, then professional training for all educational careers could not occur in a single program taken immediately after college. The faculty of education was happy to restore the Ed.M. to its original function of preparing experienced teachers for specialized positions beyond teaching. Despite this significant retreat from reorganization ideology, Holmes's devotion to high standards and the formation of professionals continued. He disguised withdrawal from the two-year plan by a new focus on student achievement that made receipt of the recast Ed.M. contingent on the passing of a vastly expanded series of final tests. The requirements for both Ed.M. and M.A.T. became astonishingly formidable. Consequently, neither degree generated sufficient tuition income to reverse the severe financial austerity forced on the School after 1932.

Henry Holmes staked all his hopes for proving his School's effectiveness on achievement tests that only helped to drive students away. Loath to lower his lofty standards, he concluded that only new endowment could assure fiscal salvation. After a brief endowment campaign failed, he pleaded in desperation for direct subsidies from the Harvard central administration. By 1939 Conant was willing to help, but his price was the removal of Holmes as dean in favor of Francis Spaulding. With Holmes finally gone, the faculty abolished almost all of the final tests. Their demise marked the end, in utter defeat and humiliation, of Harvard's faith in the power of calculated training and assessment procedures to change novices into educators.

THE TWO-YEAR master of education program increased the workload of instructional preparation and committee work, reduced the School's enrollment and income, raised charges of snobbishness among education faculty elsewhere, and won no support from Lowell. Not surprisingly, Holmes's policies were subjected to increasing faculty criticism, especially after the contents of the ill-fated Boo-Boo were widely debated. Why should experienced students be actively discouraged from attendance? Why was it necessary to propose barring women from Harvard degrees? Why was part-time study inevitably bad? Why was training the raw A.B. the most useful service the School could provide? Why was the tone of the fundraising document so conceited? To most faculty members the whole scheme seemed an ostrich-like denial of existing and intractable characteristics of the education profession.

Brewer warned against overeducating students beyond what jobs required. Guidance students cared more for personal contact with students than for "abstract intellectual study." He was even willing to concede that counselors were less important than psychologists or statisticians, if that admission would reduce the pressure on his curriculum to be more rigorous and on himself to be more scientific. Nichols was by no means surprised that doctoral dissertations in commercial education did not measure up to Flexner's lofty standards, since "a very large portion of our work is in a very real sense undergraduate work." Perhaps, he thought, outside criticism could be disarmed and unreasonable expectations reduced if the School candidly admitted that it was "really an undergraduate school operating on a graduate level."[1]

Growing departmental fragmentation was another index of low morale. Holmes detected the general conviction that everyone "must play his own game for his own advancement." Obvious symptoms of centrifugality were the proliferation of introductory courses in the face of a clear administrative mandate to reduce them, and the faculty's tendency to urge beginning students to concentrate immediately in particular fields despite School policy to defer specialization. The most successful departments withdrew into greater isolation from the rest of the institution. Alexander Inglis' young replacements in secondary education, Bancroft Beatley and Francis Spaulding, both won associate professorships at the end of the twenties through the combination of a book, constructive teaching, and strong undergraduate records at Harvard College. Their attitude was, "We'll run our show as best we can and to hell with the rest of the School." Dubious about the institution's future and their own prospects for further promotion, they considered resignation more actively than any other senior professors.[2]

The same erosion of commitment occurred within the visiting committee. Felix Warburg wholly opposed the 1927 reorganization and soon left the committee. He had no interest in a "high-brow" school, only in one that did "novel, startling things of a practical kind." Lincoln Filene was angered by Holmes's attacks on Brewer and the Bureau of Vocational Guidance. As they and others dropped out, Holmes neglected to cultivate a new generation of affluent supporters. Consulting less and less with the visiting committee he felt more isolated and became more self-righteous. Simultaneously he reduced faculty participation in decision making. A faculty vote endorsing the Boo-Boo, for example, seemed unnecessary; Holmes submitted it to Lowell as fixed policy. His withdrawal only increased internal tension. Brewer called on the faculty to adopt clear rules of procedure in the face of "one-man rule, or dictatorship." Nichols looked back longingly to the early twenties when a "democratic spirit" prevailed and the faculty itself approved all major policies.[3]

Lowell's ill-disguised contempt for the education faculty, along with the decision to add two researchers in measurement, exacerbated anxiety about the future. Might not the president's covert goal be to build a faculty only of scholars and abandon professional training altogether? Could Holmes resist such pressure? Stung by Lowell's brusque repudiation of the Boo-Boo, Holmes and Spaulding tried to rephrase the reorganization's logic more convincingly. Francis Trow Spaulding, the son of Frank E. Spaulding, had replaced L. O. Cummings as Holmes's closest confidante on questions of institutional policy. The younger Spaulding shared his father's interest in practical administration rather than research or scholarship. Like most of his colleagues, he was committed to social efficiency ideals as educational objectives and cared mainly about the majority of high school youth who would never attend college. He expressed these convictions with uncommon grace and balance. In early 1931, Spaulding was scheduled to give an important address on whether graduate schools of education should emphasize general scientific training or specific professional preparation He and Holmes worked long hours together on the speech; it became a trial balloon to help regain the ground lost through the Boo-Boo's defeat.

Harvard's abandonment of the "specific job ideal," with its superficial attention to devices and techniques, needed no apology. The immediate threat was the idea, espoused by Flexner, Lowell, and Judd, that the graduate study of education should emphasize "the academic accumulation of knowledge about education." Spaulding contended that this "academic ideal" meant the incorporation of academic subjects like history, psychology, or philosophy into schools of education without changing them in any constructive way. Sometimes the academic ideal also suggested that education itself was an academic subject. Harvard, Spaulding argued. rejected as policy foci both cookbook recipes and the accumulation of academic knowledge. Instead, it called for a training process that aimed for the "translation of educational theory into action." The sole purpose of a training program was to have "direct and transferable' bearing upon educational practice." Holmes exulted that Spaulding's formulation was an important step forward. He had called special attention to the paramount danger of creeping academicism in the education curriculum. And he had emphasized the results of professional training—the capacity to educate in an "active sense"—rather than the ingredients of the training experience. Both of Spaulding's themes influenced institutional policy in 1931.[4]

The growing academic threat was symbolized by a senior doctoral student in educational philosophy, Roger W. Holmes, who also held a faculty instructorship. Dean Holmes, no relation to the younger Holmes, regarded him as a brilliant faculty prospect and planned to advance him up the academic ladder if funds could not be raised to bring in a senior philosopher. But Spaulding, in the midst of finishing his speech defending professional training, contended that Roger Holmes's course proposal in the history of philosophy embraced the very academic ideals he loathed. Spaulding attacked young Holmes's prospectus because it resurrected historical figures "long since embalmed" and neglected a "functioning" philosophy of education for young professionals. The course seemed appropriate in a department of philosophy but not in a professional school.

The dispute soon assumed a larger dimension when the doctoral committee (consisting of Dean Holmes, Spaulding, Dearborn, Nichols, and Kelley) failed Roger Holmes's defense of his thesis plan and advised him to leave the School. He had proposed to study the Italian idealist philosopher Giovanni Gentile and then to analyze educational practice from idealist premises. From that perspective, which Roger Holmes personally endorsed, truth was a matter of individual insight and was not subject to scientific proof or verification. In the doctoral orals, Holmes's performance was judged intellectually inadequate. But beyond his logical failings, the doctoral committee questioned the acceptability of his topic even if defended adequately.

Regardless of the quality of his work, Holmes, the committee found, "would have inevitably to come to the conclusion that there is no place for education as a professional study—a conclusion which seemed . . . to rule his thesis plans out of court so far as their appropriateness in connection with a professional degree was concerned." In a letter he wisely decided never to send, Dean Holmes admitted to the philosopher Ralph Barton Perry that Roger had not "failed" in the usual sense at all. The development of his thought had put him "wholly out of step with the work of this school so that we can hardly accept the thesis he is writing without condemning a very large part of our own undertaking . . . By adopting the philosophy of Gentile Mr. Holmes becomes not merely a critic of this, that, or the other thing in our work, but an opponent of its fundamental assumptions. We grant that he may be right and we wrong . . . But we do not feel that he belongs here."

Spaulding and Holmes had injudiciously told Roger the truth, that one aspect of the decision to fail him was that his subject threatened the fundamental assumptions of the School. On receipt of this intelligence Roger's father, a prominent Harvard alumnus, immediately demanded that Lowell clarify University policy. Were doctoral students failed merely because their findings challenged accepted authority? The president assured him that his allegation was improbable and contrary to everything Harvard stood for. Still,

Lowell found it "a little odd that a man who is incompetent to get a doctor's degree should be twice given non-resident fellowships and should have been appointed an instructor to give a course in the very subject in which his thesis is rejected."

Dean Holmes now recognized the necessity to separate the issue of conformity with the School's philosophy from the issue of intellectual performance on an examination. Yet in his own mind the two were closely linked, and he spent page after page explaining to the president why Roger should leave the School "even if his position had been logically presented and defended." He was torn between what was necessary to say in order to demolish Roger's claim of unfairness and his preoccupation with the more basic policy problem of the limits of scholarly independence in a professional school. Lowell, whose regard for the School of Education perhaps now reached its nadir, merely wanted a clear statement that Roger Holmes had not been failed because of his opinions. Instead Spaulding virtually admitted to him that both Roger's opinions and their exposition had played a part in the decision to fail him. Impatiently Lowell virtually ordered the dean to produce a brief statement categorically denying Roger Holmes's assertions. Holmes complied, the case was closed, and Roger transferred to the Department of Philosophy. An essay based partly on his Ph.D. dissertation subsequently won the Bowdoin Prize for academic excellence.[5]

The purging of Roger Holmes exposed the defensive anxiety that surrounded the new plan by 1931. Unless ideological purity was maintained, the academic cancer might grow. In his annual report Holmes reiterated that research and doctoral training were the coward's way out. It would be easy to turn the School into the educational equivalent of Abraham Flexner's new Institute of Advanced Study at Princeton. But research was simply not the greatest need in American education. The real need was for "higher quality in teaching and administration" and a "sounder conception of what it means to be a schoolmaster." But how could the internal climate of discouragement be reversed?[6]

Banishing heretics was hardly sufficient. Mentally exhausted, physically ill, and emotionally drained by the death of his wife, Holmes went on sabbatical to decide what practical new initiatives might be taken. How could Spaulding's arresting focus on "action" and the actual behavior of educators be implemented? Could the sprawling curriculum ever become lean and sequential? Could the effects of instruction be assessed more convincingly? Stimulated especially by William Learned's current work in measuring school and college achievement in Pennsylvania, Holmes began to formulate a "radical" approach to the instructional process which he hoped would put Harvard's historic new plan back on course.

Final tests alone, Holmes proposed to his disbelieving colleagues, should determine fitness to receive the Ed.M. All course credits and grades should be abolished. The curriculum itself should emphasize lectures running odd lengths of time and opportunities for individual study. Residence should vary according to the time individual students needed to prepare for final tests. The School's instructional center of gravity should shift from the course to the student. Holmes thought he could implement Spaulding's focus on the behavior of educators by incorporating Learned's confidence in the objective measurement of educational products.

If final tests alone governed the awarding of degrees, the sprawling curriculum would wither away. Instruction would focus exclusively on helping students prepare for the tests. The faculty's inability to agree on a compact core curriculum would no longer matter. A small, coherent, and powerful committee would set the examinations. Not surprisingly, little faculty support emerged for Holmes's admittedly utopian scheme. Even devotees of objective measurement such as Truman Kelley advised against abandoning credits, marks, and formal courses until satisfactory final tests had been developed. But the faculty authorized experimentation with the format of the general examination. Kelley and Phillip Rulon agreed to help design objective general examinations wholly different from the essay-type general examination the School had previously used.

The new general examinations differed from the old in three distinct ways. First, the questions were largely required. Second, their goal was to test capacity to translate theory into action rather than to cover knowledge of material. Could students apply principles, ideas, or attitudes to situations with which they were not familiar? Finally, the results were assessed by objective, quantitative methods. A series of one-page "situations" were produced, each describing an educational dilemma. For the test of fundamental principles required of everyone, the situation included various decisions taken by educators in response to the dilemma. Students then rated a variety of statements about these actions according to a five-point scale. In addition to this test of capacity to make professional judgments, called the "comprehensive" examination, students were also expected to take a similar test in their special field. Here the task was not to evaluate judgments others made, but (in essay format) to make constructive proposals for action. The correct answers to the comprehensive examination were determined by the mean score of the entire faculty of education on each question. In both its comprehensive and special-field parts, the general examination consumed nine hours.

The examinations, first administered in 1933, raised a new set of pedagogical and procedural issues. They were extraordinarily time-consuming to prepare and to score. Final proof of their value depended on statistical studies of validity and reliability not yet made. Their relation to regular courses was never clear and those courses continued unchanged. Paradoxically, the examinations seemed to stand both for distrust of the existing curriculum but also for confidence that the subject of education contained correct answers to complex questions of judgment. The pedagogy the examinations implicitly endorsed was a creative response to financial adversity, for it did not require the elaborate campus Lowell had already rejected. Yet that pedagogy conflicted with Holmes's belief in professional formation through a long and well-managed residential period. In spite of these dilemmas, Holmes's spirits rose. He was convinced the School of Education had finally found the means to demonstrate its ideal of visible professional capacity. When Lowell's regime ended in 1933, Holmes offered the new objective examinations as the best possible evidence to convince the new president of his institution's value.[7]

THE ULTIMATE TEST of the reorganization was its ability to recruit young students willing to spend more time and money at Harvard than was required elsewhere in return for the greater skill and career benefits that such training presumably conferred. Holmes was convinced that the two-year Ed.M. would only lure students when they and school boards were convinced that it demonstrably improved professional performance. That was why "objective" measures of training outcomes seemed so appealing. Only when Harvard could prove that it could form educators would employing authorities "clamor for our product."

Holmes did not expect that public certification requirements would help to boost enrollments in the foreseeable future. Massachusetts had no statewide professional requirements for high school teachers, and requirements elsewhere did not recognize the master's as a two-year degree. Licensing procedures could even be liabilities. Holmes had to persuade Boston to accept the first year of the Ed.M. as the equivalent of a master's so that his students would not be penalized in seeking employment there. With no immediate help from public authority, the School tried actively to recruit students from Eastern liberal arts colleges. It redesigned its catalogue, published elegant student guides to both the reorganization and a variety of educational careers, and mailed them each year to thousands of college juniors and seniors.[8]

The early results were disappointing. Only 59 two-year Ed.M. candidates registered in 1929, the third year of the new plan, compared with 278 one-year candidates in 1926-27. Full-time students, moreover, comprised only a third of all two-year registrants between 1927 and 1932. The part-time student body was further enlarged by holdover candidates for the one-year degree who were allowed until 1934 to complete requirements under various "grandfather" clauses. Between 1927 and 1934, 637 one-year Ed.M. degrees were conferred, compared with only 146 two-year degrees. The continued presence of so many part-time students helped to maintain enrollment, but severely hindered the development of a coherent subculture of full-timers so indispensable to Holmes's theories of professional formation.

Students on the new plan differed in other respects from the expectations of the reorganization. Most were neither young (the average age was thirty-six) nor inexperienced. Their residence distribution did not approach the "national" student bodies of the business and law schools. In 1930, for example, 77 percent of education's students were Massachusetts residents, compared with 20 percent in the Business School and 16 percent in the Law School. Nor did the academic quality of new-plan students seem discernibly different from the old. A 1933 analysis found that most students had graduated from college without honors, and a later study confirmed that new-planners did not have better undergraduate records than one-year candidates.[9]

Until 1932 the School's concern with enrollment was more programmatic than financial. The institution did not depend on tuition income from new-planners. Endowment income, which never covered less than 64 percent of basic expenses between 1927 and 1932, increased from $109,000 in 1924 to nearly $122,000 in 1930. Even annual tuition income, boosted by a 1927 tuition increase (from $250 to $300) and the continued presence of old-plan candidates, was larger in every year between 1927 and 1932 than in any year before 1925. As expected, the School lost money in four of the first five years of the reorganization and saw its $100,000 surplus nearly halved. These deficits were not the result of reduced income, but of a deliberate effort to maintain expenditures at morale-boosting levels. Expense policy reflected a basic optimism about the School's future. Over $10,000 was spent to refurbish Lawrence Hall after the Business School departed, salaries were increased in 1930, and the School subsidized both the Growth Study and the Bureau of Vocational Guidance.

The Great Depression at first had little discernible impact. Indeed, the desired constituency of young college graduates seemed more impervious to the Depression than experienced teachers with families to support. But in 1932 the deepening Depression suddenly rendered all previous forecasts obsolete. The changes came with numbing speed. In mid-1932, after his budget for the following year had received Corporation approval, Holmes was informed that endowment income would be reduced 22 percent. When the school year started, tuition receipts were appreciably lower than had been predicted. Instead of a balanced budget, Holmes found himself with $129,000 of basic income to meet anticipated expenditures of $171,000.

For the first time, the School was forced to cut current expenses to minimize an anticipated deficit. Most secretaries and all course assistants were dropped. Supplies and most telephones were removed. The library budget was slashed, and the $9000 annual subsidy to the Bureau of Vocational Guidance was ended and with it Harvard's sponsorship of the *Vocational Guidance Magazine*. Total expenses were cut to $148,000, their lowest since 1925. Some faculty protested the dean's unilateral budget decisions, especially his protection of the subsidy to Dearborn's Growth Study, and demanded participation in the budget process. Unable to check a rebellion led by the colleagues he most respected, Holmes appointed an advisory budget committee to assist in the painful job of retrenchment.

Budget preparation for the 1933-34 year was even more disheartening. Anticipating another reduction in endowment yield, Lowell ordered additional cuts. During the tense first weekend in March, when Franklin Roosevelt inaugurated the New Deal, Holmes struggled in his office to decide what else to eliminate. Since Lowell would not permit the reduction of faculty salaries, the only alternative was to cut entire functions. The Growth Study subsidy was dropped, library expenses were further reduced by two thirds, and all untenured part-time faculty were dismissed. In little more than a year the School's basic expenses had fallen by more than 30 percent. The end was not in sight. In the fall, only a year before all income from old-plan candidates would cease, new-plan enrollments fell for the first time. If that trend continued, and endowment income did not soon rise, no accumulated surplus would remain to absorb annual deficits. Nichols compared the two-year plan to Prohibition, a "noble experiment" that could not endure. Another survey ranking schools of education found in 1934 that Harvard had slipped to tenth place.[10]

THESE PRECARIOUS finances forced James Bryant Conant to attend to the Graduate School of Education far earlier than his interests otherwise would have dictated. If both Eliot and Lowell began their presidencies with pronounced views on curriculum and pedagogy, Conant had no focused interest in the educational process and no program for reform. In 1933, Conant's educational ideas were mainly the product of his professional commitment to science and scholarship. By contrast, Eliot had abandoned efforts to be a research chemist. Lowell, although a renowned scholar, was at heart an urbane man of letters who resisted defining his vocation by disciplinary affiliation. Always proud that his postcollegiate education was in the law rather than academic scholarship, Lowell was never a friend of the Graduate School of Arts and Sciences or the rituals of Germanic specialization. Indeed, Lowell's valedictory to the University was to endow from his personal fortune the Society of Fellows, an effort to train scholars through elegant self-education rather than through Ph.D. programs dominated by childish requirements and credential-conscious vocationalism. Instead of Lowell's informed amateurism, Conant brought the values of the professional scholar for the first time to the Harvard presidency.[11]

Lowell regarded scholarship as a tool to civilize a potentially frivolous privileged class, but Conant imagined it as a career commitment for modern scientists, social scientists, and humanists. Despite Lowell's frequent concern for intellectual quality and his famous remark that the best way to ruin a university was to fill its faculty with merely "good" men, Conant with reason sharply criticized his predecessor's academic standards in promotion decisions. Lowell's elitism was aristocratic, Conant's meritocratic. Lowell spent a quarter century attempting to construct an ideal undergraduate educational environment. Conant concentrated instead on the selection of the most talented students and faculty. For him, at least in 1933, a university was less an environment for learning than a "collection of eminent scholars."[12]

Conant was uninterested in the academic policy issues that preoccupied the Graduate School of Education. He was not excited by the problem of making education a fit associate of law through creation of an appropriate knowledge base and training environment. Nor was he enthusiastic about the possibilities of educational research to solve this or that problem. As a professional chemist, whose own maturity coincided with the expansion of mass secondary education and the rise of schools of education, Conant fastened on the tension between content and methods in teacher education as the central issue posed by the School's existence. What was the proper relation between knowledge of a subject, the central element of vocational identity for a scientist and teacher like himself, and knowledge of education as taught in the School of Education? His prejudice that education courses only reduced the time prospective teachers spent learning their fields, without adding anything of substantive value, found early confirmation when he claimed to be able to answer the general examination questions Holmes proudly showed him without ever having taken a course in education.[13]

Another troublesome relationship between teacher preparation and academic scholarship had nothing to do with the School of

Education. Did enrollment for master of arts degrees in the Graduate School of Arts and Sciences by students interested in schoolteaching hinder the development of Ph.D. programs to train professional scholars? The numbers of teachers who undertook A.M.
rather than Ed.M. study was not trivial. One analysis, based on 62
percent of A.M. alumni, indicated that an average of twenty-four a
year throughout the twenties took schoolteaching jobs. As Ph.D.
programs grew, many members of the faculty of arts and sciences
discerned a growing gap between the interests and academic talent
of Ph.D. and A.M. candidates. Ph.D. programs maintained quality
control subsequent to admission through general examinations and
the dissertation. A.M. candidates were only required to complete a
year of coursework. Lowell and some colleagues preferred to exclude applicants with "less ambitious aims" than university professorships. By the end of the 1920s the faculty of arts and sciences
formally debated whether the Graduate School of Arts and Sciences
should become exclusively a professional school leading to the Ph.D.
degree.

Departments such as economics raised A.M. standards on their
own by requiring candidates to pass Ph.D. generals. (Since economics was not taught in secondary schools, its faculty was not "be-
sieged by secondary school teachers who want a higher degree for
purely practical purposes.") In contrast, the Graduate School's visiting committee rejected the idea of meritocratic exclusivity. Its ideal
A.M. graduate was the "cultivated, high-minded, correct living
gentleman" who studied "scholarship for the sake of scholarship"
and so learned the "art of living." The English department refused
to toughen its A.M. admission or graduation requirements. By 1933
the issue had not been resolved, although the trend was toward a
gradual raising of admission requirements without encroaching on
departmental prerogatives. Conant's bias in favor of strengthening
the Ph.D. was unmistakable.[14]

Early in his presidency, Conant learned how he could resolve with
one stroke the financial problems of the Graduate School of Education, its excessive reliance on education courses in teacher preparation, and the continuing existence of teacher education in the
Graduate School of Arts and Sciences. Conversations with Robert
Hutchins and Charles Judd revealed that the department of education at the University of Chicago had willingly surrendered power

over teacher education to the academic departments and a university-wide coordinating committee. The Chicago plan had obvious attractions for Harvard. Academic standards might rise if control over teacher education rested with the academic departments. A single University teacher education policy might reduce or eliminate the teacher education role of the A.M. degree in the Graduate School of Arts and Sciences. And if teacher education were removed from the School of Education, its smaller size would be easier to finance from endowment alone.

Lowell had never been interested in teacher education, and the subject had rarely been a serious issue at Harvard since the end of the 1890s. Now Holmes was forced to shift his concerns from professional formation and final tests of capacity, which excited him but not Conant, to an older question he had never considered in detail. Disappointed that Conant did not share his priorities, he was chagrined that Judd, who embodied the antithesis of all his efforts, had become educational consultant to his own superior. Yet Conant seemed far more approachable than Lowell, perhaps even responsive to reasoned discussion. Holmes worked to reshape the Chicago plan to conform to his own vision, while loyally acquiescing in those of its elements that Conant most admired.

Thus he conceded the wisdom of a single university policy for training secondary teachers, and agreed that academic departments should set standards for subject-matter preparation. Beyond that, however, he roundly attacked Judd's recommendation that the School of Education abandon primary responsibility for teacher education. He knew that Judd's strategy was to saddle the University of Chicago as a whole with responsibility for teacher education, in order to free the department of education to concentrate exclusively on research and the training of administrative leaders. But classroom teaching, Holmes protested, was at the very center of the educational process. Harvard's reorganization celebrated the equality of teachers with other educators; Chicago's plan suggested their inferiority. And if Judd mechanistically viewed teacher education as putting "pedagogical patches" on prospective teachers, Harvard cared about shaping them as true educators.[15]

Holmes emphasized the number of faculty positions he had committed to teacher education. Academic policy before the reorganization had downgraded the role of special methods, but the post-1927 rediscovery of the classroom teacher caused a parallel rediscovery of special methods. By the end of the twenties the School intended to appoint full-time faculty members in each of the main curriculum fields. These "straddlers" would ideally split their responsibilities (and salaries) between the School and the appropriate department in the faculty of arts and sciences.

Lowell agreed to the tenuring of special methods instructors such as Ralph Beatley in mathematics and Louis J. A. Mercier in French because the respective academic departments appreciated their contribution to elementary instruction in Harvard College and endorsed their promotion. But the departments' commitments to the straddlers were highly ambivalent. Beatley was never a voting member of the mathematics department. The English department regarded the instruction of Charles Swain Thomas as fit only for ordinary minds and excluded him from departmental involvement. Despite these tepid relationships, Holmes could accurately contend in the mid-thirties that Harvard had invested heavily in tenured special methods staff whose work research-oriented academicians would have no interest in assuming.[16]

Such practical arguments persuaded Conant that the School of Education should continue to play a central role in teacher education at Harvard. By early 1935, the president decided to create a joint program that might lead to a new degree, the master of arts in teaching. Much of the Chicago plan had been defeated, but the School was now plunged into protracted negotiations with individual academic departments to work out details. The fundamental issue was how much of the 1927 reorganization could survive the new political situation.[17]

Holmes continued to argue in these negotiations for a philosophy of teacher education which emphasized the distinction between educator and craftsman. The teacher who was merely skilled in teaching his subject was often the "worst possible obstacle in the reorganization of the curriculum or in any other line of educational advance." Holmes even admitted that the difference between an educated layman and a professional teacher was not that the latter could teach better than the former. Sometimes the layman could teach just as well without any training whatever. But no layman could "attain sound views of general educational policy without serious study of the social, psychological, and technical issues involved in creating, organizing, and conducting a system of schools."

The means to achieve that general understanding, Holmes first contended, was through all the courses that the two-year Ed.M. recommended for students planning life careers as teachers. Excluding practical training for beginners, such as practice teaching, he listed a minimum of eight essential courses in education's fundamentals. But he soon realized that he could not transfer unchanged to the joint master's degree the entire apparatus of the two-year Ed.M. The political necessity to cooperate with the faculty of arts and sciences forced him to compress those courses in a way his own faculty had been unable to do. Holmes conceded that the year of fundamentals might be reduced to three fourths of a year, and then admitted that a "heroic" effort might further reduce the core to a half year's study of educational policy, psychology, measurement, and issues of secondary education.

These concessions only opened old wounds within his own faculty and caused new ones as discussions proceeded with the academic departments. Holmes urged his colleagues to downgrade methods and stress the social aims of each subject: he wished special methods to become the "battle-ground of educational theory." But his own special methods staff, supported both by the technical specialists and by the academic departments, seemed unaccountably to prefer craftsmen to educators. Men like Beatley and Mercier were far more interested in effective classroom instruction than in vague social aims. Already the straddler in science education, Conant's old secondary teacher, N. Henry Black, had resigned his education appointment because he cared little for making science teachers into educators. Only the small minority of special methods faculty with no academic departmental ties at all, such as the young Howard E. Wilson in social studies, emphasized the social uses of special methods.

The others, well aware of their marginal status with the academic departments, wondered if their status with Holmes was any better. The straddler's job of somehow pleasing both the academic departments and education became increasingly exhausting. Why, Brewer asked, was Holmes contending for so many fundamental education courses that were "highly technical beyond the needs or imagination or utility of the newly appointed teacher in a secondary school'? Holmes nervously pleaded with his colleagues not to make their reservations public. The faculty of education would only look ridiculous to the Harvard community if its inability to agree on the basics of its own field became known. His view prevailed, and the idea of a required education curriculum—a half year of basics, a half year of practical training—returned to the School of Education.[18]

His dogged advocacy of reorganization ideals damaged Holmes's effectiveness in winning departmental support for a reasonable joint program. The School of Education's decision to require a full year of education courses, coupled with Holmes's undisguised distaste for the craft of teaching as a major program goal, fueled the resolve of several departments to demand equal graduate time for their own subjects. Holmes's contention that no graduate study whatever in the academic subjects was necessary for M.A.T. candidates who had the equivalent of Harvard undergraduate majors in their teaching fields did not make collaboration any easier. His reasoning was straightforward enough: Harvard undergraduates were forced to defer any professional study until the graduate years but had ample opportunity in college to acquire sufficient knowledge of a discipline to teach it in school. But the effect of his position was to suggest, not inaccurately, that education wanted to monopolize the content of the new joint program.

The English department was happy with its own A.M. as a teacher preparation degree and had little interest in a cooperative venture. But if Conant demanded a new program, if it was to be truly joint, and if education wanted a year for its own courses, why should English not demand nearly the same amount of graduate study? It eventually insisted on a minimum of three full-year graduate English courses, none of which could be taken in summers. Since education intended to require M.A.T. candidates to take a vastly expanded general examination, English countered by requiring the Harvard College divisional examinations in English, knowledge of three foreign languages, and tests of oral English and written composition. None of these requirements existed for regular A.M. candidates in English. Although the English requirements were atypically harsh, Conant was more interested in establishing the principle of a joint program than in resolving particular disputes bound to arise at the outset. Neither he nor the administrative board appointed to govern the degree attempted to overrule departmental standards.

The result of this competitive development of degree requirements in the two cooperating faculties was an unusually formidable program that could rarely be completed in less than two years. In comparison, the master of arts degree was less expensive, demanding, and time-consuming. As the M.A.T. requirements became publicized in the spring of 1936, many education faculty wondered if the new degree could ever increase the tuition income of the School. Conant assured Holmes that the School of Education would keep all M.A.T. tuition (as well as bear all direct costs). In addition, Conant contributed scholarship aid from University funds and agreed to work for the elimination of prospective school teachers from A.M. programs. Still, there was little possibility of restoring the ambitious objectives of the early thirties, or even granting overdue faculty salary increases, unless more income was generated.[19]

THE M.A.T. DEGREE accelerated the collapse of the ideal of complete preparation for all educational roles undertaken prior to professional service. Removing initial teacher preparation from the two-year Ed.M. to a new degree eliminated common preparation for diverse jobs and thus the effort to blur professional hierarchy. But the ideal had been near collapse anyway; the necessity to accommodate presidential desires perhaps enabled Holmes to avoid a more humiliating retreat. Upon implementation of the M.A.T. in 1936, the Ed.M. reverted to its original purpose of specialized training for educational jobs open only to experienced teachers. Harvard now conceded a training sequence it had tried for a decade to subvert. One training experience could not provide lifetime career preparation. Prospective educators would first prepare just for teaching, through either undergraduate study in institutions that offered it or through the graduate M.A.T. Then, following successful teaching experience, they would return to pursue a specialized Ed.M.

Yet Holmes's retreat from the 1927 reorganization was grudging. He did his best to suggest that the withdrawal was orderly, even logical, rather than a rout. Even before the M.A.T. was established, Holmes had responded to earlier setbacks by urging measurement of the results of training rather than by emphasizing the process of training. That commitment to a demonstrable product grew deeper as the years passed. He still believed in a lengthy residential period where values and skills could be shaped in an ideal professional environment, and even speculated about how formal training could alter personality traits. But economic reality dictated, at least for the moment, the emphasis on product rather than on process. When the former had convinced the world that Harvard meant business in training educators, then gifts and tuition income would make the latter feasible once more.

Despite considerable faculty sentiment to return the Ed.M. to its uncomplicated one-year 1920 format, Holmes pushed through requirements that made the degree dependent only on "achievement" demonstrated through performance on final tests. The two-year program was thus abolished, but no one-year degree replaced it. Harvard had taken a major step forward, he claimed, by shifting its requirements from "time or the accumulation of credits" to accomplishment. There were now no fixed course or residence requirements at all, except for the University regulation that all degree recipients take at least one year of instruction. Holmes would have eliminated even this had it been in his power to do so.[20]

To win an "achievement" Ed.M., candidates had to pass at the beginning of their studies the same general examination in education that M.A.T. candidates took at the end of their degree. This general examination was expanded to include essay-type tests in five core areas of policy, psychology, measurement, secondary education, and principles of teaching, plus the objective "comprehensive" paper. Once the hurdle of the basics was surmounted—twenty-one hours of testing was required in the six areas—Ed.M. students had to pass an additional final examination in their specialized fields. Although the comprehensive paper was only one of seven required tests, Holmes regarded it as the pivotal ingredient of the entire program. Only the comprehensive paper objectively tested the ability to *use* knowledge professionally.

As the School's stake in this part of the general examination increased, Holmes obtained a grant from the Carnegie Foundation to study its reliability and validity in measuring ability to make wise educational judgments. Much of the early analysis exposed technical problems of reliability. The scoring system assumed, for example, that each question had only one correct answer, that the "wrongness" of an answer increased in proportion to its numerical distance from the correct answer on the five-point scale, and that each test item was identical to all others in these two properties. Yet analysis of faculty responses, used as the basis for determining right answers, suggested that these assumptions were invalid. On many questions embarrassing faculty disagreement occurred. Even when test items with hopelessly disparate faculty responses were thrown out, the small faculty committee responsible for the examination was often required to use its own judgment to determine correct answers. Educational knowledge was far less authoritative than the scoring system implied.

Still more crucial was evidence of the test's validity. Did t actually *predict* ability to make wise professional judgments? To test for validity, groups of "best" and "worst" Ed.M. alumni were chosen by placement officials using the criterion of on-the-job reputation. When the mean percentile rank of each group on the comprehensive examination was computed, the results showed a positive correlation between examination performance and later professional reputation. Although the research conceded that the external criterion was not so much professional judgment as job success, it assumed that the two were closely related. The findings provided encouraging evidence that the test was in fact "differentiating between the students in the same direction that they will be later differentiated on the basis of success in teaching." Holmes enthusiastically sought additional funds for larger and more elaborate statistical analyses.[21]

While these efforts to evaluate the objective comprehensive examination proceeded, the most pressing institutional question remained the financial impact of the new M.A.T. and Ed.M. programs. Enrollment at first increased, but the added tuition return was completely absorbed by necessary M.A.T. expenditures such as salaries for part-time methods instructors. Nothing was left over to raise the School from its austere post-1933 reduced scale. It continued to lose money every year and its reserve, which made up these deficits, was only $26,000 by 1939. Moreover, enrollment began to fall once again at the end of the thirties. Economic recession had deepened, but perhaps more important was the reputation each master's program acquired for time-consuming requirements. In mathematics, where an average of one student per year received an M.A.T. degree, Ralph Beatley wondered whether there was any "point in Harvard's having a program without a product." The academic departments were unwilling to ease their requirements while

Holmes was unwilling to tamper with the twenty-one-hour general examination.

By 1937 Holmes concluded that the additional income needed to raise salaries, make new appointments, and restore morale would not soon come from tuition. New endowment seemed the only means to avert "virtual defeat" of the decade-long effort to raise standards. When the University fund drive celebrating Harvard's tercentenary was finished, Holmes once again asked permission to mount an endowment campaign of his own. Conant was hardly a friend of the School, but he now was publicly committed to the importance of collaboration in teacher education. He cautiously approved a three-year drive with no set objective and no public announcement. If a private drive failed, the University would not lose face. In that event the original Chicago plan would be resurrected and the School would shrink to a small research organization. Delighted by this severely limited but still welcome expression of presidential confidence, Holmes nonetheless understood it was "now, or never." "The theme of new endowment," he characteristically remarked, "thus reappears in the strains of the funeral march."[22]

The practical tasks of the "big push" campaign were to articulate the School's mission in compelling terms and to identify prospective donors. Holmes's rhetorical bias was to dwell on how the School had "kept the faith" of standards and quality despite hard times; its distinctive selling point was its elaborate requirements for degrees. He told Francis Spaulding that "the nub of the matter is still in the Boo boo as you & I prepared it." But as he criss-crossed the country in 1937-38, speaking to Harvard clubs, interviewing wealthy businessmen, and writing a new fundraising document, he gradually recognized that appeals to high standards made little impact. He and his campaign colleague, Howard Wilson, found themselves instead trying to dream up exciting faculty projects that might catch the attention of individual donors.

Locating those potential contributors was not easy. When Holmes had sought funds with University endorsement twenty years before, the visiting committee had been his main source of money and contacts. But in 1938 no wealthy individuals were committed to the School. In these dismal circumstances Holmes tried to emulate the popular Harvard strategy of appointing wealthy "associates," who would make small annual donations in return for policy briefings about educational issues. The short-range gains might not be great, but seeds would be sown to bear larger fruit later on. Much of Holmes's energies during 1937-38 were spent finding associates, and by the spring he and Wilson had raised $8000 in contributions.

The only quick way to raise a large endowment was through the foundations. In 1938 the School approached the Carnegie Foundation, the Guggenheim Foundation, and the General Education Board. The last seemed most promising, for the Board had both founded the School and recently made a major gift to Chicago's department of education. But Conant's personal appeal for a $2 million endowment was an embarrassing failure. Robert J. Havighurst of the board's staff laconically explained that there was a fair amount of agreement that Harvard was not the best school of education in the country. Other foundation approaches met similar fates.[23]

After the General Education Board turned the School down, Holmes and Wilson reluctantly concluded that a three-year endowment campaign could not succeed. "We need first to 'prove our ability,'" Wilson reasoned, "and to strengthen our contacts through the successful completion of a series of smaller projects . . . In effect, good public relations are more important for us right now than are appeals for large funds." Endowment would flow only after visible progress had been demonstrated. The only way such progress could conceivably be financed was through direct subsidies from the Corporation. By the fall of 1938 the School's fundraising strategy had shifted from soliciting external monies to persuading Conant to back the institution as a deficit operation. When the president balked at guaranteeing four new tenured positions, the situation became critical. Holmes was at the end of his rope.[24]

Never had his endemic optimism been put more to the test. With the precious reserve ever dwindling, even the "disgraceful" status quo could not be long maintained without additional funds. If Conant would not step in when wealthy individuals and foundations stood aside, could a professional school of education survive at Harvard? Institutional disruption seemed imminent. Spaulding lashed out at Holmes for his failure to raise money, failure to gain Conant's confidence, and failure to move the School forward in repute or influence. He planned to resign and by February 1939 had a firm offer from Chicago. All the labor of thirty years, Holmes complained, had brought forth nothing more than a "bob-tailed mouse with the rickets."

Even as he sought inspiration for one final effort to move the president's feelings, the initiative he had held since 1911 began to pass from his hands. Without his knowledge, Conant decided to argue the School's case before the Corporation. Conant asked Spaulding to write sections of his annual presidential report on the justification for a Harvard graduate school of education. In the spring of 1939, Conant offered Spaulding the deanship if he would reject Chicago. Then he secured Corporation approval of a $100,000 subsidy to enable the School to prove its worth. In those tense weeks Holmes helped Conant's plans as best he could. The humiliation of losing the deanship was nothing compared with the greater humiliation of the School's possible abolition. Indeed, Conant later recalled that Holmes himself suggested that Spaulding be made dean to keep him and keep the School. With Spaulding's concurrence, Conant made his appointment effective in 1940 to allow Holmes to complete two decades as dean and return gracefully to his professorship.[25]

THE ANNOUNCEMENT of Holmes's retirement from the deanship released a torrent of pent-up faculty resentment over his leadership. Almost everyone agreed that fifteen years of smugness about standards had to end. The problem was not that actual standards were too high. Frederick Nichols perceptively observed that they were not half as high as Holmes claimed, and that the actual content of most courses had not been affected at all by either the 1927 or the 1936 reorganization. The real problem was that Harvard talked too much about standards, and looked down its nose at other institutions too often and too conspicuously. "We take too much delight in implementing our standards," Nichols complained, "in ways which create ill will, misunderstanding, and unfavorable publicity." Never again, he counseled Spaulding, should the School be tempted to become "educational flagpole sitters, refusing to come down until the pole rots under us." John Brewer recalled Judd's comment that the School's establishment enabled the profession to don a dress suit. To this, Holmes's efforts had only added a "very high hat."[26]

Resentment focused especially on Holmes's conviction that a small student body was the inevitable price for maintaining high standards. To others that policy only guaranteed demoralizingly small classes, erosion of professional influence, and financial disaster. Spaulding agreed with his colleagues that endowment was not the only source of new income. More students had to be found. He was far less confident than Holmes that exclusive attention to curriculum building could be justified by improved faculty esprit or "forming" students in dramatic ways. Instead of a calculated training philosophy, Spaulding thought the curriculum should express the professional and research enthusiasms of the faculty. Moreover, he regarded elaborate degree requirements and examinations less as a guarantor of standards than as a barrier that discouraged able students from applying. Professor Robert Ulich, one of Holmes's closest friends, agreed that "we guide too much and select too little."[27]

In 1940 the faculty began to dismantle the final tests which embodied all that remained of Holmes's dreams. At first the five required examinations in the fundamental fields came under attack. How, the faculty asked, did these tests differ from the final examinations in regular courses most students took to prepare for them? Did they really cover education's "basics"? Why was Holmes so sure that course credits had no relation to achievement, while scores on the general examination did? Why did the School insist that students who had successfully completed courses in the basics at other institutions prove their mettle again in the Harvard tests? There was no reason to surrender to mediocrity, Nichols claimed, but on the other hand the School could no longer ignore the "critical situation that has resulted in part from a somewhat idealistic program which is beyond the demands of the times or the possibilities of the economic situation in which we have been and still are faced." Spaulding suggested that the five examinations be dropped, that material in them be covered through the remaining comprehensive paper, and that this test be placed at the end of the Ed.M. program rather than at its beginning. The changes were quickly approved, but most faculty members were still not satisfied.

Spaulding himself initiated the final assault on the objective comprehensive examination in 1941. A special faculty committee charged that the examination discredited work in education done elsewhere, imposed in effect a delayed entrance requirement, and falsely downgraded the value of existing basic courses in the School.

Even the elaborate statistical researches on reliability and validity seemed only to suggest that more research was needed. Experts like Phillip Rulon and Truman Kelley doubted that the test was a significant advance beyond thoughtful course examinations. When weighed against the need to attract additional students, maintenance of the comprehensive paper seemed indefensible. In early 1942 the examination was abolished and the Ed.M. was made routinely available in one year of study. Apart from an essay special-field examination, Ed.M. requirements were essentially the same as they had been in 1920. The School's new catalogue proudly assured prospective students that standards for success no longer differed "appreciably from those of other universities."[28]

More dismantling remained to be done even after the examination demon was exorcised. Throughout the thirties Holmes clung to the Harvard ideal that the master's degree was the highest practitioner degree in education and that the doctorate was a research degree. Outside Cambridge, however, the Ed.D. had become primarily a practitioner's degree. As doctoral programs for practitioners proliferated everywhere else, Harvard awarded in the thirties fewer than half the Ed.D. degrees it gave a decade before. Reasonable men could no longer argue in 1940 that any Harvard action could protect the Ed.D. from practitioner contamination. Spaulding proposed creating an intermediary degree or certificate between Ed.M. and Ed.D. Others urged that the Ed.D. be offered in certain fields without any dissertation at all.[29]

Holmes's failure was unambiguous, but whether his basic error lay in conception or execution remains unclear. Most colleagues, like James E. Russell years earlier, saw few parallels between educating educators and educating practitioners in more established professions. Holmes's uncritical endorsement of Lowell's pressure to model the School on elitist training patterns had, they believed, only ensured its rapid demise. No incentives arose to furnish students for the elaborate education Holmes insisted on. Schoolmen preferred part-time mid-career training because it maximized career benefits at minimum cost.

Nor would school boards provide financial incentives to hire "formed" educators. The analogy between education and professions like law rested on the assumption that people would pay to solve educational problems just as people paid to win lawsuits, increase profits, and save lives. But there was no evidence that society placed a comparable value on education. The enormous attention Holmes gave to distinguishing between better-qualified and less-qualified professionals seemed beside the point. Why spend so much time "overeducating" students when there was no greater demand for them than for those educated in conventional ways?

Holmes, moreover, spent most of his energies defining and assessing general qualities that educators should possess rather than defining what educational problems individuals with such qualifications could solve. Even those within Harvard sympathetic to raising professional standards often disagreed with Holmes's priorities. Dissatisfied with science and technique, Holmes pushed instead for broad understanding and informed judgment as central professional outcomes. He hoped to transform the profession so that professionals could produce free and socially responsible young men and women. Ultimately, the skills he most valued were moral rather than technological.

Conant would have settled in these years for mere craftsmanship in teacher education, but Holmes would not. He suggested that professional training might not be needed at all if craftsmanlike teachers were all that was wanted. Even his own colleagues were exasperated by the apparent vagueness of his moral objectives. Faculty members in administration, for example, would have preferred more focused emphasis on management or human relations skills than on broad perspectives in philosophy, sociology, or psychology. Despite its preoccupation with training, the reorganization made no effort to upgrade the technical fields. If the School had to be obsessed with final assessment, some wondered, why did it not assess skills that employers wanted to buy?

Holmes resisted applying any of these perspectives to the wreckage of his deanship. The argument that the marketplace would not support higher standards had been made, he knew, when the Harvard Business School first opened. But its graduates had proved their skill and were now in great demand. Nothing dissuaded him from the conviction that the same process was possible in education, although he confessed that the obstacles were far greater than he had imagined. Perhaps he was most disappointed by the failure of his own profession to respond to his many calls. He had been unable to break the "cake of custom" that surrounded existing training. Educators weakly accepted the "perfunctory character about the process of accumulating 'credits' toward degrees and teachers' licenses."

They accepted too the idea that public schools were little more than "happy hunting grounds for jobs" even more in 1940 than they did in 1925. Holmes angrily attacked his profession for its alleged absorption with the externals of self-interest — better pay, pensions, tenure laws, efficiency in administration — rather than with its possible impact on the lives of children and the achievement of a just and cooperative society. Like Joseph Lee, Holmes emphasized the spiritual impact of educators. Excessive concern for material gain, like excessive reliance on the application of scientific treatments, seemed destined to destroy the moral force of the profession. Somehow a "wind from some horizon of a larger view of human values" was needed to blow across schools of education. Where it might come from he could not say.

He took greatest solace from the belief that his efforts had not really failed, because they had never really been implemented. He blamed his colleagues for the absence of a truly collaborative attack on the problems of curriculum. They had been unable to agree on the basics until Conant's pressure to create the M.A.T. forced a consensus in 1936, but the core survived his retirement from the deanship only by weeks. Lowell had betrayed him by demanding higher standards in training but supporting neither morale-boosting promotions nor the construction of the campus so essential for painstaking "formation." The Depression destroyed income and enrollment at just the time when Holmes thought final tests might surmount all earlier difficulties.

In the end, the enormous pressures of reconciling Harvard expectations with those of the profession proved too much for him. Equally loyal to Harvard tradition and to the importance of all school practitioners, his effort to link the two through an ideology of elite training was unsuccessful. Colleagues saw only a weak-willed surrender of professional values to aristocratic ones. Ironically, Lowell and Conant also regarded him as too compliant. Faced almost daily with the simultaneous complaint that the School's standards were too high and too low, Holmes finally did not know what more he could do. He had kept the faith through times of trouble, and was convinced that the training ideals he exemplified would emerge again some day. Subjected to unusual collegial vituperation, he bore the brunt of blame for the frustration of many professional lives around him.[30]

9

The Lure
of Social Science

For two decades all the School's energies to cultivate impact, reputation, and stability had focused on the training of large numbers of practitioners. In the early 1920s Harvard met as best it could the perceived training needs of schoolmen; then it tried more assertively to shape schoolmen. From the dismal failure of both efforts many faculty members learned a bitter lesson they would not soon forget: the path to institutional survival led away from any preoccupation with professional training.

Even before Holmes surrendered the deanship, the emphasis of his abortive fundraising campaign shifted from the rhetoric of formation to interdisciplinary applied research. The technical expertise of a limited number of able students, grounded equally in research skill and their own experience, seemed more important than the general analytic skill of an undifferentiated mass of educators. As had always been true before, these shifts of emphasis derived from tendencies in the University as a whole. They flowed especially from Conant's growing interest in the social utility of the social sciences.

Despite Conant's early preoccupation with academic teacher education, his sense of the School's proper mission began to assume a wholly different form as the economic depression continued and the danger of European fascism grew. A cautious and pessimistic man who saw American possibilities constrained by rigid class divisions, Conant feared social disruption unless equality of opportunity was deliberately engineered by the public school system. He thought social science could provide tools to enable schools to replace the frontier as the engine of social mobility. Dean Francis T. Spaulding was cautiously excited by Conant's vision and indeed had contributed to it. Like Hanus and Holmes before him, he rode a wave of presidential enthusiasm in the hope of linking education permanently with larger Harvard interests.

The pace of change seemed abruptly checked by America's entry into World War II. Spaulding's brief forays to develop cross-faculty applied research programs were put aside and Spaulding himself departed for Washington soon after Pearl Harbor. The School's activities were disrupted as never before. Instead of enjoying a small University subsidy to enable it to start new enterprises, it was ordered to make ends meet on its own and was forced to "live off the country" by attracting as many tuition-paying bodies as possible. But despite these shocks, the war unexpectedly accelerated the tentative research beginnings. Federal contracts and war-related consulting fostered far greater faculty research activity than ever before. Internal redistributions of faculty power during the war, and the retirement of many senior professors at the end of it, eventually created an unprecedented faculty majority in favor of research.

Above all, Conant's wartime experiences reinforced and confirmed his prewar suspicion that social science (he meant social anthropology, social psychology, sociology, economics, and political science) could transform postwar American society. Even Harvard's most famous wartime educational product, the report on *General Education in a Free Society*, interested Conant less for its educational theorizing than for its conviction that a core curriculum could inculcate in youth a common faith in the American political and economic system. He privately complained that the report was too philosophical in tone, and not sufficiently explicit on how the schools could promote social mobility.

Yet Conant was always hesitant to turn the Graduate School of Education into a research institute pure and simple. To the consternation of some researchers in the School, Conant's enthusiasm was confined to the newer social sciences and did not include more traditional fields such as educational psychology. Moreover, he hardly wished to admit defeat in his public advocacy of university-wide responsibility for teacher education, and he always appreciated the leverage held by school administrators. But when Spaulding resigned the deanship at the end of the war, Conant despaired of ever making cross-faculty cooperation in teacher education work. Only then did he reluctantly decide to reorient the School wholly toward social science. He failed in a two-year effort to persuade a distinguished social scientist to take the deanship, but in the attempt found an energetic young administrator willing to carry the task through. In 1948 Francis Keppel set out to rebuild the School as a "center of thought" where social science wisdom would be directly applied to educational practice.

THE ENDOWMENT CAMPAIGN of 1937-38 forced the School to justify its existence in ways that might attract support. The deceptive security of endowment had earlier allowed it to spurn the marketplace sensitivity of Warburg and Filene in favor of the higher ground of professional formation. But by the late 1930s Holmes was obliged to *sell* that higher ground as a sound philanthropic investment. Always indefatigable at written exposition, his last annual reports were primarily advertising pleas to an amorphous constituency of wealth. Over and over he stressed how a formed educator could diagnose and treat the learning problems of individuals and also apply wise social theory to curriculum policy. But institutional justification that emphasized characteristics of well-trained professionals generated little interest. The practical problem was to find more compelling notions of mission on which the School's claims for support could be based.[1]

The most obvious marketing gambit, in the midst of the Depression, was to explore the connections between university activity and the amelioration of pressing social problems. The New Deal did not invent the idea that national economic dilemmas could be remediated through rational expert planning and the application of academic scholarship, but it gave it great impetus across Harvard University. Besides the well-publicized migration of several professors to Washington, no less than six graduate programs intending to prepare for government service were installed at Harvard in the mid-thirties. Lucius Littauer, moreover, provided Conant with an endowment to establish an entirely new graduate school for public service. Departmental competition for Littauer money, along with Conant's characteristic bias toward cross-faculty collaboration, produced plans to coordinate several faculties' research in what Conant called the social sciences toward the "larger problems of policy and administration with which modern governments are confronted."[2]

Yet for most of the thirties Holmes resisted applying this perspective to the future of the Graduate School of Education. At the outset of his career he had warmly endorsed educational science. But in the twenties he concluded that science offered only technical solutions to problems that were largely ethical, and it concentrated excessive power in the hands of a few authorities rather than in the mass of practitioners. For years he regarded a research mission as an easy but irresponsible means to secure University prestige. Assembling an eminent scholarly faculty was little more than an advertising dodge to avoid the tough problem of guaranteeing professional development.

The research record actually accumulated by the School seemed only to confirm the wisdom of its neglect. From 1922 until the mid-thirties, most research had been associated with Walter Dearborn's Harvard Growth Study. By 1934, all data were collected and final analysis neared completion. Yet senior Harvard officers, including Dearborn himself, were disappointed with the results. Despite prodigious data on 1553 children, there were no startling revelations, no discoveries of arresting correlations between physical and intellectual development, no patterns of deviation from previously found patterns of growth. Even worse, the original research design had not included measures of social development which assumed in the thirties much greater significance within psychology. For all the benefits of longitudinal analysis, Dearborn was trapped by the transience of his own categories. He neglected the study in its later stages — the final analysis was not published until 1941 — and quietly revived his earlier interest in reading disabilities. By then Holmes had lost confidence in Dearborn's research potential.[3]

Holmes's regard for the educational uses of measurement research was no higher. Truman Kelley's mathematical contributions to statistical methodology, especially in developing factor analysis, were in fact noteworthy but virtually unknown within the Graduate School of Education. Kelley cared deeply about the practical consequences of his work: his dream was to discover a structure of independent mental traits in order to allocate talent rationally and make guidance an exact applied science. His self-confidence and scientific determinism — he aspired to be the Darwin of the mind — frightened humanists like Holmes who respected his intellect but questioned its social implications. Where, wondered Holmes, did Kelley allow for emotion, drive, or purpose, or the possibility of social change? Kelley in turn angrily blamed his failure to produce the promised breakthrough on lack of financial support from the School's administration. Troubled by attracting few students and recurrent asthma, he spent just one full year at the School of Education between 1935 and 1941. The principal area of agreement between Kelley and his deans was their mutual wish to transfer his appointment to the faculty of arts and sciences. True to his social philosophy to the end, Kelley's will stipulated that the size of his sons' inheritance be determined by the IQ scores of the women they married.[4]

His diminished regard for Dearborn and Kelley notwithstanding, Holmes's anti-research bias could not withstand the pressures caused by the School's extreme fiscal distress. More dependent than ever on Conant's active support, he quickly discerned the president's growing interest in how interdisciplinary inquiry might change government policy and administration. He coveted some piece of Littauer money to prop up his moribund program in school administration, and urged the creation of new courses on taxation, public finance, and public administration to make that part of the School seem more worthy of Littauer largesse. Of course educational policy was hardly a national priority during the New Deal, and the new Graduate School of Public Administration had no intention of making education a serious part of its program. But Holmes glimpsed the philanthropic possibilities of greater involvement by the School of Education in educational policy at the state level.[5]

Holmes's reassessment of the possibilities of educational inquiry was directly stimulated by a study of secondary education in New York State conducted by Spaulding for the Board of Regents. There was nothing novel in Spaulding's utilitarian hope that the main job of high schools was to teach pupils to "*do* many things . . . of a practical and not purely intellectual sort." What mattered was his commitment to finding out whether high school graduates actually possessed the social skills of citizenship, good use of leisure, and vocation. Unlike Hanus, who a quarter century before had espoused social-efficiency goals but had access only to fledgling achievement tests in more traditional academic subjects like arithmetic, Spaulding wanted to compare social aims with the "actual outcomes" of education.

In Spaulding's study Holmes correctly discerned a tougher notion of schooling's responsibilities than men like Hanus had entertained. Accountability lay not merely in providing certain services or in professing certain objectives. Public authority should now guarantee that education "really *works*." Spaulding's focus on results rather than opportunities, utilizing a variety of tests, questionnaires, interviews, and school reports, provided ample documentation for his shocking conclusion that high schools made little impact on adult social competence. Holmes seized on Spaulding's study as a marketable example of how Harvard expertise could expose a basic educational dilemma. He reminded men of means how poorly high school students were prepared for the tasks of vocation and citizenship, and how little they learned about economics at a time when strident political threats to the American economic system were apparent from both left and right. Such problems of school effectiveness, Holmes now began to argue, could be solved only by research. The financial means to conduct that research seemed, by the end of 1937, the "central need" of the Graduate School of Education.[6]

Inquiry and planning became central themes in the fundraising campaign. Holmes enlisted the help of a newly arrived professor of the philosophy of education, Robert Ulich, to write a proposal for an Institute for Educational Research. The institute's themes—scholarly collaboration among different disciplines and across departmental boundaries, and a distinct hostility to narrow notions of educational science based in psychology and measurement—were consistent with the career biases Ulich had accumulated in pre-Hitler Germany. They also meshed perfectly with Holmes's old prejudices and new needs. The final version of Harvard's 1938 proposal to the General Education Board merged Ulich's suggestion with the programmatic focus on "educational policy and management" derived from Littauer discussions and Spaulding's New York study.

The new themes had clear implications for professional training. The General Education Board proposal, borrowing freely from ideas in other Harvard faculties, emphasized that cross-faculty research would be enriched by the presence of non-degree fellows who would be "persons in key positions in the schools." Their political potency and proximity to research activity would aid rapid dissemination of research findings. The idea of attracting advanced students who were not candidates for degrees expressed an emerging belief that the insights students brought with them upon entrance, together with their likely subsequent influence, were more signifi- cant than elaborate degree-granting training programs for large masses of professionals. Holmes never admitted that, even before his own deanship terminated, he had tacitly endorsed Charles Judd's old emphasis on research and elite expertise.[7]

Applied research began to be incorporated not only in fundrais- ing rhetoric but in institutional policy following important shifts in Conant's thinking about high schools. At first he regarded them as "selective machinery" to "sort out those who can profit most by four years of college and a subsequent professional training." Bolstering this meritocratic position by reference to Jeffersonian ideals of a natural aristocracy of talent, Conant spoke again and again of the need to select for college on the basis of intellectual ability rather than because of economic status or geographic residence. He de- vised a program of national scholarships to raise the level of aca- demic ability in Harvard College. The new Scholastic Aptitude Test, along with intensive interviewing, facilitated the discovery of talented youth without regard to the nature of the secondary educa- tion they had received. At times Conant mildly criticized the public schools for emphasizing education for citizenship more than educa- tion for leadership — in effect for allowing the selective machinery to grow rusty. But the emphasis on aptitude to select Harvard national scholars meant that success did not really depend on the quality of schooling at all. High schools did not have to be good for Harvard to raise up academic talent from the surrounding rubbish. School re- form was not, at first, an essential component of Conant's merito- cratic policy.[8]

During 1938 Conant came to know Spaulding far more intimately than before. On Holmes's initiative, he had been included in many presidential policy discussions and had accompanied Conant on speaking trips for the fundraising campaign. Impressed by Spaul- ding's tact, decisiveness, and thoughtful advocacy of the needs of secondary students not bound for college, Conant turned to him at the end of 1938 for assistance on his crucial annual report which de- fended the existence of a school of education at Harvard. In the end most of what Spaulding drafted was not used. Conant's main theme continued to be that public secondary education was the selective machinery to propel talented boys toward Harvard.

Yet Spaulding's influence was felt in two important ways. Conant's report almost entirely ignored Holmes's traditional arguments for high standards in professional training. And, for the first time, Conant admitted that the selective machinery of the schools could not work at full efficiency unless universities like Harvard understood the functions of secondary education that did not involve college preparation. It was hardly in Harvard's self-interest to ignore the powerful nonacademic pressures in schools that shaped their culture. Yet university faculties blithely ignored the "new problems of administration, of pedagogy, of educational statesmanship, forced upon the country by the sheer weight of numbers in our public high schools." There was no question, Conant wrote, "that the study of education as a social process — quite apart from the training of teachers — is as important as the study of law or of business administration."[9]

Conant's conception of education as a social process matured during 1939 as he grew more sensitive to threats against the American political and economic system. A firm defender of capitalist free enterprise at home, and a staunch foe of Nazi expansion abroad, Conant was preoccupied by the apparent fragility of American democracy. Democracy was not a self-perpetuating virus adapted to any particular body politic but a special type of organism requiring specific nutrients. One indispensable nutrient seemed increasingly absent from democracy's diet: the opportunity to improve one's lot in the society, or what Conant called social mobility.

Conant's social thought was permeated by the view, common in the thirties, that American growth in all senses had come to an end and would be replaced by a static period. The frontier had closed, immigration had ceased, the population was stable, and rapid industrialization was over. In the previous century of rapid growth, raw talent might have risen through a variety of informal channels. Now talent was in danger of being forced into rigid grooves predetermined by parental economic status. At first, Conant used his social pessimism merely to promote Harvard's national scholarship program. But after war began in Europe in late 1939, he spoke more generally of the high school as the "substitute for the frontier . . . to provide social mobility." In a static society, the high school was the key to prevent a "hereditary aristocracy of wealth" and to restore a free and classless society. In several major addresses Conant emphasized that the mobility and opportunity he had in mind were no longer confined to the natural aristocracy of intellect. All types of ability should be encouraged. At the same time, the softening of class divisions required not only a commitment to equality of opportunity but a commitment to provide all students with a common background. Youth had to be made loyal to American ideals of freedom and individualism.[10]

Not even Eliot had defined a more pressing mission for the public schools. Social danger stalked the land. The school system was nothing less than a "new type of social instrument" that had to be commandeered for the public good. Such presidential rhetoric soared beyond anything that Holmes or Spaulding had written, linked educational research with reform more tightly than ever before, and generated immense optimism within the School that the dark years of financial crisis would soon end. Conant's friend and personal assistant, A. Calvert Smith, even concluded that the potential of the Graduate School of Education was greater than any other part of Harvard. Neither Smith nor Conant was thinking of the training of teachers. The task of increasing social mobility through schooling was one for planners, administrators, researchers, and experts on complex social manipulation. As first priorities Conant urged the new dean to make the acquaintance of young Harvard social scientists such as Clyde Kluckhohn and Talcott Parsons, to consider a faculty appointment in sociology, and to plan an expansion and redirection of the School's efforts in guidance.[11]

DESPITE CONANT's dramatic conversion to the social significance of schooling and the School of Education, the overriding institutional reality in 1940 remained financial instability. When Conant introduced Spaulding to the faculty as dean-elect, he used the occasion bluntly to warn that, unless substantial new income was raised by 1944, the School's "liquidation" would be seriously considered. Fiscal underwriting by the Corporation was only a temporary measure; institutional survival was still in doubt. Privately Conant and Spaulding agreed to give prime attention over the next two years to developing dramatic new initiatives. Two years of fundraising would then follow. It was imperative to mount projects that would quickly produce impressive results. The conduct of research, Spaulding told his colleagues, would be his first concern. Decisively repudiating older ideals, he attributed quality instruction at a school of education "in very large measure [to] what its faculty does besides teaching." The key to developing an exciting research capacity was close collaboration with scholars already working in other Harvard faculties.[12]

Administration, and especially the subfield of educational finance, seemed the most promising area of collaborative program development. Holmes's efforts to pry loose Littauer money had largely failed, but two successful summer conferences on finance had been conducted. The conferences stressed equitable state school support and deliberately sought out public administrators who often had not concerned themselves before with school finance. Spaulding used the conferences for faculty recruitment and invited the more impressive participants to submit position papers on initiatives the School of Education might take in school finance. He found most interesting the suggestions of John F. Sly, a prominent national consultant on state taxation, lecturer on politics at Princeton, and former faculty member in the Harvard department of government.[13]

Sly's analysis sharply distinguished between capacity to manage routine internal operations of school systems which Harvard training in school administration traditionally emphasized, and capacity to address technical problems of school taxation. The latter was basic to the very existence of schools, but required knowledge of governmental processes that had nothing to do with schools. A new kind of educational administrator was required, Sly argued. Though not a lawyer, he needed to understand legal method. Though not an accountant, he needed to understand the language of accountancy. Though not a statistician, he needed to evaluate statistical reports and apply them to public problems. Though not a mathematician, he needed to use mathematical notation in the interest of concise demonstration. The proper training of such administrative experts—which among other things presumed knowledge of calculus—could best occur in a research environment dominated by problems of public finance and public law. Sly never belittled the traditional task of internal school management, but though experience developed better management skills than did formal university study. Harvard's special role in administration should be mainly to conduct research and transmit research skills to experienced senior practitioners.

Sly's ideas were very controversial. The New Jersey state superintendent of education, for example, implored Spaulding to entrust school administration only to individuals who were "inbred with the spirit of the teaching profession" rather than to "economists and research people." Inside the faculty Brewer and Nichols made the same plea. But Spaulding was impressed by Sly and his support from the Harvard government department. He wanted colleagues with ideas that could have an immediate public impact — he had always thought the School's fundamental lack was a faculty that would "blaze from the Atlantic to the Pacific" — and he explored the idea of appointing Sly to establish the program. Already well settled at Princeton, Sly providentially received a full professorship in the midst of his Harvard discussions. Still, he was persuaded to become part-time consultant to help develop his ideas into a new Program for Research, Service and Instruction in Educational Administration.

The full-time job he refused eventually went to another participant in the summer conferences, Alfred Dexter Simpson, assistant commissioner for finance in the New York State Department of Education. Thereafter Sly's research interests became subordinated to Simpson's desire to establish intimate working relations between the School and state departments of education, and to conduct surveys on state problems concerning educational finance. By 1941 the number of institutional consulting projects in administration was far greater than ever before. Most were funded from the School's own budget and had no research intent, but Spaulding confidently looked forward to the work's becoming self-supporting, even profitable, and more research-oriented. A happy omen was that the offices of the new program were not in the School's quarters at Lawrence Hall but in the new building of the Graduate School of Public Administration.[14]

Just as Spaulding reached out to the government department for advice on a research emphasis in administration, he reached out to other Harvard social scientists to invigorate educational psychology. He and Holmes had agreed since 1938 that interests other than Dearborn's had to be cultivated. Spaulding's central question was how high school students could develop the capacities needed to cope with the practical responsibilities of adult life. Programmatically, that meant a focus on normal individuals rather than on those with various disabilities, on adolescents rather than young children, and on the effects of unintentional social learning as well as deliberate school instruction.

The social anthropologist Clyde Kluckhohn advised that "we know a good deal about the technique of education—in the sense of the technique of imparting information. But we know scandalously little about the processes by which youngsters are *socialized*, about the processes by which ideals are transmitted and reinforced, by which characters are formed and characteristic personality types shaped." Spaulding was urged to seek young faculty prospects not at Teachers College, as Holmes had first intended to do, but rather at Yale's Institute of Human Relations. There he found C. Hobart Mowrer, who had little direct educational experience but agreed to work with Kluckhohn and Henry Murray on research problems of adolescent socialization. Spaulding also persuaded Conant to establish a cross-faculty committee to consider collaborative efforts in school guidance and agreed to shelter I. A. Richards' Commission on English Language Studies, in hopes that it might stimulate collaborative research efforts with the English department.[15]

No problem of faculty collaboration was more complex than that posed by the master of arts in teaching program. Spaulding pushed immediately to shorten the time required to complete the M.A.T. and to ease subject-matter requirements. The English department, on the other hand, was disturbed about reports of declining interest in secondary school English and growing nefarious control of state certification requirements by schools of education. To dispose finally of such troubling conflicts, Conant created a committee cochaired by Spaulding and Professor of English Howard Mumford Jones.

The "Committee on the Training of Secondary School Teachers, Especially with Reference to English" was a surprising triumph of good feeling despite its origins. Spaulding, working cooperatively and pleasantly with the equally pragmatic Jones, succeeded in shaping discussions not around the competing claims of education and English as sources of knowledge for English teachers, but around interpretations of data on the actual status of English in American high schools. With Holmes judiciously omitted from the committee's membership, hardly anything was said about the maturity and importance of education as a field. Indeed, Robert Ulich's singular contribution to the discussions was to make the reverse point that educational science had advanced little beyond profitless aping of mathematics and the natural sciences. Only 9 of the final report's 138 pages treated education as Education.

As the committee pored over its data, took field trips to inspect teacher education in the South and Midwest, and conducted interviews with experienced schoolteachers, the problem of perpetuating literary values in a mass school system became painfully apparent. The more public secondary education was analyzed, the more its "English" needs seemed to be basic skills in reading and writing. But these needs, about which substantial consensus existed within the committee, diverged dramatically from what English departments like Harvard's cared about. A mood of growing sympathy for the problem was accompanied by a sense of helplessness to do anything about it. Theodore Morrison of the English department, in a trenchant internal memorandum, argued that the center of gravity in secondary school English had shifted from "literature as the foundation of a polite tradition" to "language as an instrument of social adaptation." Morrison believed that this shift made sense for most students. But, as Jones noted, university English departments wished only to educate an intellectual elite and believed that the teaching of literature was the highest purpose they could serve.

The committee's deliberations became increasingly paralyzed as it sought to establish whether the work of the Harvard English department was at all relevant to secondary English for most pupils. For three years it issued no report, and for over a year met not at all, because it imagined no constructive recommendations. Confronted with such disparity in goals, the English department showed little enthusiasm for reestablishing collegiate control over secondary English. Its representatives agreed that the problem of secondary English was indeed important, but it was not *their* problem. Only America's entry into World War II, and the impending disruption of normal University activities, brought pressure on the group to bring its work to an end. The final report could only "note the complexity of the problem" and urge more discussion and more conferences.

Tepid as this outcome seemed, it was to have lasting policy consequences. The years of meetings seemed to confirm that the "split" between education and the arts and sciences disciplines had not been an unfortunate accident that well-meaning men could repair, but rather a reasonable outcome of the simultaneous development of mass education and the modern university. The mid-thirties' ideological battles between Holmes and the English department gave way to a mutual willingness to explore the social problems that had changed secondary English. When the English department concluded that it could little affect those problems, its need to protect the "standards" of the M.A.T. vanished.

Everyone agreed, in addition, that a degree program with so few students was absurd. The academic requirements that had made the English M.A.T. more difficult to secure than the English A.M. were gradually eliminated, as were the equally cumbersome education examinations. Requirements were eased in other M.A.T fields as well. By early 1942 the M.A.T. was presumed to be a one-year degree. It was further agreed to rely more on admissions decisions than on program requirements to assure quality control. In the future, the usual role of the academic departments toward teacher education would be benign toleration, with neither vigorous support nor active opposition.

Thus the English committee exposed the real difficulties in establishing collaborative links with arts and sciences departments representing subjects taught in secondary schools. In one sense, benign toleration played into Spaulding's hands; it was a personal triumph for his persuasive leadership style. He wanted to reduce cross-faculty acrimony and increase M.A.T. candidates, and these goals were clearly furthered by the committee's work. But he had failed to generate *intellectual* collaboration between education and the academic departments. No projects were undertaken comparable to Sly's reformulation of school administration, Mowrer's anticipated work in adolescent socialization, or the planned cross-faculty attack on school guidance. The basic lesson of the committee's work was that the future of collaboration with other departments and faculties, which during the twenties and thirties was largely exemplified by joint appointments in academic teacher education, would henceforth rest with the social sciences.[16]

Spaulding's initiatives by mid-1941 won for the School unprecedented public coverage in Archibald MacLeish's quasi-official

Atlantic Monthly defense of the Conant presidency. MacLeish characterized the main trends of Conant's leadership as "the tendency to break through the academic fences dividing fields of academic knowledge, and the tendency to recognize the function of the university in the modern world." The new activities at the School of Education were favorably cited as prime examples of these tendencies. But at the same time, America's growing role in the European war began to affect adversely the School's financial and programmatic prospects.[17]

The most immediate problem remained the size of the student body and the tuition income it provided. At first Spaulding fully agreed with Ulich's contention that the School guided too much and selected too little. He tried to raise standards through admissions decisions rather than through a structured curriculum. Just as he borrowed Conant's ideas about cross-faculty research collaboration, he also borrowed the president's ideas about training. Conant's major training initiatives—the Littauer fellowships in public administration and the Nieman fellowships in journalism—recruited successful and experienced practitioners who chose their own studies at Harvard rather than young novices who underwent a calculated training experience. Spaulding wanted to adapt this idea to school administration. He hoped also to attract larger numbers of well-educated students from upper-middle-class families.[18]

The pragmatic Spaulding never worried that selective admissions in some programs conflicted with maximizing enrollments in others. But after the Selective Service Act was passed in 1940, he understandably concentrated more on increasing numbers than on increasing quality. By the spring of 1941 he gloomily forecast an enrollment decline that could wipe out his precious Corporation subsidy for 1941-42. Following American entry into World War II, the Corporation canceled the subsidy plan and ordered the School immediately to balance its annual budget at whatever cost. Spaulding concluded, in an unhappy phrase later seized on by his opponents, that the war required the School to "live off the country."

The faculty then voted to offer courses for as little as one unit of credit, instead of the traditional four, and even to reduce the number of credits required for the Ed.M. in defiance of University statutes. Though part-time enrollments and tuition income rose through these lures, the additional income did not make up for the lost subsidy. Spaulding's new program initiatives had to be cut back. Almost all part-time and annual faculty appointments were terminated. Tenured and term appointees considered unessential for minimal operations were urged in the name of patriotism to take early retirement or unpaid leaves of absence. Marginal but crucial consultants like Sly could no longer be afforded. Projects like the committee to study guidance were dropped. Spaulding himself left for Washington in early 1942 to serve for the duration in the Information and Education Division of the army. His innovative deanship had lasted three semesters.[19]

Yet even as the war disrupted the five-year Corporation subsidy and Spaulding's careful plans for visible faculty accomplishments, the tendencies of the late 1930s continued in unplanned ways. As full-time student enrollments dropped to a low of seventeen in 1943 (although total tuition rose slightly through a combination of part-time enrollments and a new trimester schedule) the memory of the old ideal of professional formation rapidly receded. More important, the war provided unanticipated financial opportunities for the faculty to commence a variety of external research and service projects far beyond what Spaulding had imagined. Despite the reduction in faculty size brought on by dismissals, resignations, and leaves, the volume of institutional research and service actually increased in the war years. These activities included speechmaking and committee work on how education could promote the war effort, direct training of armed forces personnel through the Army Specialized Training Program, and psychological and statistical research under contract to various government agencies. Never before had the faculty of education been occupied with so many projects so unconnected with the professional training of schoolmen.[20]

As THE WAR-RELATED external activities of the faculty increased, institutional life within the Graduate School of Education became more tense. The sudden termination of the University subsidy, of Spaulding's deanship, and of Conant's personal preoccupation with education all raised up old anxieties about job security, prospects for advancement, coherent institutional purpose, and even subsequent institutional existence. Unsure how long Spaulding would be gone, he and Conant entrusted the acting deanship at first to

Holmes and then to Dearborn. Both moves proved disastrous, as opposition to their authoritarian styles provoked unprecedented faculty (and secretarial) threats of resignation. By mid-1943 Conant decided to appoint a younger acting dean with more than caretaker authority. Although most of the faculty would have preferred Nichols or Alfred Simpson to build trust and soothe tempers, Conant's practical options were confined to two vigorous and ambitious associate professors, Howard Wilson and Phillip Rulon.

After Spaulding, Howard Wilson had been Holmes's personal favorite among the younger faculty since he had joined the School as an instructor in 1928. A former high school social studies teacher, Wilson had proved remarkably energetic at writing school history texts, contributing to professional journals, speaking at educational gatherings, and serving on professional committees and commissions. At thirty-three he had been president of the National Council for the Social Studies, and was Holmes's chief lieutenant in the fundraising drive. During the war he expanded his involvement with citizenship education, emphasizing the school study of international relations in projects sponsored by the American Council on Education and the Carnegie Endowment for International Peace.

Wilson heartily approved of Spaulding's conviction that the School's influence and prosperity depended on the visibility of faculty projects. But he did not agree that these projects should emphasize research. What was most needed, he thought, was to expand "direct service" to education, an educational function "relatively new and its forms unstandardized." Wilson contemplated not simply conventional extension courses to meet local needs but an elaborate program of outreach. The effort would include aggressive solicitation of outside surveys and consultantships; a sustained search for effective methods of in-service training (such as intensive workshops); exploration of the educational uses of local agencies other than schools; and a broader commitment to the implementation of good ideas. Fundamentally, he saw educational problems as organizational dilemmas. Their solution required aggressive and creative entrepreneurship rather than systematic scholarly inquiry. In 1943 Wilson proposed a university-wide Center for Education in Citizenship, with himself as director, whose ambitious program of conferences, workshops, publications, and speeches might spearhead a national movement to promote citizenship education.

Wilson was more personable and less rigid than Brewer, but his scheme recalled the old tension between advocacy and analysis. Even in the late 1930s, Wilson had been counseled by Conant, Spaulding, and Ulich to reduce his speaking engagements and committee work in order to commence some substantial piece of research. Conant had enough confidence in Wilson to ask his participation in a major Harvard wartime project, a committee to study the objectives of general education in a free society. But Wilson, who had harshly criticized the nebulous accomplishments of the committee on the teaching of English, soon resigned from Conant's new committee on grounds that it too was preoccupied with lofty talk rather than with practical implementation. Despite an active campaign on his behalf by Holmes, Conant turned instead of Phillip Rulon to be acting dean.[21]

If Wilson felt that Spaulding overemphasized research to the detriment of implementation, Rulon was convinced that Spaulding's research moves did not go nearly far enough. Rulon, brought to Harvard by Truman Kelley in 1930 as an assistant, keenly felt the subsequent deemphasis of measurement and educational psychology. In contrast to these traditional centers of educational science, he found Spaulding's newer social sciences soft and undisciplined. Rulon had been skeptical of O. H. Mowrer's appointment in social psychology, dubious about the possibilities of a research focus in administration, and hesitant about the plans to refurbish rather than bury vocational guidance.

His own scholarly reputation rested on various evaluations of the effects of different instructional techniques. During the early 1940s, Rulon's confidence in the utility of measurement and the psychology of learning was buttressed by his personal success in obtaining major applied research contracts from the war and navy departments. The faculty's first wartime duty, he insisted, was to make similar direct technical contributions to the national effort. By contrast, Wilson's enthusiasm for new administrative structures seemed unscholarly and visionary.

Rulon and Spaulding maintained a satisfactory personal relationship, despite their policy differences, but Rulon's selection over the well-liked Wilson was generally unpopular. Many faculty and students feared or disliked him for his quick and sarcastic wit, aggressive and nonconforming personality, and unchecked faith in quantification as man's best hope to gain reliable educational knowledge. Neither Conant nor Spaulding foresaw how soon Rulon's restless impatience and insistence on precise formulations of institutional purpose would provoke an unprecedented internal debate on whether research should wholly dominate the activities of the Graduate School of Education.

Rulon's ire was triggered by the deliberations of several faculty search committees at work in late 1943. Among seven criteria listed for an appointment in secondary education, for example, research skill was mentioned only as one of several sources of evidence that a candidate was a "continuing learner." Equally important was evidence that he possess a good sense of humor "without unfortunate mannerisms of speech or conversation." Nichols hoped that his successor in vocational education could forge close ties to the Business School, but his objective was not research collaboration but maximizing enrollments in an anticipated postwar boom market for junior college business educators. The search for Brewer's successor was deadlocked between his firm antiscientism and Mowrer's wish to convert vocational guidance into psychotherapeutic counseling. The only common ground between these positions was Rulon's steadfast belief that both constituted intellectual mush.[22]

In early 1944 Rulon bluntly announced that the assumptions of all the search committees needed rethinking. The mistake, he argued, was to have defined faculty positions in terms of educational jobs or administrative divisions of educational functions. In the future all faculty positions should be defined instead by reference to educational *problems* needing solution. The central activity of all faculty members would then become research. In the thirties, the School asserted that a core curriculum could solve problems of course overlap, excessive instruction in job skills that might be learned more effectively through experience or apprenticeship, and insufficient attention to fundamental issues. Rulon's solution to the same problems lay in faculty appointment policy. A faculty of researchers would grapple with what he believed to be the basic question facing the School: how to bring up the next generation to be "acceptable" adults. The traditional focus on techniques of teaching or school management only led to an "unquestioning acceptance of the educational system of the country as is, without any reference to what the system ought to be."[23]

To Rulon it was also axiomatic that a successful research orientation required far more talented students than the School had previously enrolled. He had only contempt for the idea that a curriculum could produce a good product regardless of the quality of the raw materials. And he saw only self-defeating inconsistency in Spaulding's pragmatic efforts to build up research but also live off the country for short-term financial survival. The School could not have it both ways. Poor students invariably drove out research and researchers. Compromises on admission standards guaranteed only a "training mill" that met market needs, a second-rate student body that avoided serious courses (like his own), and a faculty that resembled the students. Rulon first championed the use of test scores as the most reliable criterion for admissions decisions at the Graduate School of Education. He was perfectly willing to accept a small research faculty if higher admissions standards led to reduced tuition income.

Everyone understood that no more basic attack on the School's appointment and admissions policies had ever been made. Holmes saw the threat and led the counterassault. What right, he asked forgetfully, did the School have to "impose" one individual's theoretical analysis of educational problems on the profession and public? Perhaps Rulon's ideas about the qualities needed in acceptable adults were interesting, but they represented after all only one possible formulation. Must not the work of a professional school be determined by the "way the profession we serve" was organized? Must not its mission be "strictly vocational," set by the "history of education as a profession, not by a theoretical analysis of education as a process occurring in the life of an individual"? He warned that policies which emphasized only research or problem solving would in the end lead to "widespread public derogation of the University and a shriveling up of the School."[24]

Only weeks from retirement, Brewer and Nichols wearily regarded Rulon's proposal as merely the latest unrealistic quest for "quality." Try as it might, the School could simply not wave away the history of the field of education as it attempted to resolve its "inferiority complex about the Harvard yard." Why deny the truth that most teachers did not have "what it takes" to apply to their day-to-day problems the complex knowledge Rulon wanted the curriculum to contain? Teachers *needed* cookbook specifics. If Rulon's standards were adopted, the familiar result would be that promising young educators would cease to attend. Brewer recalled he had "seen us twice put on a high hat, and later take it off again, and I should hate very much to see us repeat the experiment." And Nichols warned that a far worse fate than a research institute would be the illusion that a research-oriented faculty could successfully train leading school practitioners.[25]

Among the younger faculty members only Howard Wilson had a strong following and articulate opposing views. But his influence and morale were diminished when Rulon was promoted to full professor and Wilson passed over. When Wilson anxiously asked again about his proposed center for citizenship education, Rulon discouraged him and demanded that he produce a "fundamental treatise" if he too wished a full professorship some day. When Conant backed Rulon, Wilson resigned rather than endure the humiliating fate of so many other associate professors in the technical fields. By 1945 faculty attrition gave Rulon a majority generally sympathetic to his views.

Several administrative steps were thereafter taken to upgrade admissions requirements, reduce course overlap, and encourage enrollment in more general offerings. But Conant deferred basic decisions on appointment and admissions policy. Ironically the faculty shrunk precisely when the School experienced an unprecedented enrollment spurt in response to the GI Bill. As faculty capacity to deal with larger numbers dwindled, and no presidential mandate to implement his views materialized, Rulon grew restive and sought to resign the acting deanship. Holmes gloomily feared a complete collapse of morale if the School's future was not clarified. "Here we are, back nearly to the position we occupied from 1920 to 1927, yet without faculty or staff to do a good job, with quarters crowded and growing shabbier every year, and with no basic principles of operation which will make our program any better than that of any other important university department in our area." As a School, Holmes concluded, "we have little or nothing to be proud of."[26]

Conant had no intention of endorsing any major changes prior to Spaulding's return. But he also was unpersuaded by Rulon's analysis. In his policy suggestions and especially in his administrative manner, Rulon demonstrated neither interest in collaborative research across several faculties nor capacity to generate such cooperation. Where Spaulding actively initiated cooperation outside the faculty of education, Rulon possessed a bottomless ability to offend and alienate colleagues everywhere in the University. Conant never understood why Rulon took such sardonic pleasure in meeting with earthy directness the condescension toward the School of Education he routinely encountered. He seemed not merely to welcome hatred but assiduously to cultivate it. As an ambassador to the larger Harvard, Rulon was a complete disaster.[27]

Quite apart from the anxieties and resentments that such behavior probably expressed, Rulon doubted that much could be gained through collaboration with the faculty of arts and sciences. Just as he criticized his own colleagues for neglecting inquiry on educational problems, he also criticized suggestions that educational studies be organized around the categories of academic disciplines. His blustery service on both the M.A.T. administrative board and on the committee on the objectives of a general education convinced him that the interests of the two faculties were fundamentally different: one wanted to advance academic knowledge, the other to find out how to inculcate in youth needed adult skills. An acceptable adult knew about the world of nature, for example, but Rulon argued that this knowledge was not the same thing as knowledge of academic chemistry or academic biology. He was no anti-intellectual devotee of the old cardinal principles, which in fact he loathed, but instead wanted to marry the social-efficiency theme of discrete adult capacity with the cognitive resources of academic subjects. He regarded academic content as educationally indispensable, but academicians as enemies of the educational uses of their fields.[28]

Rulon also suspected close cross-faculty cooperation because he feared that education might be merged with the faculty of arts and sciences. Near the end of the war several schemes to reorganize the faculty of arts and sciences were publicly and privately considered. The dean of the Graduate School of Arts and Sciences, for example, wanted to expand his politically weak domain and suggested absorbing the Graduate School of Education as one promising strategy. Conant also considered breaking up the faculty of arts and sciences into smaller divisions better able to control departmental fiefdoms. A possible faculty of social sciences might have included education. Even though several of Rulon's research-oriented colleagues preferred some merger, the educational problems he had identified formed a "natural group" and to him made a separate school essential.[29]

Conant thought that Rulon not only undervalued cross-faculty collaboration but overvalued research. The training of teachers and other professional educators were important functions that should be continued. Conant had, after all, invented the M.A.T. degree to help bridge the gap between education and the arts and sciences in teacher education. In a major 1944 address on the fiftieth anniversary of Teachers College, he called anew for a "truce among educators." The old rigidities concerning degree requirements were gone. Conant attributed remaining frictions between the faculties to Rulon's tactlessness. They could be removed once the war ended and Spaulding was back in place.[30]

Further, Conant believed that progress in the realm of human relations depended more on the wisdom of social inventions like the M.A.T. than on the findings of experimental science. Although he fully recognized the contribution of educational research to, for example, the development of tests, he was extremely skeptical of claims that all educational processes could be studied by scientific methods. Too many variables could not be controlled. Wisdom and experience would therefore continue to be major sources of educational innovation. The preparation of wise professionals was essential.[31]

Conant further clarified his research position in the summer of 1945 when the possibility suddenly arose that Spaulding might never return to Harvard. About to leave his Washington job as Chief of the Education Branch of the army's Information and Education Division, Spaulding had been informally offered the New York state commissionership of education. The only way to keep him, Conant told the Corporation, was to continue along the lines agreed to in 1939 but with even greater emphasis on cooperation with the faculty of arts and sciences in training teachers and with a further strengthening of the School's professional position. Conant knew that Spaulding had no interest in presiding over a Harvard research institute. Either merger with arts and sciences or converting the School to something resembling a Brookings Institution would be disastrous.

Conant appealed to the Corporation to double the School's endowment to a total of $4 million and to allocate an additional million for a new physical plant. But the Corporation was divided on both the importance of education and the indispensability of Spaulding, and refused to authorize new commitments. Conant had failed and Spaulding resigned in the early fall. In the subsequent funereal atmosphere, Conant announced that he had lost not merely a battle but the entire war. He considered Spaulding's qualifications probably unique, especially his ability to make friends elsewhere in the University. Without him the School's capacity to generate exciting projects, which in turn would generate additional endowment and tuition income, seemed nonexistent. Conant gloomily feared that his only recourse was to devise some specialized field of activity to operate with a totally inadequate plant and endowment.[32]

SPAULDING'S LOSS provided an unexpected reprieve for Rulon's ideas. Conant delayed searching for a permanent dean in order to devise some new plan for the School's future that might win Corporation support. To that end he appointed a Corporation subcommittee, which asked Rulon to prepare a paper on long-range policy. Even Holmes, fearing that Conant would liquidate the School by merging it with arts and sciences, now threw his wholehearted support to Rulon. Ever ready to convert political necessity into moral certainty, Holmes claimed that only the department of education at Chicago had had the foresight to adopt the research emphasis Rulon proposed![33]

The resulting position paper of early 1946, called the "Purple Memorandum" because of the ink used to duplicate it, argued that the School's principal mission was to conduct research in six "basic and inevitable" areas: psychology; measurement, evaluation, and statistics; history, philosophy, and comparative education; educational administration; guidance and school personnel work; and problems of instruction. The memorandum took pains to stress that, despite the apparent conventionality of these categories, the School of the future would emphasize inquiry rather than job techniques. Courses in the field of instruction, for example, would not deal with procedures "which an intelligent person can learn in practice" but rather with "study of the transfer of the experiences and achievements of adult life into the area of childhood and youth."

Fifteen tenured or term appointments were needed to give proper attention to the six areas. Not only would this faculty require research support from the School's own funds—Rulon called for 10 percent of an estimated quarter-million-dollar basic budget to subsidize research expenses—it also needed protection from competing demands on its time. Although certain outside faculty activities such as major consultantships and service on policy boards were approved, most "direct service" to teachers and school systems could not be justified by the criterion of "lastingness of the influence."

Above all this faculty needed protection from a large and motley student body. "The lack of talent in many of these future workers," Rulon characteristically wrote of education students, "makes them an inferior investment of our time and energy. It simply cannot be said of the poor student that he is the best medium open to us for improving education in America." Only a small number of students who would "*foreseeably* influence education in the United States" should be admitted. Foreseeable influence as an admissions criterion, rather than intellectual ability alone, encouraged a training emphasis on careers in the "higher reaches of education where policies are made and guiding principles determined." The School would train for the "upper ranks," not for "rank and file" educational jobs. In practice, that meant abandonment of teacher education. But because of Conant's persistent advocacy of the M.A.T. the Purple Memorandum carefully avoided discussing teacher education. Yet there was little doubt that its authors hoped it would wither away.[34]

The Purple Memorandum was received with little enthusiasm. Some Corporation members viewed it as an unincisive plea to save an unimpressive senior faculty. Senior University officials whom Conant most trusted agreed with that judgment. Even the visiting committee, deathly quiescent ever since the 1927 reorganization, now revived to attack both the emphasis on research and the deemphasis of teachers. Its chairman, headmaster Perry Dunlap Smith of the Winnetka Day School, characterized research and the training of "educational technicians and 'petit' functionaries" as disastrous retreats from the main business of teacher education. The field of education already suffered from too much trivial research and too many high-salaried but ignorant "educators." What was needed was a commitment to develop the character and personality of prospective teachers through elaborate apprentice relations with outstanding master teachers. In rhetoric reminiscent of Barrett Wendell, Smith said the profession required "broad-minded, high-minded, well-rounded and well-bred individual [teachers] who know something about life and living." Other critics, less hostile to inquiry and less enamored of social breeding as the central variable in teacher development, still feared that research as Rulon envisioned it would squeeze out all forms of advanced professional preparation.[35]

Conant personally regarded the Purple Memorandum as much less ambitious than the School he had hoped Spaulding would build, but he found the narrowing of objectives prudent under the leaderless circumstances. The enrollments needed to pay for a larger faculty would only ensure perpetual low quality. Yet merger with arts and sciences would only give the correct impression of surrendering at a time when Conant had spoken so often about the importance of public education. Rulon had proposed a middle ground, and Conant now endorsed it.

The Purple Memorandum recommended a school of no more than a hundred full-time students, most of them doctoral candidates. If an additional $3 million in endowment could be raised, then 81 percent of annual income would derive from endowment. Dependence on tuition would be far less than before. At first Conant failed to persuade the Corporation to make any immediate addition to the School's endowment from University funds — his tentative suggestion of $500,000 was not accepted — but the Corporation eventually agreed to match on a dollar-for-dollar basis any outside contributions up to $1.5 million. Thus Rulon's program and budget estimate were accepted, but Harvard's support was contingent on Conant's ability to raise half the needed funds from outside.[36]

Conant's endorsement of a research-oriented school of education, albeit one that maintained teacher education, combined resigned acceptance of lowered institutional aims with a heightened sense of the significance and fundraising potential of the social sciences. After the war he extended his 1940 analysis of the relations among public education, social stratification, and social mobility. He praised the most famous educational reports of the immediate postwar period — the NEA Educational Policies Commission's *Education for ALL American Youth* and the Harvard "Redbook," *General*

Education in a Free Society—for their emphasis on how education could unify an excessively diverse and stratified society. But he thought both placed too much faith in philosophizing and curriculum improvement and ignored the more decisive (if more hidden) impact of social forces on education.

Social science studies such as Lloyd Warner's *Who Shall Be Educated?* confirmed his suspicion that the schools were not an independent force for mobility and equality of opportunity but were entangled with the social structure as a whole. They were often a barrier to mobility. It was naive, he privately said of the work of the Harvard committee on general education, to analyze education simply as an intellectual process when in fact it was preeminently a social process expressing local values and perpetuating local social hierarchies. The realistic task of modern education was not to proclaim the life of the mind as an educational ideal, but rather to maximize social fluidity and minimize a caste system. Educational problems were principally sociological rather than philosophical, curricular, or pedagogical.

So far this was only a more confident restatement of Conant's prewar preoccupation with the threat that a static society posed to political and economic freedom. Yet by 1946 he was surer than ever that newer social sciences such as sociology, social anthropology, and social psychology could not only illuminate but solve these social problems. Professors such as Talcott Parsons, Clyde Kluckhohn, and Samuel Stouffer provided Conant with the vocabulary he used to describe education as a social process (social structure, stratification, mobility, fluidity, visibility) and with concrete examples of how social science research had contributed to the war effort. This military contribution had not been as striking as that of natural science. But just as chemists, successful at making devices to wage war, now worked in medical schools to apply physiology to the improvement of human health, so might social scientists study education to enhance social mobility.

The growing Soviet threat to American security only made more urgent Conant's wish to shore up American liberty. The stakes of applying social science to public education were nothing less than ensuring that the nation continued as a vigorous and united body of free men. Conant's growing enthusiasm sometimes provoked cautious warnings from social scientists that creating a classless society by means of social science findings would not be easy and should not reduce interest in basic research. But the president nonetheless concluded that the Graduate School of Education, in close collaboration with the newly created department of social relations in the faculty of arts and sciences, had found a dramatic new purpose in the application of social science to educational policy.[37]

Neither the phrase nor the idea of social science appeared in the Purple Memorandum itself. The exclusion was not accidental. Only one faculty member, O. H. Mowrer, had personal or intellectual ties with the department of social relations. Rulon himself continued to have little sympathy for the social sciences. His immediate priorities for faculty appointments focused instead on the field of curriculum. To Rulon, it was in this area, not the social sciences, that the faculty was weakest, that the painful contrast between research and the teaching of job techniques was most pronounced, and that the analysis of *General Education in a Free Society* was most suggestive.

The general education committee had divided the ideal academic curriculum into three divisions: the physical world, man's corporate life, and his inner visions and standards. Rulon accepted this division as the basis for three new faculty appointments in the School, but the general education report provided scant guidelines for what educational research in such areas might be. Rulon knew what the faculty had to avoid — he spoke contemptuously of colleagues who had been brought up with public schools in their mouths — but was less clear about how men uncontaminated with the routines of school practice might invent new research fields out of the area of school curriculum. In late 1945, when young scholars began to leave military service, the School appointed an anthropologist, Morris H. Opler, to replace Howard Wilson in social studies education and an astronomer, Fletcher G. Watson, in science education. Both had impeccable academic training and little school experience. Committed to research as institutional policy but unsure of research issues or methods, the faculty stipulated that Opler teach in the schools to acquire educational experience and research ideas.

Conant had no objection to these appointments and employed Watson to assist him in a new general education course in natural sciences. But he did not see research on curriculum or instruction as a prime function of the post-Spaulding School. Rulon's joy that the

Purple Memorandum had been approved was soon tinged with apprehension that Conant had accepted something quite different from what the faculty had proposed. The president proclaimed that the new dean would be an eminent social scientist and appointed a search committee half of whose members were drawn from the department of social relations. Everyone soon realized that Conant relied on these social scientists — Parsons, Stouffer, and Kluckhohn — for both nominations and judgments far more than he relied on the educators. Would the postwar School, after all, become merely an appendage of the faculty of arts and sciences?[38]

The educators' fears were ultimately assuaged by Conant's failure to find a social scientist who would accept the job and his failure to raise the $1.5 million in endowment authorized by the Corporation. The second failure helped to assure the first. It was hard enough to persuade prominent men such as Robert Redfield of Chicago, Carl Hovland of Yale, or Charles Dollard of the Carnegie Corporation to shift professional identities and rescue a moribund, unprestigious institution. It was harder still when Conant had so few financial incentives to offer them.

During the two years following approval of the Purple Memorandum, he worked harder to raise funds than any Harvard president had ever worked on behalf of the School of Education. He cultivated his old New York friends Devereux Josephs, president of the Carnegie Corporation, and Roy E. Larsen, president of Time-Life, in hopes of obtaining most of the needed $1.5 million from Carnegie and a few New Yorkers, and he appealed to the reorganized Ford Foundation as well. Yet even when Carnegie eventually responded with the largest gift the School had received since 1920 — $300,000 to support operating expenses for as much as a decade — Conant considered the gift a defeat and seriously contemplated refusing it. He continued to assume that higher education, like society as a whole, would not grow during the postwar years. Temporary money would merely delay the reappearance of the old problem of fiscal instability. In a static world anything less than new endowment was unsatisfactory.

After two years of presidential effort, only $325,000 had been raised and several social scientists had formally or informally declined the deanship. A change of strategy seemed necessary. Instead of capturing a social scientist as dean, Conant now decided to seek an individual capable of persuading key senior members of the department of social relations to join the faculty of education, at least on a part-time basis, and from within help to generate new research projects and recruit new staff. Members of the faculty of education naturally protested that they did not wish to be controlled by professors in social relations, and the latter just as quickly proclaimed their genuine disinterest in such a jarring shift in professional focus. Conant's hopes were soon reduced to a dean who could somehow stimulate general collaboration between the social sciences and education.

Of all the possibilities under consideration, the most reasonable was Provost Paul H. Buck's young assistant, Francis Keppel. Keppel was well-known to Harvard's social scientists from both his administrative duties in Cambridge before and after the war, and from work in Washington during the war. Indeed, he contemplated doctoral study in the social sciences. Although only thirty-one, with no degrees beyond the Harvard A.B. and no experience in the field of education, Keppel had deeply impressed scholars like Stouffer with his administrative flair and personal charm, and they in turn urged him on Conant. Paul Buck disliked the idea of wasting his protégé on the School of Education, but admitted Keppel's meteoric rise as an outstanding young administrator. By May 1948 the two-year search was over. With $650,000 in new money—the Corporation matched the outside gifts although it rescinded its earlier vote to match additional outside gifts up to $1.5 million—there seemed no financial impediments to commencing a program of social science research.[39]

Nor were there serious political impediments. Francis Keppel had none of the professional identification of his predecessors and drew more on the advice of Conant and Buck than that of his own colleagues. Buck authoritatively summarized the new policy directions in terms Rulon would never have approved. The School of Education would henceforth emphasize "research on a high university level . . . closely related to the Social Sciences in the Faculty of Arts and Sciences" and conducted by "men fully equal as scholars and comparable in point of view to those on the Faculty of Arts and Sciences." The faculty of education could hardly object, for by 1948

the faculty hardly existed at all. Holmes and Dearborn had retired
the year before, and Kelley, near retirement, had withdrawn. Only
five tenured and three term commitments greeted the new dean.[40]

KEPPEL'S ASSIGNMENT was to create a new intellectual environment
where social scientists would gladly focus their energies on understanding and then changing education conceived as a social process.
Where Holmes had initiated curriculum planning by existing faculty members in order to shape a training environment, Keppel's
first order of business was to recruit a new research faculty. To put
an "entire team in the field" he planned to spend at least $100,000
per year of the newly available $650,000 in unrestricted income. Six
new positions were allocated to social psychology, social science, and
guidance. Avoiding formal search committees, he relied heavily on
the department of social relations for both names of prospective
appointments and for recruiting assistance.

The effort met spectacular success in the recruitment of Robert
R. Sears, social psychologist and president-elect of the American
Psychological Association, together with most of his research staff
from the State University of Iowa. On concluding that one of Sears's
associates, the anthropologist John W. M. Whiting, might replace
Opler in social science curriculum, Keppel was able to offer the
Sears group two major faculty positions along with a substantial research subsidy. The visibility, institutional support, and explicit
autonomy from specific training responsibilities that Sears won
made up for any reservations he might have had about joining a faculty of education.

The Sears appointment immediately boosted Keppel's prestige
within Harvard and exemplified the commitment to analyzing the
educational effects of social environment. Sears and his colleagues
cared about the social processes by which children acquired values,
in contrast to the usual psychological habit of isolating individual
learning from environment. Instead of exploring how school procedures could further educational objectives, Sears focused on childrearing techniques within the family. Instead of cognitive learning,
the Sears group emphasized personality formation. The name of the
School's psychological research unit was changed from the Psycho-
Educational Clinic to the Laboratory of Human Development. The

switch from Dearborn to Sears was thus a move away from school learning and schooling. Quickly Sears demonstrated skill in generating research support from the Rockefeller Foundation to supplement the School's subsidy, and commenced a major research study on the role played by identification with parents in the formation of children's values.[41]

Only Brewer's dogged refusal to resign had prevented the abolition of vocational guidance during the 1930s. The field clung to life following his retirement, despite the lack of agreement of what it was or how to do it, because of its centrality in Conant's analysis of the social function of secondary education. Believing that the proper distribution of occupations in a modern society almost guaranteed the welfare of that society, Conant went so far as to regard the matching of jobs to student capacities as the keystone of the arch of public education. Unlike Mowrer, who had dreamed that guidance might emphasize emotional adjustment and mental hygiene, Conant and Keppel both wished to retain the older emphasis on vocational decisions. They stressed how few "tested hypotheses or proven accomplishments" existed in the field, and characteristically sought planning assistance from the director of the Office of Tests in the faculty of arts and sciences, Henry S. Dyer. Dyer concluded that even the usefulness of a professional role called guidance was open to question. On his recommendation, the School decided to undertake a research reconnaissance rather than a training program. Only one of the three-man team appointed to conduct the reconnaissance had any experience at all with school guidance. The group offered a seminar entitled "Is there a Field of Guidance?"[42]

Neither social psychology nor guidance directly addressed the crucial issue of how communities affected schooling. At the center of Conant's social science enthusiasm was its potential for revealing and perhaps altering how local social structures controlled schooling's capacity to promote mobility. The milieu in which schooling operated, he emphasized again and again, was a barrier to both learning and mobility which curriculum reform alone could not change. Perhaps some teachers preferred not to motivate students with high ability but low aspirations. Perhaps family values held back the able. Perhaps, as Allison Davis argued in a 1948 Harvard lecture, intelligence tests themselves were biased in favor of students from higher socioeconomic strata. Identifying the sociological obstacles to educational mobility was perhaps the School's first task, fully analogous to the problem of "clinical identification of diseases in medicine."

Part of the needed analysis of this social disease, Paul Buck urged, could be conducted historically. For the first time the Harvard president's office saw some use for the history of education. Keppel actively sought the advice of the history department in locating a social historian to balance Ulich's learned but less relevant emphasis on the history of ideas. To conduct contemporary as distinct from historical social analysis, the School already possessed an appropriate unit. The Center for Research, Service and Instruction in Administration had conducted school surveys under Alfred Simpson's leadership and had connected Harvard with New England educational administrators. Spaulding's original research intention, as formulated by John Sly, had never been implemented. Now Keppel sought to restore and recast that research purpose. The center, renamed the Center for Field Studies, would not focus on school finance but would become a "research mechanism whereby the techniques of the social sciences, and particularly those of social psychology, anthropology, and economics are brought to bear on the relations of schools to communities throughout the United States."

The Center for Field Studies could not make the sharp break from the past that was possible for Sears's Laboratory of Human Development; Keppel had inherited the tenured Simpson and his young protégé, Assistant Professor Cyril G. Sargent. Simpson was no researcher, but Keppel realized the political values of his many field contacts for a community-oriented research enterprise. He cleverly secured Simpson's promotion to a full professorship and made Sargent director of the Center for Field Studies. He hoped that Sargent would develop new research interests in political science and sociology beyond his doctoral studies in school finance. At the same time, he consulted advisers in social relations for additional individuals to pursue a social science research thrust. Another anthropologist, Douglas L. Oliver, was appointed part-time for that purpose.[43]

Aware that research on community social structure would be expensive and time-consuming, Keppel obtained an exploratory grant from the Russell Sage Foundation to devise methods of measuring relations between schools and communities. Then Simpson's long-cultivated national contacts as vice-president of the American Association of School Administrators provided entry to more substantial research support. Many AASA leaders wished to upgrade the prestige of the school superintendency in the immediate pos war years, in part as a protective response to community dislocations, population shifts, and a wave of superintendent dismissals. Led by Superintendent Herold C. Hunt of Chicago, the AASA sought to define the superintendent's role more broadly as a community leader and approached the W. K. Kellogg Foundation for assistance. Because Kellogg believed that the American way of life depended on the stability of small communities, it proved receptive to AASA's claim that the school superintendent was the key to link the two.

Eventually the AASA helped to solicit and evaluate proposals to Kellogg from various universities. Because of Simpson's connections, Harvard was in a preferred position from the beginning. Kellogg was distinctly uninterested in research, but Harvard's research interests in local social structure fortuitously complemented the foundation's devotion to community development. Kellogg accepted the argument that practical application would soon follow social science inquiry, and chose Harvard in 1950 as one of eight universities in a $3.5 million Cooperative Program in Educational Administration. The initial three-year grant gave the Graduate School of Education nearly $200,000. Subsequent renewals brought a total of almost $600,000 by 1959. Although some Kellogg money was first allocated to develop under Simpson a network of in-service connections between Harvard and New England superintendents, the central thrust was to mount a single research project on the relations between the public schools and the power structure of one "focal community."[44]

All this faculty expansion required a conscious strategy of recruitment and retention without precedent in the School's history. Older researchers such as Dearborn, Kelley, Rulon, and Ulich had either been trained in the field of education or had spent their entire professional careers in intimate association with it. They regarded themselves not just as researchers but as researchers in education. They saw nothing odd about spending their lives within a school of education. And, excepting Rulon, they saw no contradiction between research and professional training as proper functions of schools of education. Although Ulich strongly criticized the history of American educational science, he and the others were wholly comfortable with the idea of a unified science or discipline of education.

But younger researchers like O. H. Mowrer, Morris Opler, and Fletcher Watson had neither been trained in education nor associated with the field prior to their Harvard appointments. They were outsiders. Attracting and holding their interest was a far more complicated problem than it had been for their research predecessors. Mowrer resigned in 1948 to pursue academic psychology at Illinois, despite having gained Harvard tenure and a certain full professorship. Opler left for academic anthropology at Cornell. Keppel knew very well how many distinguished social scientists had turned down his own job; the recruitment of outsiders was a new problem the School had not faced before.

Retention was as important as recruitment. Keppel wanted not simply to keep new faculty but to redirect their interests toward educational problems. It was important to establish close professional relations between new and old faculty. The "team spirit" he desired required as well an ever-present sensitivity to the feelings of faculty with more traditional educational backgrounds. In addition to securing Simpson's full professorship, Keppel carefully delegated to Rulon the selection of Kelley's successor, John B. Carroll, and appointed one of Rulon's students, David V. Tiedeman, as one member of the guidance troika. He was aware that the arrogance of outsiders might poison the environment he wanted to create. The departing Opler reminded him of the anxiety career educators often faced when scholars from the social sciences suddenly appeared in their midst. The linkages between the two groups had to be forged "carefully, quietly, and tactfully, and in this process certain types of personalities are more useful and certain others less useful."

Above all Keppel saw the need to raise faculty morale from the collective inferiority complex that Brewer and others had so long noted. He lightened teaching loads, deliberately paid young teachers more than their counterparts in arts and sciences, institutionalized the authority of tenured professors over academic and appointment policy by creating a formal committee of the senior faculty, and steadfastly resisted "joint" appointments with other faculties to avoid the inevitable drift of loyalty toward the stronger side. Keppel's habit of extensive consultation with the senior faculty, which outsiders sometimes interpreted as unsure deference, seemed a calculated morale-boosting strategy to those who knew him best. He was willing to risk promoting young faculty members quickly to solidify motivation and loyalty. Both Fletcher Watson and Cyril Sargent won tenure in the third year of their assistant professorships. In such matters, it was concluded, "one must gamble—and pray."[45]

Keppel offered remarkable freedom for researchers to pursue their own interests with few other institutional constraints. "Ideas," he often said, were the "rarest and most prized commodities in our market." Once appointed, faculty could explore wherever their scholarly interests took them. "Immediate relevance" was not a proper criterion for research or instruction. Although the contractual insulation from specific training obligations enjoyed by the Laboratory of Human Development was unique, the same downplaying of professional instruction occurred in all fields. It was hard enough to recruit social scientists trained in faculties of arts and sciences to a school of education and to ask them to redirect their research interests toward educational issues. To ask as well for a wholesale redirection of their instruction toward professional training seemed not only unrealistic but undesirable.[46]

These academic policies substantially altered the instructional program. The School did not withdraw from professional education, but it did express without apology a profound lack of confidence in existing professional knowledge. Admissions policy tried to minimize part-time and academically marginal students in search of practical job skills. Keppel revived the idea of an elite "Fellows in Education" program patterned after the Nieman fellowships for experienced journalists. Some $25,000 in fellowship costs would have been expended from the precious Carnegie funds until an award from the Grant Foundation made that commitment unnecessary.

The curriculum deliberately downgraded specialized professional training in favor of expanded electives across not only the School's offerings but the entire University's. The job-oriented specialized master's programs were abolished, and the Ed.M.'s purpose was recast as an internal selection procedure to identify able doctoral prospects. Doctoral requirements were made more flexible as well. Keppel's aim was to build a curriculum dominated by the social sciences, where the results of instruction would not be technical skill but the "art of exploring problems, getting them under control, and then finding a way to their development and solution." He sought a "fundamental discipline" that might even benefit students who subsequently did not pursue educational careers. In effect, he endorsed a curriculum that closely resembled what his colleagues might have taught in social science departments of academic faculties. From his retirement Holmes perceptively observed that "the present scheme is to *pick* students, not do anything important or unusual in training them, but expect them because of their high IQ to get all they can or could."[47]

The School no longer entrusted the career success of its alumni to the training they received. Holmes had resisted a major placement effort, although he attributed much of Teachers College's influence in the 1930s to its placement officers, and instead tried to validate final tests of professional skill. By contrast Keppel regarded placement as essential to the movement of senior alumni into positions of "leverage." He had inherited from Rulon a man capable of disguising Teachers College entrepreneurialism as Yankee reserve. Dana M. Cotton became head of placement in 1944 and soon exhibited remarkable capacity to gain the trust of schoolmen and school boards. At a time when the School's faculty contacts with the professional field of education were rapidly diminishing, Cotton's energy helped to maintain good relations with the traditional practitioner constituency. Keppel and Conant stabilized Cotton's position, extended its influence by attaching to it related duties in Harvard College admissions and the administration of the summer school, and eventually merged admissions and placement at the School under Cotton's direction. The politics of career promotion, now played with consummate skill, further unburdened the formal curriculum and faculty from responsibility for professional development.

By the end of the 1940s the research momentum contrasted dramatically not only with the training emphasis of the thirties but with Harvard's original enthusiasm for educational science nearly four decades before. That earlier effort focused on measuring educational results; its key tool was statistics. The later one stressed understanding of how social forces shaped education's impact; its methods were the social sciences. The central energy behind the first was to solidify the professional authority of schoolmen and, from Lowell's viewpoint, of college reformers like himself. Research skill in 1912 was regarded primarily as one ingredient in practitioner competence.

The research movement of the forties had no such professionalizing intention. By 1950 research was regarded as a specialized occupation remote from practice. Explicit practitioner training seemed almost antithetical to an ideal research environment. The task of engineering mobility appeared far more significant than the task of upgrading professionals. Ideas were the School's desired product, and the ordinary schoolman was no longer a decisive agent for educational change.

10

Educational Careers
and the Missing Elite

THE SINGLE-MINDED commitment to applied social science lasted only three years. The foundation support that allowed social science to expand brought with it, ironically, unexpected pressures to reconsider the place of practitioner training. In the first place, rapid faculty growth from temporary funds raised the dilemma of how to maintain those faculty positions once the "soft" money had run out. Tuition revenues subsequently assumed a larger role in long-range planning; but increased tuition implied a larger student body and, inevitably, a larger number of prospective practitioners. In the second place, the foundations Harvard cultivated proved not nearly as interested in social science as Keppel and Conant hoped they would be. The fundamental premise behind the social science rationale was a static society, defined in terms of population growth and educational aspiration. But the premise was wrong: the fifties were boom times for educational expansion.

The Ford Foundation, which had more education money to give away than anyone else, was unpersuaded by Conant's gloomy analysis. It focused its efforts on the shortage of educators caused by the postwar growth of American schooling. The Kellogg Foundation similarly gave increased attention to practitioners. Responding to these outside priorities and to his own awareness of the importance of tuition income, Keppel in 1951 decisively reemphasized the training of teachers and administrators.

The new approach to professional training deviated profoundly from the School's earlier history and gave the Keppel era its special flavor. Keppel defined the personnel problem in education as one of recruitment rather than of training. He resolved to attract to the School a larger number of graduates from the better liberal arts colleges. He bluntly asked why such graduates traditionally looked down on schools of education and the schoolteaching job. His candid answers emphasized how social-class factors affected the composition of the profession and the content of schooling. By 1952, the new institutional strategy of career recruitment was assumed to be fully consistent with the social science research agenda. The more scholarly curriculum offered by the faculty would help lure able students suspicious of traditional professional courses.

But the juxtaposition of large professional training programs and a research faculty caused substantial friction and unhappiness. A new faculty constituency arose that was more interested in tackling the personnel crisis than in research. For their part, researchers tended to focus more on basic inquiry and the advancement of their disciplines than on social problems. This centrifugal pressure threatened the harmonious applied research environment that still remained a central institutional objective. Unusual efforts were made to integrate or balance competing interests, but the principal outcome was a bewildering set of new definitions of faculty competence whose common denominator was activity other than research. By the end of the fifties Keppel had accomplished an astounding transformation of the School's scope and reputation. But that greater reputation was based less on applied research than on the strategy of career recruitment.

THE ASTONISHING BUDGET increase from $224,000 to $417,000 between 1948 and 1950 made possible a scale of operations far larger than the Purple Memorandum had envisioned. The sources of income deviated even more sharply from those earlier plans. In response to the instability of the 1930s, when endowment had consistently provided about 60 percent of total income, the Purple Memorandum recommended that over 80 percent of future expenditures be financed by endowment. But by 1950 endowment provided only 29 percent of income. The School's growth had been funded mainly by the Carnegie, Russell Sage, Kellogg, Grant, and Rockefeller foundations. In 1950 external support accounted for 43 percent of annual income.

This level of outside support was unknown since the philanthropy of concerned businessmen in the century's second decade. But where the University had then been willing to take over the salary burdens eventually created by gifts, thus making possible the growth of a permanent faculty, Conant offered no such hope in the postwar years. Temporary foundation support had allowed the School to initiate a variety of research enterprises, but could not assure their perpetuation. Yet the creation of a genuine research environment required, Keppel believed, a significant number of new professorial positions. Stable income was indispensable for that purpose. He began to imagine that his primary role would be that of a mendicant, ever seeking permanent funding sources or trying to extend temporary grants indefinitely. Conant and Keppel planned a major public endowment drive for 1952, but as the School's sense of minimal needs escalated far beyond the projections of the Purple Memorandum, the old belief vanished that endowment alone was the source of fiscal stability.

The decline in stable income as a fraction of the School's budget created a new sensitivity to the importance of tuition income. The siren lure of tuition presumably endangered research; yet tuition gradually seemed vital for the fiscal stability needed to maintain research morale. Tuition income, moreover, was rising far faster than endowment income. Despite policies that reduced the total number of enrolled students, tuition income rose because both full-time students and tuition rates increased. The GI Bill had provided an unprecedented applicant pool.of older students willing to study full time and the financial aid that allowed them to do so. Contrary to earlier predictions, the School had been able simultaneously to raise academic standards and to increase tuition income. But in 1950 this attractive condition seemed only temporary. When the GI Bill would finally run its course in 1951 or 1952, Conant predicted that student numbers would surely decline. His fear was exacerbated in late 1950 by concern that the Korean War would require national mobilization and cause a drastic decline of male students. If the pool of postwar full-timers evaporated, could some new pool be found to replace them?

That question led the School, to Conant's surprise, to devise an Ed.M. program in early 1951 which prepared elementary teachers. Nothing so radical had been considered even in the heyday of professional specializations, and Keppel was quick to reassure the president that the proposal was not a departure from the research strategy but merely a spelling out of its implications. Those implications were that the School needed a pool of students to replace those about to be lost, and hoped to find it from the women's colleges.

Everyone was aware of the tremendous national shortage of elementary teachers. The absence of teacher education programs in many of the prominent New England liberal arts colleges, when coupled with the expansion of elementary jobs in attractive suburban communities, gave Harvard a special opportunity. Perhaps it could attract young full-time students whose personal expenses, and thus financial aid requirements, would be far less than the older GI Bill students. Such women could be a "life belt" for the School if men were mobilized. Aside from these financial considerations, the young Ed.M. students would constitute a pool from which doctoral students might eventually be selected. Keppel assured Conant that the School had no serious interest in elementary teaching per se, but only wished to identify those who might one day staff teacher-training institutions and thus occupy "key points of leverage" in the educational system.[1]

The new concern for tuition income extended to secondary teacher education as well. Despite strong faculty sentiment to abolish the M.A.T. program in 1948, Keppel persuaded his colleagues to give the degree one final chance out of deference to Conant's strong feelings and oft-heard opinion that it had never been given a fair trial. M.A.T. enrollments spurted in the immediate postwar years because of the GI Bill but by 1950 were declining to distressingly familiar pre-war levels. With no national high school teacher shortage predicted until the end of the 1950s, the market for graduate-level secondary teacher education seemed no more certain than before the war. Harvard had removed virtually all of the burdensome degree requirements that had made the M.A.T. so unattractive. But apart from removing obvious barriers to attendance, the School had little experience with positive efforts to attract more students. In early 1951 these began to be explored more systematically. The School devised a plan whereby neighboring MIT students could anticipate Harvard M.A.T. education requirements as undergraduates through cross-registering for courses at the School of Education, and Keppel attempted to persuade other universities such as Yale to establish M.A.T. programs in order to publicize the idea and the label.

These signs of renewed interest in teacher preparation were still on the far margin of institutional interest. They were stimulated not by an enthusiasm for the role of teachers but by the fear that a severe tuition reduction might disrupt the research mission. When Conant and Keppel approached the Ford Foundation in mid-1951 with a general endowment request, they emphasized only the potential of the social sciences to foster equality of opportunity and a wise distribution of talent. The School's uniqueness lay in the partnership it had forged between the social sciences and educational policy, "just as clinical medicine made a partnership earlier in the century with biology and chemistry and physics."[2]

Following Henry Ford's death in 1947 and the subsequent growth in the resources of the Ford Foundation, education became a major priority. In 1951 the Ford Foundation's trustees created a separate organization, the Fund for the Advancement of Education, to direct its educational activities. Conant and Keppel realized that the financial possibilities of the Fund were remarkable but, to their chagrin, soon learned that its new officers had priorities very different from their own. President Clarence Faust and Vice-President Alvin C. Eurich had little faith that educational research could promote educational improvement. Although Eurich was an educational psychologist, he thought most work in his field had been of little value. Even where research conclusions were suggestive, as in the consistent finding that class size was not related to pupil learning, they were always ignored.

Nor did Eurich respect schools of education. While provost and acting president of Stanford, he had advocated abolition of its school of education. When chancellor of the State University of New York, he had suggested dismantling the teachers colleges there. He thought the problem of education was inherently the concern of universities in their entirety, not of separate schools. There was no distinct field of educational knowledge.

Faust and Eurich agreed that the most pressing educational dilemma was the quality of teachers. The solution was to encourage liberal arts colleges to turn out larger numbers of graduates interested in teaching and, in anticipation of the expected shortage of high school teachers, to devise new ways to utilize their talents. They were completely unimpressed with Harvard's confidence in the social sciences and, in addition, preferred to make grants for ongoing action programs rather than for endowment. At first Keppel was

disappointed, but he seized on several opportunities to talk informally with Faust and Eurich about their hopes. Despite differences
on the social sciences, they found that they shared crucial biases
about schools of education and the sources of educational reform.
Sensing some possibilities in the situation after all, Keppel began to
recast Harvard's Ford proposal to emphasize that common perspective. During the last half of 1951 a new argument for the role of the
Graduate School of Education began to emerge.[3]

The task of ensuring an intellectually able student body had been
addressed since Rulon's acting deanship through administrative
procedures such as close attention to undergraduate records at the
time of graduate admission, doctoral qualifying papers, and full-
time study requirements. As long as the School's training strategy
stressed a small body of experienced schoolmen, the problem of
quality was simply a problem of academic selection. But Keppel had
always been aware of another dimension of "quality" for which
Rulon had shown little interest. The School's procedures only allowed choices to be made among individuals who *already* had committed themselves both to educational careers and to study at a
school of education. They had no impact whatever on the initial
choice of career. Yet it was obvious to Keppel, as it had been to reformers like Horace Willard a half century before, that able and
energetic young men rarely selected careers in the schools to begin
with. Good students often learned from their parents, peers, or college teachers that precollegiate education had little appeal or prestige. That attitude seemed particularly prevalent among the affluent and ambitious students who attended expensive liberal arts
colleges.

Of course Keppel was not the first to discover the difficulty of
attracting to education privileged students with options to pursue
any profession. Older internal studies revealed that the financial
and educational background of the School's students was less ad-
vantaged than that of students in other Harvard faculties. Holmes
had attacked the problem by relying on the impact of training itself,
and Spaulding had had no time to attack it at all. Lowell always
considered the problem to be insoluble, since public education offered neither the financial rewards nor charitable incentives to appeal to talented youth of his acquaintance. Brewer and Nichols did
not regard the situation as a problem.

But Keppel's privileged social background made him unwilling to accept as inevitable the School's traditional inability to attract students who resembled his own friends and teachers. His grandfather was a successful New York art dealer; his father served as dean of Columbia College and president of the Carnegie Corporation of New York. Young Keppel spent his adolescence, which paralleled the Depression, within the protected sanctuaries of Groton School and Harvard College. But public interests, including education, were always family interests and soon became his own. Edward L. Thorndike was a close family friend and neighbor, and Keppel's father took pride in his Carnegie decision to fund Gunnar Myrdal's famous study of the American Negro. The son's upbringing exemplified the amalgam of Protestant affluence and civic concern which became increasingly known as the Eastern Establishment.

Keppel stood out from his pedagogical predecessors by linking Conant's meritocratic elitism with Lowell's aristocratic elitism. He was committed to luring a large number of academically talented students into education. But he also believed that effective educators possessed qualities of character as well as intellect, values as well as technical skill. He assumed that these latter characteristics were acquired over the entire course of childhood and youth, not suddenly during the undergraduate years and certainly not in a brief period of graduate study. Keppel's rhetoric avoided Barrett Wendell's pomposity and Perry Dunlap Smith's private school emphasis on good breeding and well-roundedness. Yet he clearly accepted their assumption that the problem of teacher quality had to be addressed by attracting those already qualified, already chosen. The "policies and programs which bring . . . future leaders to the profession may be more important than the academic programs themselves." By careful recruitment in the prestigious liberal arts colleges, perhaps the Graduate School of Education could attract its fair share of the best and brightest of young Americans to careers in the schools.[4]

THE FUND FOR THE ADVANCEMENT OF EDUCATION intended to reform teacher education by maximizing liberal studies and minimizing professional courses. Faust and Eurich hoped to shift the pattern of teacher education in the state of Arkansas to consist of four years of undergraduate liberal education, no education courses at all, and a year's supervised internship in schools. Keppel opportunistically suggested, as a complement to the Arkansas experiment that the Fund help Harvard recruit to teaching liberal arts graduates who already had experienced exactly the sort of undergraduate education that was being advocated in Arkansas. The Graduate School of Education would become a magnet to attract graduates who otherwise would choose some other vocation. The gambit proved successful. Eurich was impressed with Keppel's reasoning, and urged greater specificity on how the idea might be implemented. Near the end of 1951 a plan was mutually agreed upon.[5]

The School would attempt to persuade certain liberal arts colleges to recruit their own students to careers in public education. It was imperative to alter the attitudes of college faculty members who advised students on career choice. The immediate incentives Harvard could offer, with the Fund's assistance, were special fellowships and a selection process in which the colleges themselves would play substantial roles. Graduates would attend the M.A.T. program to receive certification. Their Harvard curriculum would emphasize opportunities for advanced study in their undergraduate majors, educational studies in the social sciences, history, and philosophy, and a practical apprenticeship. The function of this curriculum was primarily to serve recruitment by stressing disciplinary studies valued by prospective students and their undergraduate teachers. Recruitment strategy for the next decade promoted the School of Education by emphasizing how few courses in education students had to take.

Twenty-one colleges, soon expanded to twenty-nine and eventually to more than forty, accepted this ideology of training and the financial aid that came with it. It was hard for them to deny that their own students constituted education's missing elite, that access to teaching careers for their graduates should be eased, that traditional education courses were largely worthless, that rigorous graduate instruction in familiar academic disciplines was worthwhile, and that better teachers for the expanding suburban high schools served their own self-interest. The biases of Keppel and Eurich were largely their own. Keppel deliberately enlarged his ties with professional education associations in 1952 to counter the charge that Harvard had sold itself to the Ford Foundation (just as the foundation had been charged with purchasing Arkansas).

The Fund's three-year grant of $331,500 differed completely from what Conant had first proposed to the Ford Foundation seven months earlier. From the protracted negotiations had emerged a new rhetoric of mission—the career recruitment of quality students —to coexist with social science analysis of education. But there was no sense of contradiction or of retreat from research. Indeed, the School's attractiveness to able students was its very intention to remain a stimulating research environment uncontaminated by conventional training routines. It was true that the institution had adopted a new "accent on youth" and an expanded commitment to teacher education. Yet basic research and training in the behavioral sciences continued to be the "very heart" of the School's program. There would be no pressure for social scientists to adapt themselves to a professional environment any more than there would be on the M.A.T. students to do so. Scholars like Robert Sears actively supported the new ventures, and especially a small early childhood wing of the elementary program, in part because they saw in it opportunities for easier access to research subjects.

The financial impact of the grant, moreover, was not simply to add a new activity. It directly subsidized the existing program. During the year in which the grant was negotiated, tuition income declined by $8,000. Ford scholarship dollars came back to the School as a crucial new source of income to replace GI Bill money. Direct costs of certain faculty and administrative salaries could be charged to Ford resources as well. In addition, two grant-sponsored research initiatives—to study how able teachers might best be utilized and how characteristics of successful teachers might be developed through training—were staffed with existing personnel drawn from the Center for Field Studies and the Laboratory of Human Development. In such ways the Ford grant reinforced existing commitments at the same time that it made possible new ones.[6]

Keppel never lost sight of the goal of obtaining wholly unrestricted and preferably endowment support from the Ford Foundation. But the new idea of career recruitment, which had originated as a fundraising strategy to rescue a moribund endowment proposal, quickly acquired a separate momentum of its own. Stimulated by the practical necessity to renew and expand the first Fund grant, Keppel's personal analysis of the best means to reform education in the 1950s increasingly emphasized career recruitment. No educational idea, not even social science, better fitted his own values. By the end of the fifties an internal history of the M.A.T. program reported that Harvard's curriculum in teacher education seemed little changed from 1920. What was new was that career recruitment was now pursued with "missionary zeal."[7]

The test of Harvard's success was its recruits. No data were collected more avidly or displayed more frequently than information about the characteristics of the student body. Undergraduate college origins became the most significant measure of quality in a decade when highly meritocratic admissions policies were first adopted in many liberal arts colleges. By 1960 prominent private colleges or universities supplied 242 of the 293 students who enrolled in master's programs of initial teacher preparation. Harvard, moreover, tested its students again and again to assure the Fund and the feeder colleges that a new level of talent was in fact being attracted. The mean scores on the Miller Analogies Test and the Graduate Record Examinations proved not only substantially higher than national means of education students, but were almost as good as the means of graduate and professional students in physical science. A comparison of postwar Harvard College graduates who enrolled in the M.A.T. and in medical schools revealed that a slightly higher percentage of honors graduates chose the M A.T. (although the percentage of *magna* and *summa* graduates entering medicine was higher).[8]

Subsequent discussions with the Fund for the Advancement of Education concentrated almost exclusively on the tactics of finding and financing even more impressive students. In 1954, when the first renewal appeal was negotiated, special attention was given to how financial aid incentives could be permanently provided without the need for foundation assistance. The necessity to secure stable tuition income was ever present. But the strategy was not simply to fund impecunious students, since the Fund realized that the M.A.T. applicant pool to begin with was far more affluent than the national body of teacher education students. The School hoped to compete with scholarships provided by other graduate programs preparing for more prestigious careers. Financial aid was deliberately offered "without particular reference to financial need." The new plan established salaried one-semester teaching "internships" paid for by cooperating schools, and enabled those schools to meet their growing personnel shortages at modest expense. If inexperienced liberal arts graduates were immediately to teach full time for a semester, some preliminary practical experience seemed desirable. A summer program to provide this introduction was established in cooperation with the Newton school system. Thus major training innovations such as the paid internship and the Harvard-Newton Summer Program were fundamentally elements in a tuition-generating and recruitment strategy rather than planned pedagogical reforms.[9]

Having successfully secured one extension of the Ford grant, Keppel began to explore the implications of the Fund's interest in teacher utilization. Already the Fund had elsewhere supported utilization strategies such as teacher aides and classroom educational television. In the course of preparing the 1954 proposal, Keppel had reached a striking conclusion. Harvard's recruitment efforts so far had focused on changing the image of graduate teacher education and on competitive financial aid. Yet the root cause of so much undergraduate apprehension about teaching as a career was the nature of the teaching job itself. Ambitious undergraduates contemplating a variety of professional careers could not help noticing that a teacher was "rewarded very little more at the end of his service than at the time he started and ordinarily has responsibility for only the same number of pupils as he did at the start of his teaching life."

There was no sense of "promotion" at all in teaching, unless one left it altogether for the different job of administrator. Data collected from the M.A.T. class of 1954 indicated, moreover, that commitment to career public school teaching was negatively correlated with students' socioeconomic status. Perhaps, Keppel speculated, in a tactical jump that earlier analysts like Horace Willard had not made, the very structure of the teaching profession could be changed so that Harvard's "picked people will have substantial influence" *and* remain in classroom teaching. If superior teachers were designated leaders of small teams of adults responsible for instructing groups of 125 to 150 students, their ability might be better utilized. A new incentive would exist to lure and hold the ambitious liberal arts graduate. Harvard's ultimate recruiting strategy became hierarchical differentiation among teachers.[10]

The School's renewed interest in the recruitment of practitioners was not confined to teachers. At the same time that Ford officers showed greater interest in teacher improvement than in social science research, Kellogg Foundation officers began to complain that Harvard's activities in the Cooperative Program in Educational Administration overemphasized research and neglected the training of superintendents. They stipulated that foundation-supported research be "completely practical and used by the educational leaders on the job to solve the problems they face.' The program's future funding prospects depended on "solutions that are actually accomplished at the grassroots." Kellogg's pressure appeared just when the Graduate School of Education was as concerned about the size and revenue potential of its doctoral population as it was with its master's students. Although the planned research project in community social structure had not yet begun, Keppel and Cyril Sargent decided to concentrate their energies in 1951-52 on creating a new doctoral training program in school administration. Research planning would have to be deferred. The more urgent priority was to build a post-GI Bill program capable of recruiting students and convincing Kellogg that its funds were being used in practical application.

The resulting "Administrative Career Program" of 1952 was the School's first specialized doctoral program, the first doctoral program claiming to train practitioners rather than researchers, and the first not to require a dissertation. The internal push for tuition income and the external push from Kellogg accomplished what Simpson had advocated for a decade. Rulon characteristically openly opposed the new program, fearing a regression to older training values. He argued that the only reason superintendents wanted a doctorate was to call themselves "Doctor." Sears and Whiting felt uneasy as well, but acquiesced when Keppel reassured them that a more visible training program was financially necessary and would not diminish their own resources.

Although more structured than the M.A.T., the Administrative Career Program possessed many of the M.A.T.'s characteristics. Keppel was convinced that much of what was conventionally taught in courses on school administration could easily be learned on the job, that the best practicing administrators were frequently more able than professors of administration, and that proper training should emphasize the social sciences and supervised field study. Quite apart from the educational value of its curriculum, the new program had to be able to attract quality students. The School employed an officer with special responsibilities for recruitment and selection.[11]

The two new ventures proved successful financially. Tuition income rose by nearly one third in 1952-53 to its highest level in the School's history. Nevertheless, the percentage of total income supplied by tuition fell as foundation income continued to rise. Fully two thirds of all income during 1952-53 came from outside sources and not from tuition or endowment. Much of this temporary income, of course, supported activities that were properly transcient, rather than individuals or functions whose indefinite continuation seemed indispensable. Still, the School estimated that over three fourths of its entire annual expenses, or $650,000, supported activities that seemed basic or "core." Even when, in 1953, the School risked assuming for planning purposes that it could count on at least $150,000 in annual unrestricted long-term foundation support — an unthinkable assumption in 1946 — a large gap remained between assured income and basic expenses. Most of the unrestricted Carnegie grant was gone, and there were limits to tuition growth. Keppel estimated that it would now take $4.5 million of new endowment to support the core budget expenses that tuition and foundation income would not cover.

The rhetoric of the 1952 endowment drive emphasized Harvard's capacity to provide quality educational personnel in a time of national shortage. The arguments for social science research, having failed in the past to stimulate endowment gifts from either foundations or individuals, were quietly dropped. Although Conant's sudden resignation from the presidency in early 1953 wrecked campaign strategy and cast a pall over the effort, an unexpected opportunity temporarily revived optimism. Henry L. Shattuck, a wealthy Boston reformer and long-time senior Harvard official who had perhaps been the School's strongest supporter in the Corporation, proposed to rescue the campaign by using it to honor Conant. He took the lead in creating the James Bryant Conant Foundation with a $300,000 contribution, the largest individual gift the School had ever received. But even Shattuck's largesse and hard solicitations proved disappointing. By June 1954, when the drive had essentially ended, only $456,000 had been collected for the Conant Foundation and $380,000 more pledged. This was less than half Shattuck's minimum objective. Discouraged by such slow progress, Keppel resolved that fundraising must consume an even greater portion of his effort. And he worried more than before about how faculty morale would be affected by the paradox of booming but brittle "soft money" expansion.[12]

THE SCHOOL's new training obligations complicated the effort to create an environment conducive to applying social science to education and reopened the question of what attributes ideally characterized a faculty of education. Without much reflection, and far more quickly than it had anticipated, the School had been drawn back into professional obligations that previously had threatened its existence. Determined to avoid recreating a training faculty on the old terms, Keppel hoped instead that the postwar research faculty could simultaneously meet growing professional demands. But, as the decade progressed, no such simple solution seemed feasible.

A growing number of faculty members lacked interest in research. Some individuals, whose appointments and promotions were predicated on the development of research initiatives instead turned away from research in the new climate of expanded professional training. Fletcher Watson, for example, concentrated on upgrading standards within the community of science educators. Cyril Sargent did not become a researcher in sociology or political science, but administered contractual field studies and explored the applicability of the case method for instruction in administration.

Faculty appointment policy, moreover, was often opportunistic and inconsistent with the research ideal. The appointment of Superintendent Herold C. Hunt of Chicago to a professorship in administration in 1953 was considered a coup of similar significance to the appointment of Robert Sears. Hunt's value in strengthening the frayed ties with Kellogg, in student recruitment, and in placement easily outweighed the fact that he represented precisely the older model of practitioner appointment Holmes had been prevented from making by two Harvard presidents. Several additional faculty members performed crucial managerial roles in the new training programs. Keppel usually preferred a fairly rapid turnover of younger men in these positions to the frustrated ambitions of older individuals who would eventually want professorships but would lack the research productivity to secure them. Ambitious for success but with no tenure prospects before them, the administrators of training programs were easily demoralized.

As the numbers of these various nonresearchers grew, they began to argue more forcefully with Keppel and among themselves that promotion policy should be determined not solely by research capacity. More "balance" was needed. Robert Schaefer, director of the M.A.T. program, detected a "general unrest" within the faculty. There were "no high-powered counterweights in guidance, teacher-education, secondary education, etc. to our experts in measurement, human development, and philosophy." Edward Landy, a former student of Brewer's, director of guidance in the Newton public schools, and part-time Harvard lecturer, complained that the School of Education should amount to more than "merely a conglomeration of miscellaneous extensions of the psychology, statistics, sociology, philosophy, etc. departments." Programs and faculty appointments in a professional school should be organized around the "basic functioning areas of education," which were guidance, instruction, measurement, and administration. Soon the independence and alleged educational irrelevance of the Laboratory of Human Development was criticized within the senior faculty.[13]

The isolation and unease of the nonresearchers was exacerbated by important shifts in the School's research climate. Although Harvard's commitment to research continued, the special focus on applying social science to pressing social problems diminished. Instead, research became less applied, with its agendas set by the internal problems of various scholarly disciplines. This development frequently surprised observers who expected to see just the reverse in a professional school.

Anxious to hold productive scholars on his faculty, Keppel encouraged them to pursue their own interests with minimal direction. Given wide discretion, their interests in "pure" studies grew rather than receded. Robert Sears's studies of how childrearing techniques developed identification in young children yielded no short-range applications. And when Sears resigned in 1952 to become chairman of psychology at Stanford, the School chose not to move in more applied directions but to ensure the continuity of the research laboratory Sears had started. Keppel secured the tenure of Sears's principal assistant, John Whiting, and Whiting promptly led the Laboratory of Human Development into cross-cultural childrearing research more removed still from educational practice. Whiting even questioned the morality of converting social science findings into educational prescriptions. Other researchers privately expressed guilt over the lip service they had to pay to education.[14]

The same bias toward scholarly excellence regardless of application governed other appointment decisions. John B. Carroll, Kelley's successor in educational measurement, subsequently shifted much of his research effort to psycholinguistics. Although Keppel did not know how or whether Carroll's work connected to educational practice, he understood that Carroll was widely regarded as one of the most brilliant young faculty members and recommended his promotion to tenure at the same time as Whiting's. When Rockefeller Foundation funds made possible the appointments of a young historian and philosopher in 1952, the first priority was to attract the most promising scholars. Keppel hoped that the historian Bernard Bailyn would one day participate in the new program to train superintendents, but in the short run it seemed far more important to underwrite Bailyn's scholarly reorientation to the moribund discipline of history of education. The philosopher Israel Scheffler was encouraged to develop courses around his existing interests in ethical discourse and the meaning of scientific explanation while he also began to work up instruction in the philosophy of education.

Rather than gradually redirect professional identities from discipline-based scholarship to applied or problem-centered inquiry, the School's environment seemed mainly to accentuate the former affiliations. Faculty members residing in somewhat alien territory were often inclined to exaggerate their disciplinary ties. Those drawn from the newer social sciences, moreover, carried an added burden of anxiety over the scholarly standing of their fields, quite apart from the distraction of pursuing them within a school of education. Many professors wished their official titles to contain the names of their disciplines in addition to, or instead of, the word "education." Separate doctoral training programs in fields such as sociology of education were urged. And, by 1956, outside funds were being sought to develop the vestigial doctor of philosophy in education degree, based officially in the faculty of arts and sciences, into a full-scale discipline-based research training alternative to the doctor of education.[15]

Emphasis on basic or "mother" disciplines was accompanied by a trend away from using research as a tool for social reform. At the beginning of the fifties, research was justified as an instrument to foster a free and classless society. But the research commitment to reform had vanished almost entirely by the mid-fifties. The problem of social stratification was almost forgotten. The central problem of American education seemed a shortage of educational personnel. Even when newer national problems began to draw Keppel's attention later in the decade — Southern school desegregation, academic attacks on anti-intellectualism in schools and schools of education, the fear of Soviet superiority in mathematics and science — those problems were not initially perceived as agendas for educational research.[16]

The presidential transition from Conant to Nathan M. Pusey made the change clear to all. Pusey had none of Conant's cautious fears of a static society and none of his urgent interest in how the social sciences could maximize social mobility. Though vaguely supportive of the School, if not of Keppel, Pusey was less clear how it served particular Harvard or societal needs. He was, however, dissatisfied with the scholarly eminence of the faculty. Consequently Keppel became even more concerned than he might have been with the academic distinction of appointment recommendations.

As EARLY AS 1953 Keppel acknowledged the existence of "tensions" in the faculty. There was a clear polarizing tendency between non-researchers and discipline-oriented basic researchers. The same split was apparent in the student body, where prospective practitioners were far more numerous. The goal of a true community devoted to the application of research to education was threatened by centrifugal pressures. As the fifties progressed, more and more institutional energy was devoted to resolving the tensions, restoring community, and somehow rescuing or redefining the ideal of applied research. These efforts were mainly played out in guidance, administration, and teacher education.[17]

The progress of guidance was more disappointing than any of the other social science initiatives taken in 1949. No research plan had been formulated, no outside funds had been raised, and the three-man team responsible for initiating research soon broke up. In the absence of clear directions and without a senior professor in the field, Keppel asked Nicholas Hobbs, professor of psychology at George Peabody College, to make another outside assessment of the prospects of guidance at Harvard. In private talks with faculty members, Hobbs was struck by their contrasting views about the purposes of a school of education. These conflicts, he concluded, explained Harvard's marginal contribution to guidance and had to be squarely acknowledged if progress was to be made.

The core of Hobbs's argument was that the School had not made a serious commitment to guidance as a field of applied research. The clear need was for researchers who were "questioners verifiers, and seekers of new directions." He knew that some faculty members advocated training guidance practitioners at the Ed.M. level, but dismissed this on grounds that it would be "socially reprehensible" to "add to the numbers of appliers of guidance techniques, when those techniques are so urgently in need of verification and of orientation." Yet Hobbs also knew that faculty advocates of master's level training had little institutional power. They were not his main target.

The real problem was the reluctance of discipline-oriented social scientists to take applied research seriously. Hobbs learned first-hand from his conversations how much lip service was paid to the problems of schooling, how much all Harvard fields required the political power of tenured faculty members, and how much suspicion academic social scientists had of the expensive clinical facilities he believed necessary for applied research in a professional field. Hobbs had no brief for existing "pedestrian" guidance literature. Yet when he spoke of the potential components of its knowledge base, his suggestions went far beyond contemporary Harvard thought about the possibilities of professional knowledge.

To take guidance seriously, Hobbs said, the School also had to take seriously fields like personality theory, individual assessment, psychotherapy, and group dynamics. He made no mention of career recruitment as a guarantor of professional quality, nor of the uses of placement to assist the progress of alumni toward positions of ever-increasing influence. He advocated field work not as a means to avoid worthless education courses but as an activity to produce knowledge that would make professional courses essential. His analysis expressed old-fashioned confidence, reminiscent of Holmes, in the potential of knowledge to develop practitioner skill. Besides additional faculty and commitment to a clinic, Hobbs recommended creation of a four-year doctoral program to train research-oriented counseling psychologists and a three-year doctoral program to train informed leaders of guidance administration.[18]

From Stanford, Sears praised Hobbs's candor in exposing the ideological conflict that the faculty had been unwilling to acknowledge, and thought the lesson of the analysis was clear. "Either the job must be done right or the word guidance must be wiped off the Harvard slate." But if those were the only options, the outcome was foreordained. The senior faculty opposed allocating scarce resources to a new and expensive undertaking. Moreover, several social scientists believed that Hobbs's proposal for a lengthy doctoral program in counseling psychology, along with the maintenance of a guidance clinic, was simply an entry wedge for practitioner training. At the same time, those sympathetic to more practical concerns feared that implementation of the report would lead either to a more elaborate research commitment or to the erasure of guidance from Harvard's slate. Almost no one had any stake in taking Hobbs's proposals seriously.[19]

Of course Keppel understood that Hobbs's trenchant analysis was aimed at furthering the applied research goal that the School was committed to, and the dean sought to move in the general directions indicated without spending extra money or alienating his colleagues. Hobbs's rejection of the extremes of either practical training or discipline-oriented social science as the center of guidance suggested the desirability of a middle ground that would integrate the best of both. The search for a manageable compromise substantially boosted the hitherto uncertain tenure prospects of David V. Tiedeman, a survivor of the original guidance troika.

Like Watson and Sargent, Tiedeman had gradually moved toward professional service from earlier research interests. Unlike them, he had not yet received tenure when his position became clear. Even before the Hobbs report he had suggested that his future role at Harvard might be to train guidance administrators; and he acutely understood the painful conflict between research and action as well as the high stakes of his choice. Hobbs's report impressed him by suggesting a larger mission for guidance than his former focus on measuring career determinants. It helped free him, he later wrote, from the narrow positivism of measurement research. Wanting to continue guidance and stabilize it with a permanent appointment, Keppel now saw Tiedeman's strength as a balance of several desirable characteristics which somehow integrated research with professional training. Tiedeman was a devoted team player within Harvard, had made many productive associations in local and national guidance circles, and possessed a solid research background. It was rare to find men who possessed all these qualities and who were also true scholars. The right balance of attributes now seemed more important than "unusual brilliance in any single quality."

At first, the *ad hoc* committee created to advise President Pusey on the tenure recommendation demurred from this reasoning. The issue, most members thought, was simply research distinction in the field under consideration — in this case educational measurement as applied to guidance. The nominee's research contribution was unimpressive. But to one *ad hoc* member who argued for Keppel's recommendation, research distinction was not the central issue; at stake was the School's commitment to the professional field of guidance. With considerable reluctance and uncertainty, Keppel pressed the same point and eventually won reconsideration and presidential approval of the appointment. It had been Pusey's first encounter with a senior appointment recommendation from the School. He was not moved by the argument that balance rather than brilliance was the path to institutional distinction. Aside from Herold Hunt, the School had consciously deviated from the research criterion in senior appointments for the first time in the postwar era. The idea of individual balance was an administrative response, in a time of limited resources, to Hobbs's push for an applied research commitment to a professional area. Whether progress had been made was unclear. The doctoral research program was deferred, the doctoral program in guidance administration began without a research dissertation, and a master's in vocational counseling was soon reintroduced.[20]

The intention to apply social science research to educational practice was nowhere more explicit than in the Center for Field Studies' project on the power structure of a community, but in no area did the newer training obligations cause more conflict. Even without the Kellogg-induced Administrative Career Program, the intellectual obstacles to research success seemed formidable. Disagreements within the diverse young staff about interdisciplinary research design and methods of data analysis caused repeated delays in completing the project and eventual abandonment of any collaborative final report. These difficulties were exacerbated by Kellogg's insistence that the social scientists take a far more time-consuming role in the training of school administrators than they had been led to expect. Students who enrolled to become administrators rather than researchers amplified the complaint that existing instruction in social science theory and methods did not meet their needs. Professors Hunt and Sargent tended to agree. The latter, in particular, wished to teach social science concepts through direct professional service to school systems rather than through separate courses growing out of the community research project.

When, at the end of 1954, preparation of a refunding proposal to Kellogg further heightened pressure to integrate social science with professional training, the senior faculty in administration decided that henceforth social scientists would be required to participate extensively in an annual field study intended as the central "clinical" component of administrator training. The Kellogg proposal eliminated any reference to research in the social sciences as an objective. Instead Harvard would force social science to relate to administrator training by radically recasting the job descriptions of the social scientists employed in the Center for Field Studies. No one thought it would be easy to "bring the motivation of the scholar and the motivation of the responsible public servant into closer alignment." But if the efforts of some social scientists could be harnessed to address training needs, the faculty hoped that some students might eventually develop the "right balance" between research interests and administrative skill.

The team of social scientists protested that this redefinition of their role removed all incentives for young scholars to join the faculty. Perhaps, they argued, it would be better to appoint no social scientists at all to the Center. They envied the acumen of a sociologist earlier recruited to participate in the community social structure project, Neal Gross, who had almost immediately maneuvered his way out of it, thereby avoiding the substantive and training conflicts they faced. Gross had won his freedom by generating foundation support, through the help of the department of social relations, for his own separate project. Directed at the problem of role conflict in superintendents, Gross's study commanded Keppel's enthusiastic support but also called unintended attention to the dilemmas of role conflict within the faculty of education. Soon the social scientists who had committed themselves to the Center's research project — Peter Rossi, James Shipton, and J. Leiper Freeman — left the School. The priorities of 1949 had been dramatically reversed: training needs now set research policies. Partly to compensate for the demise of the Center for Field Studies as a research enterprise, the senior faculty authorized a tenured appointment in social science entirely separate from the Administrative Career Program. Everyone knew that the favored inside candidate was Neal Gross. The separate discipline of sociology of education began to emerge.[21]

As THE M.A.T. program grew in the mid-fifties, its intellectual center of gravity became the tactical functions of admissions recruitment, and financial aid. Coordinated by Associate Dean Judson T. Shaplin, both instruction and research were kept on the periphery of programmatic concern. William H. Burton, who represented the older conviction that scientific principles of teaching existed and could be conveyed to novices, felt excluded from the new priorities. "The wisdom of our ancient gods," he lamented with mock exaggeration, had been "drowned out by the shouting and the tumult of the Kelloggs and the Fords." Keppel proudly and pointedly told the Fund for the Advancement of Education that the word "principles" no longer referred to the claim that systematic knowledge existed but was merely a synonym for supervised observation and teaching.[22]

In this climate, inquiry on teacher education or curriculum did not thrive. The Fund had reluctantly sponsored a study of teacher effectiveness in 1952, which Keppel hoped would focus the attention of faculty in curriculum and methods on a research project of common interest. But the dean's office, preoccupied with career recruitment, neglected to encourage this collaboration, and project leadership passed exclusively to social scientists recruited from the Laboratory of Human Development. In contrast to policies followed in school administration, no effort was made to incorporate their research into the teacher education curriculum. Faced also with substantial methodological difficulties in correlating training experiences with subsequent teaching performance, the Teacher Education Research Project struggled in isolation and produced no dramatic results. It merely confirmed the Fund's suspicions that research in the behavioral sciences was of little practical value, and it disappeared as a funding priority in subsequent Harvard proposals.[23]

Social scientists outside the School increasingly pointed to its striking neglect of applied research in teaching and learning. Professor Jerome S. Bruner argued in 1955, for example, that the Graduate School of Education was entirely cut off from developments in cognitive psychology that promised explanations of how knowledge was acquired and how teaching might proceed. Much of Harvard University's research efforts in school instruction was carried on outside of the School of Education by psychologists in the faculty of arts and sciences, such as Bruner and B. F. Skinner. Keppel agreed with the ironic diagnosis and hoped to inaugurate a new faculty research seminar if outside funds could be obtained. Meanwhile, a small group of dissatisfied doctoral students persuaded John Carroll to take titular leadership of a Laboratory for Research in Instruction that might generate funds for research studies related to teaching and learning.[24]

Some faculty members in teacher education hoped to advance their careers not by research but by starting, as the faculty had done in guidance and administration, practitioner training programs at the doctoral level. Morris L. Cogan, who directed secondary school apprenticeship training, and Robert H. Anderson, who had similar responsibilities in elementary education, both sought to diversify their activities beyond master's level teacher education and planned advanced courses and doctoral curricula in curriculum and supervision. The perceived route to promotion within the School was to find a role apart from either research or the conduct of teacher education. This faculty strategy paralleled and complemented the growing desire to emphasize career lines for M.A.T. graduates different from, yet associated with, conventional classroom teaching. Doctoral study in teaching would legitimize the claim that master teachers or team leaders were truly different from the mass. Thus for M.A.T. alumni who did not wish a doctorate in administration, the M.A.T. would not be a terminal degree but merely the starting point on the "long road to professional leadership."

By 1955 the senior faculty agreed to authorize four tenured professorships for teacher education, but the criteria for appointment were unclear. How would the senior faculty weigh research in instruction or curriculum against the growing faculty interest in doctoral training for practitioner roles? Ambiguously, Keppel hoped that the doctoral products of these tenured professors would be "scholars" of broad educational problems but that by being scholars they would also be practitioners "in the best sense of the word."[25]

The issue came to a head in 1956 during Keppel's negotiations with the Fund for the Advancement of Education to support the idea of team teaching. Keppel hoped to secure a major endowment gift, not just for Harvard but for a number of other private schools of education, to enable them to alter the very structure of teaching careers and thus promote both career recruitment and career deployment. The Fund's interest in team teaching presented a "dramatic moment" to redefine the role of schoolteacher and stabilize the School's budget. It fully justified a "crash program" to produce the most impressive possible proposal.[26]

The crash program exposed the differences between Keppel's priorities and the career ambitions of several faculty members in teacher education. Many of the latter hoped that new Ford resources would occasion a redefinition of the role of a professor of education rather than of a schoolteacher. Long discussions in the senior faculty revealed that team teaching was more a private enthusiasm of Keppel's than a reform conviction shared by his colleagues. They did not want the proposal to "stand or fall on what was intended only as an example." The team idea should be considered merely the "first thing to be tried out." Phillip Eulon, who had always disliked the contemporary enthusiasm for teacher education on grounds that it eroded research, now doubted whether administrative tinkering with the teacher's job was a serious breakthrough and whether its impact would ever be evaluated systematically.

The senior faculty discussions concentrated not on the team idea but rather on staffing implications if Harvard wished to try out and disseminate action programs. Part of the effort, argued a subcommittee, would "involve descriptive reporting and evaluation of the *actions* taken, as distinguished from experimental research programs. A great deal of faculty energy will be expended in direct relationships with public school personnel and with concrete problems of school organization, curriculum, and the training of local school personnel." Individuals appointed to handle the program would likely "resemble more closely the administrative and supervisory personnel of school systems than the present members of the faculty." They would be at a "distinct disadvantage in research, instruction, and publication." It would therefore be necessary to develop "new criteria for tenure appointments."

The discussions had turned a subsidiary theme in Keppel's original idea—the notion of demonstrating and disseminating innovations—into a central theme. For several years Keppel had pointed to the example of medical training to emphasize the superiority of clinical or field study over didactic academic instruction. Now the analogy was pushed further to embrace the problem of implementation. Schools of education had to establish "relations with schools analogous to those long in effect between medical schools and hospitals." Harvard needed a new kind of "clinical" professor of education who possessed "operational skills as well as academic capacity." If large new Ford support was received, the senior members voted to allocate four or five new tenured appointments based on competence in managing innovative programs in schools, ability to describe the innovation as it was tried out, and capacity to cooperate with systematic research that others might undertake. They also decided to defer consideration of Robert Anderson's future until he could be assessed by the new criteria.

The new appointment policy not only opened new paths to promotion in teacher education independent of research productivity, but suggested a new strategy for school reform independent of research findings. In embracing the senior members' elaboration on his original idea, Keppel saw the value of arguing not merely for restructuring the role of teacher but for taking on implementation as a larger reform technique. In the decentralized American school system where no formal machinery existed to guarantee that useful new ideas be adopted, "everything must be done by persuasion." The best means of persuasion, Keppel now told the Fund, was sponsorship by universities of "demonstrations and pilot projects and widespread reports of results to all schools." The "clinical professor," though not directly responsible for the production or evaluation of ideas, would play a crucial role in their implementation.[27]

The programmatic and financial stakes of a single proposal had never been higher in Keppel's administration. Concurrent efforts to raise endowment, directed by Neil McElroy, the chairman of Proctor and Gamble, had met no more success than preceding efforts. Keppel's 1957 projections of the income components of an ideal core budget, when compared to similar projections made five years earlier, increased reliance on unrestricted foundation income from $150,000 to $350,000 per year and on tuition income from $170,000 to $300,000. Ford seemed the best and perhaps the only hope for large, long-term, and mainly unrestricted support. Keppel hoped to separate continued support for teacher education from support for the proposed new thrust. He wanted the Fund to endow the first and underwrite the second for a decade. But the Fund's officers remained opposed to endowment gifts. They were acutely aware that behind the exciting talk of a "breakthrough" lay Harvard's concern to stabilize its regular operations. Warily, Fund staffers combed Harvard's budget proposals for evidence of thinly disguised subsidization of faculty payrolls.[28]

Following two annual planning grants, Keppel finally obtained in early 1959 an eight-year award of $2.8 million. The final Harvard proposal integrated almost all institutional activities in teacher education and school administration within the basic theme of career recruitment. Celebrating a career progression that ideally included the M.A.T. program, a period of teaching experience, and then doctoral study, Harvard replaced Kellogg support for its administration program with Ford support and, in addition, extended Ford backing to doctoral programs in teacher education. The new grant continued all previous Ford-sponsored faculty and administrative positions, along with financial aid to teacher education, and permitted considerable expansion. A new office of recruitment was established, and the grant allowed the appointment of junior faculty members in science, social studies, and literature. In 1959-60, Ford funds alone provided 23 percent of the School's entire income. Keppel remarked that his tombstone should read "He negotiated with the Fords."[29]

In return for this astonishing underwriting and expansion of training activities, Harvard established a new agency to disseminate promising school reforms. The School and University Program for Research and Development (SUPRAD), a collaborative venture between the Graduate School of Education and the suburban school systems of Newton, Lexington, and Concord, was conceived to be an organizational equivalent to the ties between medical schools and teaching hospitals. Keppel personally viewed SUPRAD as mainly a vehicle for reordering the personnel structure of schools, and he allocated most resources to a team teaching project in Lexington. Harvard seemed puzzled about what SUPRAD might do apart from amplifying the idea of personnel restructuring, and Keppel soon worried aloud that this action agency might merely advocate fashionable innovations rather than demonstrate their efficacy with convincing evidence. The ghost of the Bureau of Vocational Guidance still stalked Harvard's halls. SUPRAD nonetheless provided an opportunity for several faculty members to redefine their Harvard roles. Robert Anderson, in particular, energetically coordinated the team teaching project, and in 1959 was rewarded with tenure. The institution had its first postwar clinical professor, in which action and advocacy were more important than research.[30]

The pressure to reconcile different notions of faculty competence had produced by the late fifties a bewildering number of new criteria for faculty appointment and promotion. The idea of "balance" in a faculty member, first made explicit in the deliberations about guidance, emphasized a variety of desirable characteristics among which research skill was only one. In teacher education, the idea of a "clinical" professorship stressed capacity to manage and promote action programs. The drift in school administration was to force social scientists to engage in systematic administrative training. Each of these different formulations was an attempt to harmonize the tasks of applied research and professional instruction, but the effect was to hasten the demise of applied social science as the dominating feature of the School's environment. The ambitious research plans in guidance, community social structure, and teacher effectiveness had not succeeded. Keppel himself detected by 1957 a "growing disenchantment with the promise of the social sciences."[31]

At the end of the fifties the School's reputation and influence rested far more on its practitioner programs, especially the M.A.T. and the Administrative Career Program, than on its research productivity. Even in discipline-oriented basic research, where the record was more visible than in applied research, it was often said with truth that projects would have been conducted anyway if the faculty had been employed in some other institution. Much of the early output in the Laboratory of Human Development, for example, merely finished at Harvard, and under the same funding auspices, what had been started at Iowa. In those rare cases where research directions had been shaped by the School itself—for example, Bernard Bailyn's pathbreaking historical study of 1960, *Education in the Forming of American Society*—they often appeared years after the faculty involved had left the School. There was little sense that the School had succeeded in building the special research environment it had attempted after 1948. Its main products, instead, were students. The 1946 Purple Memorandum had anticipated a student body of no more than one hundred full-time equivalent students, but by 1959 nearly five hundred full-time and two hundred part-time students were enrolled.

Some faculty members complained that this growth, when juxtaposed with appointment policies that stressed scholarship in academic disciplines and a confusing variety of nonresearch options, had only produced a directionless, fragmented and centrifugal institution. If a sense of common mission had ever existed, they believed, it had eroded entirely. Representatives of each kind of senior appointment argued among themselves that theirs was unfairly underrepresented. Their growing rivalries, and the uncertainty of criteria, led to embarrassing disputes with presidential *ad hoc* advisory committees that rejected both scholarly and clinical professorial nominees as insufficiently distinguished.[32]

Despite internal friction, there was little doubt that the institution's public reputation had grown enormously since the dark times of the 1930s. Nothing better expressed the nature of Keppel's achievement than the wide attention given the appointment of Calvin Gross as New York City's school superintendent in 1962. Keppel himself had chaired the search committee, and the appointment seemed to symbolize Harvard's new centrality in career recruitment and career management.[33] Gross, a Phi Beta Kappa mathematics major as an undergraduate, had been one of the first three Fellows in Education at the beginning of Keppel's administration. Later he received an Ed.D. from the School and was assisted in a meteoric rise in school administration by the School's placement services. Weeks later Keppel himself was appointed United States Commissioner of Education by President Kennedy. It seemed that education's missing elite not only had been found, but was rapidly rising to those positions of leverage which ensured effective public influence.

Epilogue:
Roots of Instability

AT THE END of Keppel's deanship the School was firmly committed to elite practitioner recruitment and the advancement of scholarly disciplines related to education. Still, this mission proved no more stable than its predecessors had. The late 1960s was a chaotic and volatile time when older purposes were challenged, sometimes discarded, and always transformed. These dislocations rivaled in intensity and effect the switch from academic curriculum reform to the socialization of education early in the century, the sudden endorsement of professional formation in the middle twenties, and the repudiation of training in favor of research during the 1940s. At the beginning of the 1970s many puzzled or exhausted faculty members wondered if discontinuity and upheaval were inherent characteristics of the Harvard Graduate School of Education. Why was drastic and wrenching change so frequent?[1]

The administration first sought to assure continuity of the late fifties' mission through obtaining long-term financial support for basic programs. President Pusey, Dean Keppel, and his successor, Theodore R. Sizer, hoped especially to consolidate earlier gains by expanding the size of the senior faculty. Its complement of ten members in 1962 was smaller than the number of tenured professors in 1940. Compared with prior efforts, their fundraising labors had remarkable success.

The School finally acquired a new campus, in part through the diligent labor and personal generosity of Roy Larsen and Neil McElroy. Endowment also rose dramatically for the first time since 1920. General Harvard prosperity allowed unprecedented redistributions of University endowment surpluses to the various faculties, and Pusey showed striking skill in obtaining outside endowment gifts for the School from even the Ford Foundation. Between 1962 and 1967 the senior faculty increased to twenty-six members. An elaborate faculty review of the School's purposes in 1964-65 under the direction of Israel Scheffler, the first such exercise since the Purple Memorandum, largely endorsed the two main thrusts of the late Keppel era.

Other ideas penetrated the School, most readily through the substantive interests of new funding sources and the shifting priorities of existing sources. Long before the endowment grew, Keppel continued to solicit short-term funds to perpetuate the advances made possible by Ford, Kellogg, and the others. That effort was successful, but its very success generated a chain of new projects that enlarged and eventually conflicted with the mission he wanted to stabilize. The most exciting new source of substantial temporary funds was the federal government.

Until 1956, the scale of federal support to the School had been limited and its influence indirect. During World War II federal contracts helped to stimulate faculty interest in research and development. After the war, GI Bill benefits increased tuition revenues. Throughout the fifties a few individuals received research support from agencies such as the National Institute of Mental Health. But as late as 1955 no more than 5 percent of institutional income derived from government sources.

Only after Congress funded the Cooperative Research Act in 1956, and the National Science Foundation supported at the same time in-service training of mathematics and science teachers, did federal concern for education per se begin seriously to affect the School. Following the Sputnik scare a year later and passage of the National Defense Education Act, Harvard understood that substantial additional federal assistance was likely. Largely through NSF in-service programs and Cooperative Research Program grants, federal aid increased to approximately 25 percent of total income for each of the years between 1953 and 1963.

Considerable faculty discussion was devoted to the probable institutional impact of federal funds. One possible problem was federal control over academic decisions, as exemplified by cold-war requirements such as loyalty oaths, disclaimer affidavits, and security clearances. But these regulations were not regarded as serious or long-term threats. They seemed always tied to specific programs the

School could reject if too obnoxious, and were also opposed by liberal politicians who dismissed them as transient. The greatest potential danger, instead, was thought to be the enticement of federal programs unrelated to the School's principal programmatic mission. Unless the School disciplined itself in its scramble for federal dollars, Keppel warned in 1959, it might "lose its central purpose and become a holding company for the solution of *ad hoc* problems defined by outside forces."[2]

Here, too, Keppel was optimistic. He hoped that personal relationships with federal officials could promote a close match between Cambridge and Washington priorities. Moreover, he hoped that the variety of potential funding agencies within the federal establishment would allow for diversity of viewpoints and even competition, so that institutions seeking support would have the same range of options available to them in the foundation world. Especially after the 1960 presidential elections, Keppel used his professional prestige and contacts within the new federal administration to advocate general, multiyear support to stabilize institutional budgets. The chances for success seemed promising, not only because the federal education bureaucracy as it related to institutional grants was unformed and malleable, but because Keppel himself soon became Commissioner of Education. Federal assistance to the School did rise greatly, especially following enactment of President Johnson's Great Society legislation. By 1967, 62 percent of all income derived from federal sources. The School's annual income first exceeded $1 million in 1958. A decade later its income surpassed $8 million; the federal contribution alone approached $4.7 million.

But the most striking aspect of this vast expansion was the general unavailability of federal funds for program support or institution building. Government priorities — and increasingly foundation priorities as well — were directed not toward stabilizing the School's programmatic mission but instead toward specific research and development projects. These were expected to produce visible educational products or services frequently outside the main currents of the School's regular activities. Among the many new initiatives undertaken, the four largest created a comprehensive secondary school for the Western Region of Nigeria ($2.4 million from the Agency for International Development); a high school physics course ($4.3 million from the Office of Education); a computer-based vocational counseling system ($1.8 million from the Office of Education); and a research and development center on educational differences ($4.1 million from the Office of Education). Just as outside foundation support in the early fifties altered Keppel's initial charge, so outside federal support in the early sixties pushed the School toward greater concern for the practical outcomes of research and development. Although some professors were concerned that the availability of grants deflected faculty from regular duties — an early example was Associate Dean Shaplin's decision to abandon directing the M.A.T. in order to participate in various international education projects — the professional advantages seemed clearly to outweigh the risks.

Both Pusey and Dean Sizer enthusiastically embraced the new possibilities. Aware that the School's present influence lay more in the leaders it recruited than in the ideas it produced, they wanted to correct the imbalance. Unlike Pusey, Sizer understood and approved the elite career recruitment strategy of the fifties. Indeed his own career (Pomfret School, Yale College, Harvard M.A.T., Harvard Ph.D. in Education) exemplified the workings of that strategy. But he also wanted to increase the impact of research on practice and policy. The momentum provided by federal project funds enabled him to support applied social science on a scale far greater than Keppel had experienced even in the heady expansion after 1948. The federal interest in applied social science at the beginning of the sixties was not at all Conant's explicit interest in promoting social mobility. Still, the growing belief that research could and should cause immediate educational improvement recalled Conant's convictions far more than it did the discipline-oriented scholarship that dominated inquiry at the School.[3]

Although the new resources for research and development were expected to deepen rather than preempt the mission Keppel had bequeathed, conflicts soon arose. Federal dollars transformed the professional roles of several senior faculty members from training practitioners to conducting action research projects. After the projects were completed, these professors were reluctant to revert to more mundane and less lavish instructional operations. A frequent outcome was the reorientation of doctoral training programs toward research and development, away from preparation for school-based practitioner roles. The apprenticeship possibilities for advanced students on projects, along with the lure of financial aid in the form of research assistantships, altered student career interests as well as those of the teachers who supervised them.

The fear of a "holding company" was ever present. Grant procedures tended to redirect financial control from the School's administration to faculty project directors, in marked contrast to the pattern of foundation training grants a decade before. When the faculty husbanded resources for its own purposes, the administration hoped that the last major project over which it exerted clear control, the research and development center, could be the "glue" to hold an increasingly disparate faculty together. The administration also fought to use at least some of the center's resources for discretionary purposes and to support existing basic programs, much as Dean Keppel had done with Ford money. Yet Commissioner Keppel's optimism that federal funds would be permitted to serve this purpose proved largely incorrect. After a protracted dispute with federal officials, the research and development center was closed down.[4]

Before its demise the center had become a serious threat to the mission of the 1950s. Many of its projects became conduits for new ideas in the School. Although some employed research designs consistent with social science methodology, others were not "research" in the sense of dispassionate, controlled inquiry. They celebrated moral passion, social activism, and optimistic reform of a new sort. Their principal themes were urban education and the limits of formal schooling.

An internal study at the beginning of 1966 revealed that the "most extended and heated issue" under debate at the center was its ability to reform urban schools. Conant's fears of class conflict had been largely forgotten at the School during the booming suburban expansion of the fifties. His analysis, moreover, had emphasized mobility for the academically talented and stratification in small towns rather than education for urban minorities. Although Harvard applauded the 1954 desegregation decision, it advanced no program of action beyond the recruitment and placement of more able school administrators for the South. But by the early sixties the old anxieties about social class had returned, in a new context. Conant's 1961 firebell in the night, *Slums and Suburbs*, dramatically applied his 1940s arguments to the case of urban blacks.

As early as 1962 the School lamented the absence of urban materials in its courses, and even briefly considered an exclusively urban
orientation for its original research and development center proposal. Urban interest accelerated through a shift of priorities within
the Ford Foundation and the funding of several urban projects
through the research and development center. The result was the
reestablishment of ties (broken since early in the century) between
the Graduate School of Education and the public schools of Boston
and Cambridge. The School appointed administrative Liaisons with
these cities, commenced curriculum projects in Roxbury, inaugurated a Harvard-Boston summer training program, and began studies on black teenagers and the effects of desegregation. Although
most of these activities were conducted by white administrators and
researchers, research and development center funds brought the
first blacks to the School's professional staff. After federal support of
these activities ceased, the Ford Foundation continued most of them
and eventually endowed a professorship in urban policy.

At the same time, these and other center projects emphasized a
second theme. Education occurred in many places outside schools
and perhaps could best be improved if schooling itself was not the
primary focus of reform. In many ways this idea was a direct legacy
of the history of educational psychology at the School since 1949.
Sears and Whiting had emphasized socialization, not schooling, and
Whiting himself resigned from the faculty in 1962 to join the more
comfortable scholarly atmosphere of the department of social relations. His successor, Gerald S. Lesser, made his interests in adolescent subcultures and the cultural roots of mental abilities central to
the research and development center agenda. The center's executive
director, a student of both Whiting and Lesser, defined his major
focus as "*expanded educational opportunities* (or environments) . . .
not restricted to schools and schooling."

The center's pre-school project, for example, stressed family
rather than school settings and addressed an age group that did not
attend school at all. Other center projects analyzed adolescent identity formation and the unintentional effects of the public schools'
social system on learning. One of the largest projects, a staff seminar
on secondary education reform (called the "Shadow Faculty" because it had a program but still no school to implement it) emphasized the restoration of links between schools and other community

agencies. All of these activities suggested the common theme of "how various educational agencies and influences can be more rationally orchestrated than is now common. One major outcome might be a classification of the limits and potentialities of schooling, *per se*." Prior to its demise, the center resolved to undertake a major study of the limits of schooling. Afterwards, with Carnegie rather than federal support, that ambition led to the analysis by Christopher Jencks and several faculty colleagues, *Inequality: A Reassessment of the Impact of Family and Schooling in America.*[5]

The emergence of both a moral commitment to urban educational reform and of growing doubts about the efficacy of schooling as a means to reform created articulate criticism of the School's established mission. If the educational value of schooling was limited, was not the program the School was attempting to stabilize flawed as well? If the problem of secondary education was the restoration of community and not academic learning, why emphasize a teacher education program organized according to the major academic subjects taught in schools? If what happened to children outside school was at least as important as what happened in school, why should Harvard practitioner programs exclusively train school-based workers such as guidance counselors and principals? If education's problems were largely urban, why were the School's recruitment and placement efforts geared primarily to a suburban clientele? If academic inquiry in discrete disciplines had little effect on solving social problems, why continue doctoral programs in just those disciplines instead of interdisciplinary programs explicitly committed to problem solving?

Had the level of federal funding been maintained, and had inflation not advanced, perhaps these new voices would simply have been added to the older mission without disrupting it. Instead, competition arose for increasingly scarce resources. The resignations of five discipline-oriented professors at the end of the decade—the largest exodus of tenured faculty in the School's history—were due in some degree to a perceived erosion of institutional respect for less "relevant" scholarship. The doctoral program in sociology of education, for example, was abolished in favor of an interdisciplinary problem-centered program in education and social policy. The Laboratory of Human Development escaped unscathed in part because it repudiated the Sears-Whiting research model and initiated topical reform themes such as children's television and moral education.

In the new climate, the ideology of career recruitment also became a less tenable justification for practitioner training programs. Most M.A.T. alumni, for example, worked in suburban school systems. Seventy-six percent of 1954 alumni reported that their pupils were mainly from professional, executive, or white-collar family backgrounds. More than that, the M.A.T. focus on school careers seemed of decreasing relevance to educational reform. Some members of the Shadow Faculty eventually transformed the social studies teacher education program into a broad concern for "learning environments" which downgraded teaching methods, curriculum, and schooling itself. By 1973 the M.A.T. itself was abolished.[6]

The guidance program was absorbed into a multifaculty attempt to prevent psychological instability by addressing its social sources; school-based individual remediation was passé. The new program in "clinical psychology and public practice' perfectly expressed the moral passion for urban reform and the conviction that decisive education occurred mainly outside school. In school administration the range of career objectives was similarly broadened beyond the superintendency to include educational and managerial jobs outside public education. Institutional withdrawal from school practice in teacher education and guidance led directly to the resignations of two other full professors.

THE NEED for some retrenchment was clear, but the character of the reduction was not foreordained. Many more cautious options were available. Yet the School decisively rejected much of the fifties' mission, just as earlier reorganizations usually rejected outright what had come before. Somehow, as in the past, there were no anchors of continuity, no self-evident functions that needed carrying on despite the immediate crisis. The strength of the institution was its extraordinary capacity to break free from tradition and take on entirely new ventures. Its weakness was the debilitating sense that nothing at all was assured, even for the brief Harvard lifetimes of faculty members and the briefer lifetimes of students.[7]

Financial vulnerability partially explains the jarring discontinuities. In most other private or public schools of education, the central university administration collected tuition and authorized expenditures. The Harvard School of Education could not rely on a centralized budget process to moderate adverse changes in its fiscal situation. It had to balance its own budget. While suffering the inherent disadvantages of fiscal independence, it lacked some of the usual advantages. Tuition policies were soon pegged to those of the faculty of arts and sciences rather than to those of other schools of education, and only in the Keppel era was the School permitted to realize any of the profits from its own summer instruction.

The School's greatest spurts of growth and energy were always made possible by new resources — the philanthropic outburst after 1912, the sizable endowment gift of 1920 which freed Holmes to dream of a training revolution, the foundation largesse of the fifties, and the federal beneficence of the sixties. But after World War II these resources became more temporary and more problematic. It seemed easier to raise funds for adventurous new initiatives than to undergird older endeavors.

Federal funding peaked in 1968 at $4.7 million and steadily declined thereafter to $1.2 million in 1975. In the first year of that decline, the School lost over $300,000 of unrestricted overhead income which paid for numerous functions that needed continuation despite the end of federal dollars. At the same time, the fraction of basic expenses assumed by noninstructional functions such as plant maintenance and library development expanded far beyond minimum-inflation planning assumptions of the early sixties. Eventually the need to reduce expenditures became insistent, and that need coincided with ideological dissatisfaction over both career recruitment and the scholarly disciplines.

But the absence of anchors of continuity to mediate temporary enthusiasm was far more complex than financial explanations alone might suggest. A deeper cause was fundamental uncertainty within the field of education itself. At Harvard, the field never resolved any of the basic organizing questions that might have legitimized stable traditions. What were the basic roles for which professionals should be trained? How could universities develop education professionals? How was reliable educational knowledge generated? What were the distinct tasks of education in American society?

Implicitly or explicitly, other Harvard professional schools developed internal consensus on at least some of these questions which satisfied themselves and the outside society for substantial periods of time. Education never satisfied itself or society that its answers were more than ephemeral. Nor did pressing responsibilities imposed from outside act as a counterweight to sudden shifts of mission. In state universities, for example, the clear obligation to turn out a predictable supply of teachers transcended any doubts about whether teachers could be trained or were the most significant education professionals. Harvard was free from such public demands. Paradoxically, the incessant internal expectation that the School conform to elite Harvard ideals of research and training only accentuated its sometimes frantic pursuit of acceptable objectives.

No lasting Harvard agreement was achieved on what educational jobs were of most worth. The answer at any moment depended on shifting institutional needs and social circumstances rather than on a stable conception of the basic job of the profession. Concerned with academic instruction for a limited number of adolescents, Eliot and Hanus first presumed that education courses existed to train beginning teachers. But Hanus, combining departmental ambition with a sense of the emerging era of mass education, soon focused on experienced teachers. While these teachers pursued the new career possibilities then opening up, they could also be recruited to the larger service of managing the socialization of education. Later Holmes understood how such considerations had separated ambitious schools of education from ordinary teachers and committed himself to bring them together again. His profound failure led the School again to reject teachers altogether. But Keppel's brilliant marriage of unexpected fundraising opportunities with a social-class analysis of teacher competence once again restored teacher education to a central institutional position.

Nonetheless, the role of the classroom teacher was rarely regarded as important in itself. Harvard's main intention was to recruit and advance a heretofore missing elite; the traditional teaching job was an obstacle to this recruitment and so had to be changed. As long as the national teacher shortage existed, the strategy worked well. But when that crisis receded by the end of the sixties and external support for the M.A.T. ended as well, no deeper commitment to teaching careers as a self-evident priority remained. An emphasis on educational jobs distant from children reemerged. Unlike earlier times, many of these jobs were located outside school systems or schools of education.

Just as the School achieved no lasting consensus about the roles it would train for, so it established no traditions of how professionals in education were developed. The schoolmen who encouraged Eliot to act in 1891 had no real confidence in the impact of training per se, but hoped that the prestige of university instruction in education would attract ambitious and able college graduates to teaching. Soon Hanus and his colleagues abandoned the idea of training as a magnet and stressed instead the technical proficiency that instruction could convey. Holmes was also confident that carefully contrived training experiences could turn novices into true educators, although his ideal curriculum emphasized general ethical and analytic capacity rather than more specialized technical skill.

Both Hanus and Holmes wanted to break decisively with traditions of training that predated university schools of education. They wanted in particular to avoid any hint that apprenticeship or submersion in particular school environments was a main source of mature professional competence. The failure of Holmes's elaborate training schemes did not lead the School to seek alternative training methods, but instead to emphasize selection and recruitment. This modern strategy stressed the limits of professional training and thus recalled the older line of reasoning exemplified by men such as Horace Willard and Barrett Wendell. Professional competence seemed primarily to be some combination of native capacity and developed personality and cosmopolitanism. It depended more on deeply held values acquired over the whole span of life than on the acquisition of particular skills in a brief moment of technical study. Holmes had grasped the significance of values and personality in teaching, but was convinced that they could be shaped through an intense professional environment. Less optimistically, Keppel preferred that students possess them on entrance.

In addition to being anti-professional, Keppel's emphasis on recruitment was elitist. At first that elitism was not disguised or apologized for. It was openly celebrated as a strategy to build internal prestige within the University and as a potent recruiting lure. But during the 1960s elitist ideology began to clash openly with emerging egalitarian values. The rejection of privilege by many of the School's students — and faculty — led to successful challenges of faculty authority in such matters as student participation in admissions and academic decisions. At a time when elected committees of students, faculty, and secretaries solemnly debated rewriting the School's "Constitution" to redistribute political power, it was hardly surprising that elitism became an epithet to be avoided rather than a banner to be marched under.

The elaborate efforts to attract students from the most selective colleges and to utilize test scores and class rank in student selection gave way to a restored 1920s emphasis on commitment and previous work experience. The retreat from elitism was accelerated also by the School's desire to admit more minority students, who did not yet attend elite colleges in large numbers, and by the claim of many students that traditional measures of intellectual capacity were inherently discriminatory against racial minorities. By the 1970s the pressing need for ever-increasing tuition revenues further diminished, in many programs, commitment to a carefully chosen student body. Accompanying the deemphasis on selection as the major strategy of professional development was the beginning of a restored interest, again reminiscent of the 1920s, in how the curriculum might successfully inculcate certain professional skills.

The School never developed a clear sense of how educational knowledge was produced. Eliot believed that Harvard already knew what proper education was from experience accumulated over the years. To him the problem was not the existence of education's knowledge base, but its implementation. Hanus soon realized that merely asserting professional authority would not suffice. Scientific evidence that could not readily be contradicted was required. Although Holmes soon became suspicious of the authoritarian tendencies and narrow agenda of educational science, he put nothing in its place. The School was a backwater of educational research until the 1940s.

After social science inquiry had become a clear priority, its benefits remained unclear. It was easy to revert to Eliot-like direct action, as Keppel did with team teaching, because no research approach seemed to offer much hope for dramatic improvements in practice. Even after the School had expended enormous federal monies in the late sixties, and had produced apparently impressive school curricula in physics and social studies, many faculty members concluded that the research and development effort made little educational difference. Somehow the right variables were not being identified. Somehow the right methodologies had not been developed. Somehow no evidence of real effect was visible. Research in education seemed a profound disappointment. Yet alternatives to the scientific generation of knowledge were never taken very seriously. The School never developed a laboratory or a demonstration school. Nicholas Hobbs's idea of a research clinic in which the complexities of actual practice could be analyzed got nowhere. The potential of SUPRAD to understand life in ordinary classrooms, or to codify rich experience, was dissipated by both confident advocacy and administrative confusion.

These disagreements about roles, skills, and production of knowledge all expressed the Harvard School's inability to sustain a coherent vision of its task in American society. In the traditional learned professions, responsibility usually meant discrete problem solving. Most of the time it was fairly clear what professional services were expected and almost as clear (except perhaps in the ministry) whether they had been satisfactorily delivered. Doctors were supposed to cure illnesses, lawyers to win cases. Education's services, in contrast, were less specific in intention, less localized in time, and less susceptible to commonsense assessments of effectiveness. Indeed, it was frequently unclear whom the clients or beneficiaries of Harvard's educational services were intended to be.

One undeniable if rarely mentioned task of Harvard, for example, was to advance the vocational interests of educators. Of course the Massachusetts schoolmen who petitioned the legislature in 1890 cared deeply for their youthful charges, but their debates make clear that their own marginal status primarily moved them to act. They wanted to convert their occupation into a career, to ally themselves with higher education, and to protect themselves from the forces of elementary education. Harvard willingly allied itself with their cause. Years later, when the Division of Education faced the peril of declining undergraduate enrollments, it deliberately recruited practicing teachers to graduate study by shaping its curriculum to meet their career needs. The career needs of adult schoolmen and the fiscal needs of the School became, for a time, synonymous with the needs of education.

In the twenties, Harvard tried to reverse that policy. It took responsibility for defining educational needs and then required prospective professionals to conform to that formulation. The School's avoidance of placement-office boosterism engendered some resentment from students who did not get full support in their quest for mobility. Holmes later lashed out against the "pedagogical racketeering" of professional courses and credentialing that made educators into mechanical civil servants. He wanted educators to be appointed for their quality alone. After World War II the placement function grew enormously as it tried to manage the career trajectories of promising alumni. But even then placement was privately regarded as serving educational needs before it served alumni needs.

From the beginning, education at Harvard also advanced the University's immediate interests. Eliot used the field almost exclusively to amplify his school reform efforts, which directly advanced the growth of Harvard College and the professional schools. Lowell hoped that educational research would validate his undergraduate reforms. Conant's M.A.T. program was in part an effort to cleanse the Graduate School of Arts and Sciences of its nonresearch aspects, and his endorsement of secondary schools as agents of social mobility meshed neatly with the rise of meritocratic admissions practices in Harvard College. Only Pusey seemed to lack a strong conception of the School's connection with obvious Harvard interests.

Beyond meeting needs of schoolmen and the University, education at Harvard had additional responsibilities to youth and to society. Until the 1950s, Harvard's efforts focused exclusively on adolescents, except for research projects like the Growth Study and tangential summer instruction. The fear of status loss provoked by too many women students enveloped elementary education and caused its early neglect. Even the nature of the School's adolescent constituency constantly shifted over the years. From an early focus on the privileged minority who attended secondary schools, Harvard dramatically shifted its emphasis to the mass of students who increasingly enrolled in high schools for reasons other than college preparation. Correspondingly, the education curriculum moved from academic curriculum reform to the socialization of education. Later on, and especially after the revival of teacher education in the fifties, the student constituency swung back to college-preparatory adolescents. Fields like play and vocational education never survived beyond the tenure of their first incumbents, any more than academic special methods courses of the early 1900s survived the onslaught of social efficiency.

Harvard's conception of education's responsibilities to society underwent similar breathtaking changes. Hanus' formulation emphasized order in a time of unsettling social change. Conant stressed educational mobility in a time of perceived social stagnation. Despite differences, both ideas were self-consciously reformist and both expressed enormous faith in schooling's capacity to shape society.

These various notions of education's tasks overlapped and frequently worked at cross-purposes. All were typically pursued without any clear sense of whether or not they were being met. Decisions to intensify or retreat from a task were not made on the basis of whether the objective seemed nearer or farther away, but on the basis of suddenly conflicting new tasks. Problems were rarely solved; they were survived.

The dilemmas of assessing institutional impact on any problem were enormous. Lowell demanded evidence of the efficacy of vocational guidance before he would promote Brewer, but all Brewer could supply was evidence of his envious role in the field's professional growth. He could say what his students did, and where they did it, but could not demonstrate that it made any difference. Holmes had faith that the market would one day prefer Harvard's well-trained graduates but shied away from defining with precision just what educational tasks they could perform. In the fifties, when school boards were finally clamoring for Harvard alumni in teacher education and administration, they primarily sought talented raw material rather than the formed product of sustained professional training.

BY THE END of the sixties the absence of firm answers to all these fundamental questions often made the School seem rootless and at the mercy of outside forces and enthusiasms. Lacking traditions of continuous professional progress or of substantial scientific achievement, the scent of discouragement was in the air, just as it had been so many times before. Some weary faculty members longed for an uncluttered and unambiguous mission—a research institute, perhaps, or a single core training curriculum—which earlier generations had also coveted and tried at times to implement. Others, assured for a time of outside project money, withdrew from concern for institutional identity to their separate spheres. To them the School seemed nothing more than a holding company. Still others harbored the suspicion that the entire enterprise was flawed and, perhaps, should be abandoned. The training of engineers at Harvard did not long survive Nathaniel Shaler's death, and Yale summarily abolished its own department of education at the end of the fifties. Was a separate and elaborate commitment to education really justifiable in an elite university?

Eight decades of sustained effort had amply demonstrated that the professionalization of education was far more complex than Eliot or Hanus had ever imagined. Exposing those complexities had been the School's greatest contribution and most compelling justification. Harvard's programmatic gyrations mirrored the uncertainties of American education as a whole more than they revealed failures of institutional vision. Indeed, the School's fiscal freedom, accompanied by intellectual obligation to the traditions of the University, only accentuated its awareness of the dilemmas of the American educational enterprise.

Although these dilemmas were debilitating to an aspiring profession in search of authority and legitimacy, they were in fact the real issues. They defined the profession's intellectual agenda. The School could not hide unclear purposes behind a confident technology, or use impressive training techniques to mask dilemmas over which professionals or which clients were most important. No illusions could be sustained for very long. In the midst of uncertainty, the School functioned as a forum where constant reassessment was not only inevitable and exhausting, but liberating and creative. In the end, Harvard's investment in education as a separate institutional center contributed to the subject and the profession not self-confidence but self-consciousness.

Sources

My principal sources were manuscript collections in the Harvard University Archives. Although Paul H. Hanus' descendents destroyed a substantial body of his letters, seventeen file boxes remain. Along with the massive Charles W. Eliot Papers, they are the backbone of the book until about 1910. From about 1912 to 1940 —the Henry W. Holmes years—the papers of the chairman of the Division and dean of the faculty of education (114 boxes) are extensive, thanks to the preservationist zeal of Holmes's devoted and legendary secretary, R. Christine Gill. These official records have been augmented by subsequent transfers of sixteen boxes from Miss Gill's office after her death; by ten boxes of miscellaneous papers; by at least ten boxes I found in various basements; and by four file drawers thoughtfully donated by Holmes's son.

After 1940 the deans' files become less organized and extensive. The original eight boxes of Francis T. Spaulding's deanship papers have been supplemented by seven additional boxes donated by his widow. The five boxes of official Phillip J. Rulon papers have been enriched by the deposit of twenty-four file drawers of records following his death. The papers of Francis Keppel's administration number only fifty-seven boxes, but they are supplemented by records of other contemporary administrative officers.

The extensive presidential papers of A. Lawrence Lowell and James B. Conant were indispensable. Although the President and Fellows graciously granted me access to the Conant Papers, that graciousness did not extend to permitting publication in this book of direct quotations from those papers. Manuscript collections of other faculty members in the Archives include the Frederick G. Nichols Papers (forty-four boxes); Walter F. Dearborn Papers (twenty-six boxes); Robert Ulich Papers (seventeen boxes); Charles Swain Thomas Papers (five boxes); Truman L. Kelley Papers (two boxes); William H. Burton Papers (two boxes); and John M. Brewer Papers (two boxes).

Papers of individual faculty members constitute only a small portion, although the most valuable portion, of the enormous and ever-increasing archival material about the Graduate School of Education. The shelflist of largely unpublished records after 1920, including the papers of standing committees and administrative departments, itself consumed twenty-three pages when this study began. An additional twenty-nine pages of shelflist was required to catalog published material, such as course bulletins. Materials on such topics as student and faculty course notes, on the Division of Education before 1920, on other departments, schools, offices, and individuals that dealt with education are also very extensive. From time to time the Archives reveal unexpected education collections only indirectly connected with Harvard, such as materials on the Vocation Bureau of Boston and the New England Association of College Teachers of Education.

Within the University but outside the Archives, important correspondence files related to the 1950s and 1960s remain in the administrative offices of the Graduate School of Education. The Houghton Library contains papers of William James and Barrett Wendell. Records of the faculty of arts and sciences were examined in University Hall. Non-Harvard manuscript collections consulted included the Hugo Münsterberg Papers, Boston Public Library; Charles F. Adams, Jr., Papers, Massachusetts Historical Society; Abraham Flexner Papers, Library of Congress; James E. Russell Papers, Teachers College, Columbia University; Henry L. Shattuck Papers, Massachusetts Historical Society; and the Archives of the Fund for the Advancement of Education, Ford Foundation, New York.

Interviews conducted to supplement manuscript material included Bancroft Beatley (October 1975); Paul H. Buck (August 1976); Alvin C. Eurich (July 1977); Francis Keppel (December 1976); R. Christine Gill (November 1961); Joseph Lee (May 1966); Paul A. Perry (June 1976); Nathan M. Pusey (July 1976); Phillip J. Rulon (February 1966); Mrs. Phillip J. Rulon (August 1976); Robert Schaefer (December 1976); Judson T. Shaplin (September 1976); Mrs. Francis T. Spaulding (January 1966); Fletcher G. Watson (August 1976); John W. M. Whiting (August 1976). Questions were answered through correspondence by O. Hobart Mowrer (January 1966) and Robert Ulich (May 1966). In addition, I received numerous letters from alumni containing reminiscences and course notes.

The most valuable published materials were the annual reports of the president of Harvard University and, beginning in 1921, the annual reports to the president from the dean of the Graduate School of Education. These not only recorded significant events and data but tried to shape future events through calculated appeals to various constituencies. The extensive educational periodical literature at the end of the nineteenth century provided a ready outlet for individual faculty thought. Within the Harvard community I relied on the *Harvard Graduates' Magazine, Harvard Alumni Bulletin, Harvard Illustrated Monthly,* and *Harvard Teachers Record* (later the *Harvard Educational Review*). The most important educational periodicals consulted were *The Academy, The New England Journal of Education, The School Review, Educational Review,* and *School and Society.*

Very few retrospective accounts of the School or its members exist. Holmes prepared a historical chapter for Samuel Eliot Morison's *The Development of Harvard University since the Inauguration of President Eliot, 1869-1929* (Cambridge, 1930). His essay naturally interpreted the School's brief history as an inexorable development toward the 1927 reorganization. After his retirement, Holmes seriously considered writing a full-scale account of the School's then less inexorable history, but his active involvement in civic education took precedence and the project was abandoned.

Hanus' *Adventuring in Education* (Cambridge, 1937) is one of the few serious autobiographies of the first generation of professors of education and is important for information on his life prior to 1891. Yet at eighty-two he was too old to need vindication; though never boring, the book has a blandness that his career did not. He knew very well, as did all his friends, how much he had left out. One of those friends, John M. Brewer, wrote a *History of Vocational Guidance, Origins and Early Development* (New York and London, 1942) which in part is an account of his own role in the movement. Walter F. Dearborn's scientific contribution was assessed by one of his most distinguished students, Leonard Carmichael, in *Walter Fenno Dearborn and the Scientific Study of Reading* (Cambridge, 1957) Beyond this, I have profited from reading, in manuscript form, retrospective accounts of guidance and science education since 1945 by David V. Tiedeman and Fletcher G. Watson, and an extended autobiographical essay by Robert Ulich.

As for education's relations with the larger Harvard, one must begin with Hugh Hawkins' study of Eliot, *Between Harvard and America. The Educational Leadership of Charles W. Eliot* (New York, 1972). Hawkins rescues Eliot' interest in schools from the oblivion to which his previous biographers had confined it. In contrast, Henry Aaron Yeomans' *Abbott Lawrence Lowell 1856-1943* (Cambridge, 1948) seems to go out of its way to ignore the Division and School of Education, as well as Lowell's serious interest in educational research. James B. Conant's autobiography, *My Several Lives: Memoirs of a Social Inventor* (New York, Evanston, and London, 1970), devotes considerable attention to his 1939 and 1946 "rescues" of the School. In a brief interview and in subsequent correspondence, Mr. Conant preferred not to comment on the School's history beyond what he had said in his memoirs. Clearly the history of twentieth-century Harvard remains largely to be written.

A recent spurt of interest in both the history of the social sciences and the history of professionalization will probably enrich our understanding of this field enormously in the next few years. The most thoughtful study of nineteenth-century schoolteaching is Paul H. Mattingly's *The Classless Profession: American Schoolmen in the Nineteenth Century* (New York, 1975). Probably the best current approach to the university study of education and educational research in the twentieth-century is through biography, specifically Dorothy Ross, *G. Stanley Hall: The Psychologist as Prophet* (Chicago and London, 1972); Geraldine Jonçich, *The Sane Positivist: A Biography of Edward L. Thorndike* (Middletown, Conn., 1968); and Walter H. Drost, *David Snedden and Education for Social Efficiency* (Madison, 1967). An older history of the most important school of education is Lawrence A. Cremin, David A. Shannon, and Mary Evelyn Townsend, *A History of Teachers College, Columbia University* (New York, 1954). A more recent and more extensive institutional account is Henry C. Johnson, Jr., and Erwin V. Johanningmeier, *Teachers for the Prairie: The University of Illinois and the Schools, 1868-1945* (Urbana, Chicago, and London, 1972).

Notes

Abbreviations

ALL   A. Lawrence Lowell
AR   Annual Report of the President of Harvard University
ARED   Annual Report of the Dean of the Graduate School of Education
BP   John M. Brewer Papers
CP   James B. Conant Papers
CWE   Charles W. Eliot
DOP   Papers in the Office of the Dean, Graduate School of Education
EP   Charles W. Eliot Papers
ER   *Educational Review*
FAS   Faculty of Arts and Sciences
FGN   Frederick G. Nichols
FK   Francis Keppel
FM   Minutes of the Faculty of Education
FTS   Francis T. Spaulding
HAP   Paul H. Hanus Papers
HCR   Annual Reports of deans or other administrative officers of Harvard University
HGM   *Harvard Graduates' Magazine*
HP   Henry W. Holmes Papers
HUA   Harvard University Archives
HWH   Henry W. Holmes
JBC   James B. Conant
JMB   John M. Brewer
KP   Francis Keppel Papers
LP   A. Lawrence Lowell Papers
MP   Records of the Administrative Board For the Degree of Master of Arts in Teaching
NEJE   *New England Journal of Education*
NMP   Nathan M. Pusey
NP   Frederick G. Nichols Papers
PHH   Paul H. Hanus
PJR   Phillip J. Rulon

RP   Phillip J. Rulon Papers
SP   Francis T. Spaulding Papers
SR   *The School Review*

All materials to or from HWH are in HP unless otherwise cited. All materials to or from CWE are in EP unless otherwise cited.

Prologue: Celebration at the Union

1. The prepared speeches, and the transcriptions of what was actually said, are in HP and HAP.

2. Harvard's principal governing board, officially named the President and Fellows of Harvard College but more frequently called "the Corporation," consists of the President, Treasurer, and five Fellows. The less powerful Board of Overseers relates to this book mainly through the "visiting committees" it appoints to examine the various departments of the University. Although visiting committees have sometimes served as investigative bodies, their primary twentieth-century role has been to provide advice and (depending on departmental skill) financial support.

3. John F. Moors to ALL, February 18, 1920, LP; CWE to Abraham Flexner, March 5, 1920; ALL to HWH, January 8, 1920; HWH to Jerome D. Greene, January 27, 1920; HWH, "Condensed Statement of Proposed Budget for 1920-21," January 22, 1920.

1. Harvard and the Schools

1. On Eliot as educational reformer see Hugh Hawkins, *Between Harvard and America: The Educational Leadership of Charles W. Eliot* (New York, 1972). On Harvard and the modern university see Laurence Veysey, *The Emergence of the American University* (Chicago, 1965). On the broadening and deepening of the arts and sciences curriculum see Paul Buck, ed., *Social Sciences at Harvard, 1860-1920: From Inculcation to the Open Mind* (Cambridge, 1965).

2. CWE, "Inaugural Address as President of Harvard College," 1869, *Educational Reform* (New York, 1898), p. 5.

3. AR 1872-73, p. 50; Edwin P. Seaver, "Report of the Committee on Government to the Board of Overseers," 1881-82, HUA; Charles F. Adams, Jr., "Report of the [Overseers'] Committee on Composition and Rhetoric," 1897, p. 19, HUA.

4. CWE, "Inaugural Address," *Educational Reform*, pp. 12ff.

5. CWE, discussion remarks, "Official Report of the Sixth Annual Meeting of the New England Association of Colleges and Preparatory Schools," *The Academy* VI:462 (November 1891); CWE, "Contributions to the History of American Teaching," ER XLII:353-356 (November 1911); CWE, "Liberty in Education," 1885, *Educational Reform*, p. 131.

6. William A. Mowry, *Recollections of a New England Educator, 1838-1908* (New York, Boston, and Chicago, 1908), pp. 96, 270; James McLachlan, *American Boarding Schools: A Historical Study* (New York, 1970), p. 228; W. C. Poland

to CWE, December 31, 1887; "The Recent Conference of College Presidents and Heads of Preparatory Schools," *NEJE* XXII:272 (October 22, 1885).

7. AR 1886-87, p. 9; William F. Bradbury to CWE, September 22, 1886. On school performance problems in other subjects see "Report of the Overseers' Committee on Rhetoric and English Literature," 1882-83, HUA.

8. CWE, "Inaugural Address," *Educational Reform*, pp. 6-7, 27; CWE, "Contributions," pp. 360-362; CWE to Nicholas Murray Butler, January 9, 1914.

9. Joseph Lovering, "The Jefferson Physical Laboratory," HCR 1886-87, p. 138; Edwin H. Hall to CWE, October 20, 1886; Edwin H. Hall to CWE, November 28, 1886; Josiah P. Cooke, "The Chemical Laboratory," HCR 1886-87, p. 129; Josiah P. Cooke, "Report of the Director of the Chemical Laboratory to the Board of Overseers," April 1890, pp. 7-8, HUA; Edwin H. Hall, "Physics," *The Development of Harvard University since the Inauguration of President Eliot, 1869-1929*, ed. S. E. Morison (Cambridge, 1930), pp. 285-286; AR 1885-86, pp. 21-22. For faculty contributions to school curriculum in other fields see, for example, Albert Bushnell Hart, "History in High and Preparatory Schools," *The Academy* II:256-265, 306-315 (1887), and Herbert Weir Smyth "Classics," *Development of Harvard University*, pp. 41, 44.

10. "Report of the [Overseers'] Committee to Visit the Academic Department," 1873-74, p. 3, HUA; CWE, "The True Function of a High School Distinct from That of a School Preparatory to College," April 7, 1876; CWE, quoted in *NEJE* III:6 (January 1, 1876).

11. "Report of the Committee on Government to the Board of Overseers," 1881-82, pp. 20-21, HUA; CWE, "Present Relations of Massachusetts High Schools to Massachusetts Colleges," *NEJE* XXI:19-20 (January 8, 1885).

12. AR 1879-80, p. 11; CWE, "What Is a Liberal Education?," February 22, 1884, *Educational Reform*, pp. 120-121.

13. AR 1882-83, pp. 10-11.

14. CWE, "Present Relations," p. 20; AR 1885-86, p. 9.

15. William A. Mowry, *NEJE* XXI:72 (January 29, 1885).

16. The average age of Harvard College graduates in 1885 was twenty-two years and seven months. The Medical School established a graded three-year course in 1871 and an optional fourth year in 1878. Eliot envisioned that both law and medical training would eventually extend to five years. AR 1883-84, p. 37; AR 1891-92, p. 10; Henry James, *Charles W. Eliot* (Boston and New York, 1930), II, 72.

17. Faculty Records, vol. 5, n.s., 1387, 1889-90, HUA; "Statement of Majority of Faculty on Vote to Reduce Course of Study of March 26, 1890," pp. 6-7, EP; Henry Putnam and Roger Wolcott, "Supplementary Report of the Special Committee [of the Board of Overseers] on Changes in the Academic Department and in Its Relations to the Professional Schools," April 8, 1891, HUA; CWE to James B. Angell, June 2, 1890; CWE, "Can School Programmes Be Shortened and Enriched?," February 16, 1888, *Educational Reform*, pp. 155, 162-170; CWE, "An Average Massachusetts Grammar School," November 28, 1890, *Educational Reform*, pp. 182-191.

18. AR 1891-92, p. 15.

19. "President Eliot on Secondary Education," *NEJE* XXXVII:291-292 (May 11, 1893).

20. A. B. Hart to CWE, May 11, 1892; A. B. Hart to CWE, May 16, 1892; A. B. Hart to CWE, March 23, 1893; Albert Bushnell Hart, "Reform in the Grammar Schools: An Experiment in Cambridge, Mass.," *ER* IV:253-269 (October 1892); FAS Records I, March 1, 1892, p. 182.

21. Nathaniel S. Shaler to CWE, October 15, 1887; Nathaniel S. Shaler to the President and Fellows of Harvard College, October 25, 1902, EP; AR 1895-96, p. 15; Nathaniel S. Shaler, "The Summer School," *HGM* I:132-133 (October-November 1892); Nathaniel S. Shaler to CWE, August 11, 1891; Nathaniel S. Shaler to PHH, October 12, 1891, HAP; "Harvard Teachers Association," August 1892, Harvard Teachers Association Records, HUA. Faculty members who enrolled during the 1890s included Edwin H. Hall, Frank W. Taussig, William M. Davis, B. O. Pierce, F. C. de Sumichrast, H. C. G. von Jagemann, James L. Love, Charles Grandgent, B. S. Hurlbut, Morris H. Morgan, Josiah Royce, Joseph Torrey, Jr., and Hugo Münsterberg.

22. Charles F. Adams, Jr., "Preparatory School Education," *HGM* I:188-189 (January 1893); Charles F. Adams, Jr., to CWE, January 9, 1893. See also Edward C. Kirkland, *Charles Francis Adams, Jr., 1835-1915* (Cambridge, 1965), pp. 194-198.

23. McLachlan, *American Boarding Schools*, p. 196; CWE to Thomas S. Fiske, December 10, 1898.

24. "Schools Examination Board," June 22, 1892, HAP; AR 1891-92, p. 15; CWE, "The Schools Examination Board of Harvard University," *HGM* I:11 (October-December 1892).

25. FAS Records I, June 21, 1892, p. 209; PHH, "Schools' Examination Board," *HGM* II:252-253 (December 6, 1893); AR 1892-93, p. 44; CWE to Nicholas Murray Butler, March 1, 1894, Butler Papers, Columbia University; Albert Bushnell Hart, "Mid-Year Retrospect," *HGM* III:348 (March 1895); PHH, *Adventuring in Education* (Cambridge, 1937), p. 138. In 1892-93 nine schools were examined: Phillips Exeter Academy, Roxbury Latin School, Groton School, St. Marks School, Milton Academy, Watertown High School, Salem Classical and High School, Peekskill Military Academy, and Miss Rideout's School of Boston. A year later the number dropped to three: Newton High School, Clinton High School, and Mount Herman School. Only one school was studied in each of the next two years: Utica (New York) Free Academy and New Bedford High School.

26. Nathaniel S. Shaler to CWE, September 1, 1894; Edwin H. Hall to CWE, May 4, 1893. Fuller discussions of the origins, content, and impact of the report of the Committee of Ten can be found in Theodore R. Sizer, *Secondary Schools at the Turn of the Century* (New Haven and London, 1964), and Edward A. Krug, *The Shaping of the American High School* (New York, Evanston, and London, 1964), pp. 39-65.

27. AR 1896-97, pp. 18-19; Edwin H. Hall to C. J. Bonaparte, March 17, 1898, EP.

28. HCR 1897-98, pp. 99-105; HCR 1898-99, pp. 102-105.

29. Charles J. Bonaparte, et al., "Report of the Special Committee on the Re-

quirements for Admission to Harvard College and the Lawrence Scientific School," January 12, 1898, p. 7, HUA; "Minority Report of the Special Committee on the Requirements for Admission to Harvard College and the Lawrence Scientific School," April 13, 1898, HUA; Charles F. Adams, Jr., to CWE, May 18, 1896; CWE to Charles F. Adams, Jr., May 19, 1896, Charles F. Adams, Jr., Papers, Massachusetts Historical Society. Hart makes the argument for a national constituency in "The New Harvard Entrance Requirements," *ER* XIV:217-235 (October 1897). A similar argument is made in James J. Storrow, "Letter of Dissent to Reports of the Special Committee on the Requirements of Admission to Harvard College, 1899, HUA; CWE to Wallace C. Sabine, May 7, 1907.

30. CWE, discussion remarks, *Addresses and Proceedings of the Twelfth Annual Meeting of the New England Association of Colleges and Preparatory Schools* (Boston, 1897), p. 114; CWE to Thomas S. Fiske, December 10, 1898; CWE, remarks at Harvard Teachers Association, March 6, 1897, Harvard Teachers Association Records, HUA; Neomer W. Brainard to FHH, December 26, 1893, Harvard Teachers Association Records, HUA; Albert Bushnell Hart, "Significant Questions," *HGM* VIII:351 (March 1900); Nathaniel S. Shaler to CWE, September 1, 1894.

2. The Harvard Normal

1. On the high school's fluidity see Edward A. Krug, *The Shaping of the American High School* (New York, Evanston, and London, 1964) p. 3; and Theodore R. Sizer, *Secondary Schools at the Turn of the Century* (New Haven and London, 1964), p. 5. CWE, "What Is a Liberal Education?," 1884, *Educational Reform* (New York, 1898) p. 89.

2. *Forty-Ninth Annual Report of the Board of Education Together with the Forty-Ninth Annual Report of the Secretary of the Board, 1884-85* (Boston, 1886), p. 21; John W. Dickinson, "The Normal School," *NEJE* XXXII:179-180 (September 18, 1890); John W. Dickinson, discussion, *Official Report of the Fifth Annual Meeting of the New England Association of Colleges and Preparatory Schools* (Boston, 1890), pp. 36-37. "Special Conference of the Massachusetts High School Masters, Held in Boston, January 18, 1890," *The Academy* V:88 (March 1890); "A High Normal School," *NEJE* XXXI:40 (January 16, 1890); Charles H. Douglas, "Status of the High School Teacher in New England," *ER* V:33 (January 1893).

3. On the centrality of college conceptions of liberal education to the definition of high school purpose, see J. W. Sewall, "The Duty of the College to Make Provision for the Training of Teachers for Secondary Schools," *Addresses and Proceedings of the Fourth Annual Meeting of the New England Association of Colleges and Preparatory Schools* (Syracuse, 1889), p. 23; Teelow, discussion, "Special Conference," p. 85; Ray Greene Huling, "The American High School II," *ER* II:138 (September 1891). On high schools and professional schools see Joseph F. Kett, *Rites of Passage: Adolescence in America 1790 to the Present* (New York, 1977), pp. 154-155.

4. Paul H. Mattingly, *The Classless Profession: American Schoolmen in the Nineteenth Century* (New York, 1975), pp. 134-168. For awareness by high school

principals of the low academic quality of normal students see J. W. MacDonald, "The Model Normal College," *The Academy* VI:33 (February 1891).

5. "Opening Remarks of the President" [of the Massachusetts Classical and High School Teachers], *The Academy* VII:189 (May 1892); John Tetlow to CWE, April 12, 1885; John Tetlow to CWE, June 14, 1885; Albert Bushnell Hart, "The Teacher as a Professional Expert," *SR* I:4-14 (January 1893). For further examples of career shifts across school and college lines see Sizer, *Secondary Schools at the Turn of the Century*, pp. 103-104.

6. Horace M. Willard, "What Can Teachers Do to Draw Men and Women of Learning and Teaching Power into the Service of Our Secondary Schools?," *Fifth Annual Meeting*, pp. 19-30.

7. Tetlow, "Special Conference," p. 85; Willard, "What Can Teachers Do?," p. 21.

8. Willard, "What Can Teachers Do?," p. 21; "Report of Committee on High Grade Normal School," February 6, 1890, Records of the Board of Education, Massachusetts Department of Education, Boston.

9. Charles Kendall Adams, "The Teaching of Pedagogy in Colleges and Universities," *The Academy* III:469-481 (November 1888). Another address at the same meeting connected the teaching of education with college self-interest. See Truman H. Safford, "Why Does the Number of Students in American Colleges Fail to Keep Pace with the Population?," *The Academy* III:482-495 (November 1888). On how education courses were used to improve the secondary schools in one Western university, see Henry C. Johnson, Jr., and Erwin V. Johanningmeier, *Teachers for the Prairie: The University of Illinois and the Schools, 1868-1945* (Urbana, Chicago, and London, 1972), pp. 44, 89, 93.

10. "Special Normal Training for High School Teachers," *NEJE* XXX:376-377 (December 12, 1889), pp. 376-377; "Special Conference," pp. 83-97; "Notes," *The Academy* I:156 (May 1886); CWE, discussion, *Fourth Annual Meeting*, pp. 31-33; John Tetlow, discussion, ibid., p. 31; John Tetlow to CWE, March 19, 1890.

11. *Fifty-Fourth Annual Report of the Board of Education Together with the Fifty-Fourth Annual Report of the Secretary of the Board 1889-90* (Boston, 1891), pp. 10-11; John Tetlow to CWE, March 19, 1890; E. H. Capen to CWE, March 18, 1890; John W. Dickinson to CWE, March 19, 1890; John Tetlow, discussion, *Fifth Annual Meeting*, p. 33; CWE, discussion, *Fifth Annual Meeting*, p. 34; CWE, "An Average Massachusetts Grammar School," November 28, 1890, *Educational Reform*, pp. 179-194; John W. Dickinson, discussion, *Fifth Annual Meeting*, pp. 36-37; Dickinson, "The Normal School," p. 80; CWE to William E. Russell, January 18, 1893; E. Hunt to CWE, September 3, 1892.

12. John Tetlow to CWE, March 19, 1890; John Tetlow, discussion, *Sixty-First Annual Meeting of the American Institute of Instruction* (Boston, 1890), p. xxiv; Edwin P. Seaver, "The Professional Training of Teachers," ibid., pp. 74-76; Edwin P. Seaver, discussion, ibid., p. 107.

13. FAS Records I, October 7, 1890, p. 46; *Fifty-Fifth Annual Report of the Board of Education Together with the Fifty-Fifth Annual Report of the Secretary of the Board 1890-91* (Boston, 1892), pp. 11-12.

14. Charles Francis Adams, Jr., "Scientific Common-School Education,"

Harper's New Monthly Magazine LXI:934-942 (November 1880). On the Quincy reforms see Michael B. Katz, "The 'New Departure' in Quincy, 1873-1881: The Nature of Nineteenth Century Educational Reform," *New England Quarterly* XL: 3-30 (March 1967).

15. Edmund J. James, *Chairs of Pedagogics in Our Universities* (Philadelphia, 1887).

16. Mattingly, *The Classless Profession*, pp. 84-168; Arthur C. Boyden, *The History of Bridgewater Normal School* (Bridgewater, Mass., 1933), pp. 38-39. The "object method" was a means to develop capacity to observe by bringing objects or pictures of objects into classrooms. On the rigidity of object teaching see "The New Mechanism," *NEJE* XII:8 (June 24, 1880).

17. John W. Dickinson, *Forty-First Annual Report of the Board of Education Together with the Forty-First Annual Report of the Secretary of the Board 1876-77* (Boston, 1878), p. 76; John W. Dickinson, *Principles and Method of Teaching Derived from a Knowledge of Mind* (Boston, 1898); George A. Walton, "John Woodbridge Dickinson, 1825-1901," *Seventy-First Annual Meeting of the American Institute of Instruction* (Boston, 1901), p. 20; Frederick Rudolph, *Mark Hopkins and the Log* (New Haven, 1956), pp. 206-207.

18. William H. Payne, "The Normal School Problem," *Education* V:382-399 (March-April 1885); William H. Payne, "The Aspects of the Teaching Profession," *Education* II:327-338 (March-April 1882); William H. Payne, "The Study of Pedagogics in the University of Michigan," *NEJE* XVII:291-292 (May 11, 1883). These essays and other writings were incorporated in Payne's most serious work, *Contributions to the Science of Education* (New York, 1886), esp. p. 278. On Payne's career see George Cleveland Poret, *The Contributions of William Harold Payne to Public Education*, Contributions to Education No. 81 (Nashville, 1930). For celebrations of educational science see William T. Harris, "Psychological Inquiry," *Education* VI:156-158 (November-December 1885); B. A. Hinsdale, "Pedagogical Chairs in Colleges and Universities," *Addresses and Proceedings of the National Educational Association* (Nashville, 1889), p. 561; and Jerome Allen, "Have We a Science of Education?," *Education* II:284-289 (January-February 1882). Hinsdale succeeded Payne at Michigan. Allen started the New York University School of Pedagogy.

19. Ferdinand Bôcher to CWE, April 26, 1891; Nicholas Murray Butler to CWE, July 27, 1890.

20. Payne, *Contributions to the Science of Education*, pp. 175-179, 185-187; Dickinson, *Principles and Method*, p. 90; Hosea Starr Ballou, "The Educational Services of the Late Hon. J. W. Dickinson," *Education* XXII:70 (October 1901). On the idealist tradition see Jurgen Herbst, "Herbert Spencer and the Genteel Tradition in American Education," *Educational Theory* XI:99-100 (April 1961); Dorothy Ross, *G. Stanley Hall: The Psychologist as Prophet* (Chicago and London, 1972), pp. 114-116.

21. For Eliot's debt to Spencer see his introduction to Spencer's *Education* (New York, 1911); CWE to Nicholas Murray Butler, January 9, 1914; Henry James, *Charles W. Eliot* (Boston and New York, 1930), I, 346-351; William Boyd, "President Eliot and Herbert Spencer," *Harvard Teachers Record* IV:33-36 (Feb-

ruary 1934). On the introspective beliefs of Dickinson and Payne, see Dickinson *Principles and Method*, pp. 8-9, and Payne, *Contributions*, p. 271. On Eliot's advocacy of practical experience over speculation, see CWE to Caskie Harrison, August 8, 1894, and CWE to Barrett Wendell, January 10, 1910, Wendell Papers, Houghton Library, Harvard. For their contrasting views on the value of educational history see Payne, *Contributions*, p. 133, and CWE, discussion, *Fourth Annual Meeting*, pp. 32-33.

22. G. Stanley Hall, "Teachers and Normal Schools," *NEJE* XIII:237 (April 7, 1881); G. Stanley Hall, *Chairs of Pedagogy in Our Higher Institutions of Learning*, Circulars of Information of the Bureau of Education No. 2 (Washington, D.C., 1882), p. 41. On Hall, see Ross, *G. Stanley Hall*, pp. 103-133. On incorporating the inductive approach into the older pedagogy, see James M. Gregory, "Is There a Science of Education?," *Education* I:384-387 (March-April 1881); J. A. Reinhart, "The Inductive Element in the Science of Education," *Education* II:173-174 (November-December 1881); Thomas W. Bicknell, "Annual Address Before the National Educational Association," *Education* V:285 (January-February 1885); N. M. Butler, editorial, *ER* II:179-180 (September 1891); and A. E. Winship, "Professional Science Versus Professional Philosophy," *NEJE* XXXIX:296-297 (May 10, 1894).

23. On Hall's retreat from pedagogy, see his remarks (in Eliot's presence) in the discussion, *Fourth Annual Meeting*, p. 31; Ross, *G. Stanley Hall*, pp. 211, 132-133; Hugh Hawkins, *Pioneer: A History of the Johns Hopkins University 1874-1889* (Ithaca, N.Y., 1960), p. 202. In 1890 Eliot remembered only the "grave doubts" that teachers present at Hall's 1881 lectures had expressed. CWE, discussion, *Fourth Annual Meeting*, p. 32.

24. William James to Thomas Davidson, January 8, 1882; William James to Thomas Davidson, April 16, 1882; William James to Thomas Davidson, May 2, 1883 — all quoted in Ralph Barton Perry, *The Thought and Character of William James* (Boston, 1935), I, 738, 742, 753; William James to Croom Robertson, November 9, 1887, quoted in Perry, *Thought and Character*, II, 85; William James to Henry Holt, February 1891, William James Papers, Houghton Library, Harvard; William James to PHH, April 6, 1891, quoted in PHH, *Adventuring in Education* (Cambridge, 1937), pp. 121-122.

25. Josiah Royce, "Is There a Science of Education?," *ER* I:15-25, 121-132 (January-February 1891); William James, *Talks to Teachers on Psychology, and to Students on Some of Life's Ideals* (New York, Norton Library Edition, 1958), pp. 23-24.

26. CWE, "An Average Massachusetts Grammar School," pp. 179-194; CWE, "Undesirable and Desirable Uniformity in Schools," July 12, 1892, *Educational Reform*, p. 297; CWE, "The Grammar School of the Future," December 1893, *Educational Reform*, pp. 308-309; CWE, "The Unity of Educational Reform," July 11, 1894, *Educational Reform*, pp. 316, 330-335. Frank H. Kasson, editorial, *Education* XIV:307 (January 1894); Frank H. Kasson, editorial, *Education* XIV:497-498 (April 1894); Frank H. Kasson, editorial, *Education* XX:306-308 (January 1900).

27. AR 1890-91, p. 12; "The Harvard Normal," *NEJE* XXXIII:328 (May 21,

1891); Josiah Royce, "Report of the Committee on a Normal Course for Graduates," FAS Records I, November 11, 1890, pp. 61-62; FAS Records I December 2,
1890, p. 67; FAS Records I, December 16, 1890. pp. 72-73.

28. Ferdinand Bôcher to CWE, April 26, 1891; ' Report of Special Overseers
Committee on Written English," October 8, 1884, HUA; L. B. R. Briggs, "The
Correction of Bad English, as a Requirement for Admission to Harvard College,"
The Academy V:312 (September 1890); Le Baron R. Briggs to CWE, December
17, 1890.

29. Josiah Royce, "Report of the Committee on a Normal Course," p. 61; FAS
Records I, December 16, 1890, pp. 72-73; AR 1890-91, p. 12; CWE to PHH,
March 25, 1891, quoted in PHH, *Adventuring*, pp. 107-109.

30. G. Stanley Hall, discussion, *Fourth Annual Meeting*, p. 51; G. Stanley
Hall, discussion, *Fifth Annual Meeting*, p. 33; PHH to Robert E. McConnell,
October 9, 1927, HAP; PHH, *Adventuring*, pp. 101-102.

31. For biographical material on Hanus see PHH to Robert E. McConnell,
October 9, 1927, HAP, and PHH, *Adventuring*, pp. 3-104. PHH to CWE, April
10, 1891; *First Annual Catalogue of the State Normal School of Colorado* (Denver,
1891), p. 19.

32. PHH, "High Schools Viewed from a Practical Standpoint," *Colorado
School Journal* II:4-5 (February 1887); PHH, "The Function of the High School,"
Colorado School Journal IV:3-5 (May 1888); PHH to CWE, March 31, 1891; PHH
to CWE, April 10, 1891; CWE to PHH, March 25, 1891; Josiah Royce to PHH,
April 7, 1891, quoted in PHH, *Adventuring*, pp. 118-119.

3. Transformations in Professional Identity

1. CWE to PHH, March 25, 1891.

2. PHH to CWE, April 22, 1891; William H. Payne, *Contributions to the
Science of Education* (New York, 1886), pp. 180-198, 343, 346; Charles Kendall
Adams, "The Teaching of Pedagogy in Colleges and Universities" *The Academy*
III:469-481 (November 1888); Anna J. McKeag, "The New England Association of
College Teachers of Education," December 3, 1921, Records of the Association,
HUA.

3. PHH to CWE, April 10, 1891; Nicholas Murray Butler to PHH, Septem-
ber 22, 1891, HAP; Nicholas Murray Butler to PHH, December 19, 1892, Butler
Papers, Columbia University; PHH to William T. Harris, February 25, 1892,
HAP; William T. Harris to PHH, February 27, 1892, HAP; PHH, *Adventuring in
Education* (Cambridge, 1937), p. 128.

4. Josiah Royce to PHH, April 7, 1891, quoted in PHH, *Adventuring*, pp.
118-119; William James to PHH, April 6, 1891, quoted in PHH, *Adventuring*, pp.
120-121. As late as 1893 G. Stanley Hall asked Hanus to lecture at the World Congress of Experimental Psychology. G. Stanley Hall to PHH, April 10 1893, HAP;
PHH, *Adventuring*, p. 128.

5. For Hanus' endorsement of Eliot's main ideas, see PHH to William T.
Harris, March 26, 1892, HAP; PHH, "Educational Aims and Educational Values,"
ER IX:323-333 (April 1895); PHH, "A Recent Tendency in Secondary Education

Examined," *SR* III:193-205 (April 1895); PHH, "Attempted Improvements in the Course of Study," *ER* XII:435-452 (December 1896). These articles were reprinted in PHH, *Educational Aims and Educational Values* (New York, 1899). For the appearance of Eliot's ideas in Hanus' theory course see Walter Lichtenstein, "Notes for Education 2," 1901, HUA; Lewis A. Bennert, "Notes for Education 2a," 1903-04, HUA. The earliest of Hanus' many public appreciations of Eliot was "President Eliot and American Education," *The Harvard Illustrated Magazine* X:198-200 (May 1909).

6. On the centrality of observation and fact gathering see PHH to CWE, April 10, 1891; PHH, "The New Department of Pedagogy at Harvard University," *ER* II:252-253 (October 1891); PHH, "The Training of Teachers and the Study of Education," *NEJE* XXXIV:356 (December 3, 1891); PHH to CWE, April 22, 1891; PHH, *Adventuring*, p. 129; PHH, "Education and Teaching," *HGM* V:221 (December 1896); PHH, "The Study of Education at Harvard University," *ER* VII: 255 (March 1894). For the contrast between Hanus' seminar and Payne's see PHH, "Education and Teaching," *HGM* II:239 (December 1893), and William H. Payne, *Contributions*, p. 343. On Hanus' professional reputation see Samuel T. Dutton, "The Training of College Graduates for the Work of Teaching," *Education* XVI:524 (May 1896); James E. Russell, "The Training of Teachers for Secondary Schools," *ER* 17:377 (April 1899); James E. Russell to PHH, October 27, 1903, HAP; Payson Smith to PHH, March 24, 1921, HAP; Walter F. Downey to PHH, March 13, 1935, HAP; Lewis A. Bennert to Paul A. Perry, February 25, 1964 (author's possession); PHH to CWE, December 21, 1897; PHH to CWE, July 20, 1905; PHH, "Questionnaire on Education 3," Committee on Improving Instruction in Harvard College, March 19, 1903, HUA.

7. FAS Records I, February 16, 1892, p. 178, March 15, 1892, p. 184, and May 23, 1893, p. 288; Josiah Royce to CWE, July 18, 1893; N. S. Shaler, "The Use and Limits of Academic Culture," *The Atlantic Monthly* LXVI:167 (August 1890); N. S. Shaler, "Lawrence Scientific School," *HGM* II:540 (June 1894).

8. Radcliffe was chartered as a degree-granting institution in 1894. By the end of the decade most education courses were available to women, either through repetition of Harvard undergraduate courses at Radcliffe or through cross-registration in Harvard graduate courses (which men and women were allowed to attend together). The appointment of George Herbert Locke as the second education instructor, made possible by Radcliffe donors, not only facilitated repetition of regular courses but permitted practice teaching to expand. When women became eligible to enroll in his courses, Hanus offered tuition waivers to local women high school teachers in return for additional practice teaching positions.

9. Enrollment data are expressed as equivalents of one-semester courses which made up one eighth of a year's academic work. Edwin P. Seaver to PHH, March 31, 1896, HAP; PHH to CWE, September 17, 1896; FAS Records III, April 3, 1897, p. 28; Byron S. Hurlbut to CWE, September 6, 1901; Byron S. Hurlbut, "Report of the Appointment Committee for 1900-01," p. 4, EP; "Student Questionnaires on Education 2 and Education 1," 1902, Committee on Improving Instruction in Harvard College, HUA.

10. PHH to CWE, September 9, 1893; FAS Records II, April 14, 1896, p.

238; Edwin H. Hall to PHH, November 15, 1898, HAP; CWE to PHH, February 8, 1899, HAP; Barrett Wendell to CWE, February 1. 1899.

11. John Trowbridge, "The Jefferson Physical Laboratory," HCR 1892-93, p. 192; Edwin H. Hall to CWE, October 1, 1895; Joseph Torrey, Jr., to CWE, May 29, 1900; Joseph Torrey, Jr., to CWE, November 30, 1900.

12. Hugo Münsterberg, "School Reform," *The Atlantic Monthly* LXXXV: 656-669 (May 1900); Barrett Wendell, *The Privileged Classes* (New York 1908), pp. 131-274; Barrett Wendell to CWE, February 1, 1899; Le Baron R. Briggs, "The Transition from School to College," *The Atlantic Monthly* LXXXV:354-359 (March 1900); Le Baron R. Briggs, "Some Old-Fashioned Doubts about New-Fashioned Education," *The Atlantic Monthly* LXXXVI:463-470 (October 1900).

13. Hugo Münsterberg, "The Danger from Experimental Psychology," *The Atlantic Monthly* LXXXI:165 (February 1898); Münsterberg, "School Reform," pp. 667-668; Hugo Münsterberg, *Psychology and the Teacher* (New York and London, 1909), pp. 60, 316-321; Wendell, *The Privileged Classes*, pp. 254-255; Briggs, "Some Old-Fashioned Doubts," p. 469; George Herbert Palmer, "The Ideal Teacher," *The Atlantic Monthly* 99:442 (April 1907).

14. Barrett Wendell, "During Vacation," *Boston Evening Transcript* (July 10, 1896), p. 4; Wendell, *The Privileged Classes*, pp. 247-252; Hugo Münsterberg to PHH, March 22, 1899, HAP; PHH to Hugo Münsterberg, March 24, 1899, HAP; CWE to PHH, June 21, 1902, HAP; PHH to CWE, June 25, 1902; ALL to PHH, October 26, 1910, HAP; Byron S. Hurlbut to CWE, August 28, 1901.

15. John H. Wright to PHH, November 15, 1901, HAP; Münsterberg, "School Reform," p. 667; Hugo Münsterberg, 'The New Psychology," *NEJE* XLI: 332 (May 16, 1895); "Championing Teachers," *NEJE* XLI:368 (May 30, 1895); William T. Harris to Hugo Münsterberg, April 22, 1898, Münsterberg Papers, Boston Public Library; Briggs, "Some Old-Fashioned Doubts," p. 470; Barrett Wendell to CWE, February 1, 1899; Barrett Wendell to CWE, February 4, 1899.

16. Briggs, "The Transition from School to College," p. 358; Münsterberg, "School Reform," p. 662; Wendell, *The Privileged Classes*, pp. 162, 269-273.

17. AR 1906-07, pp. 20-22; AR 1910-11, p. 6. By 1915 all old-plan examinations used only the CEEB tests. The new-plan scheme did not increase the access of public high school boys to Harvard, but the admissions committee believed that it prevented retrogression. See John G. Hart, "Report of the Chairman of the Committee on Admission," HCR 1918-19, pp. 232-233.

18. "Announcement of Afternoon and Saturday Courses for Teachers 1906-07," HAP; "Report of Committee on Supplementary Instruction," FAS Records VIII, November 2, 1909, p. 84; PHH, *Adventuring*, pp. 134-135; FAS Records VII, October 22, 1907, p. 214; N. S. Shaler, 'The Direction of Education,' *The Atlantic Monthly* LXXV:389-397 (March 1895).

19. Compare PHH, "The Study of Education in Harvard University," p. 250 and PHH, *Educational Aims and Educational Values*, pp. 171, 174-175. *NEJE* XXXVIII:401 (December 21, 1893); *NEJE* XXXIX:25 (January 11, 1894); "The Harvard Association," *NEJE* XLI:216 (March 28, 1895).

20. PHH, *Educational Aims and Educational Values*, pp. 175-176; PHH to CWE, July 1, 1899; PHH to CWE, June 25, 1902; "Harvard Educational Depart-

ment," *NEJE* LI:370 (June 14, 1900).

21. CWE to PHH, January 3, 1898, HAP; CWE to E. P. Seaver, July 21, 1894; CWE, "The Organization of a System of City Schools," *NEJE* XL:325 (November 15, 1894); ALL to Fanny B. Ames, August 5, 1897, LP; Henry Aaron Yeomans, *Abbott Lawrence Lowell, 1856-1943* (Cambridge, 1948), p. 49; Byron Satterlee Hurlbut to CWE, August 28, 1901; Byron Satterlee Hurlbut to Jerome D. Greene, August 22, 1901, EP.

22. Albion W. Small, "Demands of Sociology upon Pedagogy" (1896), quoted in Merle Borrowman, ed., *Teacher Education in America* (New York, 1965), pp. 129-133; Samuel T. Dutton, *Social Phases of Education in the School and the Home* (New York, 1899), pp. 6, 18-24, 203, 218-219.

23. PHH, "What Should the Modern Secondary School Aim to Accomplish?," *SR* V:377-400, 433-444 (June-September 1897); PHH, "Secondary Education," *ER* 17:346-363 (April 1899); Small, "Demands of Sociology," p. 139; Dutton, *Social Phases of Education*, p. 16; "Culture, Trade, or Culture-Trade?," *NEJE* LXVII: 509 (May 7, 1908). On the tension between the intellectual function of manual training and its role in direct vocational training see Marvin Lazerson, *Origins of the Urban School, Public Education in Massachusetts, 1870-1915* (Cambridge, 1971), pp. 74-154.

24. PHH, *A Modern School* (New York, 1904), pp. 261-262; Arthur O. Norton, "The Scope and Aims of the History of Education," *ER* XXVII:446-449 (May 1904).

25. PHH, "Division of Education," December 1910, p. 4, HAP; HWH, review of Charles de Garmo's *Principles of Secondary Education, Journal of Philosophy, Psychology, and Scientific Methods* VI:130 (March 4, 1909).

26. A. E. Winship, "The Present Educational Crisis," *NEJE* XLIX:291 (May 11, 1899); "The Profession of Education," *NEJE* LXI:154 (February 9, 1905); "Class Conscious Superintendents," *NEJE* LXI:182 (February 16, 1905).

27. "The Play Life of Joseph Lee," *Recreation* XXXI:516 (December 1937); Allen V. H. Sapora, "The Contributions of Joseph Lee to the Modern Recreation Movement and Related Social Movements in the United States," Ph.D. dissertation, University of Michigan, 1952.

28. Joseph Lee, "Münsterberg on the New Education," *ER* 20:138ff (September 1900); Joseph Lee, *Constructive and Preventive Philanthropy* (New York, 1902), pp. 2-4, 123-126, 175-177. On Lee and immigration restriction see Barbara Miller Solomon, *Ancestors and Immigrants: A Changing New England Tradition* (Cambridge, 1956), pp. 138-140. On Lee and the play movement see K. Gerald Marsden, "Philanthropy and the Boston Playground Movement, 1885-1907," *Social Service Review* XXXV:48-58 (March 1961), and Joseph F. Kett, *Rites of Passage: Adolescence in America 1790 to the Present* (New York, 1977), pp. 224-227.

29. Lee, *Constructive and Preventive Philanthropy*, p. 236; HWH, "Prophet in Education," *Recreation* XXXI:528 (December 1937); John F. Moors, "Joseph Lee," *Recreation* XXXI:536 (December 1937). On the Public School Association see George Marshall Moriarty, "The Boston Reform Movement, 1900-1910: Causes and Consequences of a Progressive Failure," Harvard College undergraduate

thesis, 1964. On Storrow see Henry Greenleaf Pearson, *Son of New England—James Jackson Storrow 1864-1926* (Boston, 1932), and Joseph Lee, "James Jackson Storrow, '85," *HGM* XXXV:73-93 (September 1926).

30. Lee, "Münsterberg on the New Education," pp. 123-140; Joseph Lee to Jerome D. Greene, March 25, 1907, EP; Joseph Lee to HWH, July 28 1907; PHH, *Adventuring*, p. 148; Margaret Cabot Lee to CWE November 3, 1900; Joseph Lee to PHH, October 14, 1901, HAP; Joseph Lee to PHH, January 11, 1902 HAP; James J. Storrow to PHH, June 9, 1904, HAP; HWH to PHH, October 16, 1904, HAP.

31. Joseph Lee to Jerome D. Greene, January 11, 1908, EP; Joseph Lee to HWH, July 28, 1907; PHH to CWE, July 19, 1907, HAP; PHH to CWE, August 9, 1907, HP; CWE to PHH, July 23, 1907, HAP; CWE to Joseph Lee, July 23, 1907; HWH to CWE, August 9, 1907, HP.

32. PHH, *A Modern School*, pp. 167-169, 205. On the Social Education Congress see the opening addresses of James P. Munroe and George H. Martin in *Social Education Quarterly* I:1-4, 8-16 (March 1907); N. M. Butler, "The Social Education Congress," *ER* 33:109-110 (January 1907); Robert A. Woods to PHH, November 8, 1907, HAP; "Fellowship in Social Education" [c. 1908] HAP

33. Lee, *Constructive and Preventive Philanthropy*, pp. 211, 202-204, 102-104; Joseph Lee, "The Boy Who Goes to Work," *ER* 38:341 (November 1909).

34. PHH, "Technical Continuation Schools of Munich," *SR* 13:578-683 (November 1905). For a full account of the Commission on Industrial and Technical Education, the report on "The Relation of Children to the Industries [of Massachusetts]" and the Commission on Industrial Education, see Lazerson, *Origins of the Urban School*, pp. 142-178.

35. PHH, *A Modern School*, pp. 103-104, 201-203.

36. PHH, *Beginnings in Industrial Education* (Boston and New York, 1908), pp. 7, 26, 78. Eliot never accepted Hall's assertion that adolescence was a distinct stage of life with marked characteristics of its own. See *The New England Association of Colleges and Preparatory Schools, Addresses and Proceedings of the Sixteenth Annual Meeting* (Chicago, 1901), pp. 89-90.

37. PHH, *Beginnings*, pp. 17, 37, 43, 46.

38. PHH, *Beginnings*, p. 83; PHH to CWE, December 31, 1907; CWE, address at the National Society for the Promotion of Industrial Education, *NEJE* LXVII:175 (February 13, 1908); "What President Eliot Said at Chicago," *NEJE* LXVII:689 (June 18, 1908); "Culture, Trade, or Culture-Trade?," p. 510; A. E. Winship, "Vocational Training in the Public Schools," *NEJE* LXXI:143 (February 10, 1910). The commission was also attacked by the state Board of Education which resented its statutory control over trade schools. In 1909 the commission was absorbed into a reorganized Board of Education. Hanus then became a member of the new state board, and chairman of its committee on industrial education. See Lazerson, *Origins of the Urban School*, pp. 168-171.

39. "Harvard Teachers Association," March 2, 1907, Records of the Harvard Teachers Association, HUA; A. Lincoln Filene to PHH, March 5 1935, HAP; Frank Parsons to CWE, March 10, 1908; Frederick J. Allen to Henry S. Dennison, May 5, 1926, HAP; James J. Storrow, "Educational Problems from the School

Committee's Point of View (I)," *NEJE* LXVII:650 (December 17, 1908); JMB, *History of Vocational Guidance: Origins and Early Development* (New York and London, 1942), pp. 62-70; Frank Parsons, "The Vocation Bureau, First Report to Executive Committee and Trustees," May 1, 1908, p. 2, EP; Frank Parsons, "A Talk to Young People," 1908, EP; Frank Parsons, "To Employers," 1908, EP; PHH, "Vocational Guidance and Public Education," *SR* XIX:51-56 (January 1911).

40. PHH to CWE, April 6, 1897; CWE to PHH, April 9, 1897, HAP; James M. Pierce to CWE, April 8, 1897; George Herbert Palmer to PHH, March 17, 1900, HAP; Barrett Wendell to CWE, February 1, 1899; CWE to Charles F. Thwing, February 14, 1900; CWE to PHH, July 10, 1901, HAP.

41. [PHH and Arthur O. Norton], *A Comparison of the Provision for the Study of Education and the Training of Teachers at Harvard University and at Other Important Universities* (Cambridge, 1906), pp. 6-10. For confirmation of Hanus' assessment of the pedagogical pecking order see "The Teachers' College Again," *NEJE* LVI:284 (October 30, 1902), and "The Great University," *NEJE* LXXIII:210 (February 23, 1911).

42. PHH, *A Modern School*, pp. 251-252; "Proposed Educational School," *The Harvard Crimson*, May 2, 1903, p. 3; L. B. R Briggs to PHH, November 27, 1905, Papers of the Dean of the Faculty of Arts and Sciences, HUA; CWE to PHH, August 3, 1903, HAP; CWE to PHH, August 22, 1903, HAP.

43. PHH to CWE, August 19, 1903; CWE to PHH, February 18, 1906, HAP; "Report of Committee on Education," April 11, 1906, in *Reports of Visiting Committees of the Board of Overseers of Harvard College CX-CCXVI* (Cambridge, 1909), p. 905; Charles Homer Haskins to PHH, December 20, 1905, HAP.

44. In Boston, for example, college training in education could substitute for one of the three required years of experience, whereas in New York City similar training could replace all three years of required experience. By 1906, twenty-three states — including New York but not Massachusetts — issued state certificates as substitutes for traditional local examinations. Sometimes the completion of professional courses was required to earn these certificates. But even when it was not, professional courses often shortened probationary periods before permanent certificates were issued or made further examinations unnecessary. See PHH and Norton, *A Comparison*, pp. 8, 12-19; William T. Foster to PHH, August 7, 1909, HAP; PHH to CWE, March 11, 1907, HAP.

45. Lawrence A. Cremin, David A. Shannon, and Mary Evelyn Townsend, *A History of Teachers College, Columbia University* (New York, 1954), pp. 97ff.

46. FAS Records IV, December 13, 1898, p. 15, and February 7, 1899, p. 50; John H. Wright to PHH, February 7, 1899, HAP; HWH, "Notes on Minutes of the Division," November 2, 1948; HWH to Charles Francis Adams, March 31, 1920, LP.

47. CWE to Abraham Flexner, March 5, 1920; HWH to PHH, October 20, 1911, HAP; PHH to HWH, October 27, 1911, HAP; PHH to Robert E. McConnell, October 9, 1927, HAP; ALL to PHH, November 24, 1909, HAP. For Lowell's judgment that Eliot's educational philosophy was primarily vocational see his eulogy, "Charles William Eliot" (1926), LP, and L. B. R. Briggs to Mrs. Joseph

Allen, March 17, 1909, Papers of the Dean of the Faculty of Arts and Sciences, HUA.

48. John F. Moors to PHH, December 15, 1909, HP; ALL to John F. Moors, November 16, 1910, LP; ALL to Joseph Lee, April 25, 1911, LP; John F. Moors to ALL, November 16, 1910, LP; John F. Moors to ALL, December 15, 1910, LP.

49. PHH to CWE, August 2, 1909; Henry S. Pritchett to Stratton Brooks, January 30, 1909, LP; W. C. Bagley to E. B. Greene, March 14, 1910, LP; Diaries of Ernest Carroll Moore, July 29, 1912, and August 12, 1912, UCLA Library, Los Angeles.

4. The Rise of Educational Science

1. [PHH and Arthur O. Norton], *A Comparison of the Provision for the Study of Education and the Training of Teachers at Harvard University and at Other Important Universities* (Cambridge, 1906), p. 27; T. N. Carver to PHH, December 16, 1905, HAP; T. N. Carver to PHH, January 8, 1906, HAP.

2. A. J. Kinnaman, "Pedagogy in Our Colleges and Universities," *The Pedagogical Seminary* IX:369-370 (September 1902); Dorothy Ross, *G. Stanley Hall: The Psychologist as Prophet* (Chicago and London, 1972), pp. 279-303; Geraldine Jonçich, *The Sane Positivist: A Biography of Edward L. Thorndike* (Middletown, Conn., 1968), pp. 213-232.

3. Lewis A. Bennert, "Notes for Education 2A", 1903, HUA, pp. 65, 79-85.

4. Hugo Münsterberg to CWE, May 5, 1908; Robert M. Yerkes to ALL, October 9, 1911, LP; Robert M. Yerkes to HWH, March 12, 1912. Yerkes also resented Münsterberg's pressure to teach psychology of the "inner states" and not confine his instruction to "external movements." Münsterberg ominously explained that anyone interested only in animal studies was no real psychologist and had no place at Harvard. Hugo Münsterberg to ALL, January 30, 1911, LP; Hugo Münsterberg to Robert M. Yerkes, January 30, 1911, Münsterberg Papers Boston Public Library; Hugo Münsterberg to ALL, December 22, 1911, Münsterberg Papers, Boston Public Library. The required fields for the Ph.D. in education were history, theory, administration, and educational institutions and contemporary activities. See PHH to Charles H. Haskins, March 8, 1910, HP.

5. PHH to HWH, July 30, 1907.

6. Joseph Lee to ALL, April 24, 1911, LP.

7. PHH, *A Modern School* (New York, 1904), p. 220.

8. PHH, "Our Chaotic Education," *The Forum* XXXIII:222-234 (April 1902); Joseph M. Rice to PHH, February 24, 1902, HAP; J. M. Rice, *Scientific Management in Education* (New York and Philadelphia, 1913), p. 18; PHH, *School Administration and School Reports* (Boston, New York, and Chicago, 1920), p. 11; PHH to CWE, September 28, 1900; PHH, "Graduate Testimony on the Elective System," in *A Modern School*, pp. 287-305.

9. The study concluded that 72 percent of the 387 respondents approved the elective system. PHH, "Graduate Testimony on the Elective System," p 294; PHH notes, on Walter Hines Page to PHH, March 19, 1908, HAP.

10. Jonçich, *The Sane Positivist*, pp. 219, 295-300.

11. Frank E. Spaulding, *School Superintendent in Action in Five Cities* (Rindge, N.H., 1955), pp. 235, 246, 249, 355-361, 377-379, 382-387. On the efficiency movement see Raymond E. Callahan, *Education and the Cult of Efficiency* (Chicago and London, 1962), pp. 42-64. Spaulding is one of the great villains in Callahan's drama of the substitution of business for educational values among school administrators. But his analysis underestimates the political nature of the superintendent's job, as many educators themselves did, and hence overestimates the extent to which Spaulding regarded appeals to efficiency as an end rather than as a means to achieve larger educational ends.

12. Frank E. Spaulding, "Reasons Why Harvard University Should Have a Well-Equipped Graduate School of Education," August 12, 1909, HAP; Spaulding, *School Superintendent in Action*, pp. 305-306; PHH, "The Discussion of the Study of School Administration at the Meeting of College Teachers of Education," *SR* XVIII:427 (June 1910).

13. Spaulding, *School Superintendent in Action*, p. 306; PHH, "Division of Education," December, 1910, pp. 3-4, HAP; HWH to W. Van Dyke Bingham, May 31, 1911.

14. Leonard Ayres, "School Surveys," *School and Society* I:577 (April 24, 1915); PHH, "Division of Education," December, 1910, p. 3, HAP; PHH to CWE, December 31, 1907.

15. Hanus' papers contain a fully documented account of his New York experiences, which he later summarized in *Adventuring in Education* (Cambridge, 1937), pp. 175-193. For additional background see "The Reminiscences of Dr. William H. Allen," Oral History Project, Columbia University; Lewis Mayers, "The New York School Inquiry," *National Municipal Review* III:327-339 (April 1914); Sol Cohen, *Progressives and Urban School Reform: The Public Education Association of New York City 1895-1954* (New York, 1964), pp. 78-85.

16. "A Great Opportunity," *NEJE* LXXIII:676 (June 15, 1911).

17. PHH to John Purroy Mitchel, June 6, 1912, HAP; John Purroy Mitchel to PHH, June 7, 1912, HAP; John Purroy Mitchel to PHH, September 12, 1912, HAP; PHH to John Purroy Mitchel, October 26, 1912, HAP.

18. Stuart A. Courtis to PHH, February 18, 1913, HAP, Stuart A. Courtis to PHH, February 25, 1913, HAP; PHH to Calvin O. Davis, June 23, 1913, HAP; Charles P. Howland to PHH, June 27, 1913, HAP; Ernest C. Moore, "The Administration of the Public Schools of New York City: A Comparison of Two Reports," *ER* XLIX:472 (May 1915); James M. Greenwood, "How New York City Administers Its Schools," *ER* XLVI:219-220 (October 1913).

19. "The New York Inquiry," *NEJE* LXXVI:546 (November 21, 1912); "The Hanus Report," *NEJE* LXXVII:154 (February 6, 1913); PHH, *School Efficiency: A Constructive Study Applied to New York City* (Yonkers-on-Hudson, New York, 1913), pp. 82-84; Andrew W. Edson, "The New York School Inquiry: A Protest," *ER* XLVI:450, 452. 454 (December 1913).

20. William H. Maxwell, "On a Certain Arrogance in Educational Theorists," *ER* XLVII:174-175, 180-181 (February 1914). Nicholas Murray Butler's *Educational Review* was a center for anti-Hanus invective. See "The New York School Inquiry: Reply of the Superintendents," *ER* XLVIII:538 (December 1914).

Hanus arranged with the World Book Company to publish the eleven-volume report, including Moore's rejected study, in 1913.

21. PHH to John Purroy Mitchel, unsent draft, May 31, 1912, HAP.

22. PHH, "Some Principles of School Administration," *School Administration and School Reports*, pp. 12-15; HWH to ALL, March 8, 1912.

23. AR 1914-15, p. 7.

24. AR 1909-10, pp. 8-9; ALL, "College Studies and Professional Training," *ER* XLII:217-233 (October 1911); AR 1913-14, p. 10; ALL to HWH July 7, 1916, LP; HWH, "Youth and the Dean: The Relation Between Academic Discipline, Scholarship, and Age of Entrance to College," *HGM* XXI:599-610 (June 1913); ALL to Joseph Lee, February 26, 1913, LP; ALL, "Measurements of Efficiency in College," *Education* XXXIV:217 (December 1913); ALL, "Scientific Study of Education," speech at Carleton College, October 13, 1916, pp. 8-10, LP.

25. ALL to Edward L. Thorndike, May 9, 1911, LP; Edward L. Thorndike to ALL, May 15, 1911, LP; ALL to Walter F. Dearborn, May 27, 1911, LP; Walter F. Dearborn to ALL, June 1, 1911, LP.

26. HWH to PHH, January 3, 1912, HAP; PHH to ALL, January 6, 1912, HAP.

27. ALL to Edward L. Thorndike, January 12, 1912, LP; Edward L. Thorndike to ALL, January 31, 1912, LP; PHH to ALL, February 7, 1912, HAP; ALL to PHH, February 12, 1912, LP; Robert M. Yerkes to HWH, March 12, 1912, LP; HWH to ALL, February 15, 1912, LP; PHH to ALL, February 17, 1912, LP.

28. HWH to ALL, February 15, 1912, LP; PHH to ALL, February 17, 1912, LP; PHH to ALL, February 21, 1912, LP; ALL to James A. Field, March 1, 1912, LP; Edward L. Thorndike to ALL, March 10, 1912, LP.

29. For biographical information on Dearborn see Leonard Carmichael, *Walter Fenno Dearborn and the Scientific Study of Reading* (Cambridge 1957). Dearborn's statistical studies that excited Lowell were *School and University Grades*, Bulletin of the University of Wisconsin No. 368, High School Series No. 9 (Madison, 1910), and *The Relative Standing of Pupils in the High School and in the University*, Bulletin of the University of Wisconsin No. 312, High School Series No. 6 (Madison, 1909); ALL to Walter F. Dearborn, April 12, 1912, LP; ALL to Walter F. Dearborn, May 17, 1912, LP.

30. HWH to PHH, November 18, 1911, HAP; ALL to Charles Hughes Johnston, April 12, 1912, LP; PHH to Ernest C. Moore, April 3, 1913, HAP.

31. For Holmes's biographical data, see HWH to J. R. de la Torre Bueno, July 16, 1942; HWH to Mrs. Husted, July 17, 1942; HWH, "Notes on Biographical Data" [c. 1948]; John F. Moors to ALL, December 13, 1910, LP; HWH to PHH, October 31, 1911, HAP.

32. Frank Thompson, "Discussion," *School Review* XX:310-311 (May 1912).

33. HWH to James J. Storrow, July 10, 1912; HWH to ALL, March 8, 1912, LP; HWH to Visiting Committee, November 25, 1912, LP; ALL to Joseph Lee, February 26, 1913, LP; William S. Learned, "Harvard's Training of Teachers," *The Harvard Illustrated Magazine* XIV:219 (January 1913); *Official Register of Harvard University* X (June 30, 1913), part 30, p. 7; ALL to HWH, October 9, 1912.

34. HWH to ALL, February 10, 1913, LP; PHH to HWH, May 18, 1912, HAP; HWH to PHH, May 16, 1912, HAP; HWH to ALL, April 4, 1914; HWH to ALL, February 16, 1914, LP.

35. HWH to ALL, March 8, 1912, LP; William Setchel Learned, *The School System as an Educational Laboratory*, Harvard-Newton Bulletins No. 1 (Cambridge, 1914), p 12ff; HWH to Joseph Lee, April 11, 1913, LP.

36. William Setchel Learned, "The Development of the Professional and Social Organization of Secondary Teachers in Germany," Harvard University Ph.D. dissertation, 1912, pp. 172, 189ff; Learned, *The School System as an Educational Laboratory*, p. 8; HWH to Prospective Contributors, July 24, 1914.

37. HWH to ALL, February 16, 1914, LP; PHH to ALL, February 17, 1914, HAP; PHH to HWH, February 20, 1914, HAP; HWH to ALL, August 5, 1914, LP; PHH, "Measuring Progress in Learning Latin," *SR* XXIV:35 (May 1916); PHH, "Courtis Arithmetic Tests Applied to Employees in Business Houses," *Educational Administration and Supervision* III:505-520 (November 1917).

38. HWH to Abraham Flexner, November 11, 1915; Abraham Flexner to CWE, November 12, 1920, HAP; PHH, "The Graduate School of Education," *HGM* XXVII:234 (December 1919).

39. Charles W. Hobbs to ALL, February 26, 1915, LP; Frank W. Ballou to HWH, April 20, 1917; HWH to Henry A. Wyman, April 14, 1917; ALL to Joseph Lee, June 15, 1918, LP.

40. HWH to PHH, October 31, 1911, HAP; HWH, "The Professional Preparation of the Teacher of Tomorrow," speech to the Convocation of the University of the State of New York, October 8, 1920, pp. 3-5; HWH, "Reform or Efficiency in the Common Schools," 1916, p. 6; HWH to Joseph Lee, December 16, 1912; Joseph Lee to HWH, January 30, 1913, LP; HWH to Abraham Flexner, November 11, 1915; HWH to E. O. Vaile, August 20, 1917.

41. Leonard Carmichael, *Dearborn*, pp. 3-4; HWH to Roger Pierce, November 22, 1915.

42. HWH to Roger Pierce, November 22, 1915.

5. New Careers for the Socialization of Youth

1. HWH, untitled address at Oberlin College, 1908, p. 4; HWH, "Culture or Efficiency," *New York Evening Post*, December 26, 1908, and January 2, 1909; HWH, "Reform or Efficiency in the Common Schools," 1916, p. 6; HWH to Mrs. Charles C. Jackson, August 13, 1923; HWH to F. R. Clow, October 29, 1918; HWH, "Main Ideas for *Education and Social Policy*," 1920.

2. John F. Moors to A. Lincoln Filene, February 25, 1915, HP; John F. Moors to ALL, May 21, 1913, LP.

3. Felix Warburg to PHH, April 23, 1914, HP; ALL to John F. Moors, May 1, 1914, LP; HWH to John F. Moors, May 1, 1914, LP; Felix Warburg to PHH, May 11, 1914, HP; John F. Moors to ALL, May 16, 1914, LP; ALL to HWH, May 25, 1914, LP.

4. Felix Warburg to James E. Russell, October 29, 1913; Felix Warburg to James E. Russell, May 13, 1914; Felix Warburg to James E. Russell, April 21, 1915

—all in James Earl Russell Papers, Teachers College, Columbia University. HWH to ALL, May 21, 1914, LP; HWH to John F. Moors, March 18, 1919, LP.

5. HWH to M. A. De Wolfe Howe, May 13, 1915.

6. Ernest Carroll Moore, *I Helped Make a University* (Los Angeles, 1952), p. 5; Ernest C. Moore, "Provision for the Education of the City Child," *School and Society* III:267-268 (February 19, 1916).

7. Ernest C. Moore, "Improvement in Educational Practice," *SR* 21:323-329, 332 (May 1913); Ernest C. Moore, "The Child in Modern Society," *School and Society* II:253-254 (August 21, 1915); Ernest C. Moore, "Is the Stress Which Is Now Being Put Upon the Practical Interfering with the Idealistic Training of Our Boys and Girls?," *School and Society* V:361-367 (March 31, 1917); PHH to HWH, April 17, 1917; HWH to W. S. Learned, May 3, 1917; JMB to HWH, December 23, 1920. Other social efficiency advocates agreed that progressive educators too often stressed methods rather than objectives. See David Snedden, *Recollections of Over a Half a Century Spent in Educational Work* (Palo Alto, 1949), p. 52.

8. HWH to ALL, March 15, 1919, LP.

9. For the development of Inglis' social ideas see *The Rise of the High School in Massachusetts*, Teachers College Contributions to Education No. 45 (New York, 1911), pp. 151-152ff; Alexander J. Inglis, "The Socialization of the High School," *Teachers College Record* XVI:1-12 (May 1915); Alexander J. Inglis, *Principles of Secondary Education* (Boston, 1918), part 2; Moore, "The Child in Modern Society," p. 254.

10. For Inglis' sensitivity to methodology see *Principles of Secondary Education*, pp. v-vii, and his review of Paul Monroe ed., *The Principles of Secondary Education*, and John Elbert Stout, *The High School: Its Function, Organization and Administration*, in *School and Society* I:30-31 (January 2, 1915). See also reviews of Inglis' *Principles* in *The Nation* CVI:541 (May 4, 1918) and *LR* XXVI:226 (March 1918). On the junior high school, see Alexander Inglis, "A Fundamental Problem in the Reorganization of the High School," *SR* XXIII:308-317 (May 1915), and Alexander Inglis, "The Junior High School," *NEJE* LXXXIV:595-597 (December 14, 1916).

11. Joseph Lee to PHH, March 26, 1915, HAP; Joseph Lee to PHH, April 22, 1915, HAP; Joseph Lee to PHH, May 25, 1915, HAP; Joseph Lee to ALL, June 21, 1915, LP.

12. For biographical information on Johnson see HWH to ALL January 19, 1916, LP. On cataloguing games see George E. Johnson, "Education by Plays and Games," *Pedagogical Seminary* III:97-133 (October 1894); G. Stanley Hall, introduction to George E. Johnson, *Education by Plays and Games* (Boston, 1907), p. xiii; Clarence E. Rainwater, *The Play Movement in the United States: A Study in Community Recreation* (Chicago, 1922), p. 244. On Johnson's administrative reputation see Joseph Lee, *Play in Education* (New York 1915), p. 185; Joseph Lee to PHH, March 26, 1915, HAP.

13. George E. Johnson, "Games Every Boy and Girl Should Know," *American Physical Education Review* XIV:65 (February 1909); George E. Johnson, "Why Teach a Child to Play?," *American Physical Education Review* XIV:500-505 (October 1909); George E. Johnson, "The Country Boy," *The Playground* VIII

404-407 (February 1915); George E. Johnson, "Suggestions for a Greater Physical Education," *American Physical Education Review* XX:508 (November 1915); George E. Johnson, *Education Through Recreation* (Philadelphia, 1916), pp. 15, 50-52, 65, 72; George E. Johnson, "Play and Recreation," *Annals of the American Academy of Political and Social Science*, LXVII:111-113 (September 1916); George E. Johnson, "A Defense of Intercollegiate Athletics," *American Physical Education Review* XXII:146-153 (March 1917).

14. On the problem of institutionalizing the play movement, see Johnson, *Education Through Recreation*, p. 85; HWH to Joseph Lee, July 25, 1917; Lorne W. Barclay to HWH, January 12, 1922; William H. Kilpatrick to HWH, May 15, 1915; Joseph Lee to PHH, May 25, 1915, HAP; ALL to HWH, June 25, 1915; HWH to George E. Johnson, June 28, 1915; PHH to Joseph Lee, July 9, 1915, HAP; HWH to Joseph Lee, March 20, 1918; Le Baron R. Briggs to HWH, March 24, 1916; HWH to ALL, January 17, 1920; Clifford H. Moore to HWH, March 15, 1920; George E. Johnson, "Outline of Child Development and Education," 1920, HP.

15. On the Vocation Bureau under Bloomfield see *Record of the Vocation Bureau of Boston* (Boston, 1914), p. 20, Vocation Bureau Papers, HUA; Meyer Bloomfield, "Notes for a Vocational Training Course," November 26, 1912, Vocation Bureau Papers, HUA; Meyer Bloomfield, *Youth, School, and Vocation* (Boston, 1915), pp. 30-32; JMB, *The Vocational Guidance Movement, Its Problems and Possibilities* (New York, 1918), pp. 22-23; Meyer Bloomfield, "Notes for Education S-7," Lecture IV, pp. 5-6, 1911, Vocation Bureau Papers, HUA. For the bureau's interest in industry-based guidance see JMB, *History of Vocational Guidance, Origins and Early Development* (New York and London, 1942), p. 72; "Harvard Bureau of Vocational Guidance," *Vocational Guidance Bulletin* XXX:1 (October-November 1917); Meyer Bloomfield, "The Aim and Work of Employment Managers' Associations," *Proceedings of Employment Managers' Conference*, Bulletin of the United States Bureau of Labor Statistics, Whole No. 196 (Washington, D.C., 1916), p. 44; HWH to CWE, June 3, 1918, EP; Roy W. Kelly to HWH, December 5, 1918; Roy W. Kelly to ALL, March 13, 1918, LP.

16. JMB, "Some Plans for Student Cooperation in School Government," *ER* XXXVII:519-525 (May 1909); Paul E. Kressly to Whom It May Concern, August 17, 1914, BP; JMB, "A Broader View of Vocational Guidance," *School and Society* V:661-663, 666 (June 9, 1917); JMB, "The Need for Vocational Guidance in Colleges," *School and Society* XI:511-513 (May 1, 1920); JMB, "Should the Schools Teach Labor Problems?," *ER* LXI:399-409 (May 1921).

17. HWH to John F. Moors, March 18, 1919, LP; John F. Moors to HWH, March 19, 1919; HWH to John F. Moors, March 22, 1919; "Minutes of the Executive Committee and Advisory Board, Bureau of Vocational Guidance," October 27, 1919, HP; Philip J. Reilly to HWH, November 14, 1919; HWH to Philip J. Reilly, November 25, 1919; JMB to HWH, April 6, 1920; "Minutes of the Board of Directors, Bureau of Vocational Guidance," May 18, 1920, HP; HWH to F. W. Hunnewell, May 20, 1920; JMB, "Memorandum for Dean Holmes from J.M.B.," October 1925, BP.

18. JMB, "Summary Statement of the Work of J. M. Brewer in Harvard University" [c. 1940], BP; "Budget of the Bureau of Vocational Guidance," 1919-20, HP.

19. JMB, *The Vocational Guidance Movement*, pp. viii, 1, 4ff; JMB to HWH, February 21, 1935.

20. JMB, *The Vocational Guidance Movement*, pp. vii, 66-67, 80; JMB, "Education as Guidance," *School and Society* XVI:712-714 (December 23, 1922); Meyer Bloomfield, *Readings in Vocational Guidance* (Boston and New York, 1915), p. v; Bloomfield, *Youth, School, and Vocation*, pp. 92-93.

21. JMB, *The Vocational Guidance Movement*, pp. 99-100, 155; JMB, "A Broader View of Vocational Guidance," pp. 664, 666-667; JMB, "Vocational Guidance in School and Occupation," *Annals of the American Academy of Political and Social Science* LXVII:62 (September 1916); JMB, "Memorandum Re Harvard University and Mr. Brewer," February 25, 1937, BP; JMB, "Memorandum for Dean Holmes from J.M.B. On Outside Contacts," October 1925, BP; JMB, "Statement to Mr. Filene about the Bureau of Vocational Guidance of the Harvard Graduate School of Education," October 29, 1930, HP.

22. Felix Warburg to James E. Russell, May 13, 1914, Russell Papers, Teachers College, Columbia University; JMB, *History of Vocational Guidance*, p. 107.

23. FGN to J. Whitley, October 2, 1926, NP; FGN to HWH, March 30, 1922; HWH to A. E. Winship, November 15, 1921; FGN to HWH, February 3, 1922; FGN, "Autobiographical Statement," 1934-35, pp. 13-14, HP; HWH, "Notes on the Meeting of the Visiting Committee for the Division of Education at the Union Club, Boston, January 9, 1920," p. 1; Henry Lefavourer to ALL, April 10, 1920, HP; "Memorandum concerning the Proposed Relation Between the Prince School, the Harvard Graduate School of Education, and Simmons College," May 6, 1920, LP; JMB to HWH, May 4, 1922; Lucinda W. Prince to FGN, May 1, 1922, NP; Lucinda W. Prince to FGN, April 14, 1922, NP; "Statement of Finances, Prince School, July 1, 1919 to July 1, 1920," HP; HWH to Jesse I. Straus, September 22, 1919; HWH to Lucinda W. Prince, June 15, 1920.

24. HWH to Rufus Stimson, June 6, 1921; HWH to Wickliffe Rose, May 21 1923; HWH to George Works, October 10, 1923; FGN to Lucinda W. Prince, November 9, 1920, NP; Lucinda W. Prince to FGN, November 15, 1920, NP; Lucinda W. Prince to FGN, November 26, 1920, NP; FGN to Lucinda W. Prince, December 4, 1920, NP; HWH to ALL, January 26, 1922, LP.

25. FGN, "Autobiographical Statement," pp. 1-23ff, HP; FGN to HWH, December 21, 1921.

26. FGN, "Autobiographical Statement," pp. 10 11, HP; FGN to HWH, March 8, 1934, NP; FGN to James M. Glass, February 1, 1933, NP.

27. FGN, "Autobiographical Statement," pp. 12-15, HP; FGN, "Commercial Education," in Harold Gernet Black, *Paths to Success* (Boston, 1924), p. 248; FGN, *Commercial Education Organization and Administration*, Bulletin No. 34, Commercial Series No. 3, Federal Board for Vocational Education (Washington, D.C., June 1919), pp. 8-15, 53-61; FGN, *Survey of Junior Commercial Occupations*, Bulletin No. 54, Commercial Education Series No. 4, Federal Board for

Vocational Education (Washington, D.C., June 1920), pp. 14, 33-34.

28. FGN to Lucinda W. Prince, November 9, 1920, NP; FGN to JMB, December 23, 1921, HP.

6. The Graduate School of Education

1. ALL to HWH, January 10, 1914, LP; ALL to HWH, June 25, 1915; F. W. Hunnewell to HWH, March 19, 1915, LP.

2. HWH to PHH, October 20, 1911, HAP; PHH to HWH, October 27, 1911, HAP; William B. Munro, "The Opening of the Year," *HGM* XX:300 (December 1911).

3. HWH to ALL, January 13, 1914, LP; ALL to HWH, January 14, 1914, LP; Charles P. Parker, *Notes on the Choice of Electives* (Cambridge, 1916), p. 4.

4. HWH to PHH, October 31, 1911, HAP; HWH to ALL, May 3, 1915.

5. HWH to PHH, May 16, 1912, HAP; HWH, "Plan for the Rearrangement of Courses in the Division of Education," 1913, p. 1; Charles H. Haskins to HWH, March 26, 1914, FAS Records; HWH, "Credit for Master's Degree on Summer School Work," August 7, 1918; Albert Bushnell Hart to HWH, April 3, 1919; HWH, "Notes for Faculty Debate," April 1, 1919; HWH to Jeremiah Burke, January 9, 1914; Jeremiah Burke to HWH, March 26, 1914; Franklin B. Dyer to HWH, April 15, 1914.

6. HWH to Charles P. Parker [c. March 1915]; HWH to ALL, January 1, 1914; HWH, "Freedom or Compulsion in the Training of Teachers?," *School and Society* II:169 (July 31, 1915); HWH to Jeremiah Burke, January 9, 1914; HWH to the Visiting Committee, November 18, 1915.

7. HWH to Charles W. Hubbard, May 7, 1915; HWH to ALL, November 29, 1915; HWH to the Visiting Committee, November 18, 1915; PHH to A. Duncan Yokum, January 10, 1914, LP; AR 1915-16, p. 16.

8. ALL to HWH, February 18, 1916, LP; HWH to John F. Moors, October 18, 1916; Lawrence A. Cremin, David A. Shannon, and Mary Evelyn Townsend, *A History of Teachers College, Columbia University* (New York, 1954), p. 97; John F. Moors to ALL, January 23, 1919, LP.

9. Jerome D. Greene to PHH, November 1, 1912, HAP; PHH to Jerome D. Greene, November 13, 1912, HAP; Jerome D. Greene to PHH, November 11, 1912, HAP; PHH to Jerome D. Greene, November 19, 1912, HAP; Charles P. Howland to PHH, November 8, 1912, HAP; Abraham Flexner to PHH, May 1, 1913, HAP; Abraham Flexner to PHH, December 5, 1913, HAP; Raymond B. Fosdick, *Adventure in Giving: The Story of the General Education Board* (New York and Evanston, 1962), pp. 116-121, 140-141, 212-225; Sol Cohen, *Progressives and Urban School Reform: The Public Education Association of New York City 1895-1954* (New York, 1964), pp. 81-83, 85; HWH to Orland Keyburtz, March 23, 1938; HWH to Samuel S. Drury, May 12, 1926; HWH to James J. Storrow, June 21, 1917; Jerome D. Greene to CWE, October 26, 1914; HWH to PHH, July 30, 1915, HAP; HWH to Felix Warburg, June 1, 1916; HWH to CWE, August 13, 1918, EP; Abraham Flexner to PHH, November 18, 1918, HP; Abraham Flexner to PHH, June 21, 1921, HAP; HWH to ALL, March 6, 1920; Abraham Flexner to Henry

James, August 22, 1935, Flexner Papers, Library of Congress; PHH to John Adams, March 13, 1921, HAP.

10. Fosdick, *Adventure in Giving*, pp. 159-160, 163; Jerome L. Greene to HWH, November 7, 1917; ALL to Jerome D. Greene, August 27, 1915, LP; Roger Pierce to HWH, November 25, 1918; HWH to ALL, March 9, 1919, LP; HWH to Abraham Flexner, April 16, 1919; HWH to ALL, April 30, 1919, LP; ALL to the Corporation, May 5, 1919, LP; ALL to Wallace Buttrick, May 10, 1919, LP; Wallace Buttrick to ALL, May 24, 1919, LP; HWH to ALL, July 23, 1915, LP; HWH to Felix Warburg, July 16, 1919, LF; Felix Warburg to ALL, June 20, 1919, LP; Joseph Lee to HWH, June 23, 1919.

11. HWH, "Reasons for Favoring a Special Degree in Education Instead of Ph.D," 1920; "Division of Education Budget 1919-20," November 4 1919 HP. Under Harvard's decentralized governance system the Graduate School of Education was an independent fiscal unit responsible for allocating income from tuition, endowment, and other sources through annual budgets approved by the Corporation.

12. JMB, "Some Notes on the History of the Graduate School of Education," December, 1943, RP.

13. Lowell did permit the doctor of philosophy in education degree to be continued in the faculty of arts and sciences, administered by a committee responsible to that faculty, for students whose educational research interests were more academic than professional. But the distinction was hopelessly confusing and there were no incentives for the School to support this vestigial organ over its own doctor of education. Hardly any students enrolled for nearly two decades. Only in the 1950s, when the research training potential of the Ed.D. seemed more problematic, was a serious effort begun to resurrect the Ph.D. in education. See Chapter Ten, note 15. HWH to Visiting Committee, November 18, 1915; "Plan of Work," pp. 21-22; HWH to James E. Russell, January 13, 1916, Russell Papers, Teachers College, Columbia University; Frank W. Ballou to HWH, December 24, 19_9; John L. Manahan to HWH, December 31, 1919; William T. Foster to HWH, January 4, 1920; "Notes on the Meeting of the Visiting Committee for the Division of Education at the Union Club, Boston," January 9, 1920, HP; W. S. Learned to HWH, January 12, 1920; HWH to Manson G over, February 2, 1920; HWH to Charles H. Haskins, March 13, 1920; HWH to Ernest V. Hollis, January 24, 1941; ALL to HWH, May 26, 1920.

14. Charles Swain Thomas, who taught English special methods, was primarily an editor at the Atlantic Monthly Press. Louis J. A. Mercier and Archibald Davison were regular members of the French and music departments with atypical career interests in teaching rather than in scholarship. In science, N. Henry Black used education to move from school to university teaching He had been a successful instructor at Roxbury Latin School and then took on at Harvard a science methods course as well as Edwin Hall's old elementary physics course. In mathematics, Ralph Beatley came to Harvard from the Horace Mann School to teach elementary mathematics and mathematics methods. Beatley's responsibilities in the mathematics department were less than half-time and he never became a full-fledged department member. Without a clear career line outside the Graduate

School of Education, Beatley's role contradicted Holmes's policy and eventually led to serious problems of personal morale. HWH, "Notes Concerning the Proposed Graduate School of Education," January 21, 1919; HWH to ALL, March 6, 1919, LP; HWH, "Notes for Faculty Meeting," December 10, 1920; L. J. A. Mercier to HWH, December 12, 1919; Archibald T. Davison to PHH, February 22, 1920, HP; Julian Coolidge to HWH, November 29, 1927.

15. HWH to the Visiting Committee, November 18, 1915; Walter D. Head to ALL, December 5, 1918, LP; ALL to Walter D. Head, December 13, 1918, LP; ALL to L. B. R. Briggs, December 1918, LP.

16. "Harvard's Educational Awakening," *NEJE* LXXVII:728 (June 26, 1913).

17. Thomas N. Perkins to HWH, June 24, 1919; HWH to Thomas N. Perkins, July 1, 1919; Bancroft Beatley interview.

18. HWH to ALL, January 12, 1916; HWH, "Notes for meeting of principals and superintendents," October 21, 1919; HWH to ALL, January 7, 1920; HWH to Clifford H. Moore, February 4, 1920; HWH to Charles H. Judd, November 4, 1920; HWH to Clifford H. Moore, January 5, 1923.

19. HWH to ALL, February 10, 1921, LP; ALL to Thomas W. Slocum, February 14, 1921, LP; HWH to ALL, May 3, 1921.

20. HWH to Felix Vorenberg, October 10, 1921; ALL to HWH, October 18, 1921, LP; HWH to Lucinda W. Prince, February 7, 1922; HWH to ALL, February 3, 1922.

21. Lucinda W. Prince to PHH, February 14, 1922, HAP; Lucinda W. Prince to FGN, April 6, 1922, NP; Lucinda W. Prince to FGN, April 14, 1922, NP; HWH to Lucinda W. Prince, May 1, 1922; FGN to HWH, April 17, 1922; HWH to FGN, April 21, 1922; Lucinda W. Prince to FGN, May 4, 1922, NP; JMB to HWH, May 4, 1922; Lucinda W. Prince to HWH, June 30, 1922.

22. HWH to Clifford H. Moore, January 5, 1923; HWH to PHH, July, 1922, HAP; HWH to FGN, May 18, 1922; JMB, "Students in the Graduate School of Education," *Harvard Alumni Bulletin* XXIV:772-773 (May 11, 1922); ARED 1922-23, p. 158.

23. JMB to HWH, November 14, 1921; "Conference with the Visiting Committee of the Board of Overseers for the Graduate School of Education," November 24, 1924, p. 3, HUA.

24. HWH, "Notes on the Graduate School of Education," March 30, 1920; ARED 1921-22, pp. 135-136; HWH to ALL, March 9, 1919, LP.

25. ARED 1921-22, p. 136; ARED 1922-23, p. 158; HWH to John J. Mahoney, January 12, 1923; HWH to ALL, March 7, 1922, LP.

26. HWH to PHH, December 17, 1921, HAP.

27. ARED 1920-21, pp. 175-176; ARED 1921-22, p. 136; HWH to Boston *Transcript*, October 30, 1916; HWH, "Notes about President Lowell's Letter of January 8, 1920"; HWH to Jerome D. Greene, January 27, 1920; HWH to ALL, April 5, 1920; HWH to John Adams, May 21, 1924.

28. ARED 1921-22, pp. 136-137; Charles H. Judd to HWH, December 24, 1919; Robert M. Ogden to HWH, June 28, 1923.

29. ALL to HWH, January 8, 1920; HWH to ALL, January 14, 1920; HWH, "Condensed Statement of Proposed Budget for 1920-21," January 22, 1920; HWH to Jerome D. Greene, January 27, 1920.

30. ALL to HWH, January 16, 1920; HWH to ALL, January 17, 1920; Jerome D. Greene to ALL, January 28, 1920, HP.

31. HWH to Joseph Lee, April 12, 1920; ALL to Graham Wallas, March 18, 1920, LP; ALL, "Note on Suggestions for an Appointment in Statistics by Harold Laski," 1920, LP; HWH, "Faculty Opinion on the Range and Scope of Instruction of the Graduate School of Education," 1921; HWH to ALL, March 29, 1920; ALL to Walter F. Dearborn, March 22, 1920, LP; HWH to ALL, April 5, 1920; HWH to Truman L. Kelley, April 9, 1920; HWH to ALL, August 19, 1920; ALL to James R. Angell, January 6, 1922 LP; AR 1921-22, p. 23.

32. HWH to Walter F. Dearborn, December 30, 1921; Max Farrand to HWH, March 30, 1922; ALL to HWH, June 4, 1929.

33. HWH to the Executive Committee of the Harvard Teachers Association, January 15, 1919; ALL, "The Relation of Secondary Schools to Colleges," *Harvard Alumni Bulletin* XXX:732-734 (March 22, 1928).

34. HWH, "Condensed Statement of Proposed Budget for 1920-21," January 22, 1920; John F. Moors to ALL, February 18, 1920 LP; R. M. Hughes, *A Study of the Graduate Schools of America* (Oxford, Ohio, 1925), p. 16.

7. The Formation of Educators

1. HWH, "Memorandum *Re* talk with Lowell," January 9, 1924; HWH to ALL, February 13, 1924; ARED 1922-23, pp. 158-159; ALL to FTS, December 2, 1931, LP.

2. ALL to FTS, December 2, 1931, LP; ALL to Frank Taussig, January 9, 1907, quoted in Melvin T. Copeland, *And Mark an Era: The Story of the Harvard Business School* (Boston, 1958), p. 7; ALL, "Reminiscences," *The Bulletin of Harvard Business School Alumni Association* XVII:137 (February 1941); Arthur E. Sutherland, *The Law at Harvard: A History of Ideas and Men, 1817-1967* (Cambridge, 1967), pp. 174-191; AR 1920-21, pp. 18-20; ALL, *What a University President Has Learned* (New York, 1938), p. 41; JMB, "Students in the Graduate School of Education," *Harvard Alumni Bulletin* XXIV:772-774 (May 11, 1922).

3. HWH to Samuel S. Drury, November 27, 1923; ARED 1923-24, p. 160.

4. "Conference with the Visiting Committee of the Board of Overseers for the Graduate School of Education," June 9, 1924, p. 4, HUA; "Conference with the Visiting Committee of the Board of Overseers for the Graduate School of Education," November 24, 1924, p. 3, HUA; Charles W. Hobbs to HWH, May 29, 1924; Frank W. Ballou to HWH, March 14, 1927.

5. HWH, "Memorandum on the Graduate School of Education," November 13, 1925.

6. HWH, "Memorandum for Faculty Discussion," January 5, 1928; *Report of the Committee on the Reorganization of Instruction*, March 1926, pp. 8-15, HUA; JMB, "Minutes of the Visiting Committee of the Board of Overseers," November 13, 1925, HP; JMB, "Notes," 1948, BP; "Conference with the Visiting Committee of the Board of Overseers for the Graduate School of Education," April 30, 1926, HUA.

7. HWH, "Notes on the Proposal for a More Unified and Thorough-Going Program for Whole-Time Inexperienced Students," April 3, 1924; "Conference

with the Visiting Committee," June 9, 1924, p. 3; "A Curriculum for Beginners," [c. 1924-25], HP.

8. L. O. Cummings to PHH, May 12, 1922, HAP; HWH, "Notes for Meeting of Candidates for Ed.D.," October 28, 1922; "Administrative Board Docket," May 23, 1922, HP; HWH, "Notes," March 5, 1924; HWH to Abraham Flexner, November 16, 1925.

9. HWH, "The Task of the Graduate School of Education," *Harvard Alumni Bulletin* XXIX:70 (October 14, 1926); ARED 1925-26, p. 157.

10. HWH to William H. Kilpatrick, April 12, 1916; HWH, "The New Social Order as Seen from the Standpoint of Education," *School and Society* XXI:9 (March 28, 1925). Learned's major reports of 1925 and 1926, which Holmes saw earlier in draft form, were published in William S. Learned, *The Quality of the Educational Process in the United States and in Europe* (New York, 1927).

11. HWH to ALL, July 31, 1924; HWH, "The New Social Order," p. 11ff; HWH, "The Teacher in Politics," *Progressive Education* IX:417 (October 1932).

12. HWH, "The New Social Order," pp. 2-5.

13. HWH, "The New Social Order"; HWH and Burton P. Fowler, eds., *The Path of Learning: Essays on Education* (Boston, 1926), p. 13; HWH, "The Training of Teachers and the Making of the Nation," *Harvard Alumni Bulletin* XXX: 163, 168 (November 3, 1927); HWH to William J. Cooper, October 18, 1930.

14. "News and Notes," *Harvard Alumni Bulletin* XXIX:10, 13 (June 3, 1926); HWH, "The Task of the Graduate School of Education," pp. 70-71; "The New Requirements at Harvard for Degrees in Education," *School and Society* XXV:707 (June 18, 1927); HWH, "The Training of Teachers and the Making of the Nation"; HWH, "Notes," October 13, 1928.

15. L. O. Cummings, "Co-operation in School Administration," Harvard Ed.D. dissertation, 1921, pp. xv, 505; L. L. Dudley to HWH, October 29, 1926; John Dewey, *The Sources of a Science of Education* (New York, 1929), pp. 47, 32.

16. "A Plan for Meeting Certain Fundamental Needs of American Education Through the Enlargement of the School," 1929, p. 6, LP; Charles H. Judd to HWH, May 5, 1926; HWH to Charles H. Judd, May 7, 1926; HWH to W. S. Gray, May 25, 1928.

17. James E. Russell to HWH, April 30, 1926; Ellwood P. Cubberley to HWH, November 17, 1929; Frank P. Bachman to HWH, May 25, 1926; Frank P. Bachman to HWH, June 9, 1926; Ellwood P. Cubberley to HWH, May 12, 1926; Stuart A. Courtis to HWH, May 6, 1926.

18. HWH to ALL, December 1928 (draft); HWH, "Memorandum on the Graduate School of Education," November 13, 1925; HWH, "Memorandum for the Meeting of the Committee Appointed by the Board of Overseers to Visit the School," November 22, 1926.

19. Committee on Admission, "Report on Procedure under the New Plan," 1927, HP; Fred C. Smith, "Statistics on Students Admitted under the New Plan," January 3, 1930, HP; Copeland, *And Mark an Era*, p. 88; Sutherland, *The Law at Harvard*, pp. 249, 320; HWH to Abraham Flexner, November 16, 1925.

20. HWH, "The Training of Teachers and the Making of the Nation," p. 162.

21. JMB, Edward A. Lincoln, and FTS, "Report of the Sub-Committee on Apprentice Teaching and Related Problems," November 18, 1926, HP.

22. ALL to FTS, December 2, 1931, LP; HWH to ALL, June 5, 1929.

23. HWH, "Memorandum on the Graduate School of Education," November 13, 1925; HWH, "General Points of View Concerning Statements or Curricula and the Organization of the Offering in a Particular Field," April 9, 1927; HWH, "Memorandum to Members of the Faculty," October 31, 1924; JME to HWH, November 3, 1924; FGN to HWH, November 5, 1924; Ralph Beatley, "Topics in the Teaching of Mathematics for All Inexperienced Students of Education" [r.d.], HP; "Topics in the Field of Secondary Education Which Ought To Be Included in the Professional Training of an Educator" [n.d.], HP; L. O. Cummings, "Principles of Educational Administration," November 1924, HP; "Suggestions for the Organization of Courses in the Common First Year," October 1924, HP; "A Curriculum for Beginners" [c. 1924-25], HP; HWH, "Required for Everybody," 1926; HWH to Members of the Subcommittees on Reorganization, October 27, 1926; HWH, "Memorandum for the Faculty Dinner Meeting," December 20, 1926; "Second Report of the Committee on the Reorganization of Instruction," January 1927.

24. Edward A. Lincoln, "Comment on the Tentative Report of the Subcommittee on the Common Curriculum," November 1926, HP; FTS, "Memorandum to the Sub-Committee on the Common Curriculum," October 30, 1926 HP; L. L. Dudley to HWH, October 29, 1926.

25. JMB to HWH, November 28, 1922; L. L. Dudley to HWH, April 5, 1926; HWH to ALL, April 9, 1926; ALL to HWH, April 12, 1926; HWH, "To be Considered in Arranging Com. Cur.," 1926.

26. For Lowell on general education see Henry Aaron Yeomans, *Abbott Lawrence Lowell, 1856-1943* (Cambridge, 1948), pp. 136-146.

27. Fred C. Smith to HWH, September 6, 1928; L. O. Cummings and L. L. Dudley to HWH, September 25, 1928; Bancroft Beatley to HWH, September 18, 1928; JMB to HWH, September 22, 1928; Archibald T. Davison to HWH, August 1, 1928; C. S. Thomas to HWH, September 20, 1928; HWH, "Bait for the President," 1931; HWH to Daniel A. Prescott, March 1932; Donald Snedden, "Comments on the Requirements for the Degree of Ed.M. — having some bearing on the Ed.D, " 1930, HP; HWH, "Memorandum on the Motion of the Dean," February 11, 1932.

28. "A Plan for Meeting Certain Fundamental Needs of American Education Through the Enlargement of the School," second draft, 1930, pp. 89-96, LP.

29. ARED 1926-27, p. 5; AR 1924-25, p. 25; JMB, "Minutes of the Visiting Committee of the Board of Overseers," November 13, 1925, p. 3, HP; ALL to John F. Moors, July 20, 1927, LP.

30. HWH, "Memorandum re L.O.C.'s Promotion to the Associate Professorship," April 7, 1927; ALL to HWH, April 12, 1926; ALL to HWH, April 23, 1927; ALL to HWH, May 27, 1927; HWH, "Notes for Conference with ALL," June 2, 1927; HWH to ALL, August 16, 1927; HWH to PHH, November 9, 1927; S. P. Capen to HWH, March 29, 1933; PHH to R. G. Jones, August 19, 1927, HAP; L. O. Cummings to HWH, December 14, 1929; L. O. Cummings to PHH, July 30, 1930, HAP; L. O. Cummings to PHH, May 16, 1931, HAP; HWH to Clyde R. Miller, August 23, 1930; [FGN], "Memorandum for the Dean," January 20, 1930, HP; HWH, "Account of Conversation with Abraham Flexner at the New York Harvard Club," February 14, 1930.

31. HWH to ALL, June 5, 1929; HWH to Joseph Lee, May 6, 1930; ALL to HWH, May 5, 1926; ALL to HWH, June 6, 1929.

32. JMB, "Memorandum *Re* Harvard University and Mr. Brewer," February 25, 1937, BP; JMB to HWH, October 22, 1925, BP; JMB, "Memorandum for Dean Holmes from J.M.B.," October 1925, BP; JMB, "Memorandum of Conference with Dean Holmes," December 31, 1925, BP; JMB to HWH, November 29, 1922; JMB, "Notes for Dean Holmes," January 27, 1926, BP; JMB, "Minutes of the Meeting of the Faculty Committee on the Bureau of Vocational Guidance," October 9, 1923, HUA; JMB, *History of Vocational Guidance, Origins and Early Development* (New York and London, 1942), p. 282.

33. HWH to ALL, May 25, 1915, LP; HWH to JMB, December 13, 1929; JMB, "The Need for Vocational Guidance in Colleges," *School and Society* XI:511-517 (May 1, 1920); JMB, *Education as Guidance* (New York, 1932); HWH, "Memorandum on Conference with Brewer," March, 1937; JMB to HWH, February 21, 1935; HWH to A. Lincoln Filene, February 11, 1932.

34. Abraham Flexner to HWH, January 23, 1930; Abraham Flexner to HWH, January 31, 1930; FGN, *A New Conception of Office Practice*, Harvard Bulletins in Education 12 (Cambridge, 1927), pp. 14-15, 32, 34-37; ARED 1929-30, p. 5; Walter F. Downey to ALL, April 4, 1930, LP; ALL to HWH, April 16, 1930, LP; HWH to ALL, March 22, 1930; FGN, *The Personal Secretary, Differentiating Duties and Essential Personal Traits*, Harvard Studies in Education 23 (Cambridge, 1934); HWH to Abraham Flexner, March 29, 1935; Abraham Flexner to HWH, April 8, 1935. Flexner's critique of schools of education appeared in *Universities: American, English, German* (New York, 1930), pp. 96-110.

35. "A Plan for Meeting Certain Fundamental Needs of American Education Through the Enlargement of the School," December 9, 1929, LP; HWH to ALL, August 1930 (draft); ALL to HWH, August 19, 1930, LP; HWH, "Notes on the Letter from President Lowell under Date of August 19, 1930, Concerning the Report on the Enlargement of the School," August 23, 1930, LP; ALL to HWH, April 8, 1931, LP; HWH to ALL, April 9, 1931, LP; S. S. Drury to HWH, January 10, 1934.

8. Professional Training and Institutional Disaster

1. HWH, "Memorandum to the Members of the Faculty of Education present at the dinner meeting of Dec. 16," January 10, 1930; L. J. A. Mercier to HWH, December 22, 1929; L. J. A. Mercier to HWH, January 14, 1930; JMB, "Some Notes on the History of the Graduate School of Education," December 1943, p. 4, RP; JMB to Truman L. Kelley, February 6, 1940, RP; JMB to HWH, February 21, 1935; FGN to HWH, February 12, 1930.

2. HWH to Joseph Lee, May 6, 1930; HWH to L. O. Cummings, March 18, 1930; FTS to HWH, June 30, 1933; Bancroft Beatley interview. Spaulding nearly went to Teachers College in 1928, to Ohio State in 1930, to Chicago in 1939, and eventually resigned in 1945. Beatley resigned in 1933 to become president of Simmons College.

3. HWH to Frederick C. Cabot, December 20, 1928; A. Lincoln Filene to

HWH, February 16, 1932; HWH to Samuel S. Drury, April 30, 1932; JMB, "Some Notes"; FGN to FTS, February 15, 1940, SP; JMB, "Report of a Conversation at Faculty Meeting," December 4, 1930, BP.

4. FTS, "Graduate Work in Schools of Education," *Harvard Teachers Record* III:123-136 (June 1933); FTS to Edgard G. Johnston, March 10, 1931, SP; HWH, "A Principle in Harness," *Harvard Teachers Record* III:120-122 (June 1933).

5. Roger W. Holmes, "Proposals for Instruction 1931-32" [January 1931], HP; FTS to HWH, January 27, 1931; Roger W. Holmes to HWH c. January 29, 1931]; HWH to Ralph Barton Perry (draft), March 2 1931; John Haynes Holmes to HWH, March 5, 1931; Roger W. Holmes to John Haynes Holmes, March 25, 1931, HP; ALL to HWH, April 10, 1931; HWH to ALL, April 11, 1931; ALL to HWH, April 15, 1931; FTS to HWH, May 5, 1931; HWH to ALL, May 7, 1931; ALL to HWH, May 8, 1931; HWH to ALL, May 13 1931; ALL to HWH, May 13, 1931; HWH to ALL, May 19, 1931; HWH to Sir John Adams, May 27, 1931.

6. ARED 1930-31, pp. 4-8.

7. HWH, "Memorandum on the Motion of the Dean," January 8, 1932; HWH to the Faculty, January 13, 1932; William Setchel Learned, *Realism in American Education* (Cambridge, 1932); HWH, "Memorandum on the Motion of the Dean," February 11, 1932; HWH, "Memorandum on Questions for the General Examination for the Degree of Master of Education," December 6, 1932; HWH, "Memorandum on the Character of the General Examination," December 20, 1933; HWH to S. S. Drury, June 14, 1932; HWH to C. S. Thomas and T. L. Kelley, May 13, 1933.

8. HWH to Joseph Lee, May 6, 1930.

9. Enrollment data are taken from summaries presented to the faculty at the beginning of each academic year. See also Howard E. Wilson, "Preliminary Report of the Apprentice Program of the Harvard Graduate School of Education," October 14, 1932, HP; Fred C. Smith, "Memorandum to Dean Holmes," May 18, 1933, HP; "Students in Harvard University from the United States, 1930-31," LP; HWH, "Data on Degrees June 1929-Jan. 35," n.d., MP; S. Willis Rudy, "The Degree of Master of Education at the Harvard Graduate School of Education," January 25, 1950, KP.

10. HWH, "The Graduate School of Education," May 8, 1932 ALL to HWH, June 14, 1932; HWH to ALL, June 29, 1932; ALL to HWH, August 4, 1932; HWH, "Memorandum on Finances," August 12 1932; HWH, "Memorandum on Economies Required During 1932-33, n.d.; HWH, "Second Memorandum on Economy," November 10, 1932; HWH, "Summary Statement on the Budget for 1933-34," March 4, 1933; HWH, "Memorandum on the Financial Situation of the School," March 8, 1933; Ralph Beatley, Bancroft Beatley, and FTS to HWH, March 9, 1933; Bancroft Beatley interview; HWH, "Memorandum on the Maintenance of the Two-Year Plan," March 8, 1933; FGN to HWH, March 10, 1933; R. M. Hughes, "Report of the Committee on Graduate Education," *The Educational Record* XV:192-234 (April 1934).

11. This distinction between amateur and professional, which emphasizes personal commitment and identity rather than scholarly competence, is developed

in Mary O. Furner, *Advocacy and Objectivity: A Crisis in the Professionalization of American Social Science, 1865-1905* (Lexington, Ky., 1975).

12. JBC, *My Several Lives: Memoirs of a Social Inventor* (New York, Evanston, and London, 1970), pp. 82-83.

13. Ibid., pp. 180-182.

14. "Data on A.M. Alumni in Teaching" [c. 1934], CP; AR 1923-24, pp. 14-15; AR 1928-29, pp. 14-16; AR 1929-30, pp. 14-18; Charles Moore, "Report of the Committee to Visit the Graduate School of Arts and Sciences," Overseers Reports, 1927-28, p. 286, HUA; Homer Gage, "Report of the Committee to Visit the Graduate School of Arts and Sciences," May 12, 1931, Overseers Reports, 1930-31, p. 32, HUA; George H. Chase, "Report of the Committee to Study the Problems of the Graduate School of Arts and Sciences, Particularly the Relation of Undergraduate to Graduate Work," May 15, 1931, HUA; JBC to George H. Chase, March 12, 1934, CP.

15. JBC, *My Several Lives*, pp. 183-184; HWH to JBC, February 14, 1934; JBC to George A. Works, March 9, 1934, CP; HWH, "Notes for Conference with Conant," April 1934; JBC, "Memorandum Concerning Training of Teachers in Harvard University, Based on Conversation with Dean Chase and Dean Holmes the Early Part of May, 1934," May 9, 1934, CP; HWH to JBC, June 28, 1934; "Docket, University [of Chicago] Senate Meeting," March 11, 1933, CP; [University of Chicago], "The Nature of the School Population" [c. 1933], CP; [University of Chicago], "Policies Relating to Teacher Preparation at the Secondary-School Level" [c. 1933], CP; HWH, "Comments on the Chicago Memoranda," September 1934; Charles H. Judd to HWH, August 8, 1935, MP.

16. Lowell's willingness to grant tenure to nonscholar specialists in elementary academic instruction was evidence for Conant's contention that his predecessor had overvalued loyal service to Harvard College. Conant consistently refused to advance such individuals from associate to full professorships. No full professor in special methods was appointed at Harvard until the end of the 1940s. Then the successful candidate had little prior school experience, held a Harvard Ph.D. in astronomy, and had passed muster through personal collaboration with the president in an undergraduate course.

17. HWH, "Notes of January 26, 1935," MP; AR 1933-34, pp. 5-6; HWH to JBC, December 31, 1935.

18. HWH, "Notes," April 1934; HWH, "Notes," January 26, 1935, MP; ARED 1934-35, p. 51; HWH to PJR, December 10, 1935, MP; HWH to E. S. Evendon, May 10, 1933; HWH to E. S. Evendon, May 23, 1933; HWH to JBC, December 31, 1935; HWH to JBC, March 17, 1936, MP; L. J. A. Mercier to HWH, May 14, 1936; HWH, "Memorandum of Conference with N. Henry Black," February 11, 1930; FM, December 11, 1935; JMB to HWH, December 13, 1935; HWH to JMB, December 14, 1935.

19. AMT Administrative Board Minutes, January 8, 1936, MP; HWH to Fred N. Robinson, January 25, 1936, MP; Fred N. Robinson to HWH, January 27, 1936, MP; Fred N. Robinson to HWH, February 8, 1936, MP; Fred N. Robinson to HWH, February 12, 1936, MP; AMT Administrative Board Minutes, February 10, 1936, February 15, 1936, and March 6, 1936, MP; HWH to JBC, February 21,

1936, MP; HWH to J. B. Munn, February 18, 1936, MP; Andre Morize to HWH, February 20, 1936, George H. Chase Papers, HUA; HWH to Andre Morize February 20, 1936; HWH to Administrative Board, March 4, 1936, CP HWH to JBC, March 11, 1936; Ralph Beatley to HWH, March 15, 1936, MP; HWH to JBC, March 17, 1936, MP; HWH to JBC, January 2, 1936, CP; HWH to J. W. Lowes, June 29, 1936, MP; J. W. Lowes, "School of Education Budget 1936-37," April 24, 1936, CP.

20. HWH to JBC, October 26, 1935, MP; HWH, "Notes for Conference with Conant," October 1, 1935, MP; ARED 1934-35, pp. 1-3; FM, December 11, 1935.

21. HWH, "Notes on the General Examination Given at Mid Years," June 12, 1934. Examples of test items with a wide spread in faculty response were: "Compromises between the educational procedures indicated by scientific findings and the exigencies of social situations and administrative feasibility are generally desirable" and "evolution should be taught [in junior high school] as an established biological fact." "Brantford question," May 1933, HP; Everett B. Sackett, "The Harvard Objective Examination of Ability to Apply Principles to Scholastic Situations," October 12, 1938, RP; Hollis M. Leverett, "Report on Work with Part VI Examination," October 1939, HP; Evan R. Collins, speech draft [c. January 1940], HP.

22. Ralph Beatley to HWH, December 7, 1939, MP; HWH to JBC, April 19, 1937; HWH to JBC, May 10, 1937.

23. HWH to FTS, September 1937; HWH, "For the Informal Faculty Meeting on September 30, 1937," p. 3; HWH, "Notes on Our Situation," May 11 1938, p. 3; A. Lincoln Filene to JBC, May 20, 1941, SP; HWH, "Notes of June 7, 1937"; Raymond B. Fosdick to Jerome Greene, April 25, 1938 CP; Robert J. Havighurst to Jerome Greene, May 13, 1938, CP.

24. [Howard E. Wilson], "A Memorandum Concerning the Further Development of the Harvard Graduate School of Education" [May 6, 1938], pp. 15-16, HP; HWH, "Notes on HEW's Memorandum to DML, May 6," May 9, 1938; HWH, "Notes for the Ten-Year Plan" [n.d., fall 1938]; "Memorandum of Conference of Holmes, Spaulding, Wilson," September 19, 1938 HP; HWH, note to himself, December 11, 1938.

25. HWH, note to himself, December 11, 1938; JBC, *My Several Lives*, pp. 187-193; FTS, "Memorandum for Mr. Conant on the Need for a School of Education at Harvard University," December 23, 1938, SP; AR 1937-38, pp. 10-12; HWH to Donald K. David, December 21, 1938; HWH to JBC, April 8, 1939; JBC, "Memorandum to J. W. Lowes," April 11, 1939, CP; J. W. Lowes, "Memorandum for the Corporation on the Graduate School of Education," April 21, 1939, RP; "Financial Outlook Through 1943-44, Proposals for University Action," April 24, 1939, HP; HWH to Howard E. Wilson, April 12, 1939; HWH to JBC, May 1, 1939, CP; HWH to JBC, June 20, 1939, CP; JBC to HWH, June 16, 1939, CP; Mrs. Francis T. Spaulding interview; Frank E. Spaulding to Susan Spaulding, February 6, 1939, SP; Diaries of Francis T. Spaulding, 1938-39 (courtesy Mrs. F. T. Spaulding).

26. FGN to FTS, February 15, 1940, SP; FGN to FTS, January 13, 1941, SP; JMB, "Some Notes."

27. FTS to JBC, October 13, 1939, SP; ARED 1940-41, pp. 13-16; Robert Ulich to FGN, January 20, 1940, DP.

28. JMB to FTS, February 16, 1940, SP; FTS to JMB, February 23, 1940, SP; FGN to JMB, May 1, 1940, NP; JMB to Colleagues, April 18, 1940, BP; "Minutes of Ed.M. Committee Meeting," April 18, 1940, NP; FGN to JMB, April 24, 1940, NP; "Statement of P. J. Rulon to the Committee on the Graduate Study of Education," October 14, 1964, RP; FM, April 23, 1940; Evan R. Collins, "Memorandum to the Faculty" [c. January 1942]; FM, January 14, 1942; *Official Register of Harvard University* XXXIX (May 28, 1942), p. 92.

29. FTS to HWH, February 22, 1942; HWH, "Memorandum on the Informal Faculty Meeting," March 23, 1942.

30. PJR to Walter F. Dearborn, March 7, 1944, DP; ARED 1939-40, pp. 1, 4, 9, 15; HWH, "Pedagogical Racketeering," *Scribner's Magazine* XCVII:157 (March 1935).

9. The Lure of Social Science

1. ARED 1936-37, pp. 5-6; ARED 1937-38, pp. 3-6.

2. HCR 1937-38, p. 293.

3. E. A. Lincoln, "Methods and Results in the Harvard Growth Study," *Harvard Teachers Record* V:27-28 (February 1935); Walter F. Dearborn, John W. M. Rothney, and Frank K. Shuttleworth, *Data on the Growth of Public School Children*, Monograph of the Society for Research in Child Development, Vol. 3, No. 14 (Washington, D.C., 1938); Walter F. Dearborn and J. W. M. Rothney, *Predicting the Child's Development* (Cambridge, 1941). Criticisms appear in B. R. Buckingham to Walter F. Dearborn, September 16, 1938, DP, and Howard V. Meredith, review of "Predicting the Child's Development," *Psychological Bulletin* XXXIX: 245-249 (April 1942). Dearborn acknowledged that the Growth Study had produced "so little" in his reply to Meredith, ibid., p. 250. HWH, "Notes on HEW's Memorandum to DML, May 6," May 9, 1938; HWH, note to himself, December 11, 1938.

4. Truman L. Kelley to HWH, September 28, 1939; George H. Chase to JBC, June 10, 1941, CP; Gordon W. Allport to HWH, February 19, 1942, SP; PJR to Truman L. Kelley, April 28, 1942, RP; Truman L. Kelley to Committee of the Corporation, January 8, 1946, HP.

5. "Report of the Committee to Visit the Graduate School of Education," May 10, 1937, HUA; HWH to Payson Smith, April 7, 1937; HWH to Payson Smith, August 3, 1937.

6. FTS to Frederick W. Porter, January 9, 1931, SP; FTS, *High School and Life* (New York and London, 1938), p. 149; HWH, "Notes," c. 1938; ARED 1936-37, pp. 7-9; ARED 1937-38, p. 12.

7. Robert Ulich was a German who, at the end of the 1920s, was councillor in the Saxony Ministry of Education in charge of universities and also professor of philosophy at the Technische Hochschüle in Dresden. He was at once a practical administrator who pioneered adult education for workers and a learned humanist who conceived of education as a unified subject integrating history, philosophy,

and social theory. His practicality, learning and disdain for quantitative educational science impressed Flexner, who first brought him to America in 1930 on a lecture tour and introduced him to Holmes. Holmes also respected Ulich and his idealist thought, and Flexner raised foundation support for Ulich to teach at Harvard when he left Germany in 1933. By 1935 Conant regarded Ulich as the School's most learned faculty member and readily agreed to a full professorship in 1936. See Robert Ulich, *On the Reform of Educational Research*, Occasional Pamphlets of the Graduate School of Education, No. 2 (Cambridge, 1937); HWH to JBC, March 4, 1938; JBC to Raymond Fosdick, March 7, 1938, HP.

8. AR 1934-35, p. 8; JBC, *My Several Lives: Memoirs of a Social Inventor* (New York, Evanston, and London, 1970), pp. 123, 424; JBC, "The Function of the Secondary School and College in Educating for Social and Cultural Leadership," *Harvard Alumni Bulletin* XXXVII:311-315 (December 7, 1934); JBC, "The Selective Principle in American Colleges, *Harvard Educational Review* VII: 165-175 (March 1937).

9. JBC, *My Several Lives*, pp. 187-190; FTS, "Memorandum for Mr. Conant on the Need for a School of Education at Harvard University," December 25, 1938, SP; AR 1937-38, pp. 3-13.

10. JBC, *My Several Lives*, pp. 207-233; AR 1934-35, p. 8; AR 1937-38, p. 3; JBC to FTS, October 7, 1939, CP; JBC, "A Free Classless Society: Ideal or Illusion?," *Harvard Alumni Bulletin* XLII:3-7 (November 17, 1939). The most complete prewar expression of Conant's linkage of schooling and social mobility was his Charter Day address at the University of California in March 1940, "Education for a Classless Society: The Jeffersonian Tradition," *The Atlantic Monthly* CLXV:593-602 (May 1940).

11. A. Calvert Smith, "Notes on July 24, 1940, Conference," CP; FTS to JBC, October 13, 1939, SP; JBC to FTS, December 12, 1939, CP.

12. FM, February 13, 1940; ARED 1940-41, p. 1.

13. FTS, "Notes for Conference with Conant," August 18, 1941 SP; FTS to John Stewart Bryan, February 4, 1941 SP.

14. John F. Sly, "Curriculum Problems in the School of Education, Harvard University," March 15, 1940, HUA; W. W. Trent to FTS, March 20, 1940, SP; FTS to Mrs. F. T. Spaulding, July 4, 1940, SP; [R. C. Gill] to HWH March 29, 1940; FTS to Robert J. Havighurst, February 19, 1940, SP; FTS to Lewis A. Wilson, June 10, 1940, SP; FTS to HWH, June 4, 1937; John F. Sly, Alfred D. Simpson, and FTS, "Research, Service, and Instruction in Educational Administration," September 1940, SP; Alfred D. Simpson, "Memorandum Concerning the Development of the Program for Research, Service and Instruction in Educational Administration," November 16, 1942, SP.

15. Clyde Kluckhohn, "Suggestions for Blurb for Hayden Foundation," January 3, 1940, SP; FTS, "Recommendation for Appointment, Orval Hobart Mowrer," June 6, 1940, CP.

16. The committee's records are in SP. In particular see Theodore Morrison, "The Teaching of English and the Training of the English Teacher," February 7, 1941. The final report was published as *The Training of Secondary School Teachers, Especially with Reference to English* (Cambridge, 1942).

17. Archibald MacLeish, "The Next Harvard," *The Atlantic Monthly* CLXVII:587 (May 1941).

18. FTS to JBC, October 13, 1939, SP.

19. HWH to FTS, October 13, 1941, SP; HWH to George H. Chase, February 28, 1942, CP; FTS to HWH, March 22, 1942; FTS, "Memorandum on Certain Financial Matters," January 13, 1942, SP; HWH, "Memorandum for the Visiting Committee," March 2, 1942.

20. ARED 1942-43, p. 1.

21. JBC to HWH, May 4, 1935; Robert Ulich to JBC, April 11, 1944, CP; Howard E. Wilson, "Proposed Memorandum to Mr. Conant Concerning the Establishment at Harvard University of a Center for Education in Citizenship," May 11, 1943, HP; Howard E. Wilson to JBC, May 27, 1943, CP; Howard E. Wilson, "Confidential Memorandum to the Faculty Committee," July 24, 1943, DP; Howard E. Wilson, "Memorandum to the Faculty," November 15, 1944, HP. Materials on the search for an acting dean are in CP.

22. P. J. Rulon interview; Mrs. P. J. Rulon interview; "Notes on Rulon Statement to Committee on the Graduate Study of Education," October 14, 1964, RP; "Specifications for a Man in Secondary Education," November 1943, RP.

23. PJR, "Memorandum to the Members of the Faculty," April 24, 1944, RP; PJR to W. H. Burton, May 17, 1944, RP; ARED 1943-44, pp. 3-16.

24. HWH, "Resolutions Offered for the Consideration of the Faculty," April 26, 1944, RP.

25. JMB to PJR, May 29, 1944, RP; FM, May 9, 1944.

26. HWH, Memorandum to Himself, November 13, 1944; HWH to PJR, January 1, 1945, RP; FM, January 4, 1945.

27. PJR to William H. Burton, December 26, 1945, RP; JBC, "Memorandum to the Corporation RE: Future of Graduate School of Education," July 20, 1945, CP.

28. ARED 1942-43, pp. 12-18; PJR, "Memorandum No. 69 to the Committee on the Objectives of a General Education in a Free Society" [n.d.], RP. Within his own School, Rulon had no quarrel with continued staffing in academic disciplines such as history and philosophy of education. Although he doubted their capacity to help solve real educational problems, he understood that their presence reinforced a research environment.

29. H. M. Jones to Robert Ulich, August 9, 1943, Ulich Papers, HUA; H. M. Jones to JBC, May 24, 1944, CP; PJR to H. M. Jones, May 12, 1944, HP; JBC, "Memorandum to Dean Buck," January 15, 1945, CP; JBC, "Memorandum to the Corporation," May 22, 1945, CP.

30. JBC, "A Truce among Educators," *Teachers College Record* XLVI:157-163 (December 1944); FM, January 4, 1945; FM, January 13, 1945; JBC, "Memorandum to the Corporation," July 20, 1945, CP.

31. JBC to Robert M. Yerkes, September 6, 1945, CP; JBC to Edwin G. Boring, July 30, 1945, CP; JBC, "Science and Society," text for speech at McGill University, October 5, 1945, pp. 6-7, CP; JBC, "The Role of Science in General Education," text for [undelivered] speech to AASA, March 6, 1946, pp. 8-9, CP.

32. JBC, "Memorandum to the Corporation," July 20, 1945, CP; JBC to FTS,

June 27, 1945, CP; FM, November 17, 1945; JBC to George A. Zock, February 28, 1946, CP.

33. Truman L. Kelley to JBC, November 20, 1945, CP; PJR to Ben D. Wood, December 3, 1945, RP; HWH to Grenville Clark, March 12, 1946.

34. "Memorandum from the Faculty to a Committee of the Corporation," March 31, 1946, RP; HWH to PJR, January 17, 1946; O. Hobart Mowrer, "The Graduate School of Education," February 25, 1946, HP; HWH to Grenville Clark, March 12, 1946.

35. Henry James to JBC, December 20, 1945 CP; Perry Dunlap Smith to JBC, January 18, 1946, CP; Perry Dunlap Smith, "Report of the Committee to Visit the Graduate School of Education," July 10, 1946, HUA; Willard B. Spalding to JBC, December 3, 1945, CP; JBC to A. L. Knoblauch, February 28, 1946, CP; Charles W. Lawrance to JBC, February 19 1946, CP; Alonzo G Grace, "The Harvard School of Education," January 1947, RP; JBC to Alonzo G. Grace, January 11, 1947, CP.

36. JBC to Grenville Clark, Henry James, and Henry L. Shattuck, April 10, 1946, CP; HWH to PJR, May 7, 1946; JBC, "Memorandum to the Corporation Re: The Future of the Graduate School of Education," May 13, 1946, CP; JBC, "Memorandum Concerning the Future of the Harvard University Graduate School of Education," June 6, 1946, RP; JBC to PJR, June 14, 1946, RP.

37. Although the specific recommendations and public impact of the Harvard Redbook were confined mainly to higher education, the report itself was principally concerned with the secondary schools. See the Report of the Harvard Committee, *General Education in a Free Society* (Cambridge, 1945); Educational Policies Commission, *Education for ALL American Youth* (Washington, D.C., 1944); W. Lloyd Warner, Robert J. Havighurst, and Martin B. Loeb, *Who Shall Be Educated?* (New York, 1944). For Conant's postwar "sociological" attitude toward public education see JBC to Robert M. Yerkes, September 6, 1945 CP; his Sachs lectures at Teachers College, especially the first lecture on "The Structure of American Society," all published in *Teachers College Record* XLVII:145-194 (December 1945); and his elaboration of these lectures, *Education in a Divided World: The Future of the Public Schools in Our Unique Society* (Cambridge, 1948), pp. 35-68; JBC to Devereux C. Josephs, December 2, 1946, CP; AF 1946-47, p. 20. On American social science during the war see Samuel Stouffer, *The American Soldier* (Princeton, 1949). On Conant's commitment to social science application and the social scientists' doubts, see Talcott Parsons to JBC, February 21, 1946, CP; Samuel A. Stouffer to JBC, October 25, 1947, CP; JBC to Samuel A. Stouffer, October 30, 1947, CP; Samuel A. Stouffer to JBC, November 4, 1947, CP; Paul H. Buck interview.

38. PJR to W. H. Burton, May 17, 1944, RP; PJR, "Memorandum to the Faculty," September 25, 1945, RP; FM, October 10, 1945 PJR to JBC, November 7, 1945, RP; PJR to Paul E. Kambly, December 21, 1945, RP; PJR to HWH, February 15, 1946; HWH to H. M. Jones, March 14, 1946, HP. *General Education in a Free Society*, pp. 262-266; JBC, "Memorandum of the Report of the Ad Hoc Committee to Advise the President on the Selection of a new Dean for the School of Education," October 22, 1946, CP.

39. JBC to FTS, November 14, 1946, SP; JBC to Devereux C. Josephs, October 9, 1946; JBC to Devereux C. Josephs, December 2, 1946, CP; JBC to Roy E. Larsen, December 18, 1946, CP; Robert Redfield to JBC, December 16, 1946, CP; HWH to PJR, January 9, 1947; JBC, "Memorandum to the Trustees of the Ford Foundation," December 1947, KP; JBC to FTS, March 24, 1948, CP; FM, April 20, 1948; FK to JBC, August 23, 1945, CP; S. A. Stouffer to JBC, March 8, 1948, CP; Talcott Parsons to JBC, April 12, 1948, CP; Clyde Kluckhohn to JBC, April 16, 1948, CP; [Paul H. Buck] "Francis Keppel. Recommendation of the Provost of the University, April 12, 1946," CP; FM, April 22, 1948.

40. Paul H. Buck to Arthur M. Schlesinger [Sr.], December 15, 1948, DOP.

41. E. G. Boring to Robert R. Sears, October 25, 1948, KP; FK to JBC, December 6, 1948, KP; FK to JBC, December 22, 1948, KP; FK to JBC, January 12, 1949, KP; FK to JBC, February 21, 1949, KP; Robert R. Sears to Deland De Vinney, September 20, 1951, KP; "Laboratory of Human Development, Graduate School of Education, Annual Report 1949-50," KP.

42. Guidance had survived between Brewer's retirement and the 1949 research reconnaissance through a federally funded Veteran's Administration Guidance Center, which counseled returning veterans about college opportunities in the Boston area and paid for a few Harvard courses. See JBC, "Selection and Guidance in Secondary Education," speech at Roxbury Latin School, May 18, 1946, CP; JBC, "Public Education: Sinews of Democrary," speech at U.S. Chamber of Commerce, May 1, 1947, CP; FM, November 9, 1948; Henry S. Dyer, "Some Thoughts on a Guidance Program at the Graduate School of Education," January 5, 1949, KP; FK to E. G. Williamson, January 21, 1949, KP.

43. FK to JBC, May 5, 1949, KP; FK to C. G. Sargent, August 5, 1949, KP; FK, "Sociological Analysis of the Community as a Basis for Developing the School Program," January 13, 1949, KP.

44. "Center for Field Studies Project" [c. 1949], KP; Arthur H. Rice, "A.A.S.A. — Kellogg Project," *The Nation's Schools* XLVI: 31-35 (November 1950); H. C. Hunt, "The Cooperative Program in Educational Administration," *The School Executive* (February 1952), pp. 72-73; W. K. Kellogg Foundation, *The First-Twenty-Five Years: The Story of a Foundation* (Battle Creek, Mich., 1955), pp. 16, 19, 100; Hollis A. Moore, Jr., *Studies in School Administration: A Report on the CPEA* (Washington, D.C., 1957); Alfred D. Simpson, "The Kellogg Grant to Harvard for the Improvement of Educational Administration," speech to New England Association of School Superintendents, October 17, 1950, KP; C. G. Sargent, "Harvard-Kellogg Project in Community-School Administration: Summary of Ideas on Research Design as of January 1, 1951," KP.

45. Morris E. Opler to FK, November 24, 1948, KP; FK to JBC, March 25, 1951, KP.

46. ARED 1952-53, pp. 7, 9.

47. See the curriculum revision reports of the Committee on the Degree of Master of Education, 1949-50, Judson T. Shaplin Papers, HUA; FK to Elliott Dunlap Smith, November 29, 1955, KP; HWH, "Notes on Minutes of the Division," November 2, 1948.

10. Educational Careers and the Missing Elite

1. FK to JBC, February 27, 1951, KP

2. JBC, "Memorandum to Mr. Paul G Hoffman for Meeting in New York, Saturday, June 2, 1951," May 24, 1951, KP; FK, 'Proposal to the Trustees of the Fund for the Advancement of Education," June 9 1951, KP.

3. See Alvin C. Eurich, *Reforming American Education: The Innovative Approach to Improving Our Schools and Colleges* (New York, Evanston, and London, 1969), and Paul Woodring, *Investment in Education, An Historical Appraisal of the Fund for the Advancement of Education* (Boston and Toronto, 1970); Alvin C. Eurich interview.

4. Keppel's principal administrative colleague, Judson T. Shaplin, thought career recruitment was a means for the School to become, at long last, a "fashionable place." He always assumed Keppel had been made dean primarily because of his impeccable connections with the University and fundraising communities. Shaplin's own social background was strikingly humble. He contributed enthusiastically to career recruitment because he valued high standards in practitioners and, like Eurich, was suspicious of educational research. Judson T. Shaplin and Francis Keppel interviews.

5. FK, "Proposal to the Trustees of the Fund for the Advancement of Education," June 9, 1951, KP; FK to Alvin C. Eurich, October 20, 1951, KP "A Cooperative Program for the Identification and Training of Teachers for the Schools" [record of discussion at December 14, 1951, meeting], KP; FK to Alvin C. Eurich, January 9, 1952, KP.

6. On the value of the behavioral sciences in a professional curriculum see Report of a Faculty Committee, *The Behavioral Sciences at Harvard* (Cambridge, 1954), p. 489. On the Fund's concern with Harvard's uses of the grant see John J. Scanlon to Phillip H. Coombs, April 27, 1955, and Clarence Faust to John J. Scanlon, May 12, 1955, Ford Foundation Archives.

7. Theodore R. Sizer, *Master of Arts in Teaching. Harvard's First Twenty-Five Years, 1936-1961* (Cambridge, 1962), pp. 22, 25, 30-31.

8. ARED 1955-56, pp. 8-9; Harvard Graduate School of Education, "Aspen Conference Report," October 1959, appendix A.

9. Joseph J. Young, "Report on Financial Aid to Students 1960 61," FM, December 5, 1960.

10. Harry Levin, Thomas L. Hilton, and Gloria F. Leiderman, "The Prediction of Teacher Behavior," Report to the Fund for the Advancement of Education, May 15, 1956, pp. 34-35, KP; Eurich, *Reforming American Education* pp. 85, 106-116; FK to Clarence Faust, August 13, 1954, KP; FK to Clarence Faust, January 17, 1955, KP; FK to Clarence Faust, January 27, 1955 KP; FK to Beardsley Ruml, June 23, 1955, KP; FK to Sloan Wilson, July 8, 1955, KP; ARED 1954-55. pp. 1-19. The fullest exposition of Keppel's rationale for team teaching is *Personnel Policies for Education* (Pittsburgh, 1961).

11. ARED 1950-51, pp. 11-12; Robert Van Duyn to C. G. Sargent, August 31, 1951, KP; FK, "Comments on Visits to Schools of Education and Certain

School Systems under a Travel Grant from Carnegie Corporation of New York,"
July 31, 1951, KP; PJR to FK, January 23, 1952, KP; FK to Hugh Masters, April 7,
1952, KP; Angelo Giaudrone, "New England CPEA Aims and Results," *School
Executive* (March 1955), pp. 102-117.

12. FK to JBC, December 29, 1952, KP; JBC to Henry L. Shattuck, January
8, 1953, Shattuck Papers, Massachusetts Historical Society; Henry L. Shattuck to
JBC, January 12, 1953, Shattuck Papers, Massachusetts Historical Society; Henry
L. Shattuck to Roy E. Larsen, March 27, 1953, DOP; Henry L. Shattuck to the
Corporation, May 29, 1953, DOP; Henry L. Shattuck, "Memorandum of Cor-
respondence Between President Conant and Henry L. Shattuck," May 19, 1953,
Shattuck Papers, Massachusetts Historical Society; Henry L. Shattuck to Paul C.
Cabot, May 21, 1953, Shattuck Papers, Massachusetts Historical Society; FK,
"Memorandum for Mr. Shattuck," June 2, 1953, DOP; FK to Henry L. Shattuck,
June 22, 1953, DOP; FK to Edward Reynolds, April 8, 1954, KP.

13. Robert Schaefer to FK, March 24, 1954, KP; Edward Landy to FK, November 30, 1953, KP; Senior Faculty Minutes, September 29, 1954, KP.

14. *The Behavioral Sciences at Harvard*, pp. 111, 378-380, 489-490; ARED
1952-53, pp. 7, 9; John W. M. Whiting interview; Nicholas Hobbs, "Report on the
Guidance Program in the Harvard Graduate School of Education," October 26,
1953, p. 18, KP.

15. This was the first assault on the Ed.D. by researchers. Previous attacks by
practitioners had focused on the degree's requirements rather than on the label itself. The active search for a Ph.D. alternative to the Ed.D. dramatized the discomfort that faculty whose graduate training was in the arts and sciences felt for what
they perceived to be a professional degree. The first generation of educational researchers, men such as Dearborn, Kelley, and Rulon, had no problem with the
Ed.D. as a research degree even though they all held Ph.Ds themselves. Their graduate studies and professional ties had been to education as a field. In their day the
Harvard Ed.D. was supposed to have been a research degree only.

The School's failure to win routine access to the Ph.D. degree (although a few
able students were discreetly channeled through the Ph.D. in Education) contributed substantially to its small impact on research training in the fifties. The lack of
Ph.D. access was unique among major schools of education; admissions officers
knew what a drawback it was in attracting research-oriented doctoral applicants.
Ironically, the cross-faculty collaborative model exemplified by the M.A.T. was
never extended to Ph.D. collaboration. Neither Conant nor Pusey saw the considerable potential of an expanded Ph.D. in Education. If they did, they neither
trusted the School with the Ph.D. nor were willing to endure the inevitable political
heat from the faculty of arts and sciences.

The Ed.D. alone thus bore the burden of both research and practitioner training. But despite the confusions and ambiguities of the situation, the blurring of
doctoral purpose eventually impressed many faculty members as a source of
strength rather than weakness. The School took pride that practitioners in training
were never isolated from researchers and research issues, and vice-versa. In an age
where confidence in both practitioner training and research training in education
was severely limited, this broader training environment was seen as a rich and fitting deterrant to naive specialization. See FK to James Perkins, January 31, 1956,

KP; "Proposal for Support of the Ph.D. in Education," 1956, KP; FK to NMP [unsent], January 8, 1956, KP.

16. ARED 1953-54, pp. 4-5.

17. ARED 1952-53, pp. 5-12.

18. FK to Alvin C. Eurich, October 20, 1951, KP; Hobbs, "Report on the Guidance Program in the Harvard Graduate School of Education."

19. Robert R. Sears to FK, November 10, 1953, KP; Edward Landy to FK, November 30, 1953, KP; [John W. M. Whiting], draft on "The Graduate School of Education," [for *The Behavioral Sciences at Harvard*, c. 1953-54], p. 17, KP.

20. David V. Tiedeman to FK [c. 1952], KP; David V. Tiedeman to FK, June 3, 1953, KP; David V. Tiedeman to FK, December 7, 1953, DOP; David V. Tiedeman, "The Topsys in Guidance I Know at Harvard," May 22, 1970 (author's possession); NMP to FK, January 19, 1955, KP; Edwin B. Wilson to FK, January 18, 1955, KP; John B. Carroll to FK, May 12, 1955, KP; FK to NMP, May 13, 1955, KP; Nathan M. Pusey interview.

21. FK to Herold C. Hunt, July 30, 1953; KP; "Minutes of the Policy Committee of the Center for Field Studies," December 1, 1954, KP; Senior Members Minutes, December 1, 1954, KP; "Memorandum to W. K. Kellogg Foundation," December 16, 1954, KP; FK to Henry T. Hill, January 7, 1955, KP; Herold C. Hunt to Senior Members, January 12, 1955, Judson T. Shaplin Papers, HUA. For one social scientist's sympathetic evaluation of the contribution of the social sciences to the Administrative Career Program, and the importance of maintaining a research emphasis to attract able faculty, see Theodore Newcomb's remarks at the CPEA Evaluation Conference, October 8, 1954, KP.

22. William H. Burton to FK, January 7, 1954, KP; William H. Burton, "The Attempted Murder of Principles of Teaching 3," 1952, Judson T. Shaplin Papers, HUA; FK to Clarence Faust, January 17, 1955, Ford Foundation Archives.

23. Harry Levin to FK, December 28, 1954, KP; Phillip Coombs to Thomas L. Hilton, May 29, 1956, KP.

24. Jerome Bruner to Talcott Parsons, "Research on the Educational Process," June 9, 1955, KP; FK to Edward C. Tolman, March 23, 1955, EP; FK to Finis Engleman, August 21, 1957, KP.

25. Robert Anderson to Judson T. Shaplin and Dana M. Cotton, September 19, 1954, KP; FK to NMP, October 13, 1955, KP.

26. "Rough Transcript of Remarks of Mr. Keppel in Telephone Conversation with Roy Larsen on December 13, 1955," KP; FK to Clarence Faust, January 6, 1956, KP; FK to Clarence Faust, February 6, 1956, KP; Clarence Faust to FK, February 10, 1956, KP; FK, "Memorandum for the Senior Members," March 16, 1956, DOP; FK to JBC, March 20, 1955, KP.

27. Senior Faculty Minutes, April 17, 1956, KP; 'Mr. Cogan's Note on the Discussion of the Senior Faculty Meeting " April 17, 1956, KP; Judson T. Shaplin, M. L. Cogan, N. Gross, D. V. Tiedeman, "Implications of Proposed Program for Personnel Policies of the Graduate School of Education" [April 17, 1956], KP; FK to Clarence Faust, April 18, 1956, KP; PJR to David V. Tiedeman, April 21 1956, RP; "Working Paper Adopted by Senior Members, May 22, 1956," KP; ARED 1955-56, pp. 2-5.

28. FK, "General Considerations," 1957, KP; Elizabeth Paschal, "Memoran-

dum on Harvard Proposal of December 20, 1956" [n.d.], Ford Foundation Archives; Lester Nelson to Alvin C. Eurich, December 27, 1956, Ford Foundation Archives.

29. FK to Clarence Faust, January 16, 1959, KP; ARED 1958-59, pp. 5-7; FK to Henry H. Hill, February 13, 1958, KP.

30. FK, "Annual Report for the Year 1957-58 Ending June 30, 1958, to the W. K. Kellogg Foundation," KP; Matthew G. Gaffney to FK, January 6, 1958, KP; ARED 1959-60, pp. 7-9; FK to Senior Members, November 16, 1961, KP; Senior Faculty Minutes, May 22, 1956; FK, "Memorandum for the Senior Members," November 5, 1958 (draft), KP; "Memorandum to the Senior Faculty from *Ad Hoc* Committee on Appointments in Elementary and Secondary Education," December 7, 1958, KP; ARED 1959-60, pp. 8-9; Senior Faculty Minutes, February 10 and 11, 1959; FK to NMP, March 12, 1959, DOP.

31. ARED 1956-57, pp. 27, 30-35.

32. Donald W. Oliver to Judson T. Shaplin, August 13, 1955, Judson T. Shaplin Papers, HUA; "Reports from Members of the Committee to Visit the Harvard Graduate School of Education," December 19, 1955, KP.

33. Fred M. Hechinger, "Behind the New York Story," *The New York Times* IV:9 (October 28, 1962).

Epilogue: Roots of Instability

1. The first section of this chapter briefly describes the major destabilizing forces of the 1960s. A full analysis of that decade is beyond the scope of my book. Many of the trends had reached no clear resolution at the time the manuscript was completed. I lacked access to certain important records and preferred not to speculate about individuals still professionally active. I was also an active participant and advocate in many of the decisions made in the late sixties. It seemed appropriate to separate here the roles of analyst and advocate, at least to the extent that is ever possible.

2. ARED 1957-58, p. 2; ARED 1958-59, p. 2.

3. For the renewed emphasis on research and research training see the Report of the Harvard Committee, *The Graduate Study of Education* (Cambridge, 1966).

4. Edward G. Kaelber to Theodore R. Sizer, January 6, 1967, DOP; U.S. Office of Education, "Summary of Evaluations by Staff and Consultants," (July 1966), DOP.

5. Harriet Feinberg, "Perspectives on the R & D Center," February 1966, HUA; John D. Herzog, "Programs and Projects, September 1, 1966-August 31, 1967," July 1, 1966, p. 37, HUA; "Quarterly Progress Report on Cooperative Research Center No. 0-04 September-November 30, 1966," p. 29, HUA.

6. "Tabulating of Responses to Follow-up Questionnaire," September 20, 1955, Teacher Education Research Project, Ford Foundation Archives.

7. Although I have emphasized how a distinct ideological critique of the Keppel mission fostered institutional change in the sixties, the dynamics of causation were not so simple. The abandonment of the late fifties' program was para-

doxically furthered by the continuing commitment of the Sizer administration to the fifties' theme of placing the faculty's intellectual quality above all considerations of practical relevance and program continuity. Decisions to stop doing certain things, and to start new enterprises, were made not only because new ideas seemed more compelling or more fundable than old ones. They were also made because the administration fully backed only those faculty members it considered most able, regardless of their field. The general direction of ideological preference was clear, but the extent of the School's programmatic dislocations was somewhat fortuitous. Had different notions of faculty quality prevailed, some enterprises might never have been abandoned.

Index